Ordnance Survey Maps   a descriptive manual

Ordnance Survey Maps
a descriptive manual

J B Harley

Southampton Ordnance Survey 1975

© Crown copyright 1975

Designed by HMSO Graphic Design
Plates and text drawings prepared by Ordnance Survey
Printed in England for Her Majesty's Stationery Office:
text by The University Press, Oxford
plates by W. S. Cowell Limited, Ipswich
cover and endpapers by Product Support (Graphics) Limited, Derby
bound by The University Press, Oxford

Foreword

Over 60 years have passed since the publication of a full and authoritative description of the whole range of Ordnance Survey maps. In 1910, *Ordnance Survey Maps of the United Kingdom* was published, with the sub-title *A Description of their Scales, Characteristics etc*. During the intervening years the subject has been covered only by a number of editions of booklets dealing with various scales of Ordnance Survey maps, the last of which were published in 1957 and have been out of print for some years.

We are aware, from the many enquiries which we receive from the public, of an increasing interest in Ordnance Survey publications. This definitive work of reference, for which we are indebted to Dr Brian Harley, a leading authority on the subject, will it is hoped fulfil the widespread desire for more detailed knowledge about our maps and thereby contribute not only to their usefulness but also to the pleasure which may be derived from their use.

B StG IRWIN
Director General
Ordnance Survey
May 1974

Contents

Detailed contents

List of figures in the text

List of tables

List of plates

Each plate is a representative portion
only of the specified map but
conventional signs are complete.

The plates of conventional signs
show those used in 1973. Maps
published earlier, or later, may show
variants of these signs.

Preface

The earliest official descriptions of Ordnance Survey maps – the ancestors of the present book – can be traced to the late nineteenth century. In 1899, for example, Colonel D. A. Johnston's *Ordnance Survey Maps of the United Kingdom. A Description of Their Scales, Characteristics, etc.*, was published, but in the 1920s a practice developed of providing separate booklets to describe the small and large scale maps. After World War II, a third booklet was added to deal with the medium scales. These three booklets were last revised and published, in 1954 (*A Description of the Ordnance Survey Large Scale Plans*), in 1955 (*A Description of Ordnance Survey Medium Scale Maps*), and in 1957 (*A Description of Ordnance Survey Small Scale Maps*). The present book – after a gap of nearly twenty years – reverts to the arrangement of providing a single description of the current maps of the Ordnance Survey. This has obvious advantages. In a cartographic sense maps at different scales, stemming from an overall policy, form a continuum; they are closely inter-dependent, both in relation to the basic surveys from which they are all derived, and in terms of production and revision. A single account can therefore reduce unnecessary duplication of basic information, and allow easy cross reference for users of the different scales.

This is not intended to be a controversial book. There have always been many shades of opinion as to how the Ordnance Survey ought to have developed and, currently, as to how its resources ought to be harnessed to meet the best needs of users. But to have explored the many alternatives would have been to transgress beyond the terms of reference of a descriptive manual which is concerned to provide an objective report on present practices. Nor, except incidentally, have I attempted to discuss the uses to which Ordnance Survey maps can be put. This would have greatly enlarged the scope of the text and yet, inasmuch as the practical and academic uses of maps are manifold, it could hardly have been definitive. The question of use is so hedged by specialist requirements that it seemed more appropriate to devote the available space to a discussion of characteristics from which independent assessments can be made as to the applications of the topographical data in Ordnance Survey maps.

In planning the book I have tried to present a concise yet rounded picture of the map production of the Ordnance Survey, rooted in legacies from the past, yet undergoing a period of unprecedented change. As much background is provided as seemed necessary to allow map users to understand the basic nature of the surveying, compilation, and production processes, but consistent emphasis is laid on the description of different map series and the inter-relationship of information they show. A principal objective is to indicate what the map user is likely to find on a particular map series and, alternatively, to signpost what is omitted. To further this end standard sub-headings have been used as far as possible in the succession of chapters (3 to 9) dealing with the main map series; thus, for example, a map user interested in the depiction of buildings or vegetation on Ordnance Survey maps at different scales would find information on each category through the index and in a series of self-contained sections. On occasions this may involve repetition, but this seemed worth while to achieve some consistency of approach. In contrast with previous descriptive booklets an attempt is made to give more of the rationale which controls the detail on maps of different scales, and especially to explain the criteria by which Ordnance Survey maps are generalized from basic to derived scales. Where appropriate, information has been set down on the standard specifications which underlie the production of each series and which determine the uniform presentation of data over the country as a whole.

The Ordnance Survey is changing rapidly in the 1970s, both in concept and practice, yet the changes themselves enhance the timeliness of any description and I make no apology for including a fair amount of information on map series which may be out of print when this book is published. It seems likely that many map users – not least libraries and major public service collections – will have retained past editions of Ordnance Survey maps and may wish to set them in context against the current range of publications. In some cases such maps will have served as a basis for recording important information and, if this is to be correctly retrieved by today's users, the relationship between conventions for detail shown on present and past series of maps needs to be understood.

I would like to thank those colleagues and friends who have smoothed research and writing over the last two years. In preparing a publication officially sponsored by the Ordnance Survey my role has often been more that of an editor than of an author.

For their patience and encouragement when the writing flagged, and for their detailed planning of the book, I am especially grateful to Miss Betty Drewitt, Deputy Director, Publications, and also to Mr A. A. Williams of the same Department. Mr W. A. Seymour, Assistant Director, Training and Information, has read the whole text in draft and the final version is greatly improved by his frank criticisms and by the hours willingly spent in discussion with the author. Detailed comments have been received from many other specialists at Southampton, and while it is perhaps unfair to single out particular names the detailed advice given by Mr Stanhope-Lovell, Archaeology Division, on Chapter 10, and by Mr R. K. Begg, Geodetic Services Division, on Chapter 11, was especially substantial. In the process of retrieving information the Survey's Librarian, Mr R. F. Thornton, has conjured otherwise elusive papers into my hands and I am also grateful to his assistants.

A major feature of the book is the provision of a representative set of map extracts and conventional signs, relating to the current publications of the Ordnance Survey at the time of going to press. The plates, reproduced in the full colour of the regular map series, together with the line diagrams, were compiled by the map production divisions of the Ordnance Survey.

Outside Southampton I owe an especial debt to the graphic designers of Her Majesty's Stationery Office, Mr David Challis and Mr John Saville, for the meticulous care with which they have guided the book through its production stages; and for sub-editorial work I must thank Mr Ernest Dellow for his careful processing of the manuscript. In matters of academic advice my debts are too numerous to list fully but I must specify the help given by my colleagues Professor William Ravenhill and Andrew Gilg of the University of Exeter who made many constructive suggestions on the text; Peter Clark, of the Mapping and Charting Establishment, R.E. from whose profound cartographic knowledge I have benefited enormously; and Yolande Jones of the Map Room, British Museum, whose assistance with the bibliography has added to the utility of the book.

In important respects this has been a co-operative venture which reflects the efforts of unnamed compilers of official instructions in the Ordnance Survey as much as its named author. It is only fair, however, to accept as mine the remaining misconceptions and errors and to confess to being a beginner both in the penetration of the many complexities and fascinations of the national survey organization and in the unravelling of the technical sequences of a massive and varied programme of map publication.

J. B. HARLEY

Department of Geography,
University of Exeter
December 1973

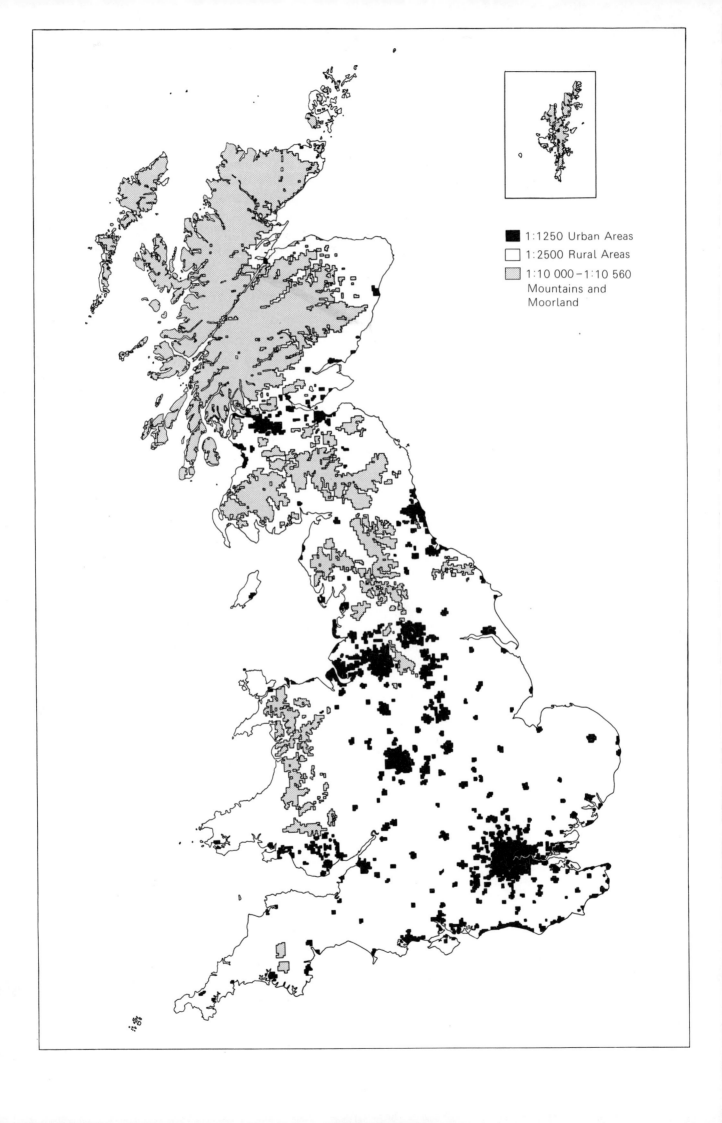

1:1250 Urban Areas

1:2500 Rural Areas

1:10 000 – 1:10 560
Mountains and
Moorland

The National Survey

Figure 1
Extent of areas of basic
scales mapping

Changing concepts

The Ordnance Survey will soon be 200 years old, but its recent history has been marked by changes, both technical and administrative, that are without precedent. So much is this true that its future historians may come to write about a 'revolution' in the technology of map-making. The *Annual Reports* of the Ordnance Survey[1] enable the process of change to be followed, if only in outline, and few of the traditional ways of doing things have remained unaltered. Of perhaps equal significance are radical changes in management practice and outlook, including a reappraisal of its financial and accounting system and of its attitude towards the services it provides for map users. Although such changes have in some respects been in progress for some time they were given formal authority in the statement made by the Secretary of State for the Environment in Parliament on 19 February 1973. It was announced that:

The Ordnance Survey will continue to function as the central survey and mapping organization in the public sector with the following aims:

(a) To produce and to maintain up-to-date basic surveys at 1 : 1250 for major urban areas and at 1 : 2500 or 1 : 10 000 for the remainder of the country.

(b) To make this survey information available at the basic scales in such forms as may be most appropriate to the needs of users; and additionally in the case of the 1 : 10 000 scale to publish and maintain a uniform series of maps covering the whole country.

(c) Otherwise to produce and make available up-to-date survey information in various forms appropriate to user needs, the cost of which can be covered by payments from users.

(d) To seek to maximize returns on all products and services subject to any limitations imposed by the Government.

In this 'new philosophy', the financial intentions have been most publicized and they could result in a reorientation of some of the activities of the national survey. The main aim is to increase the revenue derived from users and to limit the extent of Exchequer support.[2]

Some changes have been generated by the Ordnance Survey itself. The most important single change in concept is that associated with the development of the system of continuous revision. Before World War II, although piecemeal continuous revision had started in the 1920s in connection with Land Registry work, there was a tendency to regard the published large scale map as something of a 'once-and-for-all' record of fact, which, as long as it could be kept periodically up to date by a system of cyclic revision (with a twenty-year gap reckoned to be adequate for most areas) was seen to fulfil its objective. Today, more than ever before, survey and maintenance have become one process and the primary purpose of the national survey is to record change in the landscape as it occurs. The continuous revision system requires, broadly speaking, that the pace of revision shall match the pace of change and it is no longer regarded as a posthumous adjunct to the main work of the survey. Indeed, as the post-1945 resurvey of Great Britain nears completion, more and more of the Survey's manpower is being devoted to continuous revision. As new National Grid maps are completed they are brought into the system; by 1972, 52 per cent of the field surveyor strength was employed on the continuous revision of previously published 1 : 1250, 1 : 2500, and 1 : 10 000 maps.[3]

1 The first Ordnance Survey *Annual Report* was produced for presentation to Parliament for the year 1855–6 when control of the Department passed from the Board of Ordnance to the War Department. It was called for by the Secretary of State for War, who specified what information it should contain. Reports continued to be submitted to Parliament until 1921–2 when, in common with many other government publications, the *Report* ceased to be a Command Paper although it continued to be published annually. During World War II and afterwards the *Reports* were not published but, in 1954–5, publication was resumed, and the form of the *Report* has remained substantially unchanged.

2 Financial details are published in the *Annual Reports*, with net expenditure calculated after map sales and other sources of income have been deducted from gross expenditure derived from the Exchequer.

3 Ordnance Survey, *Annual Report 1971–72* (1972), 9.

Three other trends are apparent. First, for continuous revision to be effective, information collected by the system must be made available quickly. The ideal situation would be one in which there was an immediate and uninterrupted flow of information from the field survey on to the map user. While the technology fully to achieve this does not yet exist, significant advances in this direction have been made and revision data is no longer held back until a new edition of a map can be published, but is available in the form of advance revision information and lately through the SUSI system (see p. 12). Second, partly because of this need to speed the flow of information, and partly because users increasingly require data in forms best adapted to their specific purposes, the conventional map printed on paper no longer holds a monopoly position in the communication of topographic information. Successful experiments with automation in cartography (see p. 46) mean that large scale surveys will become available on magnetic tape, but even before such experiments the Ordnance Survey had decided to miniaturize the 1:1250 and 1:2500 maps in order to make these series available on microfilm. A range of other 'Services' had also been developed permitting a more flexible approach to the ways in which information could be supplied from the national survey. Large scale maps, for example, are available as 'at scale' transparencies on stable plastic material, and as enlargements or reductions in a range of scales suitable for user needs (see pp. 48 and 69).

It should be recognized that such new media, rather than merely providing an extra service for map users, have become an integral part of Ordnance Survey policy. As part of the changes in practice and procedure authorized by the Secretary of State for the Environment in February 1973 it was stated that:

The Ordnance Survey no longer has any general obligation to supply maps at 1:1250 and 1:2500 scales printed on paper. Instead it has full discretion as to the form in which the survey at these scales will be made available. Large scale survey information will continue to be supplied but the Department will take account of the variety of possible techniques of publication and will be free to decide how best to produce and market it having regard to the needs of users, to income and to proper economy.[1]

A third trend, that of the map user playing a larger role in fashioning both policy and detailed products, is explicit in the ministerial statements quoted above. The phrase 'most appropriate to the needs of users' has assumed a special significance, but it may be noted that consultative facilities have for long been available. As well as the annual consultative meetings with various types of user,[2] there is close liaison between the field regions of the Ordnance Survey (Figure 5) and local authorities. A related development is the recognition of the importance of market research, not merely to assist in selling the maps, but also to try to discover, especially with small scale popular maps, what the user thinks ought to be included. Such an exercise was conducted before the decision was taken to produce the 1:50 000 series (see p. 121) and has influenced the style and content of the final map. The Ordnance Survey now seeks in this market to keep abreast of social trends, as in the introduction of the new Outdoor Leisure Maps especially geared to recreational needs. Interaction and consultation between the Ordnance Survey and its users, ranging from government departments to private individuals, are likely in the future to be more influential in formulating broad lines of map production and publication policy.

1 A decision was taken in 1973 not to withdraw printed paper maps from publication in the absence of alternative products.

2 By 1973 six separate consultative meetings were held regularly: The Advisory Committees for Government Departments and Nationalized Industries; for the Local Authorities Associations (England and Wales); for the Scottish Local Authorities; for Large Scales Map Users; for Small Scales Map Users; and the Archaeology Advisory Committee.

Historical perspective

The primary responsibility of the Ordnance Survey is to survey and provide maps of Great Britain. The modern authority for these activities dates from the Ordnance Survey Act, 1841,[1] although the Survey is generally considered as being formally founded in 1791, with roots in the civilian and military cartography of the eighteenth century.[2] The first task executed just before the formal founding of the Survey was a scientific one – to fix the relative positions of the Greenwich and Paris observatories by means of a triangulation. During the Napoleonic Wars the military need for a one-inch map of southern England was uppermost in official thinking, but the years after 1815 brought new vistas to the Survey. The practical value of appropriate maps came to be more fully appreciated not only for the management and transfer of land but also for civil engineering and in urgent efforts to improve sanitary conditions in the growing towns of the early Victorian period. With such applications were linked scientific uses, including the mapping of geological outcrops and the recording of archaeological sites in the field, so that, by mid nineteenth century, the Ordnance Survey had assumed its modern role of providing, as a national service, the surveys and maps of Great Britain required for military and scientific purposes and for use by government and public in a variety of contexts.

One important consequence of the widening demands made on the national survey was that an increasingly sophisticated range of maps, at different scales and levels of detail, was required to meet these needs. The original 1 inch to 1 mile (1:63360) series was retained as a general map, but, as early as 1824, the specification for the Irish Survey, concerned with providing a basis for more equitable land taxation, led to the introduction of a scale of 1:10560. In 1840 the 1:10560 scale was also authorized for the survey of the remainder of northern England and Scotland (i.e. the area not covered at that date by the one-inch), but it soon became apparent that it was inadequate for all the purposes required of a national survey. A long controversy, the so-called 'Battle of the Scales' lasting for about twenty years, was to surround the choice of a suitable basic scale for the maps of Great Britain. A series of Royal Commissions and Parliamentary Committees[3] debated the alternatives and took voluminous evidence but not until 1858 was a final decision taken to adopt the 1:2500 scale for cultivated areas, the 1:10560 for uncultivated areas, and 1:500 (c. 10 ft to the mile) for towns with a population of 4000 and over. Map series on smaller scales, including the 1:63360, were to be derived from these basic large scale maps.

For approximately three-quarters of a century the Survey was engaged in implementing and adapting these mid Victorian policies and even today they have left a distinct mark on the programme of map publication. It had taken from 1853 to 1896 to complete the survey at the 1:2500 scale but, by the outbreak of World War I, the first revision had been completed. The change from survey to revision had called for some adaptation of field techniques, but it was in the methods of map production that the greatest innovations occurred, with the introduction of zincography, photography, and (from 1886) colour printing, at the Southampton office.[4] The design and content of the maps also underwent *ad hoc* development in relation to a combination of factors: some technical (as in the progressive substitution of machine stamping for hand lettering by the engraver), some owing to user demand (as in the adoption of Welsh and Gaelic orthography), and many

1 This was made permanent by the Expiring Laws Act, 1922.

2 R. A. Skelton, 'The Origins of the Ordnance Survey of Great Britain', *The Geographical Journal*, **128** (1962), 415–26.

3 Especially influential were: *Report from the Registration and Conveyancing Commission* 1850 xxxii, I; *Report from the Select Committee on Ordnance Survey (Scotland)* 1851 x 359; *Correspondence Respecting the Scale for the Ordnance Survey, and upon Contouring and Hill Delineation* 1854 xli 187; *Report from the Select Committee on Ordnance Survey of Scotland* 1856 xiv 861; *Report of the Ordnance Survey Commission* 1857–8 xix 585; and *Reports from the Select Committee Appointed to Inquire into the Expediency of Extending the Cadastral Survey to those Portions of the United Kingdom which have been Surveyed upon the Scale of One Inch to One Mile Only* 1861 xiv 93 and 1862 vi 3.

4 The best contemporary description is the *Account of the Methods and Processes Adopted for the Production of the Maps of the Ordnance Survey of the United Kingdom; drawn up by Officers of the Royal Engineers employed under Sir Henry James, Director-General* (London, 1875); this can be compared with the revised edition of the work published under the same title in 1902. See also C. W. Wilson, 'Methods and Processes of the Ordnance Survey', *The Scottish Geographical Magazine*, **7** (1891), 248–59, and J. E. E. Craster, 'Photomechanical Processes of Map Production', *The Geographical Journal*, **65** (1925), 301–14. A more modern account is H. St J. L. Winterbotham, *The National Plans* (Ordnance Survey, Professional Papers, New Series, No. 16, London, 1934).

designed to stem the rising cost of the national survey (as, for example, in the abandonment, except at local cost, of the 1:500 series of town plans in 1893).

World War I was a watershed in the history of the Ordnance Survey.[1] In particular it saw the beginning of government economies on a new scale, which were to cripple the effectiveness of the Survey throughout the 1920s and 1930s. In 1918 a Select Committee on national expenditure decreed that the revision of the 1:2500 and 1:10560 series should be placed on a forty- instead of a twenty-year cycle for all areas with a population of under 100 to a square mile. In 1922 the recommendations of the Geddes Committee intensified these economies and the establishment of the Ordnance Survey was reduced to 1000 men. Although some experimental and scientific work continued in the inter-war years, the effects were particularly severe in the revision of the basic scales which was largely confined to urban areas undergoing rapid change. It was particularly unfortunate that these cutbacks coincided with government legislation in other fields the net effect of which was to increase the demand and uses for large scale maps. The Town Planning Act (1925), the Land Registration Act (1925), the Land Drainage Act (1926), the Local Government Act (1929), the Housing Act (Slum Clearance) (1930), and the Land Valuation Finance Act (1931) all provide examples of government actions which, in one way or another, required accurate maps as part of the infrastructure to implement them. By the early 1930s it was clear that successive economies, although some activities were relatively unscathed, had left the Ordnance Survey ill equipped to meet such demands. In 1935 a Departmental Committee was set up under the chairmanship of Sir J. C. C. Davidson to consider how the effectiveness of the Survey could be restored.

The Davidson Committee

The Davidson Committee Report is a key document in understanding the development of the Ordnance Survey and indeed goes a long way in interpreting the rationale of present map publication. Its principal terms of reference were threefold. First, the Committee was asked to consider measures necessary to 'accelerate the revision of the Ordnance Survey Maps . . . to bring them up-to-date and thereafter to maintain them at a high level of accuracy'; second, to ascertain if immediate steps could be taken (even before the completion of the revision) to up-date Ordnance Survey Maps to an extent acceptable for town and country planning schemes; and third, it had 'to review the scales and styles of Ordnance Survey Maps' and 'recommend whether any changes were desirable'.[2] The urgency of the second instruction was such that the Committee produced a preliminary report in 1936, in which it recommended that 'an interim edition of the 1:2500 plans be produced for town planning purposes'.[3] This task was to be given priority, especially in areas in which town planning was 'most pressing', and extra staff were to be appointed to allow its implementation.

The *Final Report* of the Davidson Committee was not published until 1938 and World War II was to prevent systematic action on most of its recommendations until after 1945. The objectives set down in 1938 were nevertheless persevered with and have influenced the post-1945 development of the Ordnance Survey to a considerable extent. Out of eighteen recommendations the most influential in fashioning the maps are listed:

1 *The Ordnance Survey and the War, 1914-19* (Southampton, Ordnance Survey, 1919).

2 *Final Report of the Departmental Committee on the Ordnance Survey* (HMSO, London, 1938), 1.

3 *Interim Report of the Departmental Committee on the Ordnance Survey* (HMSO, London, 1936), 12-13.

(1) That the 1:2500 scale should be retained.

(2) That the 1:2500 survey should be re-cast on National instead of county sheet lines on a National projection, and that, while this work was in progress, there should be a general overhaul of the plans to eliminate the errors which had crept into the original survey in the course of revision.

(3) That a National grid should be super-imposed on all large scale plans and on smaller scale maps . . . to provide one reference system for the maps of the whole country.

(4) That the international metre should be adopted as the unit on which the grid should be based.

(5) That the large scale maps in the new National series should be square in shape.

(6) That the 1:2500 plans when re-published in the new National Series should cover one square kilometre of the country.

(7) That the one inch to the mile and smaller scales should be retained in their existing form.

(9) That the scale of six inches to the mile should be retained, and that maps on this scale should be produced in the new National Series in a square shape and containing twenty-five 1:2500 plans.

(10) That a new medium scale of 1:25000 should be tried out experimentally in certain selected areas, and, if successful, should be extended to cover the whole country in a National Series.

(11) That when the revision of the 1:2500 plans had been completed further investigation should be carried out with a view to establishing whether the requirements of urban areas would not be more adequately met by a survey at the 1:1250 scale.

(12) That when a suitable opportunity occurred, additional contours should be introduced.

(14) That the Ordnance Survey should continue to publish archaeological maps.

(16) That a system of continuous revision should be adopted for the large scale plans as soon as possible.[1]

That these recommendations provided what was in effect a new charter for the Ordnance Survey will become obvious from the detailed descriptions of particular map series in Chapters 3–10. It is true to say that some objectives formulated by the Davidson Committee were modified later either in the light of technical developments or because of internal changes in the allocation of the Survey's resources. But only from the late 1960s onwards, with the influence of technological change and the need for mapping at all scales to be suitable for use with metric units of measurement, have some of the Committee's strategies been overtaken.

A first priority involved concentration on the production of the three series of large scale maps: the 1:1250 (approximately 50 inches to 1 mile) covering large urban areas; the 1:2500 (approximately 25 inches to 1 mile) covering all cultivated areas and small towns; and the 1:10560 (6 inches to 1 mile), now being superseded by the 1:10000, covering the remaining areas of mountains and moorland. These are known as the *basic* scales, that is to say, for the areas concerned (Figure 1) they are the largest scale maps published by the Ordnance Survey and they are kept up to date by a system of continuous revision. All other map series are defined as *derived*, i.e. they are derived from the detail of the *basic* maps, to give a total range of published maps listed in Table 1.

A partial exception to the simple 'basic-derived' classification is the policy of small scales revision which has developed in recent years in order to record revision of rapidly changing features such as the road network, and the changes necessary to up-date small scale maps in areas not covered by new

1 *Final Report* (1938), 28, 29; the numbers of the recommendations are those given in the *Report*; see also M. N. MacLeod *et al.*, 'Discussion on the Final Report of the Departmental Committee on the Ordnance Survey', *The Geographical Journal*, **93** (1939), 314–32; A. G. Ogilvie, 'The Future Work of the Ordnance Survey: A Review', *The Scottish Geographical Magazine*, **55** (1939), 107–11.

large scale survey and the consequential continuous revision system. The old rule that a derived map was generally no more up to date than its parent no longer applies.

Table 1   Basic and derived scales of the Ordnance Survey

Basic scales	Derived scales
1:1250 (major urban areas)	1:2500,* 1:10560 and 1:10000
1:2500 (minor towns, cultivated areas)	1:10560 and 1:10000
1:10560 and 1:10000 (mountain and moorland)	1:25000
	1:50000
	1:63360
	1:250000
	1:625000
	1:1000000

* Production of wholly derived sheets stopped in 1973 (see p. 48).

Ordnance Survey organization

The extent to which the resources of the Ordnance Survey are devoted to various aspects of the basic scales surveys as opposed to the production of popular maps is not always appreciated by map users, who encounter maps mainly in a published form and often only as small-scale cartography. There are three directorates within the Survey: the Field Survey Directorate, the Map Publication Directorate, and the Establishment and Finance Directorate (Figure 2). The work of Field Directorate is almost wholly concerned with the production of basic scales surveys and the associated horizontal and vertical control systems. In Map Publication Directorate about 70 per cent of the work of Cartography Division and 40 per cent of the work of Reproduction Division is on the basic scales.[1]

Director General	Directorate	Division
	Establishment & Finance	Finance Management & Office Services Personnel Training & Information
	Field Surveys	Archaeology Geodetic Services Topographic Surveys
	Map Publication	Cartography Publication Reproduction
		Planning and Development

Figure 2
Functional organization of the Ordnance Survey 1973

Geodetic activities

The framework of control points, both horizontal and vertical, on which the national surveys are founded is provided by triangulation, based on the same principles as the trigonometrical work of the nineteenth century. The Principal Triangulation (published in 1858) was a selection of data from the mass

1 Ordnance Survey, *Annual Report 1972–73* (1973); plate 5 shows the distribution of staff employment at 31 March 1973.

of observations made in the earlier part of the century,[1] and the Retriangulation, forming the basis of today's mapping, was observed, computed, and adjusted between 1935 and 1962. The primary retriangulation covers the country with a network of stations which are in general about 30 to 50 km apart (Figure 3), the shortest triangle-sides being about 8 km and the longest (which connect to adjoining countries) about 135 km. This primary network is broken down successively into a secondary triangulation (giving a continuous network of stations between 8 and 12 km apart), a tertiary triangulation (with a density of control points 4 to 7 km apart), and other lower orders of control depending on the amount of development on the ground and the scale of mapping for which the points are required (in built-up areas, for example, stations can be as close together as 1½ to 2 km). Altogether nearly 22 000 stations have been observed at all levels in the retriangulation.[2]

Supplementary work on the retriangulation continues and a new adjustment, which included 180 new side lengths, was carried out in 1970 mainly for scientific purposes. New techniques are increasingly in evidence. The classical method of base measurement (by using 'Invar' tapes suspended in catenary), once a laborious and time-consuming component of a triangulation system, is now obsolete. It has been replaced by electro-magnetic distance measurement using instruments such as the 'Tellurometer', which employs a microwave system, or the 'Geodimeter', which uses modulated light waves, to measure considerably greater distances with speed and precision. The 'Tellurometer', for example, has been used to measure distances of 135 km between Great Britain and Ireland as part of the process of checking the triangulation. 'Geodimeters' are normally used for shorter distances, ranging from 5 to 50 km, according to the model employed.

Vertical control points are provided by spirit levelling which has been carried out over most of Great Britain. The country is divided along geodetic and secondary levelling lines into areas averaging 400 sq km and each area is relevelled in a cyclic system, introduced in 1956, the interval depending on the character of the country. Mountain and moorland areas are relevelled every forty years and the remaining areas every twenty years. The levelling is based on the Ordnance Datum,[3] which is the mean level of the sea at Newlyn in Cornwall, which was calculated from hourly readings of the sea level recorded on an automatic tide gauge from 1 May 1915 to 30 April 1921. This tide gauge is situated in the Ordnance Survey Tidal Observatory on the south pier at Newlyn and readings are related to the Observatory Bench Mark, which is 4.751 m (15.588 ft) above the datum.

The current levelling framework is based on two main geodetic components:

(a) The second geodetic levelling which was carried out, for England and Wales between 1912 and 1921, and for Scotland between 1936 and 1952. The values of all bench marks were connected by levelling to the Observatory Bench Mark, and thus to Ordnance Datum at Newlyn.

(b) The third geodetic levelling (Figure 4), was completed in England and Wales between 1951 and 1956. All the heights of fundamental bench marks (FBMS) (see p. 35) obtained from the second geodetic levelling were accepted unchanged. Between the FBMS, values from the third geodetic levelling were used to adjust the levels of intermediate bench marks (BMS). Thus the values of BMS between FBMS were revised, but the values of FBMS remained unchanged. In Scotland the third geodetic levelling was executed between 1956 and

1 A. R. Clarke, *Ordnance Survey of Great Britain and Ireland. Account of the Observations of the Principal Triangulation . . .* (1858), gives a full description.

2 Ordnance Survey, *History of the Retriangulation of Great Britain* (London, 1967). In addition astronomical observations by theodolite were made to adjust the triangulation of Great Britain to a datum and spheroid common to the systems of other countries. The development of artificial satellites since 1957 has provided geodesy with a new and powerful tool, enabling the triangulation network of previously unconnected land masses to be joined together. The special cameras established in Great Britain at the Royal Radar Establishment at Malvern (maintained by the Ordnance Survey), and at the Royal Observatory in Edinburgh, have participated in a number of programmes of satellite geodesy under the auspices of the International Association of Geodesy. From one of these programmes, for which observations were completed in mid 1972, a western European satellite triangulation network will, when the computations are complete, provide an integrated network of control for the fourteen countries concerned; in time it will be linked to the world-wide satellite triangulation undertaken by the USA.

3 Levelling on some of the more remote offshore islands is based on local datum; see p. 80.

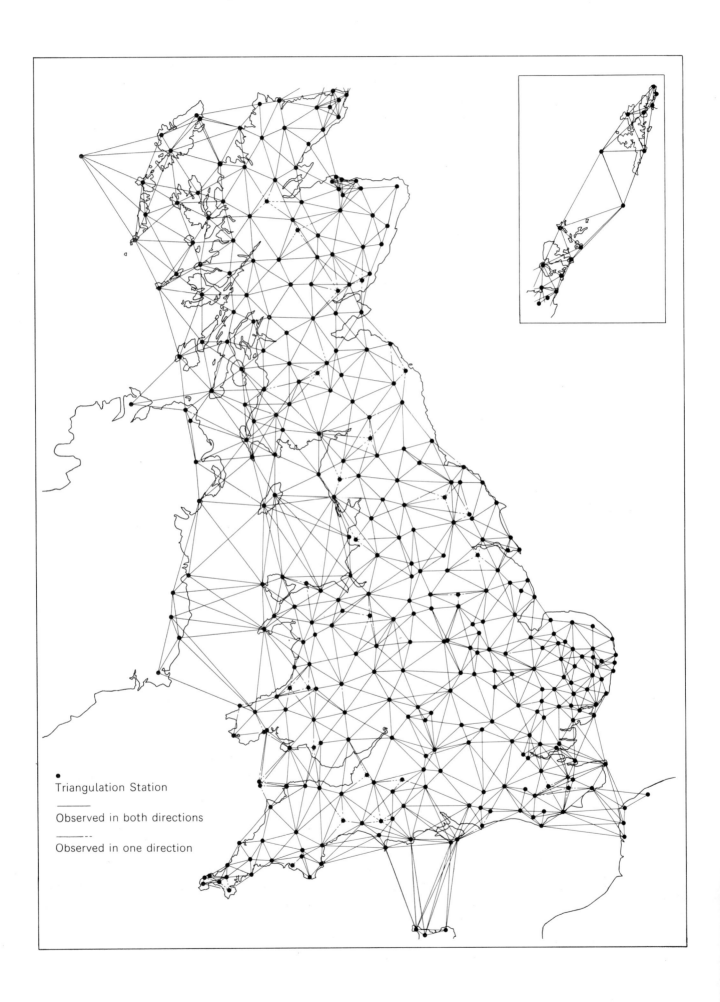

Triangulation Station

Observed in both directions

Observed in one direction

Figure 3
Primary Triangulation of
Great Britain

1958. All the heights of FBMs obtained from the second geodetic levelling were again accepted unchanged. The third geodetic levelling was used to provide additional levelling in areas not covered by the second geodetic levelling.

As far as the altitudes printed on the published maps are concerned the second geodetic levelling controlled the lower-order results prior to March 1956. Since that date, the lower-order results have been controlled as indicated in paragraph *b* above.

Topographical surveys

The topographical surveys undertaken by the Ordnance Survey may be completed wholly on the ground or by a combination of aerial and ground survey methods. Aerial survey is now the basis of the majority of new surveys[1] and is used to a lesser extent in the revision of existing mapping at the three basic scales.

The air survey[2] is divided into four main stages: obtaining the photographs, co-ordinating the plan and height points necessary to control the plotting process, plotting the map detail (including contours at 1:10 000 scale), and, finally, field completion on the ground. Aircraft are hired from private companies for the flying season (from March to October) but the Ordnance Survey employs its own camera operators and cameras, equipped with lenses of approximately $3\frac{1}{2}$-, 6-, or 12-inch focal length. The photographs in each strip overlap each other by 60 per cent and adjacent strips overlap by 30 per cent in order to provide complete stereoscopic cover. The cameras are electrically operated and include devices which enable the operator to assist the pilot to follow the planned flight path and to regulate the interval between exposures in order to obtain the correct overlap between photographs. The photography is provided at varying scales. For 1:1250 surveys the scale is 1:5000; for the revision of the 1:2500 series, 1:7500; for 1:2500 survey, 1:10000; and for the 10000 series it is 1:25000. Black and white photography is normally used[3] although experiments have been made with colour.[4]

The film is processed and paper prints are made to check the coverage and quality of the photography. The next stage varies with the map series for which the photography is to be used. In the case of new surveys glass diapositive plates, printed with the help of an electric scanner to bring out the maximum of detail from both the highlight and shadow areas of the negatives, are prepared for the plotting machines. Photographs used in the overhaul of the 1:2500 series (see p. 49), however, are produced as rectified enlargements on paper (thereby eliminating the effect of camera tilt in the aircraft) at an approximate scale of 1:2500.

In newly surveyed areas the first of the photogrammetric processes is that of deriving additional horizontal and vertical control points from the air photographs to control the plotting of detail and contours. Air photographs have in fact become a standard source for breaking down from secondary triangulation to provide control for 1:10 000 resurvey. They are especially useful in remote or inaccessible country, as in Scotland, where positions can be fixed without having to visit them on the ground. With this in mind, triangulation pillars (for example) may be painted white before a flight so that they can be identified on the photographs. The method of deriving control points from

1 R. A. Gardiner, 'The Use of Air Photographs by the Ordnance Survey', *Empire Survey Review*, **10** (1950), 242–55, for a useful summary of the development of the technique within the Ordnance Survey.

2 P. F. Fagan, 'Photogrammetry in the National Survey', *The Photogrammetric Record*, **40** (1972), 405–23, for a full description; an earlier account is A. J. D. Halliday, 'The Resurvey of the Six-inch Maps of Scotland', *The Photogrammetric Record*, **3** (1960), 320–37.

3 A special use of air survey is to map low water mark by means of infra-red photography.

4 H. C. Woodrow, 'The Use of Colour Photography for Large scale Mapping', *The Photogrammetric Record*, **5** (1967), 133–60.

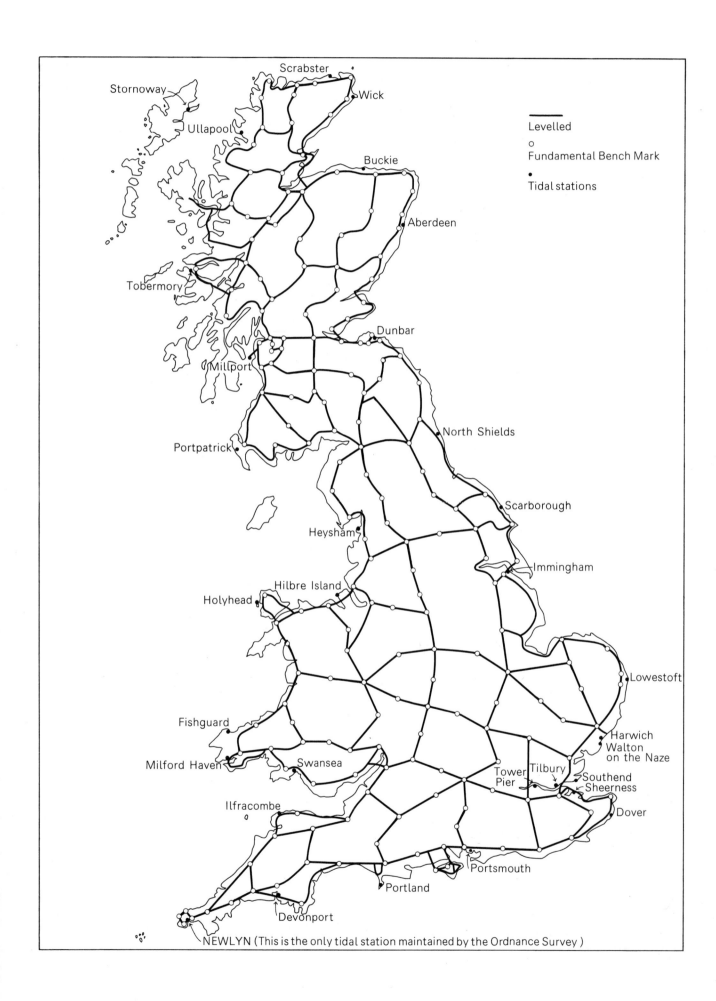

Levelled
o Fundamental Bench Mark
• Tidal stations

Stornoway
Scrabster
Wick
Ullapool
Buckie
Aberdeen
Tobermory
Dunbar
Millport
North Shields
Portpatrick
Scarborough
Heysham
Immingham
Hilbre Island
Holyhead
Lowestoft
Fishguard
Harwich
Walton
on the Naze
Milford Haven
Swansea
Tower
Pier
Tilbury
Southend
Sheerness
Ilfracombe
Dover
Portsmouth
Portland
Devonport
NEWLYN (This is the only tidal station maintained by the Ordnance Survey)

Figure 4
Network of the third geodetic
levelling

air photographs, which has been developed in the Ordnance Survey since 1947, is known as analytical aerial triangulation.[1] By means of self-recording stereocomparators precise measurements of co-ordinates are made on pairs of overlapping aerial photographs. The data are computed automatically and the end product is a list of three-dimensional co-ordinates.

The next stage is the plotting of a map. With the 1:10 000 series control points are plotted on a stable plastic sheet about the same size as the published sheet. A stereo-plotting machine is then used to derive map and contours, with the operator plotting the detail – which includes roads, buildings, the boundaries of vegetation and rock features, and antiquities – in relation to the control points. A second sheet of plastic material carrying an opaque coating is placed in exact registration with the first, and is then used for plotting and scribing the contours, the position of which can be established by the operator from the height co-ordinates supplied by the control, and by further interpolation in the plotting machine. The contours are then printed on the back of the detail sheet to assist the field surveyor in his task of map completion on the ground.

The approach to the overhaul of the 1:2500 series (see p. 49) is somewhat different in that detail already existing on the maps controls the positioning of new detail. The majority of new map detail is supplied by a combination of graphical air plotting and field survey techniques. Stereo-plotting machines may be used in areas of high-density housing development or to provide revised detail where suitable control detail from earlier surveys is sparse. The revision is again completed on the ground.

It will already be clear that despite the present contribution of air survey an important part of the job still lies on the ground. For this work the surveyors are organized into six field regions (Figure 5), responsible for the execution of surveys at the basic scales. Their task is to check the detail on the field document (the origin of which will vary according to whether they are engaged in resurvey, overhaul, or continuous revision) and to fill in what is not already shown. Where air survey is the basic source, for example, the ground surveyor has to supply details such as the ground lines of buildings and features hidden from the air in densely wooded country as well as administrative boundaries, names, and house numbers. In other cases, as with rock areas, the air survey provides only the outline of the feature and the rock detail is derived in a variety of other ways – from ground survey and sometimes from stereoscopic pairs of photographs taken at ground level.

Past methods of ground survey depended on chain survey based on dense triangulation and theodolite traverses. From 1954 onwards, however, tacheometry became the standard method of providing control detail for the ground resurvey of large scale maps. The self-reducing tacheometer is essentially a transit theodolite with the additional feature that horizontal distances can be read directly from observations on a stadia rod. Its advantages over pre-existing methods include savings in manpower and time and the relative ease with which operator error can be detected.

Today tacheometric survey is used extensively in continuous revision at 1:1250 scale and provides a framework of instrumentally surveyed detail, from which at the later stage of 'detail survey' the remaining ground features in the area are surveyed and plotted by simple methods. An area is covered with a network of tacheometer traverses, tied to previously fixed and

1 P. F. Fagan, 412–14; other descriptions include D. W. G. Arthur, *A Stereocomparator Technique for Aerial Triangulation*, Ordnance Survey Professional Paper, 20 (HMSO, London, 1955); D. J. Simpson, 'Analytical Aerial Triangulation in Practice', *Proceedings Int. Association Geodesy* (1960); W. S. Stewart and S. H. Hull, 'Analytical Aerial Triangulation in the Ordnance Survey', *Int. Archives of Photogrammetry*, 17 (1969); D. W. Proctor, 'Adjustment of Aerial Triangulation by Electronic Digital Computers', *The Photogrammetric Record*, 4 (1962), 24–33.

co-ordinated control points up to 1 km apart, enabling the legs of the traverse to be measured and the position of ground features fixed.

Tacheometric survey detail is plotted manually using a polar co-ordinato-graph. Once the instrumental detail has been plotted on the field document it is penned in red to indicate that it is control detail. The remaining map detail is completed by the surveyor on the ground using methods which combine visual alignments and intersections with taped short-distance measurements within (and controlled by) the framework of 'red' detail.

The surveyor who completes the map detail also collects and verifies names by standard procedures, records house numbers, perambulates and meres administrative boundaries, checks trigonometrical and levelling information, and transfers information provided by the Archaeology Division on to the field survey document. Such aspects are described in Chapters 3 to 10.

Continuous revision

The traditional method of keeping the basic Ordnance Survey maps up to date was by means of cyclic revision, for example, the 1 : 2500 map was originally revised on a twenty-year cycle. Following a recommendation of the Davidson Committee this system was replaced by continuous revision after World War II. Keeping abreast of development is one of the main problems, as well as duties, of the national survey and continuous revision is regarded as the first priority field task.[1] The system has three main principles: first, that changes on the ground are surveyed shortly after they occur; second, that new editions of the maps are published when required; and third, that up to date information in the form of copies of the surveyors' field sheets are obtainable on demand. All basic maps are brought under continuous revision once their first National Grid editions have been published and they are classified as either active (where continual change is expected) or inactive (where relatively little change is taking place). For the former a detailed intelligence system is maintained to record change but for the latter a simplified system is adequate. The essence of the continuous revision operation – for which purpose the country is divided into section areas – is that the field documents are kept up to date by surveying changes on the ground as soon as they reach a level which would provide economic work for a surveyor in a locality. The working documents are copies of current editions of maps, on a stable transparent plastic material, and on which additions and deletions can be made. A revised document is thus available almost immediately if wanted for drawing and reproduction and can be issued to the public as advance revision information or in the form of susi (Supply of Unpublished Survey Information) which is supplied either as a printout from a micro-film made from the surveyor's master survey drawing or field sheet or as a transparency on stable plastic material (see p. 48). A new edition is published only when this is justified by the amount of development on a sheet in relation to its age. Production is based on the principle that unchanged detail should not be redrawn but should be carried forward from one edition to the next by photographic methods. New detail is then added in exact register with the old. A measure of the importance of the work is that since continuous revision was started in 1949 over 32 000 revised maps have been published at the 1 : 1250 scale alone[2] and, added to this, the considerable volume of work undertaken by continuous revision sections for H M Land Registry must be taken into account.

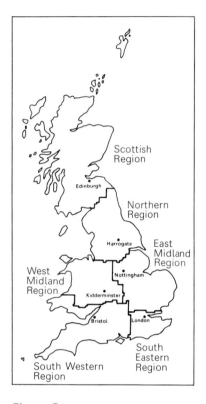

Figure 5
Field regions of the Ordnance Survey

1 W. A. Seymour and B. St G. Irwin, 'Continuous Revision of Ordnance Survey Plans', *The Geographical Journal*, **133** (1965), 76–85.

2 Ordnance Survey *Annual Report 1972–73* (1973), Appendix 1, which also gives continuous revision statistics for other basic scales.

Small scales revision

Maps at small scales (i.e. 1:50 000 and smaller), as already noted, are kept up to date by means of a revision system for changes which, for one reason or another, are not recorded by current continuous revision. Small scales revision (for example) has been necessary in areas where resurvey is incomplete or for features which are not differentiated on the basic scales. It has also been especially concerned hitherto with recording major road developments or building projects, which information can then be conveniently fed into the frequently revised small scale series. The system required that the surveys should be suitable for incorporation in the First Series (Provisional) 1:25 000 maps (see p. 91), giving a flexibility which allowed the maximum use of new information within a wide range of map series. Small scales revision is organized on a cyclic basis related to the revision cycles of the 1:63 360 map (see p. 118).

The field reviser works by comparing the ground detail with detail shown on the last published 1:63 360/1:50 000 map. The corrections or additions are made on a plastic field document which, for the 1:50 000 series, is the image of the 1:63 360 enlarged to 1:25 000 scale. This is in contrast to the revision of the 1:63 360 series which was carried out on paper copies of the latest 1:10 560 National Grid series. New detail is usually inserted by simple surveying methods similar to those described above for the ground survey of features within the framework of 'red' detail. On sheets due to be reprinted which do not warrant a full systematic revision, special revision surveys are undertaken for major roads and other important detail. Road developments, in particular, are carefully monitored with the help of information received from the Department of the Environment; surveying is carried out on the ground but, in the case of roads under construction or proposed, use is sometimes made of appropriate engineers' plans.

Map production at Southampton

As with methods of survey so with techniques of map production; the last two decades have seen rapid developments in the basic processes of the Ordnance Survey. All map production is the responsibility of the Directorate of Map Publication which, as well as these technical functions, also controls the publication and marketing of maps and related services, and the protection of Crown copyright in maps and mapping material. Map production is divided into two main operations, with Cartography Division responsible for map drawing and Reproduction Division for the printing of the maps. Each division is subdivided into further specialist units which are integrated by the planning control of map production as a whole.[1]

Cartography Division employs some 1200 draughtsmen and draughtswomen. Present techniques have dispensed with the elegance of hand lettering and copper-plate engraving but, at the same time, they have made it easier to ensure standard specifications for whole series of maps. Each map series is drawn to such a specification which sets down detailed instructions and criteria for the drawing of each feature at the particular scale; examples of specifications are given in Chapters 3 to 9.

Map production processes have the object of preserving the accuracy of the original survey, firstly by avoiding hand tracing as far as possible and relying instead on photo-mechanical methods; and secondly, by using non-distorting

1 J. R. B. Dennett, L. H. E. Hobbs, and B. F. White, 'Cartographic Production Control', *The Cartographic Journal*, **4** (1967), 96–103, describes Ordnance Survey planning of these operations as they were organized in the mid 1960s.

media, such as metal, plastics, or glass, in all stages of drawing and scribing. To increase productivity, manual methods have been replaced by automatic, mechanical, and electronic processes, whenever this is feasible and economic. The use of scribing instead of traditional drawing was an especially important development. Current scribing methods are illustrated by the role of the draughtsman in the production of the National Grid 1:2500 series maps. The working surface is a sheet of polyester plastic coated with a translucent wax-like substance; this bears a photographic image of the field document at correct scale which serves as the model for the draughtsman's work. It is placed on a table with an underneath light source and, using scribing tools with a steel or sapphire point (like traditional engravers' tools these vary with separate gravers for scribing curves, straight lines, dots, and circles), the draughtsman cuts away the wax coating along the lines of the surveyed image. The map detail is left in negative form.

Other features are dealt with separately. With buildings, for example, the draughtsman lays a sheet of masking film over the scribed sheet, holding it in position by register studs, and then cuts round all buildings which will appear stippled on the final map. The coating is then peeled off in these areas, producing a 'negative mask'. The scribed detail, the mask, and the master stipple film, together with the standard grid and border (common to all sheets in the series), are combined photographically, with registration provided by a punch register system.

On the 1:2500 series the measurement of the area of parcels of land shown on the map is also undertaken by specially trained draughtsmen. The method illustrates how automation characterizes many Ordnance Survey processes. The parcels are measured by automatic reading planimeters which incorporate electronic counters. Each parcel is measured by independent operators and the two results for each parcel are compared: where there is agreement within a certain tolerance the measurements are accepted; parcels which fail this test are remeasured. The sum of the means of all the parcel measurements on the map must agree within 0.283 hectare (0.7 acre) with the known area of the map, 200 hectares (494.21 acres). Punched tapes produced by the planimeter equipment are fed into a computer, which calculates the mean of the individual measurements of each parcel, the total area of all parcels, and also makes an adjustment for the scale of the map which varies slightly according to its position in the map projection (see p. 19). The computer then prints out the areas of the parcels, plan totals, and the totals for parishes. Areas typescript is provided automatically by the filmsetter from punched tape supplied by the computer.

The method of providing lettering and numbers is common to maps at all scales. A collation form is used by the draughtsman to specify the typeface and point size, and also the spacing. The names are then typed on a 'Monotype' keyboard which reproduces them on punched paper tape to operate the filmsetter. Names on film produced in this way are then 'stripped in', by cutting up and positioning them correctly on the map. Standard symbols, such as vegetation, are applied in a similar manner. Finally the map image is transferred to a glass base in order to maintain the accuracy of the survey and facilitate map revision.

With appropriate variation all map series are produced by combinations of such basic processes. Although some of the generalization required to produce small from larger scale maps is still undertaken by hand – and judgement is often as important as mechanical accuracy – photography remains the main ally of the draughtsman at a number of critical stages. Scribing is widely used, but a few features such as rock surfaces and slopes are still hand drawn on the 1:10 000 map. Detail to be reproduced in different colours on the final map has to be drawn separately and the marriage, with meticulous attention being paid to correct registration, takes place in the printing process.

The Reproduction Division employs about 450 men and women of different skills. The printing section, which creates the final output of much of the work of the national survey, employs about 100 men. In addition to its own map series the Ordnance Survey prints on a repayment basis maps for other government departments, in particular, the Ministry of Defence and the Directorate of Overseas Surveys. It also prints, publishes, and distributes geological and soil survey maps on behalf of the Institute of Geological Sciences, The Soil Survey of England and Wales, and the Macaulay Institute for Soil Research for Scotland.

The main printing process is offset lithography, in which a separate printing plate is made for each colour, but the use of screens, etc, makes it possible to produce shades or combinations of colours on the printed map. Printing machines are designed for various paper size ranges and for printing one, two, or four colours on each pass through the press. The processes of damping, inking, and sheet positioning are all automatic. The Reproduction Division is also responsible for printing map covers, folding maps, and casing them in hard covers where applicable.

Statistics for the printing activities of the Ordnance Survey provide a useful index of the magnitude of its operations. Available figures relate to the number of *impressions taken* rather than the number of *maps published* (a single one-inch map, for example, from a printing point of view, requires six impressions to be made, one for each colour). By this statistic, in 1972–3, the Ordnance Survey produced no less than 74 million single impressions of maps. Approximately one-third of these were for its outside customers, but this left over 47 million impressions as the total of Ordnance Survey map printing in a single year. Of the 1:50 000, one-inch, and tourist maps, no less than 32 million impressions were printed. Other operations in connection with the printed maps included the folding and casing of nearly 2.6 million maps. The growing importance of other services rendered by the Ordnance Survey is reflected by the fact that over 140 000 microfilms were made of large scale maps and a further 360 000 at scale transparencies were supplied.[1] These are some of the basic outputs of the national survey. They offer a simple yardstick by which to gauge the increasing appetite of the country for maps in the 1970s, for both practical and academic purposes, and the Ordnance Survey's primary role in meeting this demand.

Marketing

The Government statement of February 1973, that the Ordnance Survey should 'seek to maximize returns on all products and services' (see p. 1), obviously increases the importance of the marketing organization, which may be regarded as the final stage in the sequence of Ordnance Survey operations. Marketing of maps and mapping services is the responsibility of Publication Division which also has the task of putting Ordnance Survey

1 Ordnance Survey, *Annual Report 1972–73* (1973), Appendix 4.

publication policy into effect. This policy reflects the dual role of the Department as the official map publisher of Great Britain and as principal source of survey and mapping material for use by outside map publishers and others. The division, in which some 170 staff are employed, is thus structured to market the Department's publications, mapping services, and mapping material and also to administer the arrangements to protect Crown copyright in Ordnance Survey maps and to collect revenue from royalties for reproduction rights.

The distribution of Ordnance Survey paper printed maps is undertaken mainly by direct supply to the retail trade; maps in other forms and copies of surveyors' master survey drawings are supplied through retail mail order. Examples of the latter include transparencies at scale on plastic materials or miniaturized in the form of 35 mm microfilms mounted in aperture cards, electrostatic prints of enlargements or reductions of standard published maps, maps mounted either in single or composite form, map reproduction material either in the form of film for lithographic printing or, where available, on magnetic tape, and maps or map extracts specially printed to customers' own requirements. A small number of sales outlets are equipped to supply printouts from microfilm of large scale maps directly to customers. This service may be extended, and in future printouts made in this way may, to a large extent, replace the conventional printed large scale maps. Each month the division publishes the Ordnance Survey's *Publication Report* which lists new and revised editions of maps at all scales. It also issues, about eight times a year, a periodical entitled *Map News and Review* which gives information about forthcoming publications and promotional activities to trade customers.

The administration of copyright in Ordnance Survey maps and mapping material and the collection of revenue for reproduction rights is another important task. Users who require to reproduce Ordnance Survey maps fall into two broad groups; business users, who require to make copies of maps for business or professional purposes, and other map publishers who use Ordnance Survey maps or mapping material to compile their own map publications. In practice most business users are licensed to reproduce maps in their own offices and their fees are based on their average annual copying requirements. These users consist mainly of government departments, local authorities, and public utilities who require maps and facilities for copying them for planning purposes and for keeping records, as for example of drainage systems, telephone and electricity cables, and gas mains. In the private sector most holders of licences are in businesses and professions connected with land transfer and development such as architects, solicitors, estate agents, and firms in the construction industry.

The requirements of map publishers are quite different and here assessments for royalties are based on the Ordnance Survey mapping material used by the publisher which is usually redrawn and generalized. Ordnance Survey large scale maps are normally used for street plans but for road maps extensive use is made of Ordnance Survey small scale mapping.

The total revenue collected from the sale of maps and mapping services and from royalty payments amounted in 1972/3 to £1 859 000 and £999 000 respectively. In addition £1 504 000 was received in 1972/3 for survey and mapping services supplied to other government departments.[1]

1 Ordnance Survey, *Annual Report 1972–73* (1973), Appendix 7.

The projection of the Ordnance
Survey maps and the national
reference system

2

A modified form of the Transverse Mercator or Gauss Conformal is the national projection for the maps of the Ordnance Survey of Great Britain. Its development for Ordnance Survey purposes has largely occurred since 1945 and before that date a series of less suitable projections were in use. Projections are of considerable practical as well as theoretical interest to the ordinary map user, in so far as they influence characteristics in the national survey such as the system on which map series are referenced, the arrangements of the sheet lines, and the degree of conformity between sheets.

The Cassini projection and early Ordnance Survey maps

Until 1945 the projection most commonly used by the Ordnance Survey, following the practice of several other national surveys such as those of France and Austria, was the Cassini, or Cassini-Soldner projection.[1] It may be defined as a transverse application of the *plate carrée* or simple non-perspective cylindrical projection.[2] Its most important property is that scale along its central meridian, and everywhere at right angles to it, is true. Elsewhere, on the other hand, the projection distorts the scale in a roughly north to south direction, by an amount which varies as the square of the distance from the central meridian; the greater the longitudinal extent, therefore, the less suitable is Cassini's projection likely to be.

As far as the Ordnance Survey is concerned the complexity arises not so much from the general adoption of this simple projection as from the mode of its application. The essence of Ordnance Survey practice throughout the nineteenth century was that there was not one national Cassini projection covering the whole country, but a series of independent Cassini projections relating either to a county or to a group of counties. Such an approach to map projections in a national survey was widely accepted.[3] A commonly held view in the nineteenth century was that maps of small districts should be complete in themselves: large scale surveys, not only in Great Britain, but also in countries such as France and Belgium, were plotted on a series of separate meridians. It was recognized that this could give accurate results for the purposes for which the maps were designed.

The Cassini projection, introduced in 1745, was first used by the Ordnance Survey in the *Old Series* one-inch maps of England and Wales (1805–73). Although it has been claimed that the one-inch was projected on a single Cassini projection, 'so as to form a continuous series covering the whole of England and Wales',[4] this is unlikely. Winterbotham accepted the nineteenth century view that there were six central meridians for the old one-inch, stretching from Greenwich to Devon,[5] but a recent study of the *Old Series* sheets suggests that only two central meridians, probably those of Butterton Hill and Greenwich, were actually used in the construction of the maps of southern England and, in northern England, they were projected on the meridian of Delamere.[6] In the survey of Ireland (from 1825 onwards), a system of local Cassini projections in which the six-inch maps of any one county were plotted independently of those of other counties was also adopted. A point near the centre of the particular county was selected and along the meridian passing through it lay the origin of the projection relating to that county.[7] It was this technique which, after 1840, was transferred into the

1 For the one-inch maps of Scotland, Bonne's projection (a modified conical projection) was used but this had the disadvantage of creating a discontinuity along the boundary with England.

2 For a description of the Cassini projection see J. A. Steers, *An Introduction to the Study of Map Projections* (7th edn., 1949), 146–9; G. P. Kellaway, *Map Projections* (London, 1970), 32–3.

3 H. St J. L. Winterbotham, 36–8.

4 J. A. Steers, 225; chapter XII dealt with 'Ordnance Survey Map Projections and Grids'.

5 H. St J. L. Winterbotham, 70.

6 See introductory notes to J. B. Harley (ed.), *Reprint of the First Edition of the One-inch Ordnance Survey of England and Wales* (Newton Abbot, 1969–71), sheet 86.

7 Sir Charles Close, *The Early Years of the Ordnance Survey* (1926: New Edition, 1969, with an Introduction by J. B. Harley), 125–6.

large scale survey of Great Britain. To a certain extent it was an unavoidable expedient because, when the large scale surveys were put in hand, the selection and adjustment of the primary and secondary triangulation for the whole country still had to be completed and was not fully available to the detailed survey. A succession of local central meridians were as a result brought into use before the associated tertiary triangulations could be adjusted to the primary triangulation of Great Britain. They proliferated especially before the 'Battle of the Scales' was resolved, and the large scale maps of most counties in southern England, and also of many towns, were published on their own Cassini projections: it is recorded that even the Ordnance Survey buildings at Southampton had their own meridian!

The Davidson Committee and the Transverse Mercator projection

The disadvantages of a relatively *ad hoc* solution to the problem of projecting the Ordnance Survey maps began to be recognized even while it was being created. It became clear that so many meridians were an unsatisfactory development in a national survey and an attempt was made to rationalize the situation. In 1863, for example, Middlesex was combined with Hertfordshire on the meridian of St Paul's and, later, fifteen counties were combined on the Dunnose meridian. A reduction was also made in the number of meridians employed in Scotland but, even with these adjustments, the legacy of multiple meridians was large. The Davidson Committee reported in 1938 that the 1:2500 and 1:10560 series were still projected on thirty-nine different meridians[1] (Plate 1).

An inherent weakness of this system, caused mainly by the unrelated stations of the tertiary triangulation, was that significant discontinuities existed along county boundaries. In the 1891 Parliamentary inquiry on the Ordnance Survey there were complaints about inconveniences owing to this fact between Lancashire and Yorkshire,[2] and the growth of towns across ancient administrative boundaries further exacerbated the position in the twentieth century. The Davidson Committee concluded that the 1:2500 survey, although it eventually covered the greater part of the country, was not really a national survey but a number of county surveys.[3] The sheets, as the *Report* explained did not form a single series.

Every time a county boundary is changed, it involves the change of sheet lines of all the plans in that area. Since plans are completed up to the county boundaries only, the remainder of the sheet is left blank, and adjacent detail on the two sides of a county boundary cannot be fitted together. On the six-inch scale the same area may be represented on three different maps in slightly different ways. Although attempts have been made to 'fill' plans across the county boundary by re-computation of the old framework on the adjacent projection, and by replotting the detail, this course has proved very costly and inapplicable to large areas. Where changes have been made in county boundaries, and such changes are not infrequent, the employment of this process is unavoidable, and it has led to a general loss of accuracy.[4]

Another major disadvantage was that separate meridians inhibited an integrated reference system for the whole country. The case was so strong that the Committee unanimously recommended that the '. . . 1:2500 survey should be re-cast on National instead of county sheet lines on a National projection . . .'.[5]

1 *Final Report* (1938), 38.

2 *Report of the Departmental Committee to Inquire into the Present Condition of the Ordnance Survey* . . . (1893), Minutes of Evidence, 47–8.

3 *Final Report* (1938), 3.

4 *Final Report* (1938), 3. The attempt to remedy the situation is described in *The Replotted Counties* (Ordnance Survey, Supplement to Professional Papers, New Series, No. 16, Southampton, 1934).

5 *Final Report* (1938), 28.

The most suitable projection had to be selected. A Cassini projection based on a single central meridian for Great Britain was considered, but at the east and west limits of the country it would have stretched the topography by nearly 0.1 per cent in a north and south direction. Although this figure is not large – and scale in an east and west direction would remain correct – the Cassini projection was rejected for three reasons. First, there was no simple way in which correction for distortion on this projection could be made. Second, even a 0.1 per cent distortion was sufficient to affect the calculation of areas from the published maps. Third, in areas of maximum distortion, the accuracy of minor instrumental surveys, which had to be related to detail on existing Ordnance Survey maps, was likely to be affected to an extent where it became difficult to reconcile positions fixed by survey with detail on the published maps. The adoption of a single Cassini projection could have created greater difficulties than it overcame.

The Transverse Mercator, a conformal or orthomorphic version of the Cassini projection, and especially suitable for a country which has its greatest extent in a north–south direction, was accepted as the best alternative.[1] Along its central meridian scale is true and the amount of distortion, equal in an east and west as well as in a north and south direction, varies with the square of the distance from it. Meridians and parallels always intersect at right angles. The main difference, therefore, as compared with the simple Cassini, was that the projection stretched the topography equally in all directions, rather than only in a north–south direction, and this gave it the property of conformality or orthomorphism, in which there is a minimal distortion of shape over small areas and the scale, although it varies throughout the projection as a whole, is likewise equal in all directions at any one point. For large scale mapping these attributes are especially valuable.

A point of origin at Lat. 49° North; Long. 2° West of Greenwich was selected, the same as for the National Grid. One of the advantages of the projection is the ease with which the amount of distortion can be calculated[2] and, in addition, scale variation owing to projection can be lessened by a simple expedient. The method adopted is to shrink the central meridian (Long. 2° West) by the application of a 'scale factor', so as to redistribute some of the error away from the extremities of the projection. The change in scale is conveniently accomplished by reducing all dimensions of the spheroid by 0.04 per cent before calculating the projection. Along the central meridian the true scale is accordingly reduced by approximately 0.04 per cent, and it is enlarged by the same amount along the edges of the projection. The result is that the projection becomes correct in scale (i.e. there is zero distortion) along two lines at about 180 km east and west of the central meridian[3] and nearly parallel with it.

Without such a correction maps near the central meridian would be exactly on the scale of 1:2500 and those on the east and west coasts of Britain at 1:2498. Application of the 'scale factor' allows this discrepancy to be halved. The net result is that the scale of maps in the central portion of the country, in the vicinity of Long. 2° West, is about 1:2501 (approximately 0.04 per cent too small); the scale of maps on the extreme east and west coasts is about 1:2499 (approximately 0.04 per cent too large); and the intervening maps vary between these limits. Put another way, at its maximum, the remaining errors do not exceed 1 m in 2500.[4] Such distortion is hardly of practical significance as far as the published maps are concerned. It is probably

1 By 1938 the Ordnance Survey had already gained considerable experience with this projection. During World War 1 the Cassini projection, which stretched topography in one direction only and thereby distorted angles, proved unsuitable for artillery purposes. The possibility of using a conformal projection was therefore investigated and, beginning in 1931 with the Fifth Edition, the 1:63 360 map of Great Britain was redrawn on the Transverse Mercator which, by that date, had also been successfully used in a number of colonial surveys.

2 [Ordnance Survey] *Constants, Formulae and Methods used in the Transverse Mercator Projection* (HMSO, London, 1950).

3 That is, at about two-thirds of the distance between the central meridian and the edge of the projection.

4 These figures for scale only apply to the mainland of Great Britain. Scale error can reach 1:980 – for example on the west of the Outer Hebrides.

less than the normal expansion and contraction of paper caused by variations in atmospheric humidity. With regard to area measurements, a percentage correction is made for distortion, which at its maximum amounts to about 0.5 acre per square mile, and these corrected areas are shown on the published maps (see p. 56).

For some surveying operations it may be helpful to know the local scale factor at a point and it is obtained by the ratio:

Grid distance/Ground distance.

Although in theory the local scale factor is defined as being at a point, it may, for the practical purpose of minor survey or traversing, be assumed as constant for a small area of about 10 km radius. In the following table values for the local scale factor are given in terms of National Grid eastings at 10 km interval. To the accuracy given, which is sufficient for most practical purposes, the local scale factor is independent of the National Grid northings of the area.

Table 2   Local scale factors

National Grid Eastings		Local scale factor	National Grid Eastings		Local scale factor	National Grid Eastings		Local scale factor
400 km	400 km	0.99960	300 km	500 km	0.99972	200 km	600 km	1.00009
390	410	0.99960	290	510	0.99975	190	610	1.00014
380	420	0.99961	280	520	0.99978	180	620	1.00020
370	430	0.99961	270	530	0.99981	170	630	1.00025
360	440	0.99962	260	540	0.99984	160	640	1.00031
350	450	0.99963	250	550	0.99988	150	650	1.00037
340	460	0.99965	240	560	0.99992	140	660	1.00043
330	470	0.99966	230	570	0.99996	130	670	1.00050
320	480	0.99968	220	580	1.00000			
310	490	0.99970	210	590	1.00004			

The two columns of National Grid eastings indicate that two points the same distance from, but on opposite sides of, the central meridian have the same local scale factor.

Distances measured on the ground must be converted into grid distances before they are used for computations on the projection; this conversion is effected by multiplying the ground distance by the appropriate local scale factor. If the ground lengths are measured in feet they are converted to metres by the conversion factor 0.3048, and then converted to grid distances in the manner described.

Ground lengths should be reduced to lengths at mean sea level, if necessary, before conversion and vice versa. A height of 1000 ft above mean sea level will produce a difference of 1 part in 20 000.

Summarizing,

Local scale factor = Grid distance/Ground distance

Grid distance   = Local scale factor × Ground distance
                          (*Ground distance to be in metres*)

Ground distance = Grid distance ÷ Local scale factor.

The retriangulation and the national projection

The fact that a retriangulation was in progress made the Davidson Committee's recommendation about a national projection easier to put into effect. The old Cassini projections of the County Series maps were, as already noted, loosely based on the old triangulation completed in 1858.[1] While this was of sufficient accuracy for contemporary geodetic calculations, by the 1920s it was no longer of an acceptable standard. Its deficiencies were summed up by a geodesist working with the Ordnance Survey:

For all modern practical purposes there is . . . no consistent National Triangulation of Great Britain, but only a large number of semi-independent triangulations which cannot now be brought into sympathy; owing partly to the fact that too few of the old stations can now be recovered with enough certainty to connect these detached triangulations to the primary work through a limited amount of re-observation: and partly to the fact that the original observations, undertaken solely for the purpose of providing rapid control for the 1 : 2500 mapping of Counties or groups of Counties, are not sufficiently accurate to cover large areas.[2]

The old triangulation was especially weak in some areas, as in Lancashire and Yorkshire and many parts of Scotland, and in other districts the original triangulation stations had been obliterated. It was decided to produce a complete retriangulation, to which a new primary triangulation would be an essential foundation. Work on the retriangulation began in 1936 and by 1938 it covered the whole of Great Britain north to approximately the line of the Caledonian Canal. During World War II the retriangulation was virtually suspended with only a little secondary and tertiary work being completed. The primary survey was restarted in Scotland in 1948 and was completed in 1952.[3] A variety of new observations and corrections have been made subsequently, as in 1955, for example, when the primary triangulation of South Wales had to be adjusted because two primary stations had moved owing to mining subsidence.

The National Grid

Although the Departmental Committee of 1891 made a thorough investigation of the question of indexing Ordnance Survey maps on various scales,[4] not until during World War I was the problem of creating a national reference system seriously grappled with. For military purposes, a workable grid by which points could be located and referenced was essential and, out of this need, developed the so-called 'British Grid System'. This was adopted on military maps in 1919 and, in 1927, it was replaced by the 'Modified British System', which remained in use throughout World War II. In the military grid, areas were broken down into progressively smaller squares, with sides in turn representing 500 km, 100 km, 10 km, and 1 km. Letters were allocated to the 500 km and 100 km squares and numbers to the 10 km squares, so that a point reference could be given in letters and numbers.[5] This grid was in use in World War II and was overprinted on War Office editions of Ordnance Survey maps. It should not be confused with the present National Grid.

The development of the National Grid, although influenced by the War Office Grid, was also affected by Ordnance Survey experiments on its regular series of maps. A grid, for example, with lines 5000 yards apart and giving full co-ordinates, was authorized in 1929 and printed on the Fifth Edition of

1 A. R. Clarke (1858).

2 M. Hotine, 'The Retriangulation of Great Britain', *Empire Survey Review*, **4** (1937), 132.

3 For a description see [Ordnance Survey] *History of the Retriangulation of Great Britain* (HMSO, London, 1967).

4 *Report of the Departmental Committee . . .* (1893), Minutes of Evidence, *passim*.

5 J. A. Steers, 228–9, for a description.

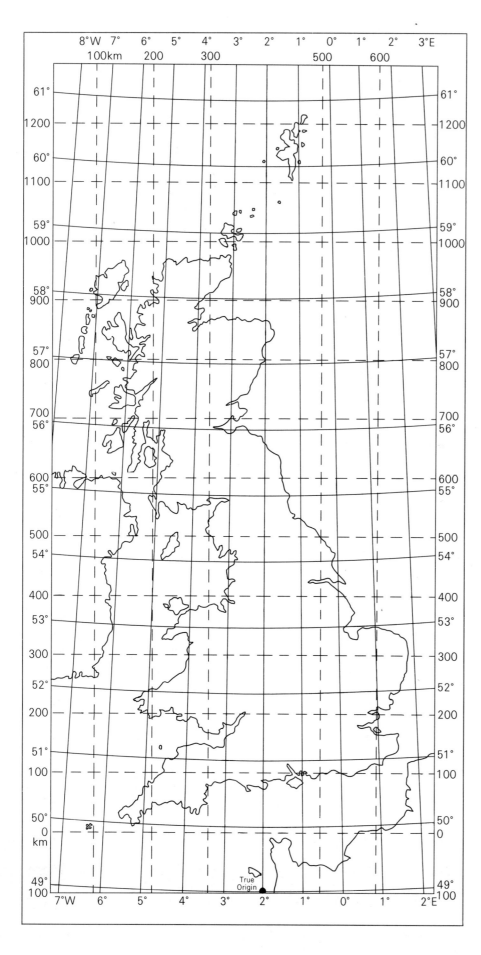

Figure 6
Relationship of the Transverse
Mercator graticule to the
National Grid system on
Ordnance Survey Maps.
The continuous lines represent
the projection; the broken
lines the National Grid.

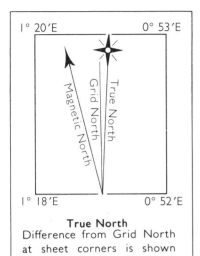

1° 20′E   0° 53′E

1° 18′E   0° 52′E

True North
Difference from Grid North at sheet corners is shown above
Magnetic North
About $7\frac{1}{2}°$ W of Grid North in 1972 decreasing by about $\frac{1}{2}°$ in eight years

Figure 7
True, grid and magnetic north
(After 1 : 63 360 sheet 176)

1 H. St J. L. Winterbotham, 'The Use of the New Grid on Ordnance Survey Maps', *The Geographical Journal*, **82** (1933), 42–54.

2 *Final Report* (1938), 2–5.

the one-inch map.[1] This series commenced publication in 1931, but together with other experiments the grid was overtaken by the Davidson Report. After reviewing the historical precedents for the use of grids on Ordnance Survey maps and assessing their practical advantages a clear recommendation was made that '. . . a National Grid should be super-imposed on all large scale plans and on smaller scale maps, to provide one reference system for the maps of the whole country'.[2] At the same time the international metre was put forward as the unit on which the grid should be based.

The relationship over Great Britain of the lines of the National Grid to the Transverse Mercator projection graticule (representing lines of latitude and longitude) is indicated in Figure 6. Although the small longitudinal extent of the British Isles prevents any serious divergence of the two systems, an exact fit of grid and graticule cannot of course be achieved. The difference in direction between the grid and graticule lines is known as Convergence; the value of the convergence is zero along the meridian 2° w but varies over the rest of the projection (Figure 7).

It may occasionally be necessary to know the angle, at any point in the projection, between the meridian and the grid line (i.e. between True North and Grid North). To calculate this accurately requires special tables; but the following formula gives the convergence to within $\frac{1}{4}$ minute of arc:

$$C' = \Delta\lambda' \times \sin \phi_p$$

Where

C' = Convergence, in minutes, of the meridian at a point, positive when measured clockwise, negative when anti-clockwise, from Grid North.

$\Delta\lambda'$ = longitude difference, in minutes of arc, between the point and the central meridian (2° w), positive when west, negative when east of the central meridian.

ϕ_p = Latitude of point.

Note $\Delta\lambda'$ should be measured to $\frac{1}{4}$ minute of arc. If less accurately known then the accuracy of the result will be of the same order as that to which $\Delta\lambda'$ is measured:

ϕ_p should be measured to 5 minutes of arc.

Example At a point in Norfolk 1° 10′ E, 52° 40′ N.

$\Delta\lambda = -190' \sin 52° 40' = 0.79512$
$C' = -190 \times 0.79512 = -151$ minutes = 2° 31′ West of Grid North.

The Grid bearing, True bearing, and Convergence are thus connected by the following relationship:

Grid bearing = True bearing + Convergence.

True bearings are measured clockwise and C has the sign as defined above.

Figure 6 shows the National Grid to be series of lines drawn parallel and at right angles to the central meridian of the projection, thus forming a series of equal squares on the paper. The number and spacing of grid lines for any map series depends on its scale. On standard Ordnance Survey maps the interval is 10 km on the 1 : 625 000 and 1 : 250 000 series; 1 km on the 1 : 63 360, 1 : 50 000, 1 : 25 000, 1 : 10 560, and 1 : 10 000 series; and 100 m on the 1 : 2500 and 1 : 1250 series. From grid lines so spaced references can be given with a precision appropriate to the scale of the map.

The method of grid reference

The distinction in Ordnance Survey usage between rectangular co-ordinates as derived from the Transverse Mercator projection and National Grid[1] references needs to be noted. Rectangular co-ordinates are used for calculations, rather than for reference purposes, but they appear in some Ordnance Survey publications and require definition.[2] Co-ordinates are a series of figures, given in two groups, which define the position of a point in terms of its distance east and north, from an origin. In applying this system to the Transverse Mercator projection covering Great Britain, the true origin of which is 2° West 49° North, a false origin is employed. Were rectangular co-ordinates to be calculated from the true origin, the positions lying west of the central meridian would be negative and the northings, although all positive, would exceed 1000 km for some points in north Scotland. To avoid inconvenience 400 km are added to all easting co-ordinates and 100 km subtracted from all northing co-ordinates. Rectangular co-ordinates quoted by the Ordnance Survey are thus related to a false or working origin, Lat. 49° 46′ N; Long. 7° 33′ W of Greenwich, slightly southwest of the Isles of Scilly. This ensures that co-ordinates of all points on the mainland of Great Britain are positive and less than 1000 km. Since the linear unit of the Ordnance Survey is the metre, co-ordinates are expressed in metres and decimals of a metre according to the standard of precision required. Figure 9(a) illustrates a simple example in which the National Grid rectangular co-ordinates of a point P, in Greater London are 538 932 East and 177 061 North.

Grid references, however, although they are also related to the same false origin off the Isles of Scilly, do not give the actual distances from this point, but employ letters and numbers in the National Grid system to denote location. The National Grid, like its military predecessors, consists of a systematic breakdown of the grid area into progressively smaller squares identified by letters and then by numbers. The largest units are 500 km squares, each designated by a prefix letter – the first letter to be quoted in the National Grid reference (Figure 8). The 500 km squares are then broken down into twenty-five 100 km squares: currently these are also designated by a prefix letter – the second letter of today's grid reference – although formerly they were referenced by figures.[3] Figure 8, representing the grid of 100 km squares covering Great Britain, identifies these letters and beneath (in brackets) the numbers they replace; the latter are shown because there are still Ordnance Survey maps in use which are referenced in this way. Under the present system no two 100 km squares can have the same combination of prefix letters.

Within the 100 km squares each smaller grid square (of 10 km, 1 km, or 100 m side) is designated by the distance of its *south-west corner* from the west (eastings) and south (northings) margins, respectively, of the 100 km square in which it lies. To enable these distances, or co-ordinates, to be easily found their values are printed in the map margins against the grid lines concerned. These provide the numbers – two, four, or six – which identify each particular grid square. A point or feature within one of the smallest grid squares can be indicated still more closely by estimating the tenths of the appropriate grid square either by eye or by means of a romer.[4]

1 On the relationship of the National Grid to other systems see D. H. Maling, *Co-ordinate Systems and Map Projections* (London, 1973); also Keith Clayton, 'Geographical Reference Systems', *The Geographical Journal*, **137** (1971), 1–13.

2 [Ordnance Survey] *Constants, Formulae and Methods*, 17 et seq.

3 The National Grid has been adopted in military as well as civilian maps and the changeover from figures to letters was made in 1951, to help bring the two systems into line. In the old references the initial numbers were separated from the remainder by a stroke in the manner 51/3877.

4 G. C. Dickinson, *Maps and Air Photographs* (London, 1969), 112–17.

Figure 8
National reference system of
Great Britain

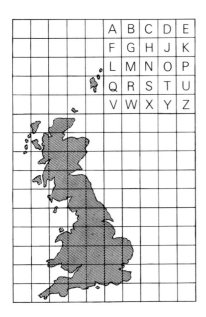

(a) 500 kilometre squares of
the National Grid

(b) Each 500 kilometre square
is divided into twenty-five
100 kilometre squares

(c) 100 kilometre squares that
cover Great Britain with
their reference letters
and (in brackets) the
numbers formerly used

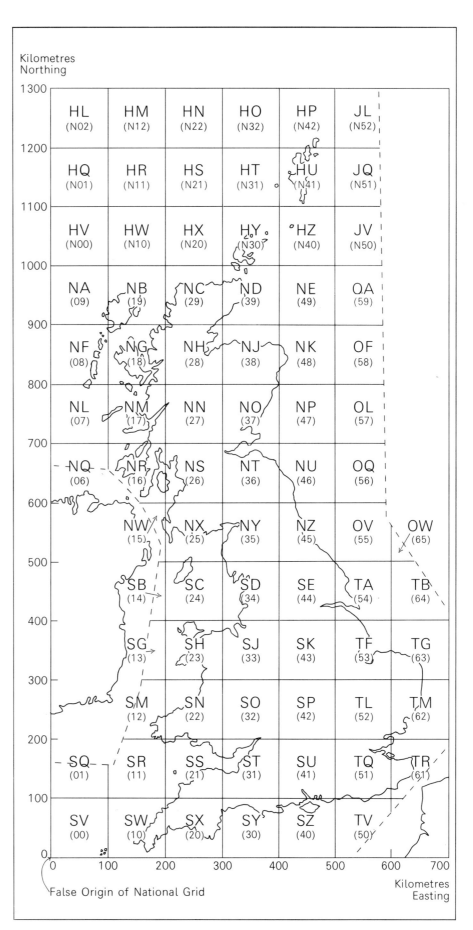

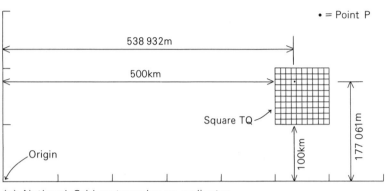

• = Point P

(a) National Grid rectangular co-ordinates
of a point P in the 100km square TQ.

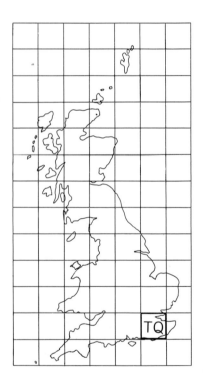

(b) 100km square TQ in relation
to the base 100km grid.

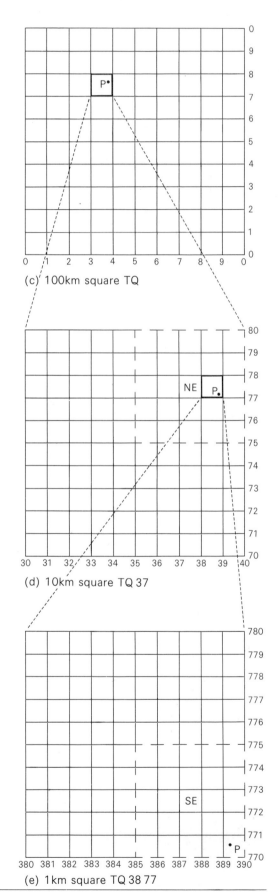

(c)′ 100km square TQ

(d) 10km square TQ 37

(e) 1km square TQ 38 77

(c) 100km square TQ

Grid intervals of 10km
Full grid reference: TQ 3877
Applicable to map scales:
1:625 000 (Part of South Sheet)
1:250 000 (Part of Sheet 17)

(d) 10km square TQ 37

Grid intervals of 1km
Full grid reference: TQ 389 770
Applicable to map scales:
1:63 360 (Part of Sheet 171)*
1:50 000 (Part of Sheets 176 & 177)
1:25 000 (Sheet TQ 37)
1:10 560 (Sheet TQ 37 NE)*
1:10 000 (Sheet TQ 37 NE)
* Withdrawn

(e) 1km square TQ 38 77

Grid intervals of 100m
Full grid reference: TQ 3893 7706
Applicable to map scales:
1:2500 (Sheet TQ 38 77)
1:1250 (Sheet TQ 3877 SE)

Figure 9
Grid references at various scales

Examples of grid references

In the National Grid reference system the initial two prefix letters immediately locate the 100 km square in which the point falls. The remaining figures, the number of which depends on the scale of the map, enable the point to be located with reference to the west and south sides of the 100 km square concerned. The point can normally be located to one-tenth of the grid interval as shown in the map margin.

When giving a National Grid reference, or rectangular co-ordinates, for any point, the distance eastwards (eastings) is always given before the distance northwards (northings). Eastings and northings must always be recorded in the same number of figures, even though some of them may be zero.

Examples of full grid references at various scales, illustrated in Figure 9, are given in Table 3.

In these examples, which serve as a summary of the system, a full grid reference is given in all cases. This is unique within Great Britain and there is no other grid reference exactly the same. If, however, the first letter (T) is omitted, all references will be repeated in the adjoining 500 km squares; if the second letter (Q) is omitted as well, the same reference will be repeated in the adjacent 100 km square. Prefix letters can only be omitted, therefore, when there is no likelihood of ambiguity arising from a reference being repeated elsewhere at 500 km or 100 km distance.

Table 3   Grid references for a point, P*, at various scales

Map scale	Grid interval of	Grid reference	Precision
1:625 000	10 000 metres	TQ 38 77	1000 metres
1:250 000	10 000 metres	TQ 38 77	1000 metres
1:63 360	1000 metres	TQ 389 770	100 metres
1:50 000	1000 metres	TQ 389 770	100 metres
1:25 000	1000 metres	TQ 389 770	100 metres
1:10 000	1000 metres	TQ 389 770	100 metres
1:10 560	1000 metres	TQ 389 770	100 metres
1:2500	100 metres	TQ 3893 7706	10 metres
1:1250	100 metres	TQ 3893 7706	10 metres

* Point P has National Grid rectangular co-ordinates (to the nearest metre) of 538 932 East and 177 061 North (see Figure 9).

Sheet numbering of National Grid maps

A further application of the National Grid is that it enables the 1:25 000 and all map series at larger scales published by the Ordnance Survey to be numbered in accordance with the grid reference of their south-west corner. Although maps at scales smaller than 1:25 000 all carry the National Grid, sheet numbering is based on different principles and does not conform to the system outlined below.

1:25 000 maps   A 1:25 000 sheet is denoted by the grid reference of its south-west corner to the nearest 10 km, e.g. TQ 37. In the *Second Series*, where each sheet represents two 10 km squares, each unit was originally numbered separately by its south-west corner, e.g. TQ 27 and TQ 37, but they are now designated in the form TQ 27/37.

1 : 10 560 and 1 : 10 000 maps The sheets in these series are denoted by the addition of quadrant letters to the 1 : 25 000 sheet reference, e.g. TQ 37 NE.

1 : 2500 maps A 1 : 2500 sheet is denoted by the grid reference of its south-west corner to the nearest 1 km, e.g. TQ 3877. For convenience of users, however, 1 : 2500 plans are normally paired into a sheet representing an area of 2 sq km and these are referenced by the south-west corner of each component 1 km square, e.g. TQ 3877 and TQ 3977 (listed in the *Publication Reports* as TQ 3877–3977).

1 : 1250 maps A 1 : 1250 sheet is denoted by the addition of quadrant letters to the 1 : 2500 map reference, e.g. TQ 3877 SE.

A fuller description of the National Grid information appearing on the various map series appears in the account of individual scales in Chapters 3 to 9. See also Plate 7.

The National Grid and the computer

Although the National Grid was originally designed as a reference system to serve in a less computer conscious age, the convenience of such a system in an age when computers are widely used – not least for mapping purposes – is now increasingly evident. The 1960s, which saw the beginnings of an effective technology for computer cartography, also witnessed the harnessing of the National Grid in Britain to new purposes, both by the Ordnance Survey itself and by other map users. The place of the National Grid in the development by the Ordnance Survey of a system of digital mapping for its large scale maps (described in Chapter 3, see p. 46) will be obvious but, in addition, outside the Ordnance Survey, the National Grid has been brought into use in the computer processing of statistical information including (in linked systems) its automatic mapping. In the mid 1960s it was found that planning authorities made hardly any use of the National Grid in connection with such operations[1] but, by the 1970s, its value in providing a simple geometric mesh of squares with a ready-made system of co-ordinate references which are ideally suited to the machine processing and plotting of data, came to be widely appreciated, especially as electronic digitizers have made it possible to find the grid reference of any point on a map with great speed and accuracy.

A particular application is that mapping by National Grid units helps to solve the problem of the inflexibility of standard administrative units which can distort the patterns revealed by data in conventional mapping and effect their comparability in space. Instead of these traditional areas, various aggregates or subdivisions of standard grid squares can form basic cells for thematic mapping[2] or, as in other systems such as LINMAP (line printer mapping),[3] in a dot system which is equally flexible. With grid mapping, the size of the mesh or grid cell can be varied with the nature of the data or research problem. In a pilot study of population enumeration on a grid square basis, for example, undertaken with the census of Scotland, a 200 m grid, easily derived from the 100 m intervals on the 1 : 2500 series, was employed.[4] On all large scale maps the fact, moreover, that co-ordinate references can be given down to 1 m has enabled an extensive application of the National Grid in the geocoding system adopted for the 1971 census. An early information paper on the census reported that:

1 G. M. Gaits, 'Thematic Mapping by Computer', *The Cartographic Journal*, 6 (1969), 51.

2 Isobel M. L. Robertson, 'The National Grid and Social Geography', *Geography*, 55 (1970), 426–33.

3 G. M. Gaits, *passim*.

4 Jean Forbes and Isobel M. L. Robertson, 'Population Enumeration on a Grid Square Basis: The Census of Scotland, A Test Case', *The Cartographic Journal*, 4 (1967), 29–37.

1 '1971 Census Information Paper 1' (General Register Office, mimeographed, May 1970).

2 '1971 Census Information Paper 5' (General Register Office, mimeographed, n.d.).

3 K. Rosing and P. Wood, *Computer Atlas of the West Midlands* (London, 1971).

4 F. Hackman, 'Scaling the Heights', *Geographical Magazine*, **44** (1972), 778–80.

5 G. A. Hackman, E. C. Willatts, and J. Worth, 'Instant Maps for Planners', *Geographical Magazine*, **44** (1972), 775–7.

Statistics from the 1971 census will be made more flexible for spatial analysis by the inclusion of a geocode for the place of enumeration of *each household. The geocodes will be National Grid co-ordinate references and will permit the aggregation of individual data, or permit other manipulations.*[1]

Among the advantages of the use of a geocode or co-ordinate reference (over enumeration districts for example) were the areal and temporal compatibility of information, the fact that household data could be more fully used without destroying its confidentiality, the use of co-ordinate reference in computations which involve locations, and the potential for computer mapping on equal area units that are spatially regular and universal. The fact that referencing down to 100 m squares is built into the National Grid at the basic scales from 1:1250 to 1:2500 had meant that a discontinuous system of full co-ordinate referencing (down to 1 m as a link code on each enumerated address) was technically feasible. In practice it was hoped to give co-ordinate references for approximately 18 million households enumerated in Great Britain in 1971 and to provide standard sets of statistics on different combinations of grid squares.[2]

That some of the pioneer studies of the National Grid in computer processing and mapping of statistics should have taken place with census data is understandable but it will be obvious that the applications are manifold. Experience has already been gained with mapping of industrial statistics[3] and with physical data,[4] to give just two further examples, while for planners an unprecedented attraction is maps which are not only more precisely tailored to their immediate purposes, but also, with a minimum of delay, can embody the latest statistical information.[5] It is clear that the National Grid will continue to play a much larger role in the computer age than could possibly have been foreseen for it by the Davidson Committee.

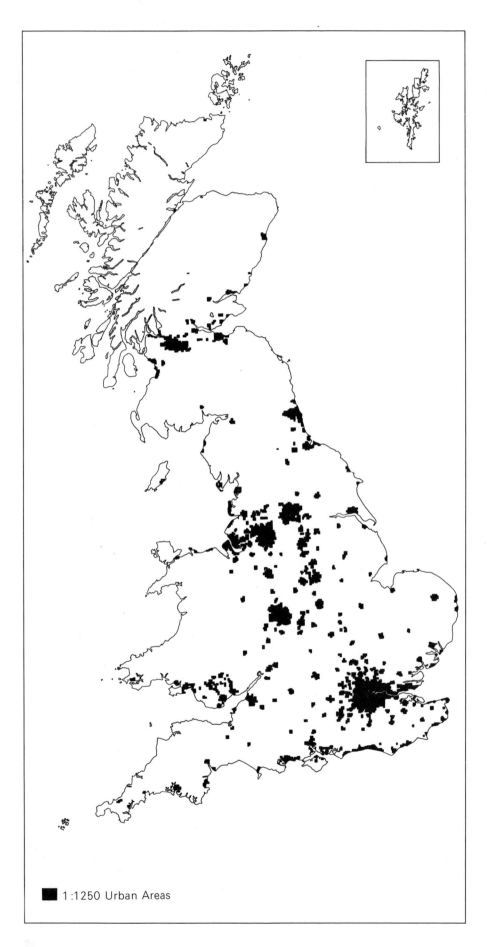

1:1250 Urban Areas

Figure 10
Extent of published areas at
1:1250 scale 1973

The 1:1250 series

The current 1:1250 series was born out of a recommendation of the Davidson Committee. Although it envisaged that priority should be given to the revision and recasting of the 1:2500 maps on National Grid lines, once this was completed, it suggested that '. . . further investigations should be carried out with a view to establishing whether the requirements of urban areas would not be more adequately met by a survey on the 1:1250 scale'.[1] The outbreak of war forestalled any action, but in the early 1940s it became apparent that the need for urban 1:1250 scale coverage was widespread. It was decided that the series should be started before the completion of urban areas at the 1:2500 scale (as suggested by the Committee), but that it would be limited to major towns and urban areas rather than including all built-up areas. A feasibility survey was conducted in the Bournemouth area to see whether the new series could be enlarged from an overhaul of 1:2500 maps or whether a complete resurvey would be necessary.[2] A decision was made in 1943 that resurvey at the 1:1250 scale was essential for major urban areas, and this resurvey, coupled with the subsequent establishment of continuous revision in urban areas, was given high priority in the post-World War II programme of mapping. The choice of scale was natural enough. Not only did a 1:1250 series possess a convenient proportional relationship to the 1:2500 maps (and to the obsolete 1:500 town plans) but also, since 1911, maps at the 1:1250 scale had been produced for specialized purposes, such as land registration, by means of direct photographic enlargement from 1:2500 maps.[3]

Maps at the 1:1250 scale cover approximately 5.7 per cent of Great Britain (Figure 10) and in 1972 there were some 50 000 sheets in the whole series. Although the initial rate of publication was slow, there was then a rapid acceleration in the programme, especially after the systematic adoption of air survey methods in 1949. The current position is that the sheets have been published for the great majority of all areas qualifying for 1:1250 survey, as shown in Table 4 below.

Table 4   Publication of the 1:1250 maps, 1948–1973

Published maps	Annual average				Total 31 March 1973	Total* in series
	1946–55	1956–60	1961–5	1966–70		
First editions all methods	1500	2440	2042	1314	47 436	51 694
Revised editions (revision started in 1949)	376	484	1137	2286	32 099	

* The statistics exclude 75 maps made for the Isle of Man.

Source: Ordnance Survey, *Annual Report 1972–73* (1973), Appendix 1.

1 *Final Report* (1938), 15.

2 G. Cheetham, 'The Post-War Programme of the Ordnance Survey of Great Britain', *Empire Survey Review*, **8** (1945), 93–102.

3 *A Description of Ordnance Survey Large Scale Plans*, 11.

4 R. P. Wheeler, 'The 1:1250 Resurvey of Great Britain', *Empire Survey Review*, **9** (1946), 235.

The criteria for areas to be mapped at the 1:1250 scale have altered since the inception of the series. They originally included all county boroughs, municipal boroughs, urban districts, and similar units with a population of over 10 000 excluding continuously built-up areas, the aggregate population of which exceeded 10 000, yet covering several administrative units. These were later brought within the scope of the series.[4] The present rule is flexibly interpreted to include all towns of over 20 000 population which would be covered by forty maps and over; a contiguous group of towns are regarded as one for this purpose. Smaller places of exceptional interest can also be mapped at 1:1250 scale.

On the edge of areas mapped at the 1:1250 scale a further problem of definition arises. It is partly solved by a rule of thumb that all continuously built-up areas with a density of 100 houses or more per 1:1250 map should be included but each urban area is still treated on its own merit. The core of 1:1250 mapping is, for example, often extended to embrace complex industrial installations, zones where development at a comparable density is scheduled, and areas in which an arbitrary termination of mapping at one scale would exclude a small area of a single administrative authority. The boundary of 1:1250 mapping is kept under continual review and is extended as urban development occurs appropriate to its scale.

Format, referencing and marginalia

Standard maps in the 1:1250 series measure 40×40 cm (c. 15¾ inches square) and represent an area of 500 m square (25 hectares or 61.8 acres). Extended sheets are sometimes used, especially where it is clear that no further survey at the scale will take place, for example, when an area is bounded by a sea or lake shore. Maps are extended in *either* a north–south *or* an east–west direction to a maximum of an additional 16 cm, but extensions are not added in both directions to the same map. Small extensions are also accommodated by a local break in the inner (but not the outer) border of the map.

Four 1:1250 sheets represent the same area as a basic 1 km square unit in the 1:2500 series. This is the key to the application of the National Grid reference system and a 1:1250 map is accordingly denoted by the addition of quadrant letters to the 1:2500 sheet number, for example, TQ3877SE. National Grid lines are shown at 100 m intervals. Full grid values are given at the corner of the sheets and the intervening values in hundreds of metres. An inner border is divided at 10 m intervals. Values for latitude and longitude are not recorded. Outer borders of sheets published until 1969 were graduated in scales of feet (west and south) and chains and links (north and east). Information in the south margin of the sheet includes an explanation of how to give a National Grid reference defining the position of a point to the nearest 10 m and a selection of conventional signs and abbreviations used on the map. On maps published prior to 1969 standard information on the dates of survey, revision, boundaries, levelling, and tides was shown on the north margin. On metric versions of the maps, published since 1969, this information, together with a 'Conversion Scale: Metres – Feet', is shown on the south margin.

Landscape at 1:1250

The 1:1250 maps are at the largest of all current Ordnance Survey scales, and, as such, particular interest attaches to the amount of detail they contain, the method of its representation, and its relationship to features actually on the ground. The fact that surface detail in towns is extremely complex, coupled with the high value of urban land, makes such considerations of considerable practical importance. Some of the attributes of the 1:1250 scale, for example that every 100 m grid square on the map represents 1 hectare on the ground or, similarly, that 1 sq inch on the map shows roughly a quarter (0.249) of an acre, are fairly well known, but misconceptions are commonly held as to the exact terms of reference of the series. Maps are sometimes loosely referred to as providing a 'complete' record of the landscape or as showing 'all' features true to scale and so on. The truth is, that like any map they omit some details, generalize others, enlarge other features to a minimum size, and use conventional signs to codify much of the surface detail. They owe their distinctive character to the fact that the detail which does appear is standardized by a set of elaborate, although not necessarily inflexible, rules adopted alike by surveyors and draughtsmen.

These rules have positive and negative aspects. On the positive side, the basic objective of the 1:1250 series is to represent all permanent detail at *ground surface level*, which can be accommodated at this scale. This means in practice that all permanent objects or buildings, the plan outline of which covers an area of 8 sq m or more, will be shown as a matter of routine. Smaller buildings or objects may be included where they are in a detached position, so as to be relatively important topographical features, and provided that they cover an area of at least 1 sq m (or their smallest side is 1 m or more in length). Detail too small to be drawn to scale in its correct position, when it is sufficiently important or prominent to be a useful feature of the map, is represented by conventional signs.

Negative rules deal with the complete exclusion of several types of feature. Firstly, in so far as 1:1250 maps are designed primarily to record the man-made features of the landscape, they do not attempt to depict natural relief, although some well-defined breaks of slope may be shown by symbols (see below). Secondly, overhead and underground details are only mapped in special circumstances. Overhead features, distinguished by pecked lines, are shown when they are of a size and character to be useful features, but where less than 1 m wide they have to be of particular importance to warrant inclusion. Underground detail, likewise depicted by pecked lines, is only included where it is a continuation (in tunnels and subways) of communications which normally run on the surface. Thirdly, a range of minor details, listed in Table 5, are normally excluded from all large scale maps. The reason for their exclusion varies, but may be related to their lack of permanence, to the fact that they are repetitive features (such as lamp posts), or merely because they are of very minor importance.

Conventional signs

Detail on the 1:1250 maps – as on all other Ordnance Survey map series – as well as being shown in plan where possible, is represented by a specially designed range of conventional signs. Such symbols and abbreviations can conveniently be regarded as a specialized language and they are so central to the whole process of cartographic communication[1] as to require detailed study by the map user. The current symbols in use at the 1:1250 scale (Plate 10) fall into several major categories, such as those relating to administrative boundaries, to vegetation, to other types of surface cover, and to other 'miscellaneous' features, including antiquities and revision and triangulation points. In addition to symbols, all maps rely on a standard set of descriptive abbreviations: these, ranging from Air Light Beacons to Youth Hostels, are printed in full in Appendix A.

At first sight most symbols appear to be self-explanatory, but Ordnance Survey practice often invests them with a more precise meaning than is

1 Arthur H. Robinson and Randall D. Sale, *Elements of Cartography* (3rd edn., London, 1969), 94–100, for a general discussion.

immediately obvious. Conventions are frequently linked to a definite specification which may have been expressed in numerical terms. A working knowledge of these specifications – standard rules by which surveyors and draughtsmen produce the maps – is essential to derive the maximum amount of information from any map series. In the sections which follow, the major conventions employed on the large scale maps are described. Not every symbol or feature is dealt with, but emphasis is laid either on symbols which embody particular definitions or where they show information unique to the large scale maps. Details of rock features and vegetation are discussed (more appropriately) in the 1:2500 chapter.

Table 5   Details excluded from large scale maps of the Ordnance Survey

---

Non-permanent ground features, e.g. temporary fences
Buildings below the minimum size
Bay windows, porches, juts, and roof projections under 1 m
Detail beneath roofs
Interior divisions, other than structural, in buildings
Overhead detail peculiar to industrial installations such as pipe lines
Natural slopes and relief features (with exceptions)
Detail in private gardens (with exceptions)
Detail beneath bridges
Minor detail within cemeteries such as tombstones and vaults unless of particular
   importance
Chimneys which do not constitute an obstruction at ground level
Minor detail in disused camp sites
Electricity transmission lines carried on single poles, except when of outstanding
 topographical importance
Flagstaffs which are not at ground level
Golf-course detail
Pipes, etc., in oil refineries
Playing apparatus in children's playgrounds
Telephone lines and poles, except when of outstanding topographical importance
Ring fences protecting single trees
Drives across sidewalks (with exceptions)
Minor roadside detail
Seasonal tracks
Minor detail in allotment gardens (e.g. plot fences, paths, and sheds)
Fruit bushes
Flower beds and rock gardens under 100 sq m in public gardens
Bollards, capstans, and mooring-posts, except when sited along rivers, canals,
 small quays or when specifically requested by a Port Authority
Mooring-rings
Catch drains alongside railways, etc.
Temporary railways in quarries, etc.
Signal posts or lights in the vicinity of large railway stations and marshalling yards
Tube railways other than the Metropolitan and District Lines
Railway water troughs
Security areas: all detail other than natural features (such as streams and woods),
 and electricity transmission lines and public ways which traverse the area, are
 excluded.

Bench marks and altitudes

A bench mark is defined as a mark the height of which relative to Ordnance Datum has been determined by spirit levelling. Bench marks are derived either from the second or third geodetic levelling (see p. 7) or from third-order levelling which provides the majority of spot heights and replacement bench marks. It is current Ordnance Survey policy to maintain the density of bench marks at about 5 per km square in rural areas and 30–40 per km square in urban areas. Over a period of twenty years about 35 per cent of rural and 10 to 15 per cent of urban bench marks are destroyed through road and building development,[1] and a cyclic relevelling policy ensures that these losses are made good at twenty-year intervals in urban and cultivated areas and at forty-year intervals in mountain and moorland areas.

A number of types of bench mark (Figure 11) are currently used by the Ordnance Survey.[2]

(a) *Fundamental Bench Marks* There are about 200 in the country as a whole which are constructed at specially selected sites. The foundations are set on stable strata such as bedrock and the likelihood of movement of the mark is thus minimized. They provide a framework of stable marks throughout the country which not only controls the whole levelling network but will, it is hoped, assist future investigations into vertical movement of the earth's crust. They are sited at intervals of about 40 km along lines of geodetic levelling throughout Great Britain. Each mark consists of a buried chamber containing two reference points, a gunmetal bolt and a flint; but these are only used in connection with the principal levelling of the Survey. For everyday use, including tertiary levelling and giving the published value, a third point refers to the brass bolt on the top of a granite or concrete pillar, about 300 mm square, set beside the chamber. On the maps they are shown in full as FUNDAMENTAL BENCH MARK 36.30 m or, in more restricted spaces, as FBM 36.30 m.

(b) *Flush brackets* These consist of metal plates about 90 mm wide and 175 mm long cemented into the faces of buildings. They are fixed, where possible, at intervals of about 1½ km along all the lines of geodetic levelling and also at important junction points along the secondary lines and in some tertiary areas. A flush bracket is also set into one of the sides of most triangulation pillars. The recorded altitude refers to the small horizontal platform at the point of the broad arrow marked on the plate face; each bracket carries a unique serial number.

(c) *Projecting bracket* This type of bench mark was used in the early stages of the second geodetic levelling, 1912–21. They are usually found on the abutments of railway and canal bridges. The reference point is the raised stud on the platform of the bracket.

(d) *Bolt bench marks* These are set in horizontal surfaces, including concrete blocks. They are 60 mm diameter mushroom-headed brass bolts engraved with an arrow and the letters 'OSBM'.

(e) *Cut bench marks* These are the commonest form of bench mark, consisting of a horizontal bar cut into vertical brickwork or similar surfaces. A broad arrow is cut immediately below the centre of the horizontal bar. They are established along all classes of levelling lines. The height value refers to the centre of the horizontal bar.

1 In cases of destruction the public are asked to inform the Ordnance Survey by writing to the Southampton office giving sufficient details, including the National Grid reference if possible, to enable such marks to be identified.

2 Others such as Stable Bench Marks (on sites least liable to subsidence in mining districts) are now obsolete.

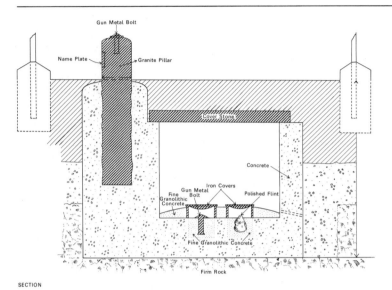

SECTION

(a) Fundamental Bench Mark

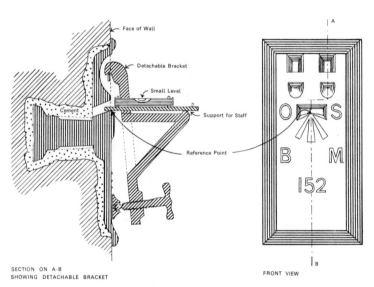

SECTION ON A-B
SHOWING DETACHABLE BRACKET

FRONT VIEW

(b) Flush bracket

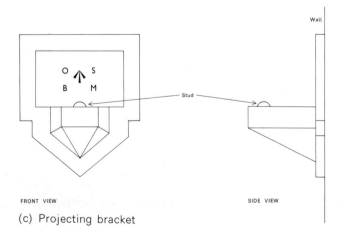

FRONT VIEW

SIDE VIEW

(c) Projecting bracket

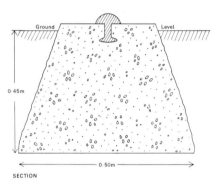

PLAN

SECTION

(d) Bolt bench mark

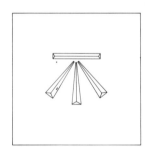

(e) Cut bench mark

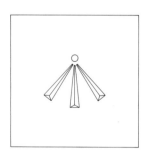

(f) Rivet or pivot bench mark

Figure 11
Current bench mark designs

(*f*) *Rivet and Pivot bench marks* Bench marks on horizontal surfaces may have a small brass rivet inserted as the reference point. These are described as 'Rivet' bench marks and an arrow symbol is cut alongside where this is possible or they may consist of a small hollow cut for a pivot to be inserted[1] at the reference point. These are termed 'Pivot' bench marks and also have the arrow symbol.

The various categories of bench marks *b* to *f* are sometimes called *Normal Bench Marks* (to distinguish them from FBMs) and they are recorded on the map in the form ⤒ BM 40.08 m.

On the 1:1250 and 1:2500 maps it is Ordnance Survey practice to show the positions and values of bench marks, but on the 1:10 000 and 1:10 560 maps only where these constitute the basic survey scale. On new and revised sheets at the 1:1250 scale, bench mark heights are given to the second decimal place (0.01) of a metre, but it will be a number of years before this aspect of metric conversion is completed for the whole series.

Contours are not published on either the 1:1250 or on the 1:2500 maps but, as a by-product of the cyclic levelling, these series print spot heights along selected roads. These heights refer to natural ground levels, and are either given to the nearest foot in the form +17 or (on metric maps) to the first decimal place (0.1) of a metre in the form +16.8 m.

Bench mark lists

New editions of maps cannot be published each time new levelling information becomes available and for cartographic reasons the maps cannot include all available bench mark information. Because of this bench mark lists are compiled for sale to those who require the latest values or need more complete information. The monthly Ordnance Survey *Publication Report* contains the areas for which revised bench mark lists have become available.

The lists are issued in units corresponding to the 1 km squares of the National Grid. Each list (Figure 12), which may consist of more than one sheet, can

Figure 12
Ordnance Survey bench mark list

ORDNANCE SURVEY BENCH MARK LIST BATCH 508 OS 808

BATCH 508 ALL BENCH MARKS ON THIS LIST FALL WITHIN KM SQ SD7530 DATUM NEWLYN PAGE 1

DESCRIPTION OF BENCH MARK	NATIONAL GRID TEN METRE REFERENCE	ALTITUDE FEET	METRES	HEIGHT OF BM ABOVE GROUND FEET	METRES	DATE OF LEVELLING
NO156 WHALLEY RD W ANG	7504 3052	473.99	144.47	0.7	0.2	1961
NO28 BURNLEY RD W ANG SW FACE	7505 3064	488.36	148.85	2.4	0.7	1961
NOS114 116 WHALLEY RD W FACE	7512 3044	476.64	145.28	1.1	0.3	1961
NO37 HENRY ST S ANG	7513 3056	498.13	151.83	1.8	0.5	1961
ANG WALL JUNC NE SIDE GORDON ST BURNLEY RD NW FACE	7513 3074	506.10	154.26	1.6	0.5	1961
WALL JUNC NW SIDE DILL HALL LANE ENT CRICKET GROUND SE FACE	7516 3009	472.46	144.01	1.3	0.4	1961
NO84A WHALLEY RD W ANG	7518 3038	478.38	145.81	1.5	0.5	1961
NO75 HENRY ST E ANG	7520 3060	535.19	163.13	1.8	0.5	1961
NO40 WHALLEY RD S ANG	7525 3030	480.63	146.50	1.7	0.5	1961
NBM NO40 BURNLEY RD W ANG SW FACE	7531 3095	473.15	144.22	2.1	0.6	1961
GREYHOUND INN NE ANG	7533 3020	486.89	148.40	1.7	0.5	1961
N ANG BLDG SE SIDE WHINNEY HILL NE FACE	7547 3030	530.55	161.71	1.5	0.5	1961
PIVOT TOP WALL 3.4M W JUNC S FACE	7547 3040	571.81	174.29			1961
STO P 1.5M N SIDE FENCE 47.2M W RD JUNC	7580 3031	613.75	187.07	1.0	0.3	1961

Date of issue 28/11/72 continued on page

In England and Wales, BM's levelled before March 1956 are based on the second geodetic levelling, and those levelled afterwards on the third geodetic levelling. Differences between altitudes derived from these two levellings may be found due to the differing adjustments, but for most practical purposes these are insignificant. An estimated correction to relate one levelling to the other, by areas, is available from the Director General, Ordnance Survey.

In Scotland BM's are based on the second geodetic levelling, with additional heights derived from the third geodetic levelling in areas not previously levelled.

To convert metres to feet, divide the metric value by 0·3048.

1 A 16 mm (approximately) diameter ball bearing should be used with these marks at the staff support.

be identified by the National Grid reference of the south-west corner of the kilometre square concerned. Some kilometre squares do not contain bench marks; on the other hand, the existence of a bench mark list does not necessarily imply that a National Grid map has been published. For each bench mark the lists give a brief description of the mark and its location, the full 10 m National Grid reference, the altitude referred to Ordnance Datum in metres and feet to the second place of decimals, the height of the mark above ground level in metres and feet to the first place of decimals, and, finally, the year in which it was last included in levelling observation. Where a bench mark has been established on a feature which has not been surveyed, the National Grid reference is approximate only; such references are marked by an asterisk.

Antiquities

In Chapter 10 a fuller discussion appears of the Ordnance Survey's archaeology policy, its practice within the Archaeology Division and also of the conventions associated with the depiction of antiquities on the main map series. It may be noted here that all classes of antiquity found on Ordnance Survey maps (Table 21) are included on the 1:1250 series, but that the principles which may influence their selection differ in some respects from other topographical features. The basic scale maps are primarily designed to record the contemporary landscape and they have to satisfy a wide range of users. Historical material has therefore to be selectively shown if the balance of the map is not to be upset. To give an obvious example, a large and conspicuous earthwork – a native fortress in pre-Roman times – is of far more general interest than the spot where a Neolithic flint flake came to light and the latter would be omitted from the map. Selection involves common sense as much as rigid rules, and the state of preservation of a visible antiquity, its value as a spectacle, its fame in the locality and the historical associations and age of its name, as well as its academic importance may all be relevant. Available space may also be an important factor and on 1:1250 sheets a reduction of antiquity content may be necessary in especially over-crowded urban areas. Subject to such general considerations the specific range of antiquities set down in Chapter 10 are depicted on the 1:1250 series.

Boundaries

It is Ordnance Survey policy to show administrative boundaries, but not private or property boundaries, on its maps. This is a statutory requirement, laid by Parliament on the Ordnance Survey and dating back to the Ordnance Survey Act of 1841, which provided for the survey and mapping of contemporary boundaries, ranging from counties down to extra-parochial districts, 'by whatsoever denomination the same respectively shall be known or called'.[1] The obligation extended to the correct naming of administrative areas. Subsequent legislation has resulted in changes both in the range of boundaries depicted, especially as new administrative areas were created and others became obsolete, and in the scale of map at which particular boundaries were required to be shown. The original requirement was to show boundaries at the 1:10 560 scale, but currently the Ordnance Survey have to publish county and parish boundaries[2] at a scale of *not less* than 1 inch to 1 mile, the boundaries of local government areas at a scale of *not less* than 25 inches to 1 mile in urban areas and at *not less* than 6 inches to

1 An Act to authorize and facilitate the Completion of a Survey of Great Britain, Berwick upon Tweed, and the Isle of Man 4 & 5 Victoria Cap 30.

2 These are civil not ecclesiastical parishes.

1 mile elsewhere. Parliamentary Constituencies are normally defined by local government areas and are also required to be published. These are minimum scales for particular boundaries to be shown: in practice all boundaries (Table 9) are shown at the 1:1250 and 1:2500 scales (although there is only a statutory need to do so on the latter). They are depicted by the range of symbols shown in Plate 10.

The legal status of boundaries on Ordnance Survey maps is a matter of practical importance. The basic position is that the publication of such administrative boundaries on various map series has never invested them with any common law or statutory significance in evidence, and indeed, the early Acts of Parliament relating to the Ordnance Survey had always declared that the rights of property should not be affected by the Surveys or published plans.[1] The development of case law[2] has, however, altered the legal situation from a case law point of view, and the 1:1250 and 1:2500 maps carry a prima facie indication to a Court of Law that a boundary existed at the map position shown, at the time of survey or revision. In addition, some 1:1250 or 1:2500 maps become, on publication, definitive maps indicating the actual legal position of the boundary as, for example, where a new boundary is related to features shown on that map and not previously shown.

One result of the Ordnance Survey's legal commitment to show public boundaries is that proper care has to be exercised in their survey and delineation. Boundaries of private property are not surveyed or recorded as such. Public boundaries, however, are often defined by private property limits including the centres of streams. Where natural changes in rivers or streams affect boundaries the normal principle of case law applies so that the natural and gradual shifts of course move the boundary with the stream; changes in a river because of artificial alterations, or owing to sudden floods, do not, on the other hand, carry the boundary with them. Boundary interpretation can also be complicated by ancient custom. Dealing with old Orders where boundaries are defined by roads, the centre of the road is defined as the centre of the road space between the hedges and not, as in modern Orders altering boundaries, the centre of the carriageway. In ancient forest districts, boundaries are mered to 'Freeboards' or 'Freebords', varying in width from 5 ft to about 25 ft, and designed for the recovery of game and the repair of fences; they are so mered on the large scale maps concerned. Boundaries of most areas terminate at low water mark and are so described in Orders altering boundaries or as shown on maps referred to in such Orders. Low water is regarded as the limit of the realm unless Parliament has extended an area seaward as (for example) for the former boroughs of Blackpool, Ramsgate, and Great Yarmouth.

Because boundaries are invisible and cannot be surveyed by direct methods, their precise location in relation to visible ground features is recorded by perambulating the boundary line and 'mereing' it to those features. This is done as part of the normal survey task for the resurvey or revision of a basic scale map. The term mereing has also been extended to apply to the written statement indicating the precise relationship of a boundary to the adjacent detail (for example, 4 ft RH = 4 ft from root of hedge) (Figure 13). Where space permits, mereings in this sense are placed parallel to the boundary, and when the type of mereing changes (as from the edge of a curb to the face of a wall) a special symbol, sometimes bent to enable it to be positioned

1 See Charles M. Clode, *The Military Forces of the Crown; Their Administration and Government* (London, 1869), **1**, 532.

2 Especially Fisher *v*. Winch 2 All ER 144 (Ct. of App. 1939 1 KB 666) and Davey *v*. Harrow Corporation, 1957 2 All ER 305.

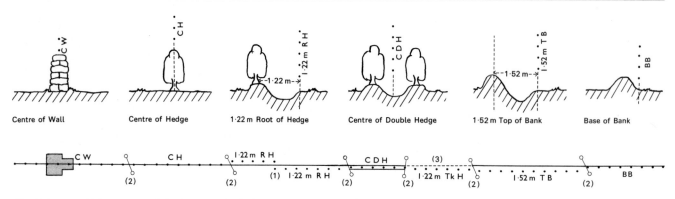

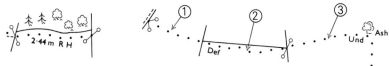

(1) Point at which property right (not mereing) changes.
(2) Point at which mereing changes.
    Sign cuts symbol at point of change.
(3) In any of these examples the hedge may be indicated on the ground by a track only.
    In these cases the hedge is indicated by pecks and Tk added to the mereing.

(a) Typical boundary mereings and cartographic representation.

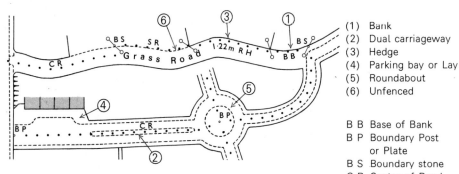

(b) Mereing related to Freeboard.

(c) Cartographic representation of Defaced and Undefined boundary.

(1) Boundary formerly mered to detail.
(2) Old feature replaced by new, (not on the same alignment).
(3) Boundary not related to detail.

Def Defaced   Und Undefined

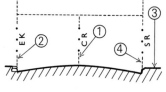

(1) Bank
(2) Dual carriageway
(3) Hedge
(4) Parking bay or Lay-By
(5) Roundabout
(6) Unfenced

B B Base of Bank
B P Boundary Post or Plate
B S Boundary stone
C R Centre of Road
S R Side of Road

(1) Centre of Road (C R)
(2) Edge of Kerb (E K)
(3) Footpath
(4) Side of Road (S R) (No Kerb)

(d) Mereings related to roads.

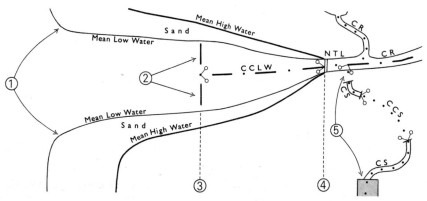

(1) Natural boundaries following M L W have no symbol, mereing or description.
(2) Mereings and mereing change signs omitted. Described where space permits.
(3) Level of sea at low water.
(4) Level of sea at high water.
(5) No mereing break for short culverts.

C C L W Centre of Channel at Low Water
C R   Centre of River (Non tidal)
C S   Centre of Stream
C C S   Centre of Covered Stream
N T L   Normal Tidal Limit

(e) Cartographic representation of boundaries following coastal features and rivers.

Figure 13
Boundary mereings

more precisely, indicates the point of change.[1] The authorized range of abbreviations for mereings is set down in Appendix A. Since 1969, boundary mereing distances have been metricated and, on all new maps, are published to the nearest centimetre, i.e. a conversion of existing mereings to two decimal places of a metre.

Buildings and house numbers

The minimum ground area for a building to be shown true to scale, in line with the general specification for the 1:1250 series, is 8 sq m. Where smaller buildings are important topographical features, however, and carry either bench marks or revision points, this minimum threshold may fall to 1 sq m (or a shortest side of 1 m or more). Similar rules (Table 7) apply to subsidiary features: walls appear to scale only where they are more than 1 m thick (otherwise they are shown by a single line representing the centre of the wall); bay windows, juts, recesses, and porches, unless they are either adjacent to a public right of way or coincident with a revision point, are distinguished only if the smallest dimension is 1 m or more; and courtyards, light or ventilation shafts, as well as extending to ground level and being accessible,[2] have to be at least 8 sq m to be shown. Below such minimum sizes, single dots are used to show the surveyed positions of a range of features, which are also either named or identified by a standard abbreviation (Appendix A). They include cranes in factories and docks, drinking fountains, letter boxes (except those built into post offices) pumps, and police telephone pillars.

Within the outline, buildings were ruled on older large scale map series, but a stipple is now applied to these features on the 1:1250 series. The majority of roofed structures, covered tanks, and solid masonry such as bridge buttresses and walls wide enough to be surveyed by two lines, carry stipple and are flanked by continuous lines. Roof car parks are not stippled if access to the roof is external to the building; when access to multi-storied car parks is within the building they are shown as normal roofed buildings, but external approach ramps are not stippled. For glasshouses a special cross-hatched symbol is in use but there must be an area of glass sufficiently large to be represented by at least one full diamond of the symbol; below this glass roofs are stippled. Ruins are not stippled. The limits of overhead detail are represented by pecked lines.

Since 1946, house numbers have been published on the 1:1250 series. The postal numbers of all buildings and parts of buildings are collected as part of the field survey with the exception of suffixes and fractional numbers (for example 93a) related to the same building. The many irregularities in street numbering, with numbers in a sequence being missed out, with duplicated or temporary numbers, or even with one house having two numbers each in different roads, requires considerable care to be exercised in this work. To avoid overcrowding, not all house numbers are published, but the selection allows the whole sequence to be inferred. One number is shown at the plan edge, at the beginning and end of every road, on each side of every road junction, and on each side of any break in a regular sequence of numbering. Otherwise approximately every sixth number is shown, although the number 13 is always published where it occurs.[3] Numbers of flats are given to cover the whole range in the building. Where a building has no postal number, a name is entered on the map if applicable.

1 Because of space limitations short-distance changes in the nature of a mereing are not indicated; the predominant feature is published, as for example where a hedge is replaced by wire fencing in short sections only it would be designated as hedge throughout.

2 Where they are inaccessible and detail has been derived from site plans they are shown by pecked lines.

3 Because of the tendency of house occupants for superstitious reasons not to display the number.

Communications

'Ways' on the large scale maps are divided into three categories: roads, tracks, and paths, each with a specific meaning. Roads are defined as metalled ways for vehicles. Tracks are defined as unmetalled ways, usable by vehicles, but not necessarily suitable for all-weather use. A path is an established way other than a track or road, clearly marked and permanent, perhaps paved or gravelled, and defined by stiles, gates, guide posts, or permanent gaps. Of these features, all roads are shown on the 1:1250 series, including metalled drives of 40 m or more in length; all tracks are likewise depicted, together with unmetalled drives of 40 m or more in length; and all paths are represented in their correct alignment. Unmade paths which are liable to vary in position, are plotted as straight lines between fixed points such as stiles and gates.[1] Exceptions are made for the deviations necessary to avoid obstacles such as clumps of trees, ponds and boggy land, or, in hilly districts, to follow the natural line of least resistance.

Many subsidiary features associated with roads, subject to standard minimum dimensions, can be shown to scale on the 1:1250 maps. Where a feature is less than 1 m in width it is enlarged conventionally to that width – as in the case of bridges, the dividing strip between dual carriageways, unmade paths, and steps (a tread of less than 1 m is shown by conventionally dividing the distance between the top and the bottom at intervals of about 1 m). Verges are drawn to scale. Kerbs that are less than 0.3 of a metre high are shown by a pecked line, but above this by a firm line. Other features to be systematically mapped include cattle grids, ferries (shown by pecks with annotation indicating foot or vehicular), fords (annotated with an indication if they are not suitable for motor vehicles), gates and toll gates, mileposts and milestones (by dots and abbreviations MP or MS), sidewalks, and made paths in verges. Department of the Environment road numbers are now shown on the 1:1250 series. Rights of way are not distinguished on large scale maps; a statement in the sheet footnotes is made to this effect.

Standard-gauge railways are drawn to scale by firm lines. A narrow gauge railway is defined as less than 1.435 m and is shown by a single line with cross bars. The same convention applies to tramways. Among minor features of the railway system to be depicted at the 1:1250 scale are bridges and viaducts (to scale), buffers, level crossings, mileposts and stones with distances, signals and switches, and turntables. On the other hand, overhead wires of electric railways and conductor rails are ignored and detail covered by railway station roofs – including lines – is likewise omitted. Stations and halts are represented as normal building detail. Numerous closures of railways and tramways have required appropriate definitions. Where rails exist in a usable state they are annotated 'Railway (disused)', 'Rly (dis)' or 'Tramway (disused)'. Where, however, the rails have been removed, but the alignment has not been converted to a road or track, the residual feature is named 'Dismantled' railway or tramway. Lines that have been concreted over or macadamized are ignored.

Tunnels along railways (or roads) which normally run on the surface are indicated by pecked lines to show their approximate alignment and are named. On the other hand, underground railways, such as the majority of the deep-level tube railways in London, are ignored except where they come to the surface, in which sections the normal railway conventions apply. The Metropolitan and District Railways are an exception to this rule,[2] and

1 No longer applies in England and Wales; only visible footpaths are now shown (1973).

2 A legacy from the original 1:1056 survey and its subsequent revision, when this detail was added at the request of the companies concerned.

their underground sections are shown by pecked lines, plotted from manuscript copies of the obsolete 1:1056 plans of London maintained by the Ordnance Survey. Where an underground Metropolitan or District station is combined with another tube station, pecks are drawn to show the limits of the Metropolitan or District platform level only.

Names

The Ordnance Survey has always assumed responsibility for deciding what place names are to appear on its maps and how they shall be spelt.[1] Indeed, except in the case of certain administrative names, which follow the spelling of the Act of Parliament by which they were created, there exists no national body in the United Kingdom responsible for laying down the names and spelling of places appearing on official maps or in other official documents. For Welsh and Gaelic names, however, the Board of Celtic Studies, University of Wales, and the School of Scottish Studies, University of Edinburgh, respectively, act in an advisory capacity to the Ordnance Survey.[2] A decision about a name is primarily guided by local custom and usage, so that the final spelling is that most generally useful and acceptable in the locality concerned.

A threefold distinction is made by the Ordnance Survey within the names it collects and publishes. Firstly, *administrative* names are given to local government and other administrative areas. They are collected as part of the procedure which establishes administrative boundaries and generally follow the official names adopted by local authorities, as prescribed in various Acts of Parliament. At the 1:1250 scale, unless an area or a detached part of an area falls wholly within one map, administrative names are omitted from the body of the map, but are printed in the sheet margins.

Secondly, *descriptive* names define the character or use of a feature (otherwise unnamed) as, for example, Allotment Gardens or Recreation Ground. Consistency of usage for the same objects in different maps is accomplished both by the use of a standard list of descriptive names, from Abattoir to Zoological Garden, and also, where appropriate, by employing standard abbreviations (Appendix A).

Thirdly, *distinctive* names (although some administrative names fall within this category) comprise the main body of proper place names; they may be of great antiquity and often have a quality of uniqueness – as, for example, River Thames or Park Lane Methodist Church. The main research effort of the Ordnance Survey has lain here. To establish the most acceptable name forms the surveyors make appropriate inquiries and consult the best 'authorities' and although the evidence collected in this way is never in principle mandatory, it is frequently accepted. Any conflict is resolved by the Ordnance Survey itself. In the nineteenth century, Ordnance Surveyors added many thousands of names to the maps of Great Britain for the first time, but, today, existing large scale maps of the Survey provide a basic authority for names on new or revised editions. Investigation accordingly focuses on new or altered names; the basic assumption is that place names tend to change but rarely and should not be subject to passing whims. For genuine changes the surveyor seeks visual evidence (as where the name is displayed on a notice board), documentary evidence (written bill heads and other publications), oral evidence (as from local government officials and owners), as well as the signed approval of these persons in some cases.

1 J. B. Harley, 'Place-names on the Early Ordnance Survey Maps of England and Wales', *The Cartographic Journal*, **8** (1971), 91–104, describes the development of Ordnance Survey techniques in this respect.

2 [Ordnance Survey] *Place Names on Maps of Scotland and Wales* (Southampton, 2nd edn., 1973), provides a glossary of the principal Gaelic and Celtic words used on Ordnance Survey maps: for Welsh names Elwyn Davies (ed.), *A Gazetteer of Welsh Place-Names* (Cardiff, University of Wales Press, 1958) also contains a glossary of chief elements on Ordnance Survey maps.

Once the revision of names is complete in the field, they are subject to editing[1] and, as the names applicable to local features are almost infinite, a selection has to be made for even large scale maps, by the criterion of general interest as much as space. Omissions include the names of shops and restaurants, burial grounds when adjacent to churches, minor hotels and public houses, names of houses which have postal numbers but are not of particular interest or importance, names of buildings within large installations, proprietary names unless required for identification, field names unless of particular interest or historical importance, and Forestry Commission names where they are purely administrative in character. On the 1:1250 and 1:2500 series names of extensive districts, such as the Cheviot Hills or the Peak District, cannot be depicted, and the names of housing estates are not usually recorded where the roads have been named. Other names are excluded for security reasons. This list is not exhaustive, but it assists in defining more closely the terms of reference of the written content of the large scale map series.

Water features and the depiction of high and low water marks

Maps at the 1:1250 and 1:2500 scales aim to represent as fully as possible the characteristics of both natural and man-made water features. They depict not only springs, streams, rivers, and lakes, but also canals and reservoirs, as well as objects such as locks, bollards, capstans, and mooring posts.[2] Floating objects are only shown when, as in the case of pontoons and landing stages, their plan positions are fixed and they are attached to permanent detail which is above water level at low tide.

The conventions include the fact that the outline of lakes and ponds is plotted by a firm line at *normal winter level;* the *top water level* of reservoirs is shown; but the outline of tidal ponds is recorded at *low water.* Rivers and streams are shown by two lines where they are 1 m or more in width and are known as 'double streams': below this threshold 'single streams' are depicted by one continuous line. Permanent drains and ditches follow the same convention, i.e. below 1 m in width they appear as 'single ditches', and above as 'double ditches'.[3] Width is related to *normal winter level* and if, therefore, the stream is surveyed in summer it is the permanent channel, eroded of vegetation, rather than the water width, which is measured. Direction of flow is indicated by an arrow at least once on every sheet but, where ambiguity could occur, as where a stream might be confused with a fence, extra arrows are added.

The sources of all streams are annotated with standard terms, namely: 'collects', where the source is a bog or marsh; 'spring' (Spr) where the source is a natural spring; and 'issues', where it is an emission from an agricultural drain, or where the stream re-emerges from underground. Where a stream disappears underground the spot is annotated 'sinks' and, where it spreads, as on a sand or shingle beach, or in a marsh, it is described by the term 'spreads'. Springs are drawn to scale if of sufficient size; otherwise they are represented by a small open circle. Mineral springs and wells are named to indicate their nature (e.g. chalybeate). Other miscellaneous conventions are that in Ordnance Survey usage the term 'mill race' is given to the water leading to a mill, and 'mill stream' to the water leaving it; the term 'waterfall' is applied only to natural features; canal and river locks are surveyed with their gates in a closed position; navigation aids such as perches,[4] pilot

1 There are rules, for example, for spelling and compounding, as when a substantive in a name is descriptive of the object to which it is applied (for example, Red Bridge describes a bridge, and is not compounded as Redbridge). The reverse applies when a substantive name is not descriptive of the object (for example, in Millbrook).

2 Bollards, capstans, and mooring posts will normally be shown only if they are 0.3 m or over high on quays and along rivers and canals; they are indicated in docks only at the request of the Port Authority.

3 Catch drains alongside hedges and railway lines, and single drains in water meadows, are not shown.

4 Poles set in estuaries to indicate the course of the deep-water channel.

beacons, and navigation lights are shown by dots in tidal rivers; but the large scale maps no longer distinguish between navigable and non-navigable rivers.

The delimitation of high and low water marks on Ordnance Survey maps is a matter of considerable practical importance. To give just two examples, the legal position of administrative boundaries is frequently related to low water level and, in tidal rivers, the Department of the Environment, rather than the local authority, is responsible for coastal protection work up to normal tide limit. The tidal lines appearing on the large scale maps are, therefore, derived from special ground or air surveys, depending on the nature of the foreshore. As high tide generally leaves a clear mark until the next high water there is not much difficulty in surveying this line by normal ground survey methods. Low water, however, presents greater difficulty, because of the limited time at the surveyor's disposal and the inaccessibility of the low water mark on some beaches. Air photographs are therefore taken of the coastline, at a time when the tide is at low water; ordinary black and white photographs do not always distinguish clearly between shallow water and land and infra-red film is used to overcome this difficulty.[1]

For the particular lines which are surveyed and published legal authority dates back to the mid nineteenth century. In 1854 the Lord Chancellor, in giving judgement on the limits of foreshore around England and Wales, defined its boundaries as following the high and low water marks of a medium or average tide, i.e. of a tide half-way between a spring and a neap tide. In Scotland there has been no legal definition of foreshore boundaries but ancient custom establishes their extent as limited by mean spring tides. The Ordnance Survey therefore shows the high and low water marks of a mean or average tide in England and Wales and of an average spring tide in Scotland.[2] Before August 1935 the lines so surveyed in England and Wales were called 'High and Low Water Marks of Ordinary Tides' and, on the 1:2500 and 1:10 560 maps, these descriptions or their abbreviations (HWMOT and LWMOT) were always shown against them. In August 1935 the term 'Medium' replaced 'Ordinary' as a better description, and the abbreviation on the large scale maps of England and Wales became HWMMT or LWMMT. Since March 1965, however, the term 'Mean' has been adopted in place of 'Medium' and the words 'Mark' and 'Tide' omitted. Thus the present descriptions in England and Wales are 'Mean High (or Low) Water', abbreviated to MH (or L) W. In Scotland the lines were called 'High and Low Water Ordinary Spring Tides' (HWMOST and LWMOST); since 1965 this has been shortened to 'Mean High (or Low) Water Springs', abbreviated to MH (or L) WS. In tidal rivers the Ordnance Survey also determines the points to which mean tides (or in Scotland spring tides) flow at high or low water. The highest point is annotated 'Normal Tidal Limit' (NTL), but the low water description is not shown to that portion of the channel of such a river above the point where the river reaches the level of the sea at low water. It is Ordnance Survey practice to show all these tide lines definitively on large scale maps, except where they pass beneath a permanent structure such as a bridge, a jetty, or a landing stage supported on piles.

Revision and Advance Revision Information (ARI) maps

Ordnance Survey planning allows at least one completely new edition of all 1:1250 maps to be published every twenty-five years but, in practice,

1 Shallow water absorbs infra-red radiation effectively, allowing the low water mark to stand out clearly.

2 High water mark shown on Admiralty charts is that of mean spring tides, and low water mark is that of Admiralty Chart Datum.

the working of the continuous revision policy[1] enables this to occur more frequently for many sheets. The objectives of continuous revision have already been described (see p. 12), and it will be seen that the policy applies with particular force to the 1:1250 series. All sheets are classified as 'active', that is to say, it is assumed that they cover areas where rapid change is likely to occur and a detailed intelligence system, including liaison with local authorities, is maintained to record these changes. All revision work is undertaken at the same scale and to the same standard of accuracy as on the original maps. Its initiation in a particular locality depends on the presence of an economic minimum of work to be undertaken, usually defined as one day's work for a surveyor of the continuous revision section.

Revision surveys in areas covered by the 1:1250 maps are made available in two forms. First, new editions are published once the changed detail has reached an appropriate level: this is not an arbitrary threshold but has a carefully assessed numerical basis, in which each feature which is to undergo revision is converted to standard 'house units'. To give a single example, a new motorway or dual carriageway would rate from 5 to 10 'house units' per 100 m of its length and, as soon as a map has accumulated a certain number of changed 'house units' – on a sliding scale according to the date of the previous survey – a new edition is authorized. These maps are identical in style to the maps they replace.

A second form in which continuous revision is supplied to map users is by 'Advance Revision Information' (ARI) maps (Plate 39). These are photocopies[2] from the field sheets which are maintained by the surveyors and contain the most up-to-date information. Any ARI map is available for purchase until the final reproduction stage for a new edition of a sheet has been reached. Because an ARI map is made from a field sheet (although every effort is made to complete it) line quality and completeness do not reach the standard of the published map and, moreover, ARI maps cannot be regarded merely as slightly incomplete versions of printed maps. Although all important changes as required by the customer are included, minor changes may not have been surveyed, new features may be still unnamed, the field sheets may not have been fully checked before being copied, information about administrative boundaries and levels may be less up to date than the rest of the detail, and parts of the National Grid lines may be missing. No table of conventional signs and abbreviations appears in the margin of an ARI map and, moreover, some conventions differ from their counterparts on the published sheets. Vegetation, for example, rather than being shown by the usual symbols, is merely defined by a pecked line and its nature indicated by abbreviations (such as c for Coniferous, NC for Non Coniferous, and so on), qualified in the case of scrub or woodland by the addition of '(c)', '(m)', '(o)', or '(scat)' to indicate a close, medium, open, or scattered density. With buildings, too, instead of the stipple of the published map, hatching defines the external lines of new developments. Many of the other abbreviations on the ARI maps are, however, identical to those in use with the finished maps.

Large scale digital maps

It is Ordnance Survey policy to supply the information in the large scale surveys in forms alternative to (and indeed eventually replacing) the traditional paper sheet produced by lithography (see p. 2). Among the new media by which information from the national survey can be communicated

1 W. A. Seymour and B. St G. Irwin, 76–85.

2 Either on paper or on a polyester film with matt surface. Enlargements to the 1:500 scale are available from the 1:1250 ARI maps.

the development of large scale digital mapping is especially important. Although preliminary research in the Ordnance Survey was concerned with deriving small scale maps by computer generalization from large scale maps that had been digitized, the greatest practical success has been achieved with coding and storing the data on selected 1:1250 and 1:2500 maps and then producing printout maps by means of a precision plotter.[1] The experimental work in these operations had reached a point in 1972[2] where the points, lines, and text of a conventional map could all be digitized, with the program not only sorting the data into National Grid squares but also automatically rectifying distortion and, by means of a conformal transformation, adjusting the machine co-ordinates, x and y in millimetres, to the National Grid co-ordinates on the Transverse Mercator projection.

Experimental digital maps, relating to part of London, were plotted at 1:1250 scale,[3] but, in 1973, the first sheet was published under the pilot scheme at 1:2500 scale and related to part of Herefordshire (Plate 40).[4] This map shows exactly the same detail as a regular series National Grid sheet (see p. 52) but differs from it in that all the 'hard detail' (line, point, and alpha-numeric detail) is produced by plotter from magnetic tape. The remaining information such as vegetation symbols and area data is still produced manually and added at the printing stage, but it is expected that further development will enable all the information depicted on large scale urban maps to be incorporated into magnetic tape.[5]

For the map user the main innovation is that a magnetic tape can be purchased as well as a printed copy of the map (or the transparency and microfilm forms which are described below). The significance lies not only in the fact that the Ordnance Survey has developed a technology to produce maps by automatic means, but also, in particular, that basic survey information is available in computer-compatible numerical form. For large users of urban topographic surveys this facility has considerable potential. Planning authorities and service industries are devising new systems of data banking and related data processing but, for all computer users, there is the advantage of flexibility. Once the data of any particular map are stored in a topographic data bank, they can be recalled for printout maps programmed to a predetermined selection of detail,[6] at different scales, and in various combinations of areal unit (based on the National Grid) which escape from the rigidity of fixed sheet lines. A local authority appropriately equipped can, for example, print out merely the information relating to roads and buildings if it is required. Revision materials can also be fed into the data bank (with savings in production costs) and, similarly, specialist data supplied by the user could be programmed into the printout map. For the large public-service user the potential of the system, as compared with the traditional paper map, has been defined as one which:

. . . provides the purchaser with the means of drawing the map he requires for any particular purpose instead of having to accept what the cartographer has designed as a compromise between the many conflicting requirements.[7]

Special services

The development of modern photographic, electrostatic, and microfilm equipment has also enabled the Ordnance Survey to offer its large scale surveys in forms other than the conventional printed map. The 1:1250 maps

1 In 1973 a Ferranti Master Plotter with a light spotter projector for the final drawing.

2 R. C. Gardiner-Hill, *The Development of Digital Maps* (Ordnance Survey, Professional Papers, New Series, No. 23, Southampton, 1972); for earlier developments see M. St G. Irwin, 'Developments in Automated Cartography at the Ordnance Survey', *The Cartographic Journal*, **8** (1971), 133–8.

3 R. C. Gardiner-Hill, Figure 7.

4 By the end of 1973 a total of 79 sheets – 46 1:1250 and 33 1:2500 – were available on magnetic tape.

5 E. P. J. Williams, 'The Publication of Urban Topographic Surveys in Great Britain', *The Cartographic Journal*, **10** (1973), 49–53.

6 R. W. Breward, 'A Mathematical Approach to the Storage of Digitised Contours', *The Cartographic Journal*, **9** (1972), 82–3, illustrates one potential use.

7 R. C. Gardiner-Hill, 3; also E. P. J. Williams, 'Digitized Ordnance Survey Maps', *The Geographical Magazine*, **44** (1972), 780–1.

are available in the form of both transparencies and 35 mm film. The transparencies, which are the same size as the paper sheets and show the same detail, are reproduced on plastic material of good dimensional stability and with matt drawing surfaces. They are designed for map users, such as local authorities, who require record or working maps on which to show special information such as the alignment of water mains, electricity or telephone cables.[1] Advance Revision Information maps are also reproduced in transparency form. The 35 mm service offers a copy of the 1:1250 sheet miniaturized as a 35 mm diazo negative mounted in an aperture card. Apart from the advantage of being able to view the maps, it allows considerable economies to be made in the storage of map material.[2]

Other specialist needs are catered for by the enlargement and reduction services.[3] Enlargement of 1:1250 sheets are supplied, on request to the Ordnance Survey, at the scale of 1:500. It should be recognized that such enlargements are no more accurate than the parent plans from which they have been derived. Facsimile reductions of 1:1250 maps to a 1:2500 scale are also supplied under similar conditions. The service is especially designed to alleviate the problem caused by component parts of 1:2500 sheets becoming out of date in areas where they are derived by photographic reduction from 1:1250 maps.[4] It is not possible to up-date a derived 1:2500 map every time a basic 1:1250 map is revised and, as a result, the derived maps can be rendered significantly out of date. To overcome a delay in revision at the 1:2500 scale the Ordnance Survey therefore provides, on either paper or film, reductions of 1:1250 maps which enable map users – for example by sticking a new quadrant over the old – to up-date the component parts of 1:2500 sheets as necessary.[5]

1 'Supply of Transparencies', Ordnance Survey Leaflet No. 14 (1972).

2 '35 Millimetre Microfilm Service', Ordnance Survey Leaflet No. 33 (1972).

3 'Supply of Enlargements of Large Scale maps', Ordnance Survey Leaflet No. 15 (1972).

4 In 1973 the Ordnance Survey ceased production of new 1:2500 derived maps and also revision of existing 1:2500 derived maps.

5 Fuller details are given in 'Reduction Service', Ordnance Survey Leaflet No. 6 (1972).

Ordnance Survey maps at the 1:2500 scale originated in the mid nineteenth century. Today they are still the most detailed maps to be published for much of Great Britain (Figure 1) and there are more sheets in this series than in any other. Only in major urban areas, where the 1:1250 provides the largest published scale, and in mountain and moorland districts, where the largest scale falls to 1:10000 or 1:10560, are they replaced as the basic national map series.

A regular programme of survey had been finally settled in 1863, at the end of the 'Battle of the Scales', but proceeded so slowly that, in 1880, owing to the urgent need for accurate plans for land registration purposes, the establishment of the Ordnance Survey had to be increased with the object of bringing forward the date for the completion of the original 'County Series' 1:2500 maps to 1890. In addition, in 1886, the Treasury authorized a system of 1:2500 revision on the basis of a twenty-year cycle; the first revision, started in the Home Counties in 1891, was completed in 1914. A second revision was put in hand in 1904 and a third in 1911, but neither of these was completed. A combination of wartime conditions, and the period of austerity and retrenchment which followed it in the 1920s, meant that the Ordnance Survey was unable to maintain its planned revision programme.

The Davidson Committee made two major recommendations for the 1:2500 maps. First, although lack of revision had lessened the current utility of the series there was a unanimous opinion in favour of its retention. Second, the Committee recommended that '... as soon as it can be conveniently arranged the 1:2500 survey should be re-cast on National instead of county sheet lines on a National projection' and that, while this work is in progress 'a general overhaul' of the plans would be undertaken 'to remove the discrepancies along county boundaries and to eliminate the errors which have crept in to the original survey in the course of its revision.'[1]

In the event, in addition to 'overhaul' and the production of 1:2500 scale National Grid maps derived from the 1:1250 series, many sheets in the series have been produced by resurvey methods where overhaul has proved to be impracticable. Even so, overhaul – defined by the Ordnance Survey after 1945 as the process of refashioning the old County Series 1:2500 maps to adequate modern standards – has made a major contribution to the total programme. Its object was '... to provide a series of plans covering the smaller towns and developed rural areas, on a national sheet line system and in sympathy with the retriangulation, to an acceptable level of accuracy as quickly and cheaply as possible'.[2] Following experimental work from 1945 to 1951, various routine stages were developed in the overhaul process. They included the adjustment of the detail on the old maps to the control points of the retriangulation, the recompilation of the maps on the national Transverse Mercator projection and with sheet lines corresponding to the National Grid, the elimination of errors (particularly those caused by distortions of materials and inadequacy of old revision methods), the revision of detail and, finally, the fair-drawing of all the maps to a new specification.

The first of the new National Grid maps was published in 1948.[3] Thereafter, the overhaul programme gathered pace, but a large amount of conversion still remains to be completed for which a target date of 1980 has been set. The development of the 1:2500 series in the post-World War II period is set out in Table 6 and illustrated in Figure 14.

1 *Final Report* (1938), 8.

2 [Ordnance Survey], *The Overhaul of the 1:2500 County Series Plans*, Professional Papers, New Series, No. 25 (Southampton, 1972), 6.

3 This was a map derived from the 1:1250; publication of the basic first edition began in 1949 and revision of the overhauled series began in 1950.

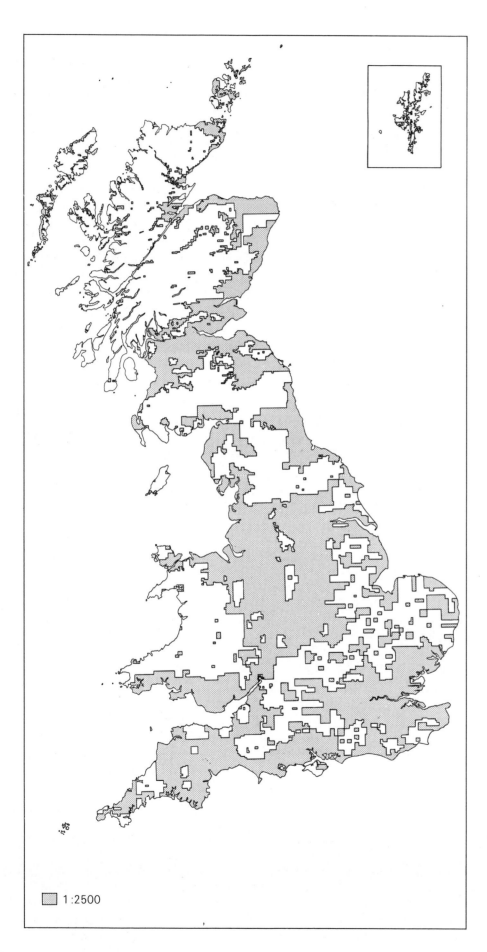

1:2500

Figure 14
Extent of published areas at
1:2500 scale 1973

The sequence of publication of the 1:2500 series was further varied in 1969 by the introduction of metric maps. Coupled with the survival of some pre-1939 maps, and with the development of basic and derived series of post-1945 maps, this has meant that four styles have been published at the 1:2500 scale:

(a) The original series, named the COUNTY SERIES because of the independent origin of each county meridian and the fact that the maps are numbered separately for each county.

(b) The post-1945 maps *derived* from the basic 1:1250 survey in major urban areas and based on the National Grid. As from February 1973, however, new publications and revisions of regular mapping at 1:2500 scale were discontinued in those town and urban areas covered by the 1:1250 survey. Reductions to 1:2500 scale of individual 1:1250 sheets continued as a standard service supplied in the form of transparencies or electro-photographic prints.

(c) The post-1945 1:2500 *basic* maps for smaller towns and cultivated areas and also referenced on the National Grid.

(d) The metricated versions of *b* and *c*. Bench marks and spot heights are given in metres and areas in hectares (as well as in acres); boundary mereings are also given in metres. All new and revised maps are published with these conversions, but it will be a number of years before the process is completed.[1]

Although this fourfold classification is important in terms of the provenance of some of the maps, and while there are differences in the representation of some features, the fundamental distinction is that between the COUNTY SERIES and the NATIONAL GRID SERIES.

Table 6   Publication of the 1:2500 maps 1948–73

Published maps	Annual average				Total 31 March 1973	Total* in series
	1946–55	*1956–60*	*1961–5*	*1966–70*		
First editions Basic	823	2200	4576	5767	99 537	170 163
First editions derived from 1:1250	484	570	437	255	10 303	
Revised editions Basic and Derived	60	80	443	902	11 687	

* All figures relate to square kilometres but the majority of maps are published in 2 × 1 km format. The statistics exclude 40 maps made for the Isle of Man.

Source: Ordnance Survey *Annual Report 1972–73* (1973), Appendix 1.

COUNTY SERIES

Format, referencing and marginalia

A County Series sheet covers an area on the ground of 1 mile by 1½ miles. The scale has the traditional advantage that 1 sq inch represents approximately 1 acre on the ground.

The sheets are numbered relative to the 1:10 560 County Series (see p. 73) so that any one 1:2500 map is identified in three stages: by the county name, by the 1:10 560 sheet number within that county, and by the number of

1 F. M. Sexton, 'The Adoption of the Metric System in the Ordnance Survey', *The Geographical Journal*, **134** (1968), 328–42.

the 1:2500 map in that 1:10560 sheet,[1] for example:

Aberdeen 46/14

The arrangement is illustrated by Plate 2 from which it will be seen:

(*a*) That the full 1 : 10560 sheets in each county are numbered, beginning in the north-west of the county and finishing in the south-east; Roman numerals were used for this purpose.

(*b*) That each full 1:10560 sheet is divided into sixteen 1:2500 sheets from 1 to 16, again from the north-west to the south-east corner of the sheet.

A guide to the coverage of the 1:2500 County Series, including small areas of land published as insets or additions on adjacent plans, is provided by base maps of the 1:100000 administrative sheets which are published for England and Wales with the sheet lines overprinted in orange. In Scotland the County Series is indexed in the Central Lowlands on 1:63360 outline sheets showing sheet lines in orange;[2] for the remainder of Scotland they are shown, county by county, on maps at 1:126720 scale.

The arrangement of the series also reflects a number of changes of policy in the nineteenth century. From 1855 to 1872, for example, the 1:2500 sheets were published as parish plans (with the area outside the parish being left blank). Moreover, one result of the projection of the sheets on a county basis is that some sheets containing county boundaries omitted detail in the adjacent county. Between 1913 and 1919 a start was made on the systematic reduction of the number of meridians used for the 1:2500 map. This resulted in amended sheet lines and numbers; the sheets affected were distinguished by the prefix 'N' to the sheet numbers. The practice of completing maps on the borders of counties with detail from adjacent maps on a different meridian (producing what were known as 'filled plans') was discontinued in 1922.

Apart from the sheet lines no grid appears on the maps, nor is the latitude and longitude shown in association with the single line border.[3] The numbers of adjacent 1:2500 sheets are given outside the middle of each border. The south sheet margin contains supplementary information including a linear scale graduated in chains, links, and feet, various notes about the dates of original survey, revision, and reprinting, and footnotes reporting the mean level of the sea used in the calculation of altitude, as well as the mode of description of bench marks. There was also an abbreviated table of 'characteristics and symbols' used in the map, but the full range of symbols was available only as a separately published sheet (see Plate 4).

Once the overhaul started no further significant revision was undertaken on maps in the County Series. Until recasting on National Grid sheet lines is complete the Ordnance Survey will supply, as a service on request, National Grid co-ordinates for the sheet corners of any County Series map. This information enables users to relate the County Series to the National Grid and is provided in the form of co-ordinates listed for the sixteen 1:2500 sheets in a 1:10560 county sheet.

NATIONAL GRID SERIES
Format, referencing and marginalia

The smallest sheet size for the 1:2500 National Grid Series maps – irrespective of whether they were derived from the basic 1:1250 survey in major

1 This reference system formerly extended to the (now obsolete) town plans at large scales: the 1:1056 plans were numbered 1 to 100 within the 1:10560 sheet; the 1:500 plans from 1 to 25 within the 1:2500 maps.

2 On the 1:63360 Outline sheets see p. 119; the sheets published with county series sheet lines are 40, 43, 50, 53, 54, 55, 56, 59, 60, 61, 62, 63, 67, and 72. These index sheets, for both England and Wales and Scotland, replace the 'county index diagrams' referred to in *A Description of the Ordnance Survey Large Scale Plans* . . . (1954), 6.

3 The numbers which frequently appear outside the neat lines on 1:2500 maps are the numbers of parcels abutting to the sheet edge.

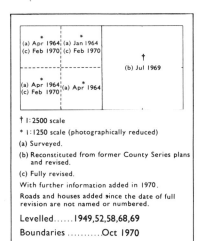

† 1:2500 scale

* 1:1250 scale (photographically reduced)

(a) Surveyed.

(b) Reconstituted from former County Series plans and revised.

(c) Fully revised.

With further information added in 1970.

Roads and houses added since the date of full revision are not named or numbered.

Levelled......1949,52,58,68,69

Boundaries ....Oct 1970

Figure 15
Compilation data for 1:2500
National Grid Series

urban areas, from resurvey, or from the overhaul of the County Series – measures 400 × 400 mm (15.75 inches square) and represents an area of 1 km square (100 hectares or 247.1 acres). As a general rule, however, two maps are paired and published as one sheet to represent an area of 2 sq km. With some of the earlier National Grid maps an extended layout was used as in coastal areas where a sheet with a large blank area was avoided. Such maps are extended in *either* a north–south *or* an east–west direction to a maximum of an additional 160 mm; currently extensions to the standard layout are limited to an area that can be accommodated by a local break in the inner (but not the outer) border.

In so far as the basic sheet units at the 1:2500 scale represent 1 km square, they could be indexed simply by means of the 1 km squares shown on the Seventh Series 1:63 360 maps and now on the 1:50 000. A single 1:2500 sheet is identified on the National Grid by giving the grid reference of its south-west corner to the nearest 1 km, for example Plan TQ 3977; maps in the 2 km format are denoted by references to the south-west corner of each component 1 km unit, for example 'Plan TQ 3877 and Plan TQ 3977'. National Grid lines are shown at 100 m intervals. Full grid values are given at the corner of the sheets and the intervening grid values are given to 100 m, excluding the 100 km figure. An inner border is divided at 10 m intervals. Values for latitude and longitude are not recorded. Outer borders of sheets published until 1969 were graduated in scales of feet (west and south) and chains and links (north and east). Information in the south margin of the sheet includes an explanation of how to give a National Grid reference defining the position of a point to the nearest 10 m, a selection of conventional signs and abbreviations used on the map, a note on the vegetation classification, and (on later versions of the maps) a 'Conversion Scale Hectares-Acres'.[1] Standard information on the dates of survey, revision, levelling, and boundaries, and, where appropriate, of tidal details, also appears in the sheet footnotes to every 1:2500 map. Where a sheet is derived (even in part) from the 1:1250 survey, the dates of survey or revision of the component basic sheets appear in a diagram on the sheet (Figure 15).

Landscape at 1:2500

Although the 1:2500 maps are often referred to as the 'twenty-five inch' series, their exact scale is 25.344 inches to 1 mile. They aim to depict the permanent features of the man-made landscape at ground level,[2] as faithfully as possible, and without 'deliberate distortions of scale'.[3] The 1:2500 maps indeed share many of the attributes of the 1:1250 series so that emphasis will be laid on the differences; it can be assumed (unless differences are specifically mentioned) that similar rules govern the depiction of particular features on both series of maps.

An obvious result of the reduction of scale by half is an increase in the minimum thresholds above which features are shown correctly in plan rather than being depicted by conventional signs, or, in the case of some minor features, being omitted completely. The rule that features have to cover an area of 8 sq m or more to be shown in plan is in fact the same for the 1:2500 as for the 1:1250 series, but, in practice, the minimum threshold often has to be increased on the 1:2500 scale. This is true, for example, of the major exception to this rule: where smaller buildings and objects in a detached position are relatively important topographical features they can

1 Some pre-metric maps contained the hectares–acres conversion scale (e.g. SH 6280/6380 A edn.).

2 A limited amount of underground and overhead detail is also shown.

3 *A Description of the Ordnance Survey Large Scale Plans* (Chessington, Surrey, 1954), 14.

be shown in plan (although they are less than 8 sq m) but at different thresholds on the two scales. On the 1:2500 series this is either 4 sq m or with the shortest side measuring at least 2 m, as opposed to values of 1 sq m and 1 m respectively, for the same dimensions on the 1:1250 series. The different thresholds on the two scales are exemplified in Table 7.

Table 7   Examples of minimum thresholds on the 1:1250 and 1:2500 series

1:1250 Threshold	1:2500 Threshold	Features
1 metre	2 metres	Juts and recesses on buildings, bay windows, porches, roof projections, the width of walls (below which centre line only is shown)
1 metre	1.4 metres	Bridges, centre section of dual carriageways
2 metres	4 metres	Sloping masonry (distance between top and base)
5 metres	10 metres	Hedges (extension from roots for feature to be shown by vegetation symbols)
10 metres	20 metres	Orchards (smallest side for feature to be distinguished)
3 square metres	6 square metres	Base of pylons
0.25 hectare	1 hectare	Vegetation (below which is classified* in one way only)

* i.e. although a mixture of vegetation symbols may be shown the area is not subdivided to show the location of the different types.

Conventional signs

The conventional signs employed at the 1:2500 scale are the same as on the 1:1250 series, as are the standard abbreviations in use (Appendix A). The only difference in the range of signs is owing to the fact that area information is peculiar to the 1:2500 series (see p. 56).

Taking the 1:2500 series by itself, more significant differences have developed between the conventions used on the County Series and those on the National Grid Series. The main reason is that several symbols on the County Series maps (Plate 4) are now obsolete. They include the linear symbols for some administrative boundaries, styles of writing depicting different categories of names, the shading of roads and water, and the hatching which was used to infill buildings. Moreover, in common with other Ordnance Survey maps, the symbols for furze, bushes, underwood, osiers, and rough pasture were discontinued after 1963, when new symbols for bracken, coppice/osiers, heath, scrub, and rough grassland were introduced (see p. 66).

Altitudes and bench marks

On the 1:2500 National Grid maps the information on altitudes and bench marks is rendered in the same manner as on the 1:1250 series. In areas where the County Series maps are still current, however, there is more variation both in the provenance of the data and their reliability. This reflects first the use of data from earlier levellings and, secondly, the use of the old Liverpool datum. According to date of publication, the 1:2500 maps (and the series derived from them) have obtained their altitudes from three main levellings (and associated lower order observations) surveyed as shown in Table 8.

Table 8   Primary levelling in Great Britain

	England Wales	Scotland
First primary levelling	1840–60	1840–60
Second geodetic levelling	1912–21*	1936–52
Third geodetic levelling	1950–68	1956–68
Cyclic relevelling	1956–	1959–

* Except parts of East Anglia and Kent, completed 1946–51.

Changes were especially significant as between the first and second levellings, owing to relatively inaccurate instruments and techniques in the first levelling and, to a lesser extent, to variable movements in the land surface. Other changes are linked to the fact that on the oldest maps, altitudes were computed from Liverpool datum, the mean of high and low water mark taken at Liverpool in 1844. This was unsatisfactory, as much from the short duration of the observations taken to establish it (ten days only), as from the location of the station on a tidal river. Thus, when the second geodetic levelling was put in hand,[1] Newlyn datum, as defined in Chapter 1 (see p. 7), was established. In 1922 the process began of converting heights published on new editions of Ordnance Survey maps to Newlyn datum, but, as far as the 1:2500 series was concerned, the policy could not be implemented for many years. In 1929 a compromise solution was adopted, in which the *difference* between the levels derived from the two datums was published in the sheet footnotes; this varied with locality, but was given so as to be accurate to the nearest 0.1 ft over the limited area of any 1:2500 sheet. Before 1929, bench mark levels were given to one decimal of a foot, but thereafter to two decimals of a foot, for example, BM 574.35; after 1929 surface heights were shown along roads in the manner +392.

Data from the third geodetic levelling has been used on National Grid maps published since March 1956. Again, owing to slight differences in adjustment, there may be small systematic differences between the two levellings although, for many practical purposes, these may be of little consequence. An estimate of the corrections necessary to bring altitudes based on the second geodetic levelling into approximate agreement with those based on the third may be obtained from the Ordnance Survey. In Scotland, bench mark values and altitudes on many sheets are still based on the second geodetic levelling: only on more recently published 1:2500 National Grid maps has data derived from the third geodetic levelling been incorporated, including areas not previously levelled.

Antiquities

On the National Grid 1:2500 series the same range of antiquities is shown as on the 1:1250 scale, though the rural areas covered by the former allow rather more scope for the publication of antiquities than do the heavily built-up areas of the latter. In any case depiction of archaeological information is similarly governed by the general principles described in Chapter 10.

It is more difficult to generalize about the archaeology on the County Series 1:2500. Depending on the date of the original survey the antiquity content

1 See Colonel Sir Charles Close, *The Second Geodetic Levelling of England and Wales 1912–21* (HMSO, London, 1922); also H. St J. L. Winterbotham, 41–3, . . . (1934).

may result from different terms of reference than those obtaining at present. Before 1951, for example, the working terminal date for an antiquity to be shown was 1688 and, although the original authority for this cannot be traced, it was probably adopted in the nineteenth century. The terminology for divisions of prehistoric and historic has also changed during the life of the 1:2500 series. The earliest classification recognized 'Roman antiquities', 'Druidical or Saxon antiquities', and 'Norman or subsequent antiquities';[1] by 1899 these had become Roman; Prehistoric; Danish or Saxon; and Norman or subsequent.[2] During the present century, however, a new classification came into use with three categories of antiquity being shown: Prehistoric (prior to A.D. 43), Roman (A.D. 43 to 420) and Saxon and Medieval (A.D. 420 to 1688). And from 1950 onward only two types of lettering have been used to distinguish antiquities, one for pre-Roman and post-Roman (up to 1714) and one for Roman.

An equally important consideration for today's users is that the archaeology on the County Series, especially on sheets published before the appointment of an Archaeology Officer in 1920, is unreliable by modern standards. This can be gauged not only from outside critics[3] but also from Ordnance Survey concern with the proper depiction of archaeology. A circular of April 1886, for example, pointed to 'the case of certain ancient entrenchments in Hampshire having been erroneously styled Roman Camps' and urged that 'Division Officers should exercise great caution before describing any objects as Roman antiquities'. The 1905 Instructions of the Survey, in turn, gave more explicit guidance on the recording of antiquities. Despite these efforts the accuracy of archaeological information on the County Series must be regarded as variable.

Areas

The system by which each parcel of land is numbered, its area calculated from the map,[4] and this value printed on the sheet is peculiar to the 1:2500 series and helps to render it an important tool in the conveyancing and registration of land.[5] The Ordnance Survey large scale maps, which show practically all permanent fences and hedges, are particularly suitable for use as the basis of the description of the land to which each title refers. Today the first registration of title to land is compulsory on sale in those areas so designated and, on a very limited basis, is permissible in non-compulsory areas. It is planned to extend the system to the whole of England and Wales as soon as this is possible and, by 1973, about 4 million separate titles had been registered and compulsory registration extended to areas having a population of some 22 million people. During the year 1972–3, 19 060 requests from H M Land Registry for revision and other information were dealt with by the Ordnance Survey. The Ordnance Survey is also responsible for maintaining a statistical record of the total areas of certain administrative units,[6] of the areas of inland water (lakes, ponds, rivers, etc.) and of tidal water and foreshore. For areas on the maps, as much detail is given as possible, bearing in mind economy in measurement and the need to avoid obscuring other features. In much of the countryside, areas of the actual enclosures can be given but, in built-up areas, which would have too many single parcel numbers for convenience, arbitrary zones called 'Town Areas'

1 See, for example, Ordnance Survey of England, *Book of Reference to the Plan of the Parish of Bishop's Castle, Shropshire* (London, 1884), explanatory remarks prefacing the book.

2 Colonel D. A. Johnston (1899), 13.

3 F. Haverfield, 'The Ordnance Survey Maps from the Point of View of the Antiquities Shown on Them', *The Geographical Journal*, **27** (1905), 165–76, sums up some of these criticisms.

4 In this sense the areas as published are 'paper' areas which do not take account of factors such as slope and height above datum. They are accurate within specified limits which are derived from a comparison of the totals of individual parcels (measured as described in Chapter 1) with the apparent area of the map. The residual difference between the measured and the apparent area of the map is known as the 'apparent closing error'; it must not exceed 0.5 acre and where it does the map is remeasured. The true closing error (obtained after adjustment for projection) is distributed among the separate parcel areas of the map.

5 On land registration see C. J. Sweeney and J. A. Simpson, 'The Ordnance Survey and Land Registration', *The Geographical Journal*, **133** (1967), 10–23.

6 Total areas are calculated for counties, boroughs, urban and rural districts, wards, and parishes in England and Wales; and counties, burghs, districts, county council electoral divisions, wards, and parishes in Scotland.

are measured as though they were one parcel (although within such areas inland water and tidal water are numbered and measured separately).

A parcel is accordingly defined as any area which is measured and published on the plan; it may be a single feature, usually an enclosure, or it may consist of several adjacent features grouped together. As a general rule parcels are bounded by lines of natural detail, such as hedges or streams (although in creating 'Town Areas' other features such as railways are used), but they are sometimes bounded artificially as by administrative boundaries or the sheet edge. Each parcel is given a reference number. Where adjacent features are linked to make one parcel the process is known as bracing and is indicated by a brace – an elongated symbol – placed across the common division. No limit is stipulated to the number of features which may be braced into one parcel but, none the less, the composition of parcels is governed by several rules. Firstly, area measurement takes place within the civil parish in order that its administrative area can be calculated, and where a parish boundary or any other administrative boundary divides an enclosure, each part is treated as a separate parcel. No portion on one side of a boundary is included in, or braced to, a parcel falling on the other side. In Scotland, parcels falling astride 'county of the city' boundaries are similarly treated.

Secondly, just as there are minimum thresholds for detail to be shown to scale, so too there are minimum areas below which certain features are not measured separately, but are braced with an adjacent parcel. For example, where a lake, pond, reservoir, or an island in a river is less than one-tenth of an acre (0.040 hectare) it will be braced; and, similarly, where fenced occupation roads and tracks are less than 10 chains (200 m) in length they are braced to the adjacent parcel, while unfenced occupation roads and tracks are braced irrespective of their length. These examples illustrate that the selection of parcels and the use of braces is governed by practical convenience in measuring: the parcels have no significance whatsoever in regard to property ownership. In any case there are exceptions to such thresholds and some features are *always* separately numbered and measured irrespective of their size. They include railways in rural areas (in built-up areas they may form part of 'Town Areas'), all public roads, whether fenced or unfenced, and foreshore and tidal water (foreshore is the land between MHW and MLW: tidal water is water below MLW but within the administrative boundary).

Thirdly, although some conventions (as will be shown) have changed, a fairly standard set of symbols is now used in the representation of area data on the 1:2500 series (Figure 16). A single brace is generally used to denote the extent of a parcel, the head and tail of the symbol being positioned on either side of the line dividing the features being braced. A *centre* brace is used where the feature is not wide enough to be separately numbered (for example, a double hedge) and where half the feature is therefore in each of the adjoining parcels; the division between such parcels is taken as the centre line of the double braced feature. An *open* brace is used to link portions of a parcel that are divided by another parcel, for example when a river is crossed by a road or railway. Where there is no continuous line, such as a hedge or a wall, to bound a parcel on the ground, an 'imaginary' line is indicated by 'measurement pecks'. The perimeters of 'Town Areas' are now defined by a symbol like a pedestrian crossing beacon placed at regular

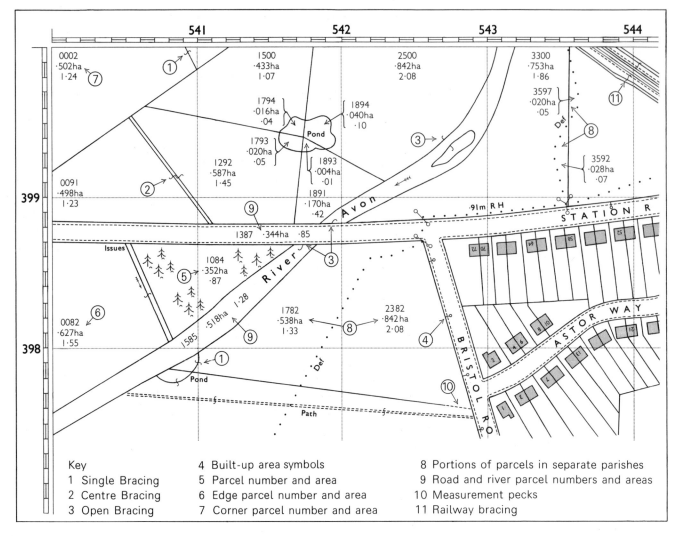

Key
1 Single Bracing
2 Centre Bracing
3 Open Bracing
4 Built-up area symbols
5 Parcel number and area
6 Edge parcel number and area
7 Corner parcel number and area
8 Portions of parcels in separate parishes
9 Road and river parcel numbers and areas
10 Measurement pecks
11 Railway bracing

intervals along the edge of the urban parcel. (Previously they were defined by a 'T' symbol and up to 1909 by various colour bands, stipples or hatching.) Braces are not normally used within Town Areas.

To appreciate other policy changes on areas it is helpful to consider the County Series and the National Grid Series 1:2500 maps separately.

COUNTY SERIES

Parcels have always been numbered and measured on the 1:2500 maps and indeed the public requirement for accurate data on areas was a basic *raison d'être* for their introduction.[1] At first parcels were numbered consecutively throughout each parish with the numbers printed on the maps and, until 1884, the areas, together with the land use of each parcel, were recorded in separate Parish Area Books. This system was discontinued after 1884 and areas, to three decimal places of an acre, were printed on the maps below the parcel numbers. For parcels broken by the sheet edge the component areas were totalled and the whole acreage of the parcel was published on each map.

Some changes were introduced to accompany the revision of the series beginning in 1891. Unaltered parcels retained their existing numbers and areas. New parcels formed by partition of an existing parcel also retained the

1 *Report from the Registration and Conveyancing Commission*, British Parliamentary Paper, 1850

Figure 16
Methods of bracing and
numbering areas on 1:2500
series

parent number but suffixes a, b, c, etc. were added to distinguish new divisions. Where older detail had been altered, some parcel numbers were cancelled, and some parishes, the boundaries of which had been changed, were renumbered. After World War I, when revision was confined to areas where the need was most urgent, it was no longer possible – inasmuch as one map might be revised but not its neighbour – to show the total areas of parcels broken by sheet edges. From 1922 areas of parcels were measured to the map edge only. This policy was carried on in the National Grid Series maps and has continued to the present day.

NATIONAL GRID SERIES

After 1945 a new system of numbering parcels was introduced on the National Grid Series maps. All parcels within a map (including parts of parcels broken by the map edge) were given a four-figure number which represented the grid reference of their approximate centre to the nearest 10 m. The same numeration applied to parcels consisting of continuous features such as roads, rivers, railways, built-up areas, foreshores, and large tracts of moorland which, although cut by the map edge, were treated as being confined to one sheet. An important advantage is that each parcel has a unique reference number and can be easily located on the National Grid. Since 1950 areas have been published to two decimal places of an acre only, rather than three as formerly.

On all maps numbered after 31 December 1958 a further refinement has been introduced for parcels falling astride a sheet edge. The principle is that each broken parcel has one number and not, as before, as many different numbers as there were maps on which a parcel falls. The system is:

(*a*) A parcel which includes the corner of a single map (1 km square) is allotted a number from 0001 to 0006 depending on the position of the map in the National Grid. The system is so devised that a number allocated to a corner parcel will not be repeated elsewhere on any other map surrounding that parcel.

(*b*) Other parcels which are divided by the map edge are allotted the four-figure grid reference of the mid point of the portion of the map edge intercepted by the parcel, unless the latter is part of a continuous feature, when it is treated as before as being confined to the map.

(*c*) Where a parcel is divided by the sheet edge into more than one part on any map, each part is given the same reference number.

It should be noted that the system applies to parcel *numbers* only: *areas* of components of broken parcels are still shown individually.

Since 1969 metric values have been introduced for areas. In each parcel areas are given in hectares as well as in acres, with the hectare value printed directly below the parcel number, and the acreage below that. Areas are given to three decimal places of a hectare and, as before metrication, to two decimal places of an acre.

In mountain and moorland areas, parcel areas are calculated and recorded from the basic 1:10 000 or 1:10 560 surveys. Unlike the 1:2500 series, however, these values are not printed on the maps, although they are used in the statutory calculation of administrative areas. They can be obtained on application to the Ordnance Survey.

Boundaries

The present-day method of surveying boundaries and the symbols and abbreviations used in their mereing are the same on the 1:2500 as on the 1:1250 series. A further measure of the similarity of the two series in this respect is that they share a common table of conventional signs (Plate 10). The 1:2500 series may, however, be distinguished, firstly, by the fact that a statutory obligation existed for the Ordnance Survey to publish this scale with the boundaries noted below. Secondly, owing to the greater age of the series, considerably more historical perspective is required in their interpretation, especially in areas where County Series maps are still in use. As well as changes in the published boundaries and their symbols, there have been changes in convention and in the styles of lettering employed for administrative names. The subject is a complex one, related to a long series of Acts of Parliament affecting boundary status, and to differences in administrative geography in England and Wales on the one hand and Scotland on the other. In general terms, however, the development of boundary representation can be divided into four periods, although it must be noted that new symbols have been introduced irrespective of period and, moreover, especially as the revision programme fell behind, there were often timelags in implementing changes in convention.

BEFORE 1879

Until 1879 the 1:2500 series included the ecclesiastical (so-called mother or ancient) parishes, the civil parishes or townships, the subdivision of townships, together with the hundreds (and similar subdivisions such as rapes and wapentakes), and registrar's districts (Figure 17). On some of the early sheets in northern England the areas of these units were calculated to high water mark and the banks of rivers. Although recognized in Scotland for many years, only in 1868 did the Poor Law Amendment and Boundary Acts extend parish, county, and parliamentary areas to low water mark and the centre of rivers for England and Wales.[1]

1879–1944

In 1879 the depiction of many ancient boundaries was replaced[2] by a system in which the boundaries of civil parishes, the smallest effective unit of local administration, were to be shown (Figure 17). The substitution did not occur immediately and for many sheets was only completed concurrently with the first revision of the series. The system of boundary depiction also altered with the creation of new administrative areas. The Local Government Act of 1888 was responsible, *inter alia*, for the introduction of administrative counties and county boroughs. Urban and rural districts[3] were approved for addition to Ordnance Survey maps, respectively, in 1887 and 1899 but, again, they were only incorporated as the revision of sheets took place. Other changes were of a temporary nature; the boundaries of lands common to two or more parishes, for example, omitted from 1:2500 sheets published between 1890 and 1907, were subsequently reinserted on further revision. According to the date of their last major revision County Series maps may reflect these changing practices.

Figure 17
Boundary symbols on 1:1250 and 1:2500 maps

1 Although the Acts were made in 1868 plans containing the changes did not appear until 1878 and it was only in 1883 that rules for the extent of the sea in rivers were formally set down by the Ordnance Survey to form a corollary to the Acts. By these rules parish boundaries were taken to the point in tidal rivers where the level of the river coincided with the level of the sea at low water.

2 On Treasury instructions dated 15 April 1879.

3 Known originally as Urban Sanitary and Rural Sanitary Districts; Sanitary was used until 1894 when the titles were changed by the Local Government Act of that year.

(a) Before 1879

Name of area	Boundary	Writing
County and County Corporate	— — — —	C
Ridings and Quarter Sessional Divisions	—+— —+— —+—	R
Liberties	— . — — . .	L
Parliamentary County Divisions	— — —	P
Superintendent Registrar's Districts	A —x— — — . x	R
Registrar's Districts	B —v— — — . v	R
Hundreds or other similar divisions e.g. Rapes, Wards, Wapentakes etc.	— — —	H
Boroughs (Parliamentary)	Boundary described — —	B
Divisions of Parliamentary Boroughs	Boundary described — —	D
Boroughs (Municipal)	Boundary described — —	B
Municipal Wards	. . — — — .	W
Cities returning members	Nil boundary described	C
Cities, Episcopal and Prescriptive, not returning members	Nil boundary described	C
Market Towns	Nil	B
Other Towns	Nil	B
Parishes, Ancient or Mother	▪ ▪ ▪ ▪ ▪	P
Civil Parishes or Townships	. . . . .	T
Divisions of Townships	— . . — .	T
Subdivisions of Townships	— . . . . —	T'

(b) 1879-1944

Name of area	Boundary	Writing
County	— — —	C
County Administrative Division	—+— —+— —+—	S*
County Boroughs (England)	Boundary described — — — — —	
County Boroughs (Scotland)	Boundary described — — —	€
Parliamentary County Division	Boundary described — — —	P
Borough (Parliamentary)	Boundary described — — —	B
Division of Parliamentary Borough	Boundary described — —	D
Borough (Municipal)	Boundary described — — — —	D
Municipal Ward	Boundary described . . — . — .	W
Urban District and Burgh (Scotland)	Boundary described — — — —	U
Rural District	Boundary described v — v	R
Civil Parish	. . . .	P

* On margin only

Where the administrative county boundary coincides, as is usually the case, with parish boundary, the characters for both are used alternately thus —.—., and where any other boundary coincides with that of a parish, the character for the latter only is used, but the other boundary is described. Where Urban and Rural area boundaries coincide "Co. Boro. Bdy.," "Munl. Boro. Bdy.," or "U.D. Bdy." is typed along the boundary on the urban side, the Rural District boundary being indicated by the symbol v only, placed on the rural area side about three chains apart.

1944–50

To coincide with the introduction of large scale maps on the National Grid, a new set of boundary symbols was devised (Figure 17), differing both in the style of lettering, which was less ornamental than hitherto, and in the range of boundaries depicted. Some boundaries were shown for the first time after 1944, including the wards of urban districts in England and Wales.[1] In Scotland after this date the burghs were grouped into two main classes: 'counties of cities' and all other burghs whether large or small, and district council areas were included on Ordnance Survey publications for the first time.[2]

1950–73

The boundary symbols introduced after 1944 were retained in the main, but, after 1950, a new nomenclature for Parliamentary divisions[3] was adopted (Figure 17). On all 1:2500 maps published since 1950 the boundaries listed in Table 9 have been included as a statutory obligation.

1 In July 1945.

2 In the first place, on the 1:625 000 Administrative Areas map published in March 1944 and, after 1947, on all 1:2500 sheets.

3 Representation of the Peoples Act 1948 brought in new titles effective in 1950.

(c) 1944 to 1950 and 1950 to 1974 combined.

England and Wales

Designation	Boundary	Marginal	Body name
Geographical County	(Not described)	—	
Administrative County with Parish 1 with Geo County	Ad Co Bdy	ADMIN CO	—
2 across Geo County	Ad Co Bdy		
County Borough & Parish	C B Bdy	CO BORO	
County Districts: Municipal Borough	M B Bdy	M B	B
Urban District	U D Bdy	U D	
Rural District	R D Bdy	R D	
Civil Parish (to 1966)	(Not described)	P H	P
Civil Parish (1966 onwards)	(Not described)	C P	C P
Ward-Boro or U D (not based on ph)	Ward Bdy	WARD	W
1944-1950			
Parliamentary Co (not with Ad Co or ph)	Parly Co Bdy	PARLY CO	—
Parliamentary Division (not with ph)	P Div Bdy	DIVISION	—
Parliamentary Borough (not with ph)	P B Bdy	PARLY BORO	
Division of Parliamentary Boro (not with ph)	Div of P B Bdy	DIVISION	D
1950 onwards			
County Constituency (not with ph)	Co Const Bdy	CO CONST	
Borough Constituency (not with ph)	Boro Const Bdy	BORO CONST	C

Notes:
1. Not inserted separately on the margin when co-extensive with, and of the same name as the Geographical County on any one plan.
2. Where a County Borough, Municipal Borough, or Urban District is co-extensive with, and bears the same name as a Civil Parish, the names will be conjoined on the body and margin.
3. Where County Borough or County District boundaries coincide with Geographical & Administrative County, the symbol for the latter is used.
4. Where other boundaries coincide with the Civil Parish, the symbol for the latter is used.
5. When describing the boundary between a County Borough and the Administrative County with which it is associated, the description of the latter is omitted. In all other cases boundaries will be fully described.
6. Coincident boundary descriptions will be conjoined.
7. Metropolitan Boroughs will be described as Met B on body, margins and descriptions.

Scotland

Designation	Boundary	Marginal	Body name
County (County Council) (alone)	Co Cnl Bdy	see note 1	—
County (County Council) (coincident with ph)	Co Cnl Bdy		
County of City (not with ph)	Co of City Bdy	Not abbrev	B
County of City (with ph)	Co of City Bdy		
Burgh (not with ph)	Burgh Bdy	BURGH	
Burgh (with ph)	Burgh Bdy		
District Council Area (not with ph)	Dist Bdy	DISTRICT	—
District Council Area (with ph)	Dist Bdy		
Civil Parish (to 1966)	(Not described)	P H	P
Civil Parish (1966 onwards)	(Not described)	C P	C P
Ward-Burgh (not with ph)	Ward Bdy	WARD	W
1944-1950			
Parliamentary County (alone)	Parly Co Bdy	PARLY CO	—
Parliamentary Division (alone)	P Div Bdy	DIVISION	—
Parliamentary Burgh (alone)	Parly Burgh Bdy	PARLY BURGH	
Division of Parly Burgh	Div of Parly Burgh Bdy	DIVISION	D
1950 onwards			
County Constituency (alone)	Co Const Bdy	CO CONST	
Burgh Constituency (alone)	Burgh Const Bdy	BURGH CONST	C

Notes:
1. Where county areas such as Geo County, County Council Area and Parly County (before 1950) are co-extensive and of the same name on any one plan a single county name is shown (e.g. Banffshire).
Where a plan contains part of a Co of a City, the "shire" name is inserted across the boundary of the latter and the Co Council name also inserted in its appropriate position (e.g. Lanark County).
2. Where a burgh comprises two or more towns, or is considerable in extent, the name is inserted centrally (e.g. Motherwell and Wishaw Burgh). In small compact burghs, the burgh name may be omitted if identical with the town name. In such cases the name book should be endorsed accordingly.
3. Where Co of a City boundary coincides with Co Council boundary, the latter is shown.
4. Royalty and other similar boundaries, where approved will be shown in non-parochial character (line 8) and described, except when coincident with other boundaries.
5. When describing the boundary between a Co of a City and the Co Council Area with which it is associated, the description of the latter is omitted. In other cases boundaries will be fully described.
General: Where local government and parliamentary boundaries of a burgh coincide, the description is Parly & Burgh Bdy before 1950 and afterwards is Burgh Const & Burgh Bdy.

Table 9   Boundaries* shown on the 1:1250 and 1:2500 series (1973)

England and Wales

Geographical county, administrative county, county borough (CB)†, London borough (Greater London only) (LB), municipal borough (MB), urban district (UD), rural district (RD), rural borough (RB), civil parish (CP), ward (borough and urban district), county constituency (CC), borough constituency (BC)

Scotland

Geographical county, county council area, county of city, burgh, district council area, civil parish (CP), ward (burgh), county constituency (CC), burgh constituency (BC)

Isle of Man

Borough, town, sheading, village district, parish district, ward

* The basic Act for the depiction of boundaries remains the Ordnance Survey Act of 1841, made permanent in 1922; all other legislation is construed as being corollary to the basic Act.

† Standard abbreviations are used; they are shown in brackets after the name.

Buildings

The depiction of buildings on the County Series 1:2500 maps has been subject to a number of changes.[1] On the first edition, published up to 1892, buildings were shown either in outline or with colour applied by hand (red for brick and stone; black for wood and iron). During the first revision of the series buildings were hatched and this convention, characterizing maps published between 1892 and 1906, was coupled with the practice of 'shading'[2] buildings within the south and east sides from 1898 to 1908. From 1906 to 1922 buildings were stippled and, from 1922 to 1930, they were again hatched. Colour printing in grey was adopted in 1930. Some of these conventions, according to the age of the maps, may be encountered on County Series sheets still in print.

A stipple replaced the grey colour fill for buildings on the National Grid Series maps. On those sheets derived from the 1:1250 series the style and content is identical with the parent series. On the basic 1:2500 sheets the main difference is an increase in the minimum size at which buildings are shown correct to scale rather than conventionally. The thresholds, set out in Table 7, apply not only to the principal buildings or structures, but also to subsidiary features including archways, bay windows, porches and recesses, and projecting roofs. House numbers have been included on basic sheets published since 1959.

1 H. St J. L. Winterbotham, 61; Plate 13, . . . (1934).

2 That is, thickening of the bounding line.

3 While on the 1:1250 scale, for example, roadside verges are shown where possible to scale, on the 1:2500 National Grid maps 1 m becomes the minimum width for this to occur.

4 On maps published until July 1958, road destinations were given on the sheet edge in some cases. They comprised the name of, and the distance to, the next important place from the point where an 'A' or 'B' road left the map.

Communications

On the National Grid maps the specification for railways, roads, tracks, paths, and similar features is virtually the same for the 1:1250 and the 1:2500 basic maps.[3] The only new category of information (excluded from the 1:1250 series) is that the road classification numbers of main roads are printed inside the map margin, at road junctions, and at other points where the course of the classified road might otherwise be ambiguous.[4]

On the County Series maps similar changes in convention characterize communications as other features. With railways the main problem on many sheets is purely one of a lack of revision related to closure of lines. With roads, however, changing Ordnance Survey conventions must be noted at the

1:2500 scale. From 1884 to 1912 roads (like buildings) were shaded,[1] but the exact position varied from county to county. The shading was sometimes central to the bounding feature; elsewhere it was added to the roadside; and, occasionally, to the field side of the road. The practice of adding shading to roads on the 1:2500 series was discontinued in 1912.

Names

Although the basic policy for the derivation and publication of names is the same for the 1:2500 as for the 1:1250 series, there are several differences in practice. Of the three types of published names – distinctive, descriptive, and administrative – the differences particularly relate to administrative names. On the 1:1250 series such names are relegated from the body of the map to the sheet margin: on the 1:2500 series, with the exceptions noted below, administrative names are printed on the face of the map. Among administrative areas in Table 9 the names of counties of cities, counties, municipal or metropolitan boroughs, burghs, urban districts, civil parishes, and wards are each shown once on the body of the map on which the centre of the area falls; they are printed in the margins of all other maps containing a part of the area. Parliamentary constituencies, rural districts, and district council names are only shown on the body of the map when an area, or a detached part of an area, falls wholly on one sheet.

The size and shape of some administrative areas require special treatment. Where a parish is too small for the name to be positioned normally a letter 'a' is inserted in the centre of the area and the name published in the nearest open space; where this happens twice on a single map the second parish is referenced 'b' and so on. A detached part of a parish is shown by the parish name with the abbreviation (det) printed beneath it; should there be more than one detached part to the same parish they are numbered (Det No 1), (Det No 2), etc. Detached parts of other administrative areas are shown by a similar system. In the case of islands the name of the mainland parish to which the island belongs is positioned below its own name.

Another indication of categories of administrative areas was provided by the size and style of lettering. On County Series maps lettering tended to be large and ornate, a design which was facilitated by the generous sheet size, but which was altered in association with major changes of boundary policy. The names within each group of boundaries employed their own styles of lettering, for example, Roman capitals in ornamental, open, shaded, hatched, and solid varieties for boroughs from 1879 to 1943; Egyptian capitals for urban districts from 1887 to 1943; and italic capitals for civil parishes from 1879 to 1943 (Figure 17). After 1944 the styles and sizes of type were redesigned for the National Grid Series, although they continued to indicate the status of the administrative area in some cases.[2] Type faces generally became smaller – related to a smaller sheet size – and were spaced in a more compact manner. For borough names, Times upright faces, coupled with the use of abbreviations (Table 9) were adopted and Roman capitals were substituted for Egyptian in the case of urban districts (Figure 17). In 1969 Times type was superseded by Gill Sans as one of the distinguishing features of the new maps with metric measurements. The effect of these changes in design has been further to differentiate the look, respectively, of County and National Grid Series maps at the 1:2500 scale.

1 That is, a thickening of the bounding line. In 1912, to facilitate the enlargement of 1:2500 maps to the 1:1250 scale, shading was omitted from the former; and they were also drawn with finer lines thereafter and with the size of lettering reduced.

2 Parishes were in fact distinguished by style of type until 1963 when the abbreviation CP (Civil Parish) was introduced.

Ground surface features

On the current 1:1250 and 1:2500 maps 'ground surface features' are defined by the Ordnance Survey to cover the following: boulders, cairns, caves, chalk pits, clay pits, cliffs, dunes, gravel pits, grottoes, marl pits, mud, mussel beds, natural arches, opencast workings, quarries, refuse tips, rock, sand, sand pits, scree, shingle, slag heaps, slopes, spoil heaps. The introduction of the metric map, in April 1969, was accompanied by a major change in the representation of these features. Its main result was to limit the use of symbols employed on the published map to those for boulders, cliffs, rocks (including quarries), and hachures for slopes (Plate 10). Areas of sand, shingle, and dunes, formerly represented by symbols, were thereafter shown in outline only and described by those terms. In addition, all ground surface features between high and low water marks were likewise indicated by annotation only.

Before 1969 many ground surface features had been produced by a process of controlled freehand drawing. Detail added by this method was known as 'ornament' and the aim of the ornamental draughtsman was to pen a symbol conveying an impression of the three-dimensional feature which he was portraying, yet sufficiently standardized to ensure comparability between sheets. Although there were changes in detail, and some symbols were already obsolete by 1969, the basic style of ornament detail had survived from the conventions employed on the County Series maps at the beginning of the present century. Until 1969, for example, when the symbols were discontinued, sand and gravel pits had been consistently shown by graduating from large symbols at the top to smaller at the bottom – thus giving the effect of a pit – and by employing a sharp and irregular symbol for gravel and a rounded one for sand.

With boulders or stone blocks, and with rock features, caves, and cliffs, it is the current practice to use standard symbols on film but some interpretation of the actual character of the ground surface above mean high water is still made. Large and conspicuous boulders or isolated stone blocks are surveyed individually and appear in position on the published map. With areas of boulders or stone blocks above mean high water the surveyor records their density on the scale:

Close   average distance apart less than 10 m
Medium   average distance apart 10–20 m
Open   average distance apart 20–30 m
Scattered   average distance apart 30–40 m

and standard symbols represent the densities on the map. With cliffs and rock faces the surveyor merely records the upper and lower edge (not, as was traditional, attempting to record the varying character of the strata) and the feature is published with a symbol for the upper edge, a pecked line for the lower, and the description 'Cliff' between. For caves and natural arches the symbol ⊗ has been in use since 1951 and the features are annotated. Symbols are also used for inland rock features, but patches of rock less than 0.25 hectare on the 1:1250 series (1 hectare on the 1:2500 series), may be mixed with standard vegetation symbols with 25, 50, or 75 percentages estimated in the field for representation on the map.

The current practice for slopes is that artificial slopes are shown by symbol when they are permanent features (for example if they are overgrown or form embankments carrying permanent features) and are over 1 m in height. Artificial slopes are always shown if a boundary is mered to them. Natural slopes, on the other hand, are only shown if an administrative boundary is mered to the feature or if they are coastal slopes in which case they will be annotated but not shown by symbol. The slope symbol (Plate 10), which aims to show only the *extent* of slopes and not their relative steepness, is a modified version of the hachure originally employed to show relief on early Ordnance Survey 1:63 360 maps. Hachures are also used in the representation of cuttings and embankments.

Vegetation

The character of all areas of vegetation is shown on the 1:1250 and 1:2500 maps, subject to the conventions described below, and with the exception of vegetation associated with land under cultivation, including improved pasture. While the objective of the maps is to portray the general nature of such areas of vegetation with accuracy they do not set out to delineate minor variations, nor is it practicable for the Ordnance Survey, even on its large scale maps, to represent the great range of vegetation types found in Great Britain. Apart from the scientific manpower necessary to map species in the field, even in botanical terms the intergradation between different types and the changes due to biotic variables are difficult to map so that the separation of different areas is often an arbitrary and artificial process. Ordnance Survey maps therefore confine themselves to showing vegetation types which are widely understood, are easily identifiable from field survey or aerial photographs and, to ensure some continuity, have been traditionally shown on official maps.

Since the introduction of the 1:2500 series there have been several changes in the depiction of vegetation, with a trend towards simplification already evident in the late nineteenth century. In 1888, for example, the separate symbol for birch wood was discontinued and minor vegetation features (such as hedgerow timber, omitted after 1892) were also eliminated during the first revision of the series. The collection of vegetation information for the County Series maps is described by the 1905 Instructions of the Survey and it may be noted that the surveyors did not employ the numerical classification of vegetation types, described below as currently in use, although distinctions such as those between close, medium, and open woodland were already recognized.

Changes made during the life of the National Grid series 1:1250 and 1:2500 have been more far-reaching. In 1958, for example, the present density scale for woodland, described below, was introduced. And in 1963, after discussion with the Nature Conservancy, the whole range of vegetation types shown on Ordnance Survey maps was amended to bring it more in line with modern ecological thinking. The categories before that date, each with separate symbols, were bush, coniferous tree (surveyed and non-surveyed), non-coniferous tree (surveyed and non-surveyed), furze, marsh, saltings, orchard tree, osiers, reeds, rough pasture, and underwood.[1] The new symbols sought to simplify this list but at the same time to give the maps a better scientific basis from a botanical standpoint. Some of the pre-1963 categories, such as brushwood and underwood, had dated military significance[2] yet were not useful botanical descriptions. They were absorbed into other categories: bushes, underwood, and furze into scrub; and osiers into

1 [Ordnance Survey] *A Description of the Ordnance Survey Large Scale Plans . . .* (1954), Plate X.

2 They were originally used, respectively, for stuffing paillasses and making fires, when an army was quartered in the field.

coppice (although osiers were to be named where space permitted). At the same time, bracken and heath were added as new categories. The vegetation categories currently shown are summarized in Table 10.

Table 10   Vegetation types currently distinguished on Ordnance Survey maps

Type	Definition
Bracken	Heathy terrain where bracken predominates
Coniferous	Woodland areas dominated by coniferous species
Coppice	An area of non-coniferous wood or thicket consisting of underwood and small trees such as hazel, grown for periodical cutting. Since 1963 osiers, previously given a separate symbol, were incorporated with coppice
Heath	Open ground, uncultivated and unwooded, and covering a wide range of botanical types
Marsh	Non-coastal marsh, in a variety of swampy locations, waterlogged throughout the year, and may be variously known as fen, moss, flow, swamp or bog. Peat cutting lines are not shown on Ordnance Survey maps. Marsh symbols are sometimes mixed with those for heath or rough grassland
Non-coniferous	Woodland composed of deciduous species. This symbol is also employed with the coniferous symbol to define areas of mixed woodland
Orchard trees	Cultivated fruit trees of any kind; no indication is given of density or pattern and they are represented by a standard symbol
Reeds	Confined to reeds growing in open water on the edge of a lake, pond, or river; reeds on the landward side of the water's edge are not shown
Rough grassland	Rough, uncultivated grassland in both upland and lowland situations
Saltmarshes	Stabilized and colonized areas of vegetation in the inter-tidal zone; in some areas described as 'salterns' or 'saltings'. On maps published since 1969 vegetation below mean high water has been shown without symbols, by annotation only
Scrub	Areas with associations of shrub species. Since 1963 areas of bushes and underwood (formerly shown separately) have been classified as scrub, and the type therefore covers a wide range of other species

Because woodland and scrub are prominent landscape features they have always been portrayed in detail. In particular (since the nineteenth century on the 1:2500 series) the relative density of woodland cover has been shown. Up to 1958 the effect of differing density was achieved by varying the spacing between clumps of trees of standard size: since 1958 the surveyors have recorded the density of coniferous, non-coniferous, and scrub vegetation in terms of numerical criteria. In a fourfold scale, 'close' is defined as an area with trees or scrub up to 5 m apart; 'medium' as 5 to 17 m apart; 'open' as over 17 m; and a further category 'scattered' is recognized. Standard stick-on symbols are linked with this scale in a '4–3–2–1' system, in which clumps of 4, 3, 2 or 1 symbol(s) denote close, medium, open, or scattered woodland (Figure 18). Neither coppice nor orchard stands are differentiated in this manner, and another exception occurs on slopes depicted by hachures; the natural density of woodland is ignored here and only sufficient symbols inserted to show the character of the vegetation. Other conventions are that within woodland areas, plantations are not distinguished from other woodland; the limits of clearings are shown by pecked lines; and paths, tracks, and fences of a temporary nature do not appear.

A distinction is also made between 'surveyed' and 'not surveyed' trees. Trees which are prominent landmarks, have historical interest, or help to define administrative boundaries are surveyed to an accuracy of 1 m and are depicted by the 'surveyed' tree symbol; the foot of the tree indicates its position on the map and an appropriate descriptive name, such as 'ash' or 'oak' is added. Where isolated trees are conspicuous features they are located to within an accuracy of 5 m but are shown by the 'not surveyed' tree symbol, which is also used to represent trees in rows or avenues. In either case the 'not surveyed' tree symbols may be omitted where more important detail has to take precedence. In avenues where trees are less than 15 m apart, they are positioned at a conventional distance of about 15 m; if they are spaced at over 15 m they are shown in position to within 5 m; the first and last trees, together with those at the end of breaks, are also shown to this level of accuracy.

Revision and Advance Revision Information (ARI) maps

Once a new National Grid 1:2500 sheet is published it is placed under continuous revision.[1] The policy in 1973 was that at least one new edition of every 1:2500 sheet will be published every fifty years, but in practice, in many areas of the country, depending on local developments, the basic sheets are revised more frequently. The recording of ground changes is organized at two levels of intensity at the 1:2500 scale. At the higher or 'active' level the same detailed system of intelligence is employed to record changes as in areas where the 1:1250 is the basic scale. Three types of 1:2500 sheet are classified as active: first, those covering minor towns; secondly, those covering areas where land registration is compulsory; and thirdly, those where significant change, defined as a concentration of changed detail which would take one or more days' survey to revise, is known to be taking place. At the lower or 'inactive' level, where changes are scattered and of little importance in themselves, a simplified intelligence system is maintained, the main object of which is to reveal significant change when it occurs, so that qualifying sheets can be reclassified as active. The classification is thus by no means immutable: in areas of rapid change, as on the fringe of major urban areas, 1:2500 sheets can be upgraded for survey and publication at 1:1250 scale and inactive maps can become active.

The standard of accuracy of the revision survey is intended to be the same as the original survey. All sheets are revised in accordance with current rules so that the opportunity may be taken (for example) to show house numbers or to reclassify vegetation and ground surface features in line with the latest specification.

Non-coniferous (close)

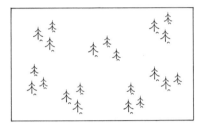
Coniferous (medium)

Non-coniferous (open)

Coniferous (scattered)

Figure 18
Conventions for density of vegetation on 1:1250 and 1:2500 maps

1 J. C. T. Willis, *An Outline of the History and Revision of 25-inch Ordnance Survey Plans* (HMSO, London, 1932) describes pre-Davidson methods of revision of the series.

Advance Revision Information (ARI) sheets, which are photographic copies from the continuous revision field sheets, are supplied, as for the 1:1250 series, in advance of publication of new editions. They are available as sheets representing single kilometre squares (the unit of field survey) and not in the 2 × 1 km format now generally used for publication at 1:2500 scale. The limitations of ARI sheets have already been described for the 1:1250 sheets, but a particular problem with those at the 1:2500 scale is that parcel numbers and areas may be incorrect because of changes since the original publication.

Special services

At scale transparent copies of 1:2500 published sheets and of field documents can be made on plastic material, with those of field documents being restricted to the single kilometre format.

In areas where 1:2500 is the basic scale enlargements to 1:1250 and 1:500 scales of both established sheets and field documents can be supplied. These enlargements measure 1.067 × 0.610 m (42 × 24 in); this means that for enlargements to 1:1250 scale each kilometre square is produced in two parts, north and south or east and west, with small overlap. Enlargements to 1:500 scale each cover an area 500 m east to west and 250 m north to south, i.e. one-eighth of a kilometre square.

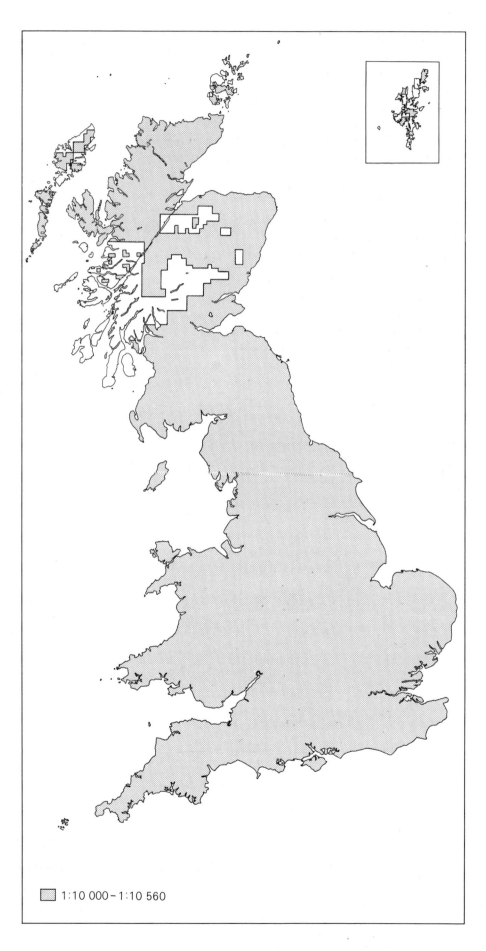

Figure 19
Extent of published areas at
1:10 560 and 1:10 000 scales
1973

☐ 1:10 000 – 1:10 560

The six-inch or 1:10 560 map, apart from the first edition one-inch (1:63 360) series, is the oldest of the Ordnance Survey map series. In 1840, following the survey of Ireland, the scale was adopted for the still unsurveyed territory of northern England and of Scotland. After the decision that a 1:2500 series should become the basic scale for all cultivated areas, subsequent 1:10 560 maps of such districts were derived from the larger scale parent maps. The 1:10 560 remained as the basic scale, however, in mountainous and moorland areas (Figure 1), and in coastal tracts embodying extensive areas between high and low water marks. The 1:10 560 is thus the largest scale to cover the whole of Great Britain down to low water mark, as will be its successor the 1:10 000. It is also – another characteristic of outstanding general importance – the largest scale on which contours (albeit excluding much of Scotland) have been shown since their introduction by the Ordnance Survey in the mid nineteenth century. Contoured 1:10 560 maps have become firmly established for a variety of purposes, both educational and for civil engineering, local government, and town and country planning.

Earlier editions of the 1:10 560 maps followed the cycle of 1:2500 revision. The routine up-dating of the series was accordingly delayed by World War 1, and by the subsequent effect of the 'Geddes Axe'. If anything the 1:10 560 maps suffered more than any other scale from these measures. In 1922 cyclic revision was confined to town areas, with the result that uncultivated areas, where the 1:10 560 was the basic scale, were especially neglected. This state of affairs persisted to the 1930s, but the Davidson Committee, noting that the 1:10 560 series had been in existence for a hundred years and was used extensively for records of all kinds – as by local authorities to illustrate statutory boundaries – had no hesitation in recommending its retention. The complete series, like the 1:2500 series, could be recast to conform with the National Grid; existing 1:10 560 plates were to be printed from until such time as the new style map was available.[1]

Some of the Davidson Committee's recommendations are still being implemented today. The task of converting all the 1:10 560 sheets, initially over 10 000, into the Regular Series format and incorporating the results of resurvey and overhaul is so large that it is being accomplished in stages and a Provisional Edition was issued as an interim measure. Since 1969, as part of the Ordnance Survey's programme of metrication, the simple conversion of old to new 1:10 560 maps has been overtaken by the introduction of the 1:10 000 scale. In some areas this scale is a direct replacement for the pre-1939 1:10 560 editions. The development of the post-Davidson National Grid Series 1:10 560 and the 1:10 000 series is set out in Table 11 and illustrated in Figure 19.

As a result of post-1945 developments the 1:10 560 maps have been published in both County Series and National Grid Series versions.

COUNTY SERIES

(a) *As an unmodified pre-1939 County Series*, but confined to parts of the Scottish Highlands and Islands. In March 1973 the remaining area so covered stood at approximately 5000 square miles; by 1982 the remaining sheets in the series will have been phased out.

(b) *Post-war 'provisional' series* (which should not be confused with the

1 *Final Report* (1938), 11–13.

Table 11   Publication of the 1:10 000 and 1:10 560 mapping 1948–73*

Published maps	Annual average				Total 31 March 1973	Total† in series	Comment
	1946–55	*1956–60*	*1961–5*	*1966–70*			
1:10 000 and 1:10 560 Regular Series, First Edition Basic	–	–	70	67	999	1393	Survey and publication of the basic areas started in 1958
Regular Series, First Edition, derived from large scale plans	38	34	82	257	3214	9084	Publication of the derived series started in 1953. The total includes sheets that are part derived and part basic
Regular Series, Revised editions	–	–	–	26	226	–	
Provisional Edition on National Grid sheet lines	450	774	467	–	4994	4994	Of the original 7250 sheets in this edition, 2256 have been superseded by Regular sheets

current Provisional Edition in (*a*) below). It was initiated in 1939, follow-ing the recommendation of the Davidson Committee, and was charac-terized by National Grid lines rouletted[1] in black and National Grid data printed in red. County sheet lines were retained and the form of publica-tion was in quarter sheets (Plate 5). Some sheets were revised from the 1:10 560 surveys carried out for civil defence purposes (the so-called 'ARP'[2] revision); in the case of buildings these new details were distinguished from the older base map by the absence of hatching.

NATIONAL GRID SERIES

(*a*) *Provisional Edition*: the second (and current) style of the Provisional Edition of the 1:10 560 maps was compiled from the County Series. It was designed to provide, as quickly as possible, an up to date map from the best available information. The sheets were produced by fitting the material of the County Series sheets, together with revision data, into the frame-work of the National Grid with a minimum amount of redrawing. Where-ever available the edition incorporated the revision undertaken between 1948 and 1957 at the 1:10 560 scale for the publication of the Seventh Series 1:63 360 map.

(*b*) As a *Regular Series*, upon the publication of which corresponding *Pro-visional Edition* sheets are withdrawn. The *Regular Series* has been produced in a number of ways – by derivation from larger scale National Grid sheets, by overhaul from the *County Series* coupled with revision at the 1:10 560 scale, and from new air survey. The type of material used in the compila-tion forms the basis of the distinction between the *Derived Regular Series* – covering areas where 1:1250 and 1:2500 series sheets are available on National Grid lines – and the *Basic Regular Series* – equating with areas where the basic scale of survey is 1:10 560.

(*c*) *Part Regular*: there is also a category of hybrid sheets (classified by the Ordnance Survey as Provisional) compiled in part from regular and in part from provisional material according to their availability for the sheet

* An index at 1:1 250 000 scale is issued at six-monthly intervals to show the availability of 1:10 560 and 1:10 000 National Grid sheets.

† All figures relate to sheets of 5 sq km size. Publication at 1:10 000 scale started in 1969, and the totals of basic and derived sheets include 1354 sheets published at this scale.

Source: Ordnance Survey, *Annual Report 1972–73* (1973), Appendix I.

1 That is, the line consists of small, closely spaced dots.

2 Abbreviation of 'Air Raid Precau-tions' in common use in World War II.

as a whole. The criterion for conversion is that where seven or more of the 25 km squares in a whole sheet have regular material available, a *Part Regular* sheet is authorized.

In so far as all sheets in the 1:10 560 *Regular Series* are drawn to a standard specification, the distinction between basic and derived sheets is often of theoretical interest only to the map user; some of the exceptions are noted in the account of particular features which is given below. Of greater importance were the changes effected in the design of the 1:10 560 *Regular Series* from the early 1960s, which were introduced to facilitate its direct reduction to the 1:25 000 scale. These are also described below.

COUNTY SERIES

Format, referencing and marginalia

Maps in the *County Series* were originally published as 'full' sheets each measuring 36×24 in and representing an area of 6 miles by 4. Until 1882 all the 1:10 560 maps of England and Wales were engraved in this large format: thereafter, until 1920, with the exception of a few sheets in Lancashire and Yorkshire, only 'quarter' sheets, of 18×12 in size, were issued. In 1920 full sheets were reintroduced, but their publication ceased again in 1925 as a result of representations from many users. The history of the sheet size for the 1:10 560 maps of Scotland is similar, except that some of the Highland districts are still published in full sheets.[1] The key to referencing was the fact that each county, or in some cases a group of counties, had its own meridian (Plate 1) and was drawn on a separate Cassini projection. Full 1:10 560 sheets were thus numbered consecutively throughout each county. 'Quarter' sheets were denoted by the full sheet number with the addition of suffixes NW, NE, SW, and SE. County index diagrams were formerly published at the quarter-inch scale showing the incidence of the 1:10 560 and 1:2500 sheet lines and the boundaries of civil parishes. In those cases where the county coincided with the limits of the area controlled by individual central meridians, the surveys ended at the county boundaries, and sheets abutting to the boundary were only completed to that line leaving the rest of the sheet blank.

No grid was shown on the face of the maps, but latitude (in 30 second intervals) and longitude (at 1 minute intervals) were given in association with the otherwise plain border of the quarter sheets. The sheet margin contained supplementary information including an index to adjacent quarter sheets, linear scales graduated in feet, chains, furlongs, and miles, and various notes about dates of survey and revision. A small selection of 'characteristics and symbols' was also included.

NATIONAL GRID SERIES

Format, referencing and marginalia

The introduction in 1953 of a Provisional Edition of the 1:10 560 map on National Grid sheet lines was accompanied by a change of format with the redesigned sheets each representing an area of 5×5 km and measuring 473.5 × 473.5 mm within the neat lines. With some sheets an extended layout is used especially where, as in coastal areas, this avoids sheets with large

1 Full sheets covered the Isle of Man, Caithness, Inner Hebrides, Inverness-shire, Isle of Lewis, Isle of Skye, Roxburgh, Shetland Islands, and Sutherland. Full sheets were also available for parts of the former counties of Berkshire, Brecon, Buckinghamshire, Carmarthen, Derby, Durham, Essex, Glamorgan, Gloucester, Hereford, Hertford, Leicester, Middlesex, Monmouth, Northumberland, Oxford, Stafford, Warwick, Wiltshire, Worcester, Yorkshire, Aberdeen and Banff, Argyll, Dunbarton, Forfar, Linlithgow, Orkney Islands, Perth, Ross and Cromarty, and Stirling.

blank areas. Each standard sheet occupies a quadrant of a 10 km square of the National Grid and can therefore be indexed on smaller scale Ordnance Survey maps. Thus, as the 1:25 000 maps are based on a 10 km square, the National Grid 1:10 560 maps, with sides representing 5 km, cover a quarter of this area and are linked to the map reference of their 'parent' 1:25 000 sheet: for example, if the 1:25 000 sheet number is TQ 47, the 1:10 560 sheet occupying its NE quadrant would be TQ 47 NE. More extensive indexes are provided by the 1:63 360 sheets on which each 10 km grid line is emphasized – and, in turn, by the 1:625 000 maps which are gridded at 10 km intervals.

National Grid lines are shown at 1 km intervals. Full grid values are given at the corner of the sheets, and the intervening values in kilometres, by the last two figures of the kilometre values from 00 to 99 inclusive. An inner border is divided at 100 m intervals. All sheets also show latitude and longitude in association with the inner border; abbreviated values are given at 1 minute intervals and full values, in degrees and minutes, accompany the 1 minute interval nearest to the sheet corners. Outer borders are graduated in scales of feet (west), yards (south), furlongs (east), and links and chains (north). A note on the relationship between true, magnetic, and grid north appears in the south margin of the sheet, together with an explanation of how to give a National Grid reference correct to 100 m, two panels of conventional signs, an index diagram to adjoining sheets, a 'survey diagram' (Figure 20), where appropriate, giving the dates of survey of component larger scale sheets and, beneath, revision notes on other information in the map.

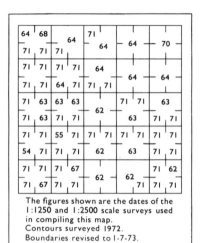

The figures shown are the dates of the 1:1250 and 1:2500 scale surveys used in compiling this map.
Contours surveyed 1972.
Boundaries revised to 1-7-73.

Figure 20
Survey diagram for derived 1:10 560 and 1:10 000 series

Landscape at 1:10 560

At the 1:10 560 scale 0.474 mm on the map represents 5 m on the ground and 1 sq inch on the map represents 17.778 acres on the ground. Six inches to 1 mile is the precise scale (in contrast with the 'twenty-five-inch' maps, the true scale of which is 25.344 inches to a mile). Many features on the 1:10 560 series are depicted at their actual scale but, for others, generalization is necessary, involving the selection and simplification of material to eliminate unwanted detail. Only in this way can the character and clarity of the maps be achieved. Since 1961 in particular the Regular Series has had to be drawn with further generalization for direct photo-mechanical reduction to the 1:25 000 scale. Such considerations influence the content of the 1:10 560 maps in three ways:

(a) in the minimum dimensions or areas (compared with the 1:2500 maps) at which detail is correctly shown in plan form, without either conventionalization or enlargement;

(b) in the elimination and simplification of certain minor details which appear on the larger scale maps at 1:1250 and 1:2500;

(c) in the adoption of minimum dimensions – as for streets and the distance between buildings – involving an exaggeration of the true width of these features.

MINIMUM DIMENSIONS FOR DETAIL

Some aspects of the current specification for the Regular Series map illustrate the effect of reduced scale on the ground size at which features can be shown to scale. Five metres is taken as the minimum dimension below which detail at 1:10 560 scale is either shown conventionally – as by a dot – or, if it is in a detached position and an important topographical feature, exaggerated in scale and shown at the minimum size. Above this threshold, detail is shown in true plan. In practice, however, as Table 12 illustrates, the threshold depends on the type of feature.

Table 12   Examples of minimum thresholds on the National Grid Regular Series 1:10 560 mapping

1:10 560 Threshold	Features
5 m in width	Rivers and streams, ditches, drains, canals, bridges and viaducts; projections, recesses, spaces between buildings
9 m in width	Firebreaks in woods
10 m plan width from top to bottom	Sloping walls, weirs on double streams
10 m square at base	Pylons
20 m in length	Steps
50 m in length (minimum distance to be shown by firm line)	Old walls and banks which are still prominent features
100 m in length (minimum for feature to be shown)	Metalled drives
Circa 1 hectare in area (minimum for feature to be distinguished)	Mud, marsh and bog, bracken and heath

ELIMINATION OF MINOR DETAILS

The 1:10 560 series is also generalized by the omission of minor details where they are either less than the minimum dimensions noted above or are of insufficient general importance to be shown at the small scale (Table 13).

A qualification is that in areas where the 1:10 560 map forms the basic scale, even minor features can be shown where they are judged to be of value to the map user.

MINIMUM DISTANCES BETWEEN PARALLEL LINES

A third aspect of the 1:10 560 specification is that minimum distances are maintained between features represented on the map by parallel lines. This helps to preserve clarity at the 1:10 560 scale and on the derived 1:25 000 series. In such cases the actual distances between parallel lines of the features are exaggerated on the map, with the extent of exaggeration sometimes varying between the basic and derived 1:10 560 series, albeit not sufficiently to make much practical difference to the map user. These minimum distances are illustrated in Table 14 relating to sheets published in the 1:10 560 Regular Series since 1961.

Table 13   Details shown on the current* 1:1250 and 1:2500 series but omitted from the 1:10 560 and 1:10 000 series

Anchorages for Radio and TV Station masts
Bollards, buoys, capstans, dolphins, mooring posts or rings
Cranes, except travelling cranes, hoists
Drinking fountains, water taps, pumps, troughs, water points
Flagstaffs, flowerbeds, sundials
Gas-governors
Hoppers, inspection pits, light beacons, lighting towers
Minor street detail, e.g. fire alarms, letter boxes, police call boxes, bus shelters
Navigation posts, lights, and beacons
Railway switches, buffers, retarders, railway mile posts and stones, signal lights and posts, loading gauges, mail pick-ups
Saluting batteries and guns
Sand drags
Ventilators
Weighbridges
Yair, Yaire (Salmon trap)

* On earlier editions of 1:10 560 series the composition of this list has varied from time to time.

Table 14   Conventional minimum clearances on the National Grid Regular Series 1:10 560 mapping (post-1961)

Minimum clearance between lines	Features
0.5 mm	Single track railways, buildings
0.6 mm	Sidings and tramways, minor roads, canals and other parallel lines
0.75 mm	Multiple track railways
1.0 mm	Roads
1.2 mm	Named roads in town areas

Conventional signs

Conventional signs employed at the 1:10 560 scale have in general followed the style of the 1:2500 series, especially in the case of the 1:2500 and 1:10 560 County Series. While the 1:10 560 symbols were necessarily smaller, both the style of lettering – as to denote administrative areas and antiquities – and the form of the symbols were remarkably similar (Plates 4 and 6). The main differences lay in the range of information portrayed. On the 1:10 560 maps symbols for boundary mereing are excluded from derived sheets (on the basic sheets they are only omitted if there was no room to show them) and other minor details, together with their abbreviations, are also excluded (Table 13).

After 1961 a new design for the Regular Series 1:10 560 was adopted, with the primary purpose of allowing direct reduction of its drawings to the 1:25 000.[1] It introduced not only a greater degree of generalization and further omission of minor details, but also a redesigning of the style of lettering and of the scope and character of the conventional signs as a whole (Plate 17). To give just three examples (full details are incorporated in the account below of individual features) houses were stippled instead of hatched, some road widths[2] were increased, and linear symbols introduced for railways.

1 Until 1967 the compilation and drawing of the 1:10 560 Regular Series was undertaken at 1:2500 but, thereafter, the drawing scale became 1:5000.

2 Only those roads needing a colour filling at 1:25 000 scale.

A consequence of the redesigning is that for a time part regular maps continue to incorporate two styles. On those sections of a sheet derived from National Grid 1:2500 material the new symbols are in use but, where County Series 1:10 560 were used in compilation, the old style symbols may remain unconverted. On such a sheet, for example, buildings may be shown by either hatching or stippling, according to the character and age of the map from which they were derived.

Contours, bench marks and altitudes

In one important respect – in the depiction of contours – the 1:10 560 series is parent to smaller scale maps. Contours are shown neither on the 1:1250 nor the 1:2500 series but, since contouring was first employed in 1839–40 on the original 1:10 560 survey of Ireland, and after 1853 adopted in Britain, it has remained as a distinctive feature of successive 1:10 560 map series. The major exception is that contours were not shown on 1:10 560 County Series sheets of the Highlands and Islands of Scotland, i.e. approximately that part of Scotland not covered by the 1:25 000 First Series (Figure 22). Contours have been subject to more changes of policy than most features on Ordnance Survey maps, alike with respect to method and to the vertical intervals at which they were instrumentally surveyed. These changes have determined the contour content of the obsolescent 1:10 560 County Series, and to a less extent the characteristics of contours on the post-war National Grid Provisional Edition (Table 15).

Contrasting policies were sometimes pursued simultaneously in different counties, with the result that contours on the County Series 1:10 560 were far from uniform. The main differences in contour interval over the country as a whole are summarized in Figure 21. In counties south of Lancashire and Yorkshire there was a fair (although not an entire) uniformity of practice, but to the north there are considerable variations. Nor were the differences solely in contour interval. Most of England and southern Scotland was

Table 15 Changes in instrumental contouring policy at the 1:10 560 scale, 1847–90

Period	Vertical contour intervals (VI)
1847 to 1856	25 and 50 ft From 50 ft to 400 ft at 50 ft VI From 400 ft to 600 ft at 100 ft VI From 600 ft to 1200 ft at 200 ft VI
1854 to 1869	From 25 ft to 100 ft at 25 ft VI From 100 ft to 500 ft at 50 ft VI From 500 ft to 1000 ft at 100 ft VI From 1000 ft to highest point at 250 ft VI
1857 to 1869	50 and 100 ft From 100 ft to 1000 ft at 100 ft VI From 1000 ft to 2000 ft at 250 ft VI From 2000 ft to highest point at 500 ft VI
1869 to 1890	As from 1857 to 1869, except that contours were only surveyed instrumentally up to 1000 ft

Source: H. St J. L. Winterbotham (1934), 46–7.

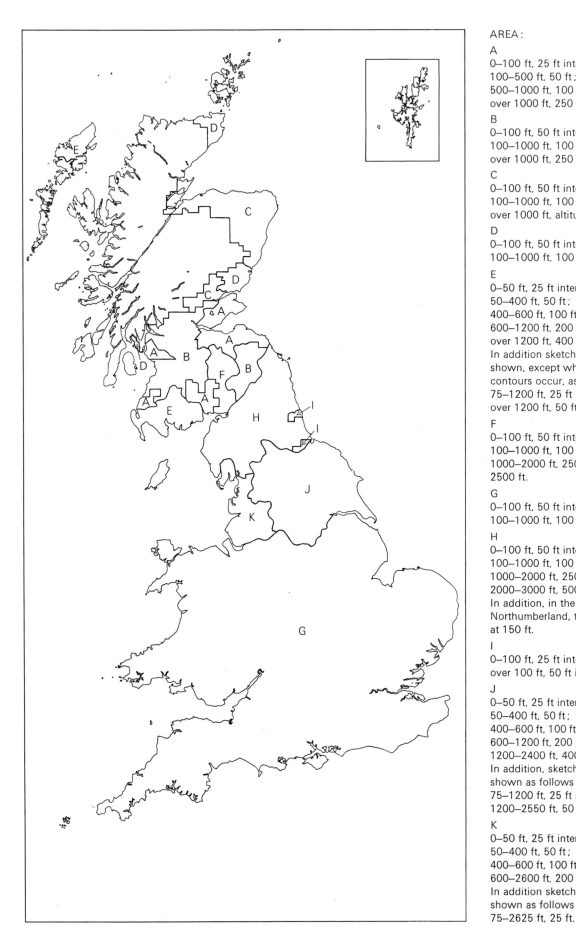

AREA:

A
0–100 ft, 25 ft intervals;
100–500 ft, 50 ft;
500–1000 ft, 100 ft;
over 1000 ft, 250 ft intervals.

B
0–100 ft, 50 ft intervals;
100–1000 ft, 100 ft;
over 1000 ft, 250 ft intervals.

C
0–100 ft, 50 ft intervals;
100–1000 ft, 100 ft;
over 1000 ft, altitudes only.

D
0–100 ft, 50 ft intervals;
100–1000 ft, 100 ft intervals.

E
0–50 ft, 25 ft intervals;
50–400 ft, 50 ft;
400–600 ft, 100 ft;
600–1200 ft, 200 ft;
over 1200 ft, 400 ft intervals.
In addition sketched contours were
shown, except where instrumental
contours occur, as follows
75–1200 ft, 25 ft intervals;
over 1200 ft, 50 ft intervals.

F
0–100 ft, 50 ft intervals;
100–1000 ft, 100 ft;
1000–2000 ft, 250 ft;
2500 ft.

G
0–100 ft, 50 ft intervals;
100–1000 ft, 100 ft intervals.

H
0–100 ft, 50 ft intervals;
100–1000 ft, 100 ft;
1000–2000 ft, 250 ft;
2000–3000 ft, 500 ft intervals.
In addition, in the county of
Northumberland, there was a contour
at 150 ft.

I
0–100 ft, 25 ft intervals;
over 100 ft, 50 ft intervals.

J
0–50 ft, 25 ft intervals;
50–400 ft, 50 ft;
400–600 ft, 100 ft;
600–1200 ft, 200 ft;
1200–2400 ft, 400 ft intervals.
In addition, sketched contours were
shown as follows
75–1200 ft, 25 ft intervals;
1200–2550 ft, 50 ft intervals.

K
0–50 ft, 25 ft intervals;
50–400 ft, 50 ft;
400–600 ft, 100 ft;
600–2600 ft, 200 ft intervals.
In addition sketched contours were
shown as follows
75–2625 ft, 25 ft.

Figure 21
Vertical intervals of nineteenth
century surveyed contours

(All contours were instrumentally
surveyed except where shown)

instrumentally contoured at lower altitudes, but in large parts of northern Scotland and the Islands contours were either non-existent or were derived from sketching and an inferior method of surveying known as water levelling. Water levelling, which was also used for surveying contours in southern England over 1000 ft, was both quicker and cheaper than spirit levelling, but is generally acknowledged to be far more inaccurate.[1] Late nineteenth century disagreements about both the techniques of contouring and the most appropriate vertical intervals have thus left an uneven legacy for the Ordnance Survey revisers of the twentieth century.

After the basic programme of contouring was completed – in England and Wales in 1891 – there were piecemeal additions to the stock of published contours and changes in their representation at the 1:10 560 scale. The Departmental Committee of 1892, for example, collected conflicting evidence on the subject,[2] but recommended an increase in the number of contours and a few additional contours over 1000 ft were surveyed as a result. From time to time special-purpose contouring was also incorporated into the 1:10 560 sheets: in 1903 lake-bed contours were derived from the Pullar Trust surveys; and a survey of the 20 ft contour in the Ouse drainage area in 1926 was later added to sheets in Norfolk, Suffolk, Huntingdon, and Cambridge. A demand for extra detail was also met by the insertion of contours at interpolated intervals, drawn in the main from hill sketches. From 1894 instrumental and interpolated contours were represented on the 1:10 560 sheets respectively, by chain and ordinary dots. Other changes of convention included the printing of contours in blue in 1909, but this was superseded by the adoption of red in 1912.

When the Davidson Committee considered contouring, nineteenth century changes of policy were still rendering the 1:10 560 contours inadequate for many purposes. The recommendations of the Committee were, however, somewhat ambivalent. On the one hand, they believed that additional contours should be introduced: on the other hand, inasmuch as engineers and others required independent checks on height, they argued that, provided '. . . the accuracy of the work conforms to certain well-defined limits . . . a minute precision . . . is not required'. No technical advice was offered and they left the 'details to be settled when the time is ripe for the Department to undertake the work'.[3]

The main decision, taken in 1943, was that contours on the Regular Series 1:10 560 map were to be surveyed at 25 ft vertical intervals and that the same data were to be included on the 1:25 000 map. Recontouring has been greatly assisted by the development of air survey techniques. A topographical method of surveying contours, by plane table and Indian clinometer, was adopted to speed up the publication of contours for the 1:25 000 Provisional Edition, but this was discontinued in 1946, in the October of which year contouring by air survey methods was commenced.

On the current 1:10 560 sheets the upshot is that contours are still derived from material of different provenance. Contouring from air survey continues, yet there is still some reliance on nineteenth century instrumental contours. It has been found that the nineteenth century contours are usually most reliable in areas of little relief, so that in hilly and mountainous districts the main source of contours is necessarily air survey. The origin of contours in any particular sheet is given in the sheet footnotes, which specify whether the data is from regular survey material, or from previous 1:10 560 county

1 K. M. Clayton, 'A Note on the Twenty-Five Foot "Contours" shown on the Ordnance Survey 1:25 000 Map', *Geography*, **38** (1953), 77–83; H. Collier, 'A Short History of Ordnance Survey Contouring in Scotland', *The Cartographic Journal*, **9** (1972), 55–8.

2 *Report of the Departmental Committee . . .* (1893), *passim*.

3 *Final Report . . .* (1938), 17.

surveys, in which case it is noted when instrumental contours did not extend above 1000 ft.

It must be borne in mind that reduction to the 1:25 000 scale requires some generalization of contour form and, on the Regular Series, conventions have been adopted since 1961 to break or simplify contours where they cross double-line water features, cuttings or embankments, roads, and railways. Contours and contour values are currently printed in brown and, except with contours derived from the County Series, the line thickness of every 100 ft contour is accentuated. Values are inserted to enable the height of any contour to be found quickly and easily, but without overcrowding the map; the 100 ft contours only are numbered in hilly districts where contours lie close together. The policy with respect to the publication of bench marks on the 1:10 560 sheets varies: on the Regular Series derived sheets, bench marks are not published; on the basic and part basic sheets, however, bench-mark detail is shown (as on the larger scales) by an arrow symbol, the point of which coincides with the position of the bench mark and is at right angles to it. Values are given to two decimal places of a foot, prefaced by the letters BM, but when a bench mark is coincident with a triangulation station – for example on a pillar – the bench mark symbol is omitted and the letters BM and the value are given. No distinction is made between fundamental and other types of bench mark at the 1:10 560 scale.

Surface heights are shown on both the basic and derived maps, but with difference of practice according to source material. On sheets with regular contours the heights determined by ground survey are published in black; those determined by air survey are published in brown, the latter convention having been adopted in 1966. On derived sheets with County Series contours, however, spot heights represent a selection. The draughtsmen work to definite principles, taking heights at the summits and bottoms of roads, at marked changes of slope and river crossings, on permanent topographical features such as the tops of hills, saddles, and valley junctions and, elsewhere, at appropriate intermediate intervals. There has been a tendency to show fewer spot heights on recent editions of the 1:10 560 maps and, in many areas, a greater number were published on the first edition County Series 1:10 560 maps of the nineteenth century. Altitudes are also subject to changes owing to the conversion from Liverpool to Newlyn Datum. Some difficulty was experienced in computing the systematic difference between the old and new levels but, on 1:10 560 maps compiled since April 1929, this difference, to the nearest 0.1 ft over the area of a 1:10 560 quarter sheet, was given in the sheet margin. On the Regular Series sheets most altitudes are based on Newlyn datum, apart from the maps of offshore islands remote from the mainland, where heights are sometimes based on locally determined datums. Such local datums are Stornoway for Harris and Lewis; Loch Maddy for North and South Uist and Benbecula; Loch Scresort for Rhum; Lerwick for Shetland; and for the Orkneys – with two datums – Kirkwall and Stromness. The survey origin of the spot heights and information on datum is given in the sheet footnotes.

Antiquities

The draughtsmen are supplied either with a 1:10 560 'working model' of the archaeological detail (for derived sheets) or with field documents (for basic sheets), together with correct names and descriptions for these features. The archaeological objective of the 1:10 560 series is to depict the same categories and types of individual features as on the larger scales (see p. 150), although lack of space may require omission or generalization of some features. The overall selection is made according to the degree of 'importance' of the features (as classified in Chapter 10) and the amount of congestion in the area concerned. Individual stone or earth works may also be generalized, but particular care is taken to preserve the special characteristics of these features (Roman camps, for example, have rounded corners and they will be so depicted) although other detail may have been shed in the process of modification. 'Remains' are shown by firm lines as surveyed; other sites, if defined, are represented by pecked lines, but otherwise by symbols. Frequent use is made of the standard slope symbol in the depiction of tumuli and other earthworks.

Boundaries and administrative areas

The 1:10 560 maps have been subject to changes in boundary delineation similar to those already described for the 1:2500 maps. The replacement of ancient ecclesiastical parishes by civil parishes in 1879, the initiation of rural and urban districts in the 1880s, and the discontinuation of the boundaries of Poor Law Unions after 1930, were, for example, in time reflected on editions of the 1:10 560 maps. The redesigning of the 1:10 560 Regular Series after 1961 was also characterized by new boundary conventions, and the changes are brought out if we compare the previous 1:10 560 boundary symbols (Plate 6) with those in the current specification (Plate 17). The latter are much bolder and have thicker line gauges; in addition a reduction was made in the total number of symbols by eliminating separate symbols for rural districts and Scottish burghs.

There is a statutory obligation laid on the Ordnance Survey to show currently the boundaries set out in Table 16 on maps at the 1:10 560 and 1:10 000 scales. The main difference in boundary depiction on the larger scales (Table 9) and the 1:10 560 Regular Series is the omission from the latter of ward boundaries in boroughs and urban districts. Minor differences include the naming of geographical counties[1] on the body of the 1:10 560 maps and, also to aid simplification at this scale, the practice of either combining boundary symbols or – where two or more boundaries coincide – of omitting the boundary lower in the administrative hierarchy in favour of the higher one. Thus, for example, when a parish boundary (shown by dots) coincides with the boundary of a local government area such as an urban district (shown by bars), an alternate dot and bar symbol is used. Where two or more boundaries depicted by bars coincide, however, the symbol for the senior local government boundary is adopted. When administrative counties, London boroughs, county boroughs, or county of the city boundaries coincide with that of the geographical county, the symbol for the last-named is published. The symbol for parliamentary constituencies is used only when it is not coincident with another local government boundary. Administrative area names or their abbreviations are named in the body of the sheet central to the area and districts. Exceptions to this rule are rural and other districts unless they appear on offshore islands falling wholly within one sheet.

Where boundary symbols clash with other detail the maps follow established conventions. If civil parishes run along a line of detail or pass through 'ornament', the dots are accentuated; where a municipal or 'district'

---

1 On the larger scales they are not named on the maps.

Table 16 Boundaries shown on the 1:10 560 and 1:10 000 series (1973)

England and Wales

Geographical county,* administrative county,† county borough (CB), London borough (LB), municipal borough‡ (MB), urban district (UD), rural district, rural borough§ (RB), civil parish‖ (CP), county constituency, borough constituency

Scotland

Geographical county, county council area, county of city, burgh,¶ district council area,** civil parish (CP), county constituency, borough constituency

Isle of Man

Borough, town, sheading, village district, parish district

---

* The term has no statutory definition. The Ordnance Survey definition links it to the areas of jurisdiction of Lords Lieutenant.

† The Greater London administrative area, although not an administrative county, is treated as such on Ordnance Survey maps.

‡ Sometimes known as 'non-county boroughs'.

§ Rural boroughs or 'boroughs included within rural districts' were created by the Local Government Act of 1966 and were not shown on Ordnance Survey maps before this date.

‖ There are no civil parishes in Greater London. The Inner and Middle Temples continue to be shown as 'places' within the City of London.

¶ For local government purposes Scottish burghs are divided into two classes, 'large burghs' and 'small burghs'. They are, however, distinguished only on the special administrative maps of the Ordnance Survey.

** District council areas were not indicated on the County Series 1:10 560.

boundary, whether or not in combination with a parish boundary, coincides with a line of pecks representing another feature, these latter pecks are omitted, but the name (e.g. Path) is retained in an appropriate position. On the other hand, where a line of detail, such as a multiple track railway, is of equal thickness to the boundary symbol, or a boundary runs along high water mark, the boundary symbol is omitted. Boundary symbols are also broken where they cross names. Lines of boundaries are usually named on the map only where the symbol is omitted or where the boundary concerned is that of a rural borough.

At the 1:10 560 scale mereings are not shown on the derived sheets, but they form an integral part of the representation of boundaries on the basic and part basic sheets. In such areas the maps employ the same abbreviations and symbols as on the larger scales (see p. 40). Compared with the larger scales, however, there may be some generalization along those boundaries where frequent changes of mereing are necessary.

Buildings

The reduction of buildings from the 1:2500 to the 1:10 560 scale results in several changes in representation. First, where the 1:10 560 maps form the basic scale there is a lower threshold[1] – 5 m – below which recesses, projections, and spaces between buildings are not surveyed and, on derived sheets, where these features would measure less than 0.75 mm (0.6 mm in the case of spaces between buildings) on the published sheet, they are also omitted. Second, conventional minimum dimensions (Table 14) serve to maintain the clarity. Some buildings are accordingly exaggerated from their true size and none is represented by a minimum size of less than 1 mm square on the derived sheets and 0.5 mm square on the basic sheets. The same consideration applies to the minimum distances – for derived and basic sheets 0.6 mm and 0.5 mm respectively – which are maintained between buildings and between other objects and buildings.

A third method of generalization relies initially more on the judgement of the draughtsman than on the application of minimum values. In simplifying residential areas an effort is always made to retain the character of an area. Adjacent houses of the same type, for example, are depicted in a similar fashion, and are not blocked in with markedly different houses, although this may require the artificial enlargement of gaps between houses to separate

1 With the object of allowing the maximum amount of detail to be shown in areas where 1:10 560 is the largest published scale.

groups of different character. The grouping of houses is also related to their spacing on the ground. Houses, or blocks of terraced houses, which would have appeared at less than 1 mm apart on the 1:10 560 Regular sheets, are generalized into one terrace; houses 1 to 2 mm apart are generalized with three or four forming one building; houses 2 to 3 mm apart are generalized by showing two as one building; but houses 3 mm or more apart are shown individually. Where a line of buildings would have been placed less than 3 mm from a road it is moved to the road edge, but above this distance away it remains in a position off the road.

Garden fences are simplified by retaining those running to the centre of a pair of semi-detached houses and omitting those which run between each pair. The principle of showing every other fence is also applied to terraced houses (although in some cases the gardens may be so narrow that more fences will have been omitted to conform to minimum spacing between parallel lines)[1] and to rows of detached houses; where individual houses are widely spaced, all fences may be shown. Other practices which assist in the generalization of built-up areas include the omission of internal divisions in buildings (except in large buildings where a division may be included to separate a named portion) and of selected names of houses, public houses, and garages, and leaving as undistinguished from the remainder of a building, archways and covered passages within its framework.

Fourth, at 1:10 560 scale, the method of representing buildings has differed from that on the larger scales. On the National Grid Provisional Edition of the 1:10 560 and first Regular Series sheets, buildings were hatched and shaded on the south and east sides. Public buildings were shown in solid black. After 1961, a stipple was used for buildings – as at the larger scales – on the redesigned Regular Series. The symbol for public buildings – a stipple edged by a thick black line – has no counterpart at the larger scales, but it is only used where such buildings can be named. Public buildings at the 1:10 560 scale are currently defined to include: art galleries, assembly rooms, cathedrals, chapels, churches, civic centres, colleges, drill halls, employment exchanges, exhibition halls, fire stations, government and municipal offices, hospitals, law courts, libraries, markets (covered: not cattle markets), museums, observatories, police premises, post offices, railway passenger stations, royal palaces, schools, synagogues, Territorial Army centres, town halls and universities. In all these categories only the main block or blocks will be shown in heavy outline, the remainder being edged in a normal line gauge.

Communications

All roads, including metalled drives 100 m or more in length, are shown on the 1:10 560 series. Wherever possible, they are represented to scale, but in the case of narrow roads their width is exaggerated to a minimum distance (Table 14). The limits of roads are shown – as traditionally – by firm lines if fenced and by pecked lines if unfenced; roads under construction are also shown by pecked lines and are described on the map as 'Under Construction'. Unlike the 1:1250 and 1:2500 series no attempt is made to show sidewalks; grass verges may be shown in between a metalled roadway (in such cases bounded by a pecked line) and the boundary fence (shown by a firm line), but only where their combined minimum width permits it.

1 Back alleys and terraced houses in areas of nineteenth century working-class housing may sometimes have been shown below minimum width to preserve their character and layout and to maintain a consistency of treatment.

The 1:10 560 map incorporates information on the status of roads as classified by the Ministry of Transport (now the Department of the Environment),
with the result that details change from time to time to follow the official
classification. The methods used for the depiction of roads are designed to
distinguish the following: motorways; trunk roads, principal and other classified roads (with dual carriageway where necessary); roads with 14 ft of
metalling or above (where not included in the previous categories); tarred
roads with under 14 ft of metalling; and minor roads in towns, drives or unmetalled trackways. Road numbers for motorway and A and B roads are
published on the map in a number of positions – usually just within the sheet
edge, at road junctions as necessary to clarify the route, and above the lines
representing the road; modification of these practices is sometimes necessary
in built-up areas. Road destinations and mileages are included in the sheet
margins adjacent to the official classification, but destinations are not given
for motorways and may be omitted in built-up areas.

Paths and tracks are shown on the 1:10 560 and 1:10 000 series by single line
pecks unless fenced, in which case double pecked lines are drawn to scale
subject to the minimum clearance between parallel lines. Within parks and
public gardens only the principal paths are shown. Special treatment was
formerly given to certain important paths or tracks such as the Pennine Way,
but currently the standard description 'Path' is employed.[1]

Railway symbols on the National Grid Provisional Edition, which were
modelled on the conventions of the County Series, differ from those on the
current Regular Series. Since 1961 no attempt has been made to represent
the intricate layout of individual lines, and multiple tracks are currently shown
by a single line (where many tracks run parallel to each other, however,
the number of these symbols may be increased with a minimum distance
of 0.75 mm between them). Single line railways are shown by a double line
with bars and spaces; and mineral lines and tramways by a single line of
a thickness approximately half that for multiple tracks. Sidings are generalized by depicting only the outer and the main switch-over tracks, and by
conventionalizing the remaining groups of parallel tracks to a minimum
width of 0.6 mm apart. Narrow gauge railways are shown by a single line
with cross bars.

Station buildings are also generalized in line with the principles described
for other buildings, and certain minor railway details, shown on the larger
scales, are omitted completely (Table 13). Those underground railways
depicted by pecks on the larger scale maps are also omitted on the 1:10 560
series.

Names

The source material for names on the derived sheets is the parent larger scale
map, but in compiling the basic sheets and the basic parts of part basic sheets
the information is obtained as for the other basic scales. From the total stock
of names collected the policy at 1:10 560 scale is to show as many as possible.
In eliminating names the usual practice is to retain all those which are of
sufficient importance to be shown at 1:63 360 or 1:50 000 scale and to leave
out – in overcrowded areas – minor descriptive names which do not meet this
criterion. Where a descriptive name is omitted the associated symbol, such
as a dot, which would have represented it at 1:10 560 scale, is also excluded.

1 Public rights of way are not indicated
on maps at this scale. See p. 101 for
details of public rights of way on
1:25 000, 1:50 000 and 1:63 360 maps.

Rocks, cliffs and slopes

On the County Series maps and the Provisional Edition derived from them, rock features, screes, and slopes were hand-drawn as ornament, but these methods have been largely superseded on the Regular Series. In 1958 a careful study – which disregarded all previous forms of depiction – was made of the best way to treat rock features at the 1:10 560 scale. The term 'rock features' was defined to include rock faces, flat and outcropping rock, and boulders and screes and, within areas so defined, a systematic examination was made of air photographs to develop the best means of illustrating the same shapes in a line drawing. The result was a new technique of rock drawing as far as Ordnance Survey maps were concerned which – apart from the cliff symbol – owed little to previous practice.

The new technique has analogies to contouring, with the steeper the slope the closer the linework, and a realistic impression of form is obtained over the whole range of shapes. With rock faces an important distinction was made in 1958 between vertical, concave, and convex faces. A vertical face cannot be depicted in true plan and the draughtsman produces an exaggerated picture of the top of the cliff strata. With concave rock faces the top of the face is defined by a shaded firm line and with strata being shown in a decreasing gauge of line towards the lower limits. For convex faces the effect is the reverse of the concave, but, the heaviest lines again serve to show the steepest part of the feature at the bottom of the slope. Although the convex and concave conventions represent the extremes of rock slope, they enable most graduations of rock surface to be depicted, being perhaps, least effective with sharp ridges and peaks.

On areas of flat and outcropping rock, the extent to which rock features are mixed with other vegetation cover is indicated on the map, and approximate percentages of the various types are recorded in the field for this purpose. Prominent isolated boulders are surveyed in the 1:10 560 basic survey, but only when they are larger than approximately 25 sq m; in the published maps they are depicted with a shadow on the south and east sides. Larger areas of boulders are classified according to their density as 'close' (average distance apart less than 20 m), as 'medium' (between 20 and 100 m), and as 'open' (more than 100 m apart).

The portrayal of scree is also flexible to enable local characteristics, as far as possible, to be recorded. In general, larger symbols are shown at the bottom of the scree slope, with a graduation to smaller symbols at the top; the draughtsman can, however, vary the design to show prominent scree runs, patches of vegetation on partly stabilized slopes, and also to identify coarser screes where boulders are intermixed. For rock features along the coast – including cliff and rock faces, flat or sloping rocks and boulders, and arches under rocks – a range of basic symbols are again employed but, within the limitation of the scale, varied to show features such as the direction of the strata, or patches of boulders fallen from cliffs. With such boulders, as with flat rocks, shading is applied to the south and east sides of the symbol. The entrance to rock arches (annotated 'Natural Arch') is either drawn as surveyed or indicated by a circle symbol, and cave and pot-hole entrances are also shown by a circle symbol.

Artificial slopes (as at 1:2500 scale), are shown by hachure symbols when they are permanent features, and subject to a minimum threshold of either

10 m along the slope and 2 m in height or that their minimum length must exceed 0.6 mm on the published map. Slopes less than this are usually omitted, unless they are named, are part of an antiquity or of a system of flood banks, or bear an important relationship to similar features within the sheet, in which case the symbol showing them is exaggerated to the minimum threshold.

Vegetation

On the earliest characteristic sheets to the County Series 1:10 560 maps, orchards and gardens, woods, fir plantations, 'rocky heathy pasture', 'furze or whins', 'furze or whins with rocks and trees interspersed', 'rough or heathy pasture', marshes, and bog or moss, were all distinguished by separate symbols.[1] Thereafter – as on the 1:2500 County Series – and partly due to the use of mechanical stamps in copperplate engraving, the trend was towards simplifying and omitting minor vegetation features. Since 1945 the Provisional Edition and Regular Series have also followed the changes of practice on the larger scales including the adoption of a new range of vegetation types in 1963 (see p. 66).

The 10 560 Regular Series, like the larger scale series, employs a density classification to assist in the delineation of vegetation areas, but such density distinctions are not made unless an area is 1 hectare or over on the ground or, on the published map, is 1 cm square or larger. The standard template symbols have their own design, which differs from the '4–3–2–1' system on the larger scales, and are graded for the several vegetation types into close, medium, open, and scattered. In mixed woodland the distinctions are not employed within one area, and the mixed woodland symbol is applied throughout at the closest density to be found within the whole area. With patches of trees mixed with other vegetation, such as scrub, the two standard vegetation symbols are also mixed at one appropriate density. Marsh may also be represented in a mixed symbol. The field surveyors estimate the degree of dampness of marsh according to approximate percentages (25, 50, or 75) of other species such as heath or rough grassland in the vegetation cover and this determines the proportion of the two symbols on the published map.

The vegetation content of the 1:10 560 Regular Series is also simplified through the adoption in the field of a minimum threshold of approximately 1 hectare where the series provides the basic map cover. Below this value, an area of vegetation will neither be mapped nor described, and the rule applies equally to the survey of bracken, heath, marsh, osiers, reeds, saltmarsh, rough grassland, scrub, woodland, and orchard. Moreover, on both basic and derived maps, isolated trees are not shown unless they are important landmarks (for example, on an administrative boundary) or are named and described. In parkland and ornamental grounds, a selection of single trees indicates the general nature of the land use, with no attempt made to provide a detailed survey of individual features; trees along roads are also omitted where the symbols would have obscured the limits of the road, names, or other detail such as fences. In the case of avenues, trees are spaced conventionally at intervals of approximately 4 mm on the map.

1 'Ordnance Survey Characteristic Sheet for the Six-Inch and One-Inch Plans.' Various dates after 1854, copies in the Map Room, British Museum.

Water features

In surveying for the basic 1:10 560 Regular Series sheets, rivers and streams are shown to scale by double lines if 5 m or more wide and, by a single line, if less than 5 m. Streams will not have been surveyed up a hillside beyond the point where they have well defined channels. In the case of the derived sheets, rivers and streams are drawn to scale by double lines to the point, as the width decreases, where they would be 0.6 mm wide on the published map and, below this, by a single line. The change from a single to a double stream is tapered, but when a stream changes width frequently within a sheet it is generalized according to its dominant character.

On the 1:10 560 Regular Series terms such as 'collects', 'issues', and 'sinks' are only used sparingly where the source of a stream or its course would otherwise be ambiguous. Springs, however, are generally marked and described and are only omitted where they fall inside roads. Ditches and drains are also shown by means of double and single lines with a 5 m threshold on basic sheets but, where there is a close network, only sufficient may be retained to indicate the general pattern. Canals are depicted to scale or, if less than 5 m in width, are exaggerated to that width.

Areas of inland water – lakes, lochs, and ponds – are represented by an accentuated line around the perimeter; a narrow band of stipple 5 mm in width is applied inside this line, which in smaller water features fills the area. Narrow strips or very small areas of water, occupying less than approximately 1 sq mm on the map, are omitted, although if they are at least 2 mm in length they will be enlarged if space permits to a minimum width. Published levels refer to the winter water level (or the top water level in the case of natural reservoirs) and are usually given in feet above Newlyn Datum (for example, 'Winter water level 89 feet above Newlyn datum 1963'); where a local datum is used this will be specified.

THE 1:10 000 SERIES

A major step forward in the Ordnance Survey's programme of metrication was the publication of the new map at the 1:10 000 scale which commenced in 1969. For mountainous and moorland areas it is intended that the 1:10 000 map will become the basic scale, superseding the 1:10 560; for the rest of the country it will also become a standard derived map. The distinction between derived sheets (compiled from the 1:1250 or 1:2500 surveys or both), the basic sheets (compiled from the 1:10 000 or 1:10 560 surveys), and part basic sheets (from a mixture of these scales) are therefore the same as for the 1:10 560 series. The survey for the basic maps at 1:10 000 was commenced in the Highlands of Scotland and in these areas 1:10 000 sheets will replace the County Series directly. In other parts of the country the 1:10 000 maps are being produced by conversion from the 1:10 560 Regular Series.

Format and referencing

The sheet lines for the 1:10 000 series are shown on the published 'Index to Ordnance Survey maps at scale of 1:10 560'.[1] Each sheet normally represents an area (like a National Grid 1:10 560 sheet) of 5 × 5 km and forms a quarter of a 10 km square. This standard sheet measures 500 × 500 mm within the neat lines. Extended sheets are also produced by adding 1 km either east or

1 See p. 72. This index will also show the availability of the 1:10 000 sheets as publication proceeds.

west and/or north or south and producing sheets representing either 5×6 km or 6×6 km. Small extensions in standard or extended sheet layouts break into the border. In exceptional cases, as where an island falls on two or more sheets, it may be published as a whole by joining parts of the relevant sheets in a standard or extended sheet size and, in addition, small islands are published as insets.

National Grid lines are drawn on the 1:10 000 sheets at 1 km intervals and where a 10 km or 100 km grid line falls within a sheet – as on an extended or combined sheet – it is accentuated. Grid values are shown within the border, with full grid values, carrying the suffix 'm', being shown at the sheet corners. One hundred metre intervals are represented at the inner border. The sheet numbering system is identical with that of the 1:10 560 Regular Series (see p. 74) and in the form:

SHEET NY 17 NE

On extended and combined sheets the objective is to avoid, wherever possible, an unnecessary repetition of index letters and figures. The various permutations in use, according to type of sheet, are exemplified below:

Single extension	*Either*	*or*
	NT 37 SE	NO 50 SW
	& part of 37 NE	& part of NT 59 NW
Double extensions	*Either*	*or*
	NF 60 SE	NC 27 SE
	& parts of 60 NW, 60 NE,	& parts of NC 27 SW
	& 60 SW	& NC 27 NE
Combined sheets	*Either*	*or*
	Parts of HU 30 NE & 40 NW	Parts of NA 90 SE & NF 99 NE

In addition to the National Grid all 1:10 000 sheets show values for latitude and longitude at 1 minute intervals within the border. The values nearest to the sheet corners are shown in full but intermediate values are in minutes only; degree values below 10 are shown by a single figure, e.g. 5° not 05°, but single minute figures are preceded by 'o'. Distinctive marks of the 1:10 000 marginalia are the metric key, the description HEIGHTS IN METRES on the north margin, and the use of a side panel legend. Other information is the same as on the 1:10 560 Regular Series – apart from scales of imperial linear measures in the outer borders (see p. 74) which are excluded.

Landscape at 1:10 000

Many of the aspects of the specification for the 1:10 560 Regular Series as redesigned after 1961 apply to the 1:10 000 series. This holds true, for example, for the methods of generalization, including minor details which are eliminated completely, and for the minimum thresholds above which features are shown to scale.

The increase in scale (1:10 560 to 1:10 000) has resulted in some fractional increases in the minimum distances maintained between parallel lines.[1] That the majority of the other conventions are the same is revealed by even a quick comparison of symbols for the 1:10 560 Regular Series and the 1:10 000 (Plates 17 and 18). Among identical conventional signs are those for antiquities, bench marks, buildings, water features, electricity transmission lines, mereing signs, roads and railways, boundaries, and rock features. Some of the differences are noted below.

1 For example (1:10 560 value given in brackets: see Table 14), the minimum distances for minor roads and canals are increased to 0.63 mm (0.6 mm), those for multiple track railways to 0.79 mm (0.75 mm), and those for named roads in town areas to 1.27 mm (1.2 mm).

Metric values on the 1:10 000 series

One of the most important differences between the 1:10 000 and the 1:10 560 series is the adoption on the former, wherever possible, of metric values. In terms of area 1 sq cm on the 1:10 000 map represents 1 hectare (2.471 acres) on the ground. Linear conversion is facilitated by the inclusion of a 'Conversion Scale' in the reference panel.

Altitude values are given in metres above mean sea level at Newlyn (except where a local datum is employed). Levelling information is published as bench marks and surface heights. Bench marks are shown in metres to two places of decimals on basic and part basic sheets only; the value is preceded by 'BM' and followed by 'm'. Surface heights are given to the nearest metre.[1] The winter water level of lakes and inland lochs, and the top water level of natural reservoirs, are also given to the nearest metre. In those cases where the position of a dot symbol for a surface height coincided with other symbolized items (for example, a railway or a boundary) the dot may have been moved to one side.

Contours and their values on the 1:10 000 – as on the Regular Series 1:10 560 – are printed in brown. Contour data, in the short term at least, still have to be derived from several sources – air survey, ground survey, or the old County Series 1:10 560 maps – with differing degrees of reliability. Contours are shown at vertical intervals of 5 or 10 m or 25 ft (expressed in metres) according to the type of country and the source material available. They are depicted as continuous lines with a thicker gauge for the 25 m, 50 m, and 100 ft (30 m) contours than for the intermediate ones. Contours derived from the 1:10 560 County Series[2] are all drawn in a thin gauge, but still by continuous lines. All contour values are shown in metres with 'm' following the number, although these may have been converted from contours originally surveyed in feet.

Boundary mereings also incorporate values in metres.

Vegetation

Inasmuch as vegetation symbols have been redesigned on 1:10 000 sheets published since March 1970, the treatment of vegetation marks an important departure from the specification of the 1:10 560 Regular Series. The purpose of the change was to secure a further simplification of style with reduction to the 1:25 000 scale in mind. Two principal changes have taken place. First, although the basic 1963 classification of vegetation types is still applicable, the symbols in all cases have been enlarged. One result of this is that more areas are created in which it is impossible to show different types of vegetation – as mixed woodland types – by a mixture of their appropriate symbols. In such cases the symbol for the 'lower' type of vegetation is omitted on an established order of precedence set out below:

Trees will take precedence over Coppice
Coppice will take precedence over Scrub
Scrub will take precedence over Heath and/or Rough Grassland
Rough Grassland will take precedence over Bracken

Second, there are only two density classifications of vegetation on the 1:10 000 series. The distinction on the Regular Series 1:10 560 between close, medium, and open categories has been abandoned and these are all given

1 When the series first appeared they were given to the nearest 0.5 m.

2 In this case the interval may be variable: in Shropshire, for example, there are some 100 ft contours (expressed in metres) derived from the County Series.

the same density pattern. Scattered vegetation is still shown in more open form.

Revision

As far as the 1:10 560 Regular Series and the 1:10 000 series are concerned only the basic sheets come under the continuous revision system, and the revision of derived sheets generally follows that of the larger scales. When the Provisional Edition 1:10 560 sheets are due for reprint (but for which 1:1250 or 1:2500 post-World War II survey is not wholly available) limited revision is incorporated. This is normally confined to important changes in roads, railways (new developments not just closures), reservoirs, major installations, and boundaries. On the Regular Series, County Series contours may also be replaced if resurveyed contours are available when a new edition is published. An expanding revision programme is now in hand to deal with derived 1:10 560 Regular Series published sheets which are considered to need a new edition. These sheets are converted to 1:10 000 and fully revised using the latest 1:1250 and/or 1:2500 material. All revision material is inserted to conform to the current specification for the series, and its nature and date is recorded in the sheet footnotes.

Special services

The Advance Revision Information Service (issued for the 1:1250 and 1:2500 series) is not available for the 1:10 560 and 1:10 000 series. There is, however, a special enlargement and reduction service designed to minimize inconvenience during the period of conversion from the 1:10 560 to the 1:10 000 scale. For map users along the junction between 1:10 560 and 1:10 000 mapping, the Ordnance Survey will supply, on electro-photographic paper or on plastic, enlargements of the 1:10 560 maps to 1:10 000 or reductions from 1:10 000 to 1:10 560 scale. The 1:10 560 and 1:10 000 series maps are also available as transparencies, showing all the published detail with the exception of contours.[1]

1 See Ordnance Survey: 'Enlargement and Reduction Service for 1:10 560 and 1:10 000 Scale Maps', Leaflet No. 12; 'Supply of Transparencies', Leaflet No. 14; for further details.

The 1:25 000 series

6

The origin of the 1:25 000 series can be traced back as a military map to 1914. In that year production of a map series at 1:25 344 (a true 2½ inches to the mile scale) was begun for War Office purposes in East Anglia and later extended to cover all the eastern counties.[1] It was produced by the Ordnance Survey but was not available for public use. In the early 1930s a new series[2] was put in hand at the 1:25 000 scale, again for military rather than civilian purposes, and this became the model selected by the Davidson Committee when they recommended in 1938 that:

> *. . . maps of selected parts of the country should be produced and put on sale on the scale of 1:25 000, and, if these are successful, that a complete series on this scale should be published with fixed sheet lines conforming to the National Grid.*'[3]

The basis for the recommendation was the view expressed by a number of witnesses that the gap between the scales of 1:63 360 and 1:10 560 was too great. Schools, in particular, had found 1:10 560 too large a scale to give a general picture of the country, yet the 1:63 360 was too small to afford sufficient detail. It was also considered that the general public would welcome the 1:25 000 map for walking purposes and, moreover, as early as 1939 its value for regional planning was recognized.

During World War II the coverage of the War Office edition of the 1:25 000 maps, begun in the 1930s, was rapidly extended to meet the needs of defence and rearmament, especially in urban areas where the revision programme of the regular Ordnance Survey maps was most in arrears. The sheets in this series, known as the War Office Edition or GSGS 3906, were based on the War Office Cassini Grid, rather than the National Grid, and this reference system was superimposed on the map at 1 km intervals. Each sheet represented 10 × 15 km and the detail was printed in black, apart from contour lines and values, which were printed in brown. Neither the raw material (and hence accuracy) of the maps in the series nor their appearance were standard. They were a stop-gap publication, albeit derived from the best available sources, issued in a time of emergency.

The sheets were direct reductions from the quarter sheets of the County Series 1:10 560 maps, incorporating additions from War Office maps, from surveys made for special defence purposes, or from unpublished revision undertaken for the Ordnance Survey 1:63 360 maps. The result, by the yardstick of other Ordnance Survey maps, was of indifferent cartographic quality, related to the speed of production and the fact that direct reduction from the 1:10 560 sheets rendered finer features and minor names almost illegible in some places. Notwithstanding these deficiencies, and the criticisms they sometimes engendered, the value of the maps for civilian as well as for military purposes became widely accepted.[4] With the ending of the war, the Davidson Committee's recommendation to add the series to the existing range of Ordnance Survey scales was adopted and quickly implemented. Until such time as the new maps[5] could be produced for the whole country, however, GSGS 3906, the War Office 1:25 000 map, was put on general sale and was widely used by planners, geographers, and others.

First Series (Provisional Edition)

The first post-war 1:25 000 series, often called simply the Provisional Edition, was designed to provide, within a reasonable time, a properly produced

1 As GSGS 3036. The sheet lines were quarters of the Third Edition 1:63 360 Large Sheet Series. Over seventy sheets were produced in all.

2 GSGS 3906.

3 *Final Report . . .*, 13.

4 *A Description of Ordnance Survey Medium Scale Maps* (Chessington, Ordnance Survey, 1947), 13.

5 In *A Description of Ordnance Survey Medium Scale Maps . . .* (1955), 16, the series was in the final stages of being phased out.

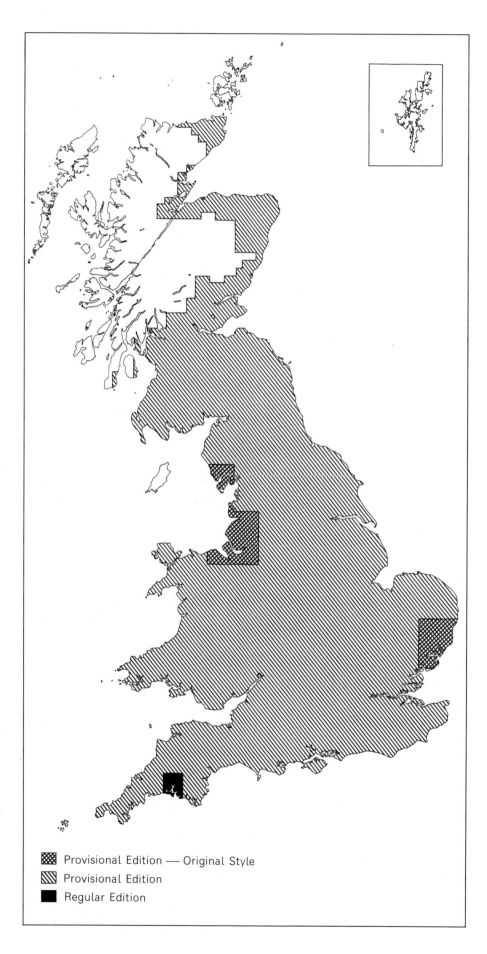

Figure 22
Coverage of 1:25 000
First Series

Provisional Edition — Original Style
Provisional Edition
Regular Edition

map from the available survey material. It was 'Provisional' not in the sense of the quality of production – the maps were completely redrawn in a manner designed to suit the scale[1] – but because the edition was planned to remain effective only until superseded by a regular edition based on the resurvey and overhaul of the basic large scale maps of Great Britain. This meant in practice that the First Series was derived from three main map sources – first, from the most up to date of the published 1:10 560 county sheets, including in some areas the 'Second World War Six-Inch Emergency Edition'; second, from GSGS 3906 at the 1:25 000 scale; and third, from field revision executed at 1:10 560 scale to provide material for up-dating the 1:63 360 and other smaller scale map series. In format and specification the sheets were uniform, with a standard sheet representing an area of 100 sq km, but so diverse was the revision material that the up to dateness of the series always varied markedly in different parts of the country.

Owing to their experimental nature, there have been a number of changes in the design of the 1:25 000 maps. From the outset the Provisional Edition was coloured but the range of colours was subsequently increased. The first sheets to be published, some ninety in areas of East Anglia and north-west England beginning in November 1945 (Figure 22), were printed in three colours: black, brown, and blue. In this 'original' style, the principal field boundaries, the outlines of all roads and tracks, railways, buildings (solid black for some public buildings and hatched in black for others), woods, brushwood, furze, and orchard symbols, and administrative and National Trust area boundaries were shown in black. Orange was used for contour lines and values, for sand and shingle and, in various permutations – solid and by means of pecks – for the depiction of classified roads. Ministry of Transport Class 1 roads were shown in solid orange; Class 2 roads by broken filling and minor metalled roads by short pecks. Blue was reserved for water features and their names, including areas of marsh, reeds, and osier beds and, combined with a brown stipple, to represent mud.

During the period of the 'original' style several minor modifications were made. On early sheets, for example, the use of broken fillings was confined to Ministry of Transport Class 2 roads and was only applied at a later date to minor metalled roads, as noted above, although on reprinting, earlier sheets were brought into line.

The later Provisional style covered the whole of Great Britain except the Highlands and Islands of Scotland and the Isle of Man – areas where the 1:10 560 County Series were particularly inferior and lacked contours in large areas (Figure 22). It was introduced partly as a result of constructive criticisms of the original style and the main innovations were the use of an extra colour – grey – and the adoption of a different fount of type for the lettering. Grey was used in place of black for field boundaries, for the in-fillings of non-public buildings (as a grey tint), for woods (by tree symbols) and for the brushwood, furze, and orchard symbols (but with the tree symbols in ornamental parks remaining black) (Plates 19 and 21). The result of these changes was to put less important features into the background and to display to greater effect the more important, as well as to give built-up areas a cleaner and more finished appearance.

As the coverage progressed towards completion in 1956, a revision of the published sheets was put in hand from revision undertaken for the smaller scale maps (see p. 118). Revised sheets of the whole series were issued between

[1] F. J. Monkhouse, 'The New Ordnance Survey Map Series Scale 1:25 000', *The Town Planning Review*, **21** (1950), 70–81, for a general description; also G. Cheetham, 'New Medium and Small Scale Maps of the Ordnance Survey', *The Geographical Journal*, **107** (1946), 211–24.

1950 and 1965. In addition, revised sheets were subsequently reprinted to incorporate important changes such as major road developments.

The chronology of publication, together with that of the Second Series, described below, is summarized in Table 17 and illustrated in Figures 22 and 23.

Table 17   Publication of the 1:25 000 mapping 1946–73

Published maps	Annual average				Total 31 March 1973	Total in series
	1946–55	1956–60	1961–5	1966–70		
First Series, Revised	143	209	66	–	1883	1883*
Second Series	–	–	–	14	139	1399†

* Of the original 2027 sheets in the series 144 had by March 1973 been superseded by sheets of the Second Series.

† Publication started in 1965.

Source: Ordnance Survey, *Annual Report 1972–73* (1973).

First Series (Regular Edition)

In 1957 a start was made with the publication of a Regular Edition of the First Series. As far as the 1:25 000 scale was concerned these were the first maps to be based wholly on the 1:10 560 National Grid Regular sheets. The format was identical to that of the Provisional Edition with each sheet representing an area of 10 × 10 km. The scope of the information was also the same, but from a design point of view an innovation was the introduction of a fifth colour – green – as a tint for wooded areas.

Soon after the publication of the first sheets, however, work on the Series was discontinued, partly on technical grounds to allow the development of the methods described below for the Second Series, and partly on policy grounds, because resources had to be diverted to higher-priority mapping.[1] The net result was that a block of only eleven sheets in Devonshire – two pilot sheets together with nine others – was produced (Figure 22). These eleven Regular Edition sheets, together with those remaining from the Provisional Edition, were collectively renamed the First Series in 1968.

Second Series

While the eleven sheets of the First Series (Regular Edition) were being produced, experiments had started in 1956 to establish if a satisfactory 1:25 000 map could be obtained by direct reduction from the fair drawings of the 1:10 560 Regular sheets. Out of these experiments was born the Second Series. At first, with a view to economy in production and in response to requests for a larger sheet size, a format representing 20 km east to west by 15 km north to south was proposed. In 1960 an experimental sheet, Ilfracombe and Lundy, was issued in this format in a five-colour design.[2] Despite the advantages of this size from a production point of view, it required an inconvenient system of numbering inasmuch as the system could not be related simply to the numbering of 10 km grid lines, and the format was dropped. In 1961 a sheet size for the series of 20 km east to west by 10 km north to south was adopted. This provided a sheet twice the size of that of the First Series, contributing in some measure to economies in production, yet at the same time enabling the existing National Grid numbering to be retained in a modified form. Each sheet was to be named. Pilot sheets were

1 *The Ordnance Survey Annual Report 1959–60* (1960), 14.

2 *The Ordnance Survey Annual Report 1960–61* (1961), 14; two others were taken to proof stage but were not published.

published in 1962 for parts of Sussex (TQ 21/31) and of Sutherland (NC 45/55)[1] and the first fourteen regular sheets in the new series appeared in December 1965.

In addition to a larger format the maps embody three other principal changes. First, new conventional signs are used for motorways and dual carriageways, and also for public rights of way which were introduced on Second Series sheets of England and Wales. Second, the grey colour of the First Series was dropped and vegetation symbols, together with house fillings, represented by a stipple, reverted to black. Green – experimented with on the First Series (Regular Edition) – was retained in a brighter and stronger shade and was applied to rights of way symbols and as a stipple to woodland areas. Third, conventional signs and abbreviations are printed in a panel placed in the west margin of the Second Series sheets, thereby extending their size to 965 × 559 mm. In many respects the 1:25 000 First and Second Series are fundamentally different maps. Whereas the First Series was a derived map in its own right, the second was primarily a reduction of the National Grid Regular 1:10 560 sheets (and increasingly since 1969 of 1:10 000 sheets). The two series are therefore described separately in the account of particular features which follows.

FIRST SERIES

Format, referencing and marginalia

The coloured sheets are in two styles, flat, or folded in covers which originally carried publicity material. Later it was decided to dispense with the board cover and to use instead an integral cover. This was to be printed on the reverse of the sheet with an index showing the original extent of the series, and a note on the National Grid. The conventional signs which had been printed on early sheets of the Provisional Edition but omitted from 1948 onwards, being shown on a separate card, were also to be included. This new format was introduced in 1970. The integral cover did not, however, protect the sheet sufficiently and in 1972 it was arranged for the folded sheets to be supplied in plastic pouches which had the added advantage that the opened sheet could be read through the plastic cover. On the First Series (Regular Edition) the conventions were printed in the south margin of the sheets. Each sheet normally represents an area 10 × 10 km, with a size 400 × 400 mm within the neat lines. Some sheets have been extended, where the inclusion of small portions of coastline avoids the issue of separate sheets for small areas of land.

All sheets are also published in an outline edition (see p. 103), printed in grey and available in flat form only.

An index map at 1:1 250 000 scale showing the availability of all sheets in the series is published every six months.

National Grid lines are shown at 1 km intervals. In the National Grid system the sheets are numbered by the Grid reference of their south-west corner to the nearest 10 km, e.g. TQ 37.[2] The inner border is diced in black and white at 100 m intervals and information on latitude and longitude, at 1 minute intervals with values to the nearest second at the sheet corners, is also associated with the inner border. The outer borders are graduated with scales

1 *The Ordnance Survey Annual Report 1962–63* (1963), 7.

2 In earlier editions the 100 km squares were denoted by figures.

of miles and furlongs (north and east), yards (south), and feet (west). There is a marginal index to adjoining sheets, a note on the relationship of true, magnetic, and grid north (and an indication printed in blue, in the margins, of this relationship) and footnotes on the dates of revision of the component 1:10 560 sheets and of features such as major roads.

Landscape at 1:25 000

That 1 sq inch on a 1:25 000 map represents 99.639 acres on the ground gives a measure of the extent to which generalization and elimination of selected detail is necessary to achieve a satisfactory representation of the landscape. On the First Series this generalization was achieved with the most up to date 1:10 560 maps as the basic source, developing a specification which frequently entailed a degree of selection or simplification which went beyond a purely mechanical reduction of the parent map. Not all details were derived from the 1:10 560 series: for example, seaward detail below high water mark – for which no 1:10 560 coverage existed – had to be derived from large scale Admiralty charts or air photographs; and major road and other important developments were obtained from the data of the small scales revision programme (see p. 13).

Two features immediately distinguish the representation of the ground surface from the larger scales. The first is the extensive use of colour – with separate black, grey, blue, and orange plates being made – as an integral part of the system of conventions, although colour is often used to add clarity or sophistication rather than to replace large scale symbols which in basic design remained unmodified (Plates 6 and 21). A second innovation at 1:25 000 scale is that standard symbols were introduced for some features which were shown in plan at 1:10 560. This was so, for example, with churches and chapels, with ruins (where the symbol occurred on the parent map), and with railway stations, while symbols were also used to differentiate trigonometrical points according to their location on churches, chapels, lighthouses, chimneys, and other buildings.

Altitudes and contours

Heights are given in feet above mean sea level at Newlyn. Where they are associated with trigonometrical stations the figures are printed in italic, but otherwise in roman type face. The published spot heights are a selection from the parent 1:10 560 maps and, in addition to those related to trigonometrical points, they are usually inserted at changes in relief – as at the summits and bottoms of roads, at valley junctions, and on the tops of hills. Contours are included at 25 ft vertical intervals. Pending resurveying, however, contours have had to be derived from a number of sources. For large areas the old contours on the 1:10 560 series were used, but where they were unavailable, in areas where they were known to be inaccurate or their vertical interval (Figure 21) did not match the 1:25 000 specification, the contours had to be obtained by other means. These included ground survey, air survey (as data became available from the resurvey), and sometimes from interpolation. The latter method accepted the position of heights on the 1:10 560 as fixed points and then used the form lines on the hill sketches[1] to draw in intermediate contours; sometimes a type of interpolation was used, merely conforming to the shape of available instrumental contours.[2] On earlier issues

1 The hill sketches – for various parts of the country at 1:63 360, 1:31 680, and 1:10 560 scales – were sketched in the nineteenth century. They are preserved in the manuscript store at Southampton.

2 K. M. Clayton (1953), 77–83.

of the First Series the heights of instrumental contours were given in the key but were not included on the sheet when the key was left off. The line thickness of every 100 ft contour is accentuated, but in built-up areas all contours are drawn in pecked rather than continuous lines. Where the information for natural freshwater lochs in Scotland was available bathymetrical contours and their values are shown.

Boundaries and administrative areas

There is no statutory obligation for the Ordnance Survey to show boundaries on the 1:25 000 series and this consideration may have influenced policy. The only boundaries to be shown were those of the geographical counties, county boroughs, counties of city (Scotland), and civil parishes, together with the limits of National Trust properties. The size of lettering used to name towns on the body of the map is related to population in the latest census. The largest lettering is used for places of 300 000 and over, with successive lower thresholds (and smaller lettering) at 100 000, 30 000, and 10 000. All administrative areas are named and positioned, with geographical county names in the sheet margins only, and county borough names, county of the city and civil parish names printed once on the body of the map as near the centre of the particular area as other detail permitted; on adjoining sheets these names are shown in the margin central to the area on that sheet.

Buildings

In the original style, buildings were hatched and shaded on the south and east sides, but for current sheets the convention is replaced by a solid grey filling within the black outline of the building. Public buildings – designated to include barracks, cathedrals, civic centres, colleges, government buildings, hospitals, libraries, municipal buildings, museums, royal palaces, police stations, post offices, railway stations (passenger), schools, Territorial Army centres, town halls, and universities – are shown in solid black, but only where there is space for them to be identified by name or abbreviation. The generalization of groups of buildings did not always follow the same rules as for the 1:10 560 series and the layout reflects the judgement of the draughtsman to some extent. Buildings are grouped so as to avoid ambiguity and the divisions between buildings or blocks of buildings, together with garden fences and back alleys, are omitted where it improves the clarity of the map.

Communications

The clear depiction of communications has always been regarded as a primary objective of the 1:25 000 series and, among methods designed to achieve it, roads are exaggerated to minimum widths and special symbols and colours employed to aid classification. Five road categories are differentiated on the First Series, namely, motorways, trunk and main roads, secondary roads, and (without classification) good metalled roads and poor metalled roads.[1] For motorways under construction there is a special pecked symbol (uncoloured) and for unfenced roads the traditional convention of a pecked rather than a continuous line was adopted. All classes of roads are enlarged to minimum conventional widths, except within built-up areas where the generalization remained as on the 1:10 560 source material. Road numbers

1 A slightly modified classification for roads was introduced on the First Series (Regular Edition) and on the experimental Ilfracombe sheet. Apart from motorways – which in any case were not present in the area of the published sheets – a fourfold distinction was made between Class 1 and Class 2 roads, other tarred roads (not classified), and minor roads in towns, drives, and untarred roads. In all categories fenced and unfenced roads were distinguished.

H

are printed on the body of the map and in margins where the road leaves the sheet. Road directions to the nearest places also appear in the margins.[1] Footpaths are shown with the disclaimer that 'The representation . . . of a road, track or footpath, is no evidence of the existence of a right of way.' Railways[2] are differentiated as multiple track (defined as two or more lines), single track, and narrow gauge; where mineral railways joined a standard gauge railway they are shown as normal standard gauge single track lines (or depending on their length) as sidings; in other cases they appear as narrow gauge railways (Plate 21).

Rock features and vegetation

Cliffs, rocks, flat rocks, and slopes are treated as 'ornament' and are modelled on the style of large-scale depiction current at the time of their drawing. Where necessary, especially with man-made features including flood banks, cuttings, embankments, and slopes of antiquities, the draughtsman exaggerates the feature to achieve clarity.

Three types of woodland, coniferous, deciduous, and brushwood, are shown by symbols printed in black (grey on the later four-colour style) and bounded by continuous or dotted lines according to whether the area is fenced or unfenced. (Plate 21). There are separate (black) symbols for parkland, for orchard and for furze, and (shown by the same symbol) for rough pasture, heath, and moor on the original style; on the later style sheets, grey was substituted for black for this range of vegetation types, but symbols for marsh, reeds, and osier beds continued to be printed in blue. The changes in vegetation classification made in 1963 (see p. 66) were not implemented on any First Series sheets, although on the First Series (Regular Edition), two new vegetation categories (mixed woodland and underwood) were introduced, while the brushwood symbol and the distinction between fenced and unfenced areas was discontinued.[3]

Water features

Water features are printed in blue. The generalization necessary in reducing from the 1:10 560 scale was, subject to certain standing instructions, the responsibility of the sheet draughtsman who was allowed to make a certain amount of simplification. Thus, although he followed the depiction of double and single streams on the 1:10 560, single streams were drawn in 'atlas' style, that is to say, some natural sinuosity was smoothed out. Even double line streams were sometimes conventionalized to maintain a minimum width for reproduction, and, where streams ran alongside other detail, they could be moved slightly to permit reduction, except where they carried administrative boundaries, in which case the other detail was moved. Other generalization includes a selective elimination of terms such as 'rises' – retained only for the principal streams – and likewise only sources of important rivers are described. Drains are depicted, but, where they occurred in association with roads, only those which formed part of a general drainage system are included; even then they are sometimes displaced to allow metalled roadways to be shown at the specified conventional width. Canals are drawn with no further generalization beyond that of the 1:10 560 source material.

1 Directions for B roads were added only in those cases where an A road did not appear in the same margin.

2 The representation of railways was initially made to conform to the current 1:10 560 Regular Series specification on the First Series (Regular Edition).

3 At the same time a green tint was adopted for woodland symbols, although the symbols for orchard, rough pasture and furze (in grey), and for marsh, reeds, and osier beds (in blue) remained unaltered from the Provisional Edition. On the experimental Ilfracombe and Lundy sheet the only change was that the green tint was abandoned for underwood.

Revision

The maintenance of the First Series has not since 1966 included full revision of all features. However, when sheets are reprinted important changes (defined as those which, if omitted, would seriously impair the usefulness of the map) are incorporated. They include developments such as motorways and other major roads, railways, reservoirs, and extensive afforestation. If no major revision is required stock is maintained from facsimile reprints of existing sheets.

SECOND SERIES

Format, referencing and marginalia

This series is published in both coloured and outline (see p. 103) editions. The coloured sheets are published flat, or folded with covers which show on the front an index to adjoining sheets, and elsewhere publicity material.

An index map at 1:1 250 000 scale showing the availability of sheets is published every six months (1973 position shown in Figure 23).

Each sheet is bounded by kilometre grid lines of the National Grid and represents an area 20 km east to west and 10 km north to south. For coastal sheets a 10 × 10 km format is sometimes retained as being more convenient with a 4 km extension in either east or west direction where necessary, and where an additional sheet is saved by this device. As a result there are three sheet sizes in regular use for the Second Series:

Area represented

20 × 10 km	80 cm (31.496 in) × 40 cm (15.748 in)
10 × 10 km	40 cm (15.748 in) × 40 cm (15.748 in)
10 × 14 km	40 cm (15.748 in) × 56 cm (22.047 in).

Small extensions are accommodated by local breaks in the margins of any sheet and, in addition, offshore islands can be included as insets on the nearest convenient sheet.

National Grid lines are drawn at 1 km intervals with 10 km lines (where not coincident with the neat line) being emphasized in a thicker gauge. Full grid values are given at the corner of the sheets, and the intervening values in kilometres by the last two figures of the kilometre values from 00 to 99 inclusive. The inner border is diced black and white at 100 m intervals. Each sheet is identified by a title and its National Grid reference, consisting of two letters and two or four figures, according to format. The two letters identify a 100 km square; the figures refer to the eastings and northings of the southwest corner of each 10 km square. For example:

TORBAY SX 86/96

Where sheet lines do not correspond to the lines of the 10 km squares, sheet numbers refer to all 10 km squares involved. For example:

SALCOMBE SX 73 & parts of SX 63 & SX 83.

Latitude and longitude are indicated in association with the inner border; abbreviated values are given at 1 minute intervals and full values, in degrees and minutes, accompany the 1 minute interval nearest to the sheet corners. Outer borders are graduated in scales of feet (west), yards (south), furlongs (east), and metres (north). A note on the relationship between true, magnetic,

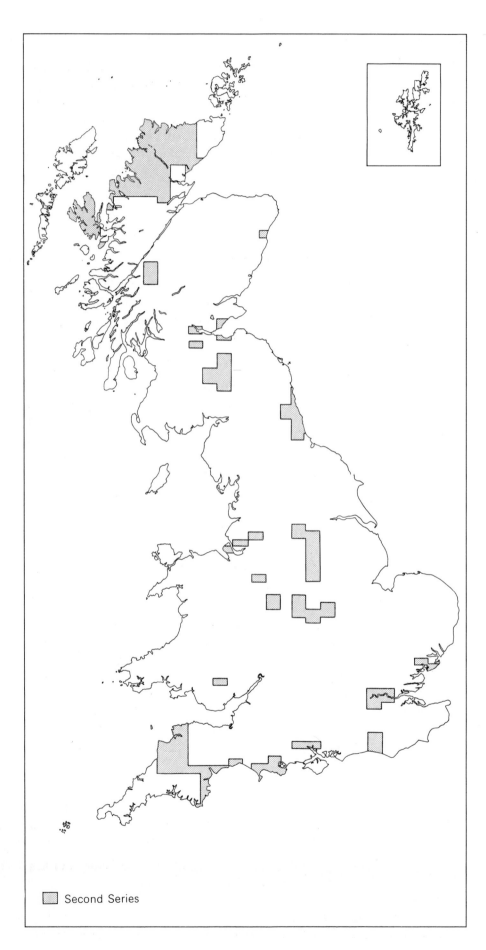

Figure 23
Coverage of 1:25 000
Second Series 1973

Second Series

SE 21 NW 1966 *	SE 21 NE 1966	SE 31 NW 1966	SE 31 NE 1965 *
SE 21 SW 1967 *	SE 21 SE 1966 *	SE 31 SW 1965 *	SE 31 SE 1966 *

The sheet numbers and publication dates shown are those of the Six Inch to One Mile Maps from which this map is compiled.

Date of survey 1952-62 with partial revision 1968.

* Contours were not surveyed at these dates but were taken from the 1:25 000 Provisional Edition.

Major roads revised 1969.

Figure 24
Marginal source diagram for
1:25 000 Second Series sheet

and grid north is in the margin on the west of the sheet. Apart from the reference panel with conventional signs, other marginalia comprise an index[1] to adjoining sheets in the southern margin and, below the reference panel in the west margin, 'Compilation Notes', including a diagram with numbers and dates of the component 1:10 560/1:10 000 sheets (Figure 24) and also the date of revision of major roads.

Landscape at 1:25 000

The essential characteristic of the Second Series is that its base is a direct reduction from the 1:10 560 Regular Series or, after their introduction in 1969, from the 1:10 000 series. Although a simple concept, with eight (see p. 73) 1:10 560/1:10 000 sheets reducing to one at 1:25 000 scale, the series has required considerable experiment in both design and production methods and a progressive adjustment between the contents of parent and derived maps. The trial sheets in the series as well as the first sheets to be published, indicated that the component 1:10 560 base material needed revision and a modification of specification to be suitable for reduction. The redesigning of the 1:10 560 symbols in 1961 was a response to this need and some of the older 1:10 560 Regular sheets had to be redrawn before they could be used in the production of 1:25 000 Second Series maps. In a similar manner the post-1970 vegetation symbols on the 1:10 000 series were redesigned to facilitate the production of the 1:25 000 map.

The current production method results in most of the detail on the Second Series maps being derived from direct reduction. This is true of outline detail, of contours, of water features, of house fillings and (when from the 1:10 000) of vegetation. Second Series maps thus embody much of the specification of their parent scale (Chapter 5) and the details are not repeated here. The main differences between parent and derived map can be summarized under three headings:

CONVENTIONAL SIGNS

With maps in the Second Series, conventional signs are printed in a reference panel occupying the western margin of the sheet, and the design of this has undergone several modifications since 1965. A standard layout is headed by roads and railways and beneath, in turn, boundaries, symbols, rock features and vegetation, and heights and abbreviations. Most conventions are identical with the parent maps (Plates 17 and 18), but for some features (as on the First Series) symbols replace depiction in plan. These symbols (Plate 22) are for churches and chapels, for bus and coach stations (first given a separate symbol on the Second Series), and for lighthouses and lightships.[2]

DETAIL NOT SHOWN ON THE 1:10 560 / 1:10 000 BASE

Four main categories of information are derived from sources other than the 1:10 560 or 1:10 000 base:

(a) *Public rights of way*   The National Parks and Access to the Countryside Act, 1949, and later the Countryside Act, 1968, set up and developed a system for establishing public rights of way; the Ordnance Survey agreed to show these rights of way, as depicted on the definitive maps prepared by local authorities, on its 1:25 000 (Second Series), 1:63 360, and 1:50 000 maps. The 1949 Act defined four terms relating to rights of way. Firstly, 'footpath'

1 When sheets are sold folded the index to adjoining sheets is cut off as it is printed on the cover.

2 Their position is obtained from Admiralty charts or from the Admiralty list of lights.

was defined as a highway over which the public had right of way on foot only, other than such a highway at the side of a public road. Secondly, 'bridleway' was defined as a highway over which the public had rights of way both on foot and on horse or leading a horse, with or without the right to drive animals of any description along the highway. Thirdly, 'public path' was to refer to a highway which was either a footpath or a bridleway; and fourthly, a 'road used as a public path' was taken to mean a highway, other than a public path, used by the public mainly for the purposes for which footpaths or bridleways are so used.

The other relevant provision of the 1949 Act, as qualified by the 1968 Act, was that local authorities were required to prepare definitive maps showing the categories of 'footpaths', 'bridleways', and 'roads used as public paths', and to record changes of status in these categories. The legislation applied neither to Scotland, nor, except in certain cases, to county boroughs in England and Wales. There were special provisions for London, but in some exempted areas in England and Wales a voluntary definition of rights of way has taken place. In those areas for which, since 1965, such definitive maps have been available, the Ordnance Survey shows on the 1:25 000 Second Series the three categories of footpaths, bridleways, and roads used as public paths. On the 1:25 000 Second Series, rights of way are plotted from the definitive maps without further checking by local surveyors and printed either in green superimposed on the ordinary black pecked lines in use for paths or roads or, where no black detail exists, simply in green. The caveat is still entered in the sheet footnotes that the representation of other roads, tracks, or paths is not evidence of the existence of a right of way.

(*b*) *Details of National Trust properties*   Properties belonging to the National Trust (England and Wales) and National Trust for Scotland are shown and are either named as such or are abbreviated. The initials (NT and NTS) within the perimeter are in red to indicate that the property is always open to the public or in blue if it is in the opening restricted category (Plate 22).

(*c*) *Seaward detail below high water mark*   In some areas there is no cover at 1:10 560 scale for this detail, in which case it is derived either from large scale Admiralty Charts or from air photographs.

(*d*) *Major developments occurring since the publication of the latest 1:10 560/ 1:10 000 base map*   Details of major road improvements and other changes of comparable importance are derived from the continuous revision data for the parent sheets concerned.

DETAIL OMITTED FROM THE 1:10 560 / 1:10 000 BASE

Although the specifications for the 1:10 560 and 1:10 000 series were redesigned to aid reduction to 1:25 000, some base detail, in particular that of contours and names, has to be further simplified or omitted to obtain the desired clarity. When the parent 1:10 560 sheets do not include newly surveyed contours at 25 ft vertical intervals these are taken from the First Series where the contours, although of mixed origin and reliability, are uniformly at 25 ft vertical intervals. A selection may be made of the spot heights published at 1:10 560. Similar considerations apply to the depiction of names and generally only a selection from the 1:10 560 base will have been included. A rule has been adopted that at least all names which appear on the 1:63 360 map should appear on the 1:25 000 map. Particular attention is given to administrative names[1] and also to the names of antiquities. The names of buildings, however, such as those of hotels, inns, and public houses (or their abbreviations) are often omitted, especially in towns and, similarly, names of small woods in predominantly wooded areas are eliminated to avoid overcrowding. No attempt is made to show the relative densities of woodland areas (see p. 86).

Revision

The policy on revision for the Second Series is related to the amount of change on a particular sheet. On sheets where major changes are occurring (defined to include new information about rights of way as well as major road developments, railways, reservoirs, extensive afforestation) revision takes place when there is an appropriate amount of detail available from large scale continuous revision or small scale cyclic revision. All sheets are reviewed at five-yearly intervals.

SPECIAL EDITIONS OF THE 1:25 000 MAPS

Although the 1:25 000 series has been successful as a multi-purpose map, the scale has also been used for special maps designed to serve particular map users more precisely than the ordinary sheets.

Outline edition

Outline editions are published for both First and Second Series maps and have the same geographical coverage. Printed in grey in both cases, they show the same detail as the parent map apart from contours and road fillings absent from both series and, in addition, vegetation detail (shown in green on the coloured map) which does not appear on the outline edition of the Second Series. Their purpose is as a working tool for planners, field study groups, and others who require a suitable base for recording in the field and plotting additional data.

Administrative areas edition

The administrative areas edition is now largely obsolete, but was established after World War II as a national cartographic record of administrative boundaries. It consisted of the outline edition of 1:25 000 sheets overprinted in red with administrative information. In England and Wales this information comprised the boundaries of administrative counties and county boroughs in a heavy line; metropolitan and municipal boroughs, urban and rural districts in a medium line; civil parishes in a thin line; and borough and urban district wards in a thin pecked line. Each administrative area was either named in red or, for administrative county areas and for civil parishes not identical in area with boroughs or urban districts of similar name, with the name underlined in red. In Scotland the corresponding administrative boundaries and names were overprinted in a slightly different colour to distinguish them from English boundaries along the international border.

After 1948 administrative areas editions were published only for sheets containing wards or parts of wards of boroughs and urban districts. Production

1 The names of county boroughs, municipal boroughs, urban districts, large and small burgh (in Scotland), and civil parishes, appear once only on the face of the map, positioned in the sheet containing either the greatest area of the particular administrative unit or its built-up centre. On any adjacent sheet, such names appear in the margin. When the name of an urban built-up area is the same as that of the administrative unit, the status of the latter is shown in brackets, in abbreviated form, adjacent to the physical name, for example, BURGESS HILL (UD & CP). The names of administrative counties, rural districts, district councils, borough, burgh, or county constituencies, however, appear marginally only, unless the area is wholly contained within a sheet or exceptional circumstances prevail which render it desirable for the name to appear on the body of the map.

of new and revised sheets and of reprints was suspended before 1955.[1] Only the territory of the Greater London Council is today covered by administrative areas maps at the 1:25 000 scale; there are twenty-five sheets in the GLC series recording all administrative boundaries from that of the Greater London Council down to those of London borough wards. The style is that of the original administrative areas edition, with boundaries and administrative names overprinted in red on a grey outline base. An index to the series is available from the Ordnance Survey.

Outdoor Leisure maps

Starting in 1972 with the publication of 'The Dark Peak', the Ordnance Survey launched a new tourist type map, based on the 1:25 000 series, known as 'Outdoor Leisure Maps'.

In 1973 'The Three Peaks' map was added and others were in preparation. They provide another instance of the trend to publish maps closely designed to meet specialist needs[2] and, as with other tourist maps, they recognized the fact that regular series maps cannot adequately fulfil leisure requirements. Sheet lines, for example, may cut across areas of special public interest, or the conventions exclude information of critical interest to tourists. The sheets, based on current mapping, represent areas 20 × 26 km and are available (in coloured editions only) as flat and folded sheets. The covers of the latter contain information and hints for travellers and both maps employ special symbols overprinted in magenta or blue on the ordinary base to show tourist features. These include access land in National Park and National Trust property, long-distance footpaths, mountain rescue posts and youth hostels, camp and caravan sites, places of interest such as waterfalls and caves, and also the location of information centres and viewpoints. The depiction of all such items is not standard on the Outdoor Leisure maps, but is varied to enable the inclusion of local features of special interest.

Isles of Scilly

A special map of the Isles of Scilly is published at this scale in the First Series style. It covers every isle and islet in the archipelago.

1 *A Description of Ordnance Survey Medium Scale Maps*, . . . (1955), 15.

2 The Dark Peak map was planned in conjunction with the Peak Park Planning Board.

•

The one inch to one mile maps

Maps at a scale of 1 inch to 1 mile (1:63 360) were the earliest to be published by the Ordnance Survey and occupy a special place in its history and technical development. Until their replacement by the 1:50 000 series, they remained as the Department's main small scale series best-seller and have been used widely for administration, defence, and planning, and also for educational and recreational purposes. The modern style has developed over many years. Beginning in Kent (1801) and Essex (1805), sheets extended to cover the whole of England and Wales and were completed with the publication of the map of the Isle of Man in 1873. The first 1:63 360 maps of Scotland were published from 1856 to 1887.[1]

The early sheets were relatively unsophisticated monochrome productions, printed in black from engraved copper plates. Relief was indicated solely by hachures and other information which is today taken for granted was also missing. From the 1830s onwards, however, the design of the *Old Series* underwent a slow metamorphosis: smaller 'quarter' sheets were introduced in the early 1830s; parish boundaries were first inserted in the 1840s; and latitude and longitude were incorporated in the margins of many sheets during the 1850s.[2] The modified style of the mid nineteenth century maps was perpetuated in the New Series, the publication of which commenced in 1872, and also in the first complete national revision which was undertaken in the last decade of the nineteenth century. The first steps towards colour printing were taken in 1889, when an alternative series was produced with hachures printed in brown.

Thereafter far-reaching experiments with the design of the 1:63 360 series were put in hand. Following the Report of the War Office Committee of 1892, five-colour sheets were published for south-east England from 1893–4 onwards. The contoured series with hachures over-printed in black or brown was kept in print but lithographic techniques were then harnessed to produce a fully coloured version for the whole country. This was printed in six colours: brown for hachures, together with contours in red, roads infilled with brown, water in blue, and a green tint for woods.[3] A permanent result of the adoption of colour printing was that the small sheet size (12 × 18 in) became uneconomical (except for the monochrome outline versions without hachures) and the 'Third Edition' was also published as a 'Large Sheet' series (mainly 27 × 18 in), formed by the amalgamation of existing maps.

Although post-1918 economies curtailed these developments, including experiments with sheets printed in no less than thirteen colours (such as those of Killarney and Somerset), the 'Fourth Edition', published between 1918 and 1931, consolidated the main innovations.[4] A large sheet size was retained (with some rearrangement of sheet lines especially in Scotland) and the series was renumbered to give 146 sheets in England and Wales and 92 in Scotland. Copperplate printing became obsolete for the 1:63 360 series and the maps were printed in seven colours from either stone or zinc: black was retained for outline detail and green employed for woods, orange for contours, red and brown for different road categories, and two different blues for water features. Hachures were abandoned and parish boundaries were temporarily discontinued; otherwise, as in the use of colour and in the adoption in 1919 of a more objective road classification,[5] the series was deliberately designed to appeal to a wider range of users. It was officially

1 J. B. Harley and C. W. Phillips, *The Historian's Guide to Ordnance Survey Maps* (London, 1964), 7–10, 42–3.

2 *Reprint of the First Edition of the One-Inch Ordnance Survey of England and Wales*, edited by J. B. Harley (Newton Abbot, 1969–71), *passim*, describes some of these changes.

3 J. Farquharson, 'Twelve Years' Work of the Ordnance Survey, 1887 to 1899', *The Geographical Journal*, **15** (1900), 565–98, provides an introduction to these developments.

4 W. J. Johnston, 'The New One-Inch and Quarter-Inch Maps of the Ordnance Survey', *The Geographical Journal*, **55** (1920), 192–200; John Mathieson, 'The New One-Inch to a Mile Ordnance Survey Map (Popular Edition)', *The Scottish Geographical Magazine*, **48** (1932), 98–103.

5 Following the Ministry of Transport Act, 1919, after which the official nomenclature for 'A' and 'B' roads was adopted. In 1919 they were first incorporated into the 'Ministry of Transport Road Map' published by the Ordnance Survey at a scale 1:126 720.

designated as the 'Popular Edition' and, in the words of a contemporary Ordnance Survey description, was intended to be 'indispensable' to 'Motorists, cyclists, pedestrians, tourists and travellers generally'.[1]

A continuing effort to widen the market for 1:63 360 maps was reflected in the design of the 'Fifth Edition'. The maps were available in several styles: in a small sheet outline edition (c. 1931–5); in a coloured version (similar to the Popular Edition) with relief shown solely by contours; and, most ambitiously, in a new large sheet 'Relief Edition' (c. 1935–8), which combined the use of contours, hachures, hill shading, and layer colouring and, at the same time, was redrawn to employ a new style of lettering and additional conventional signs. The ordinary coloured version also had the new lettering and other improvements and it has been said of the 'Fifth Edition' that:

Quarries, wireless masts, isolated telephone boxes and electric power lines filled out the landscape detail; new symbols for Youth Hostels and National Trust property reflected a growing tourist market; parish boundaries came back, latitude and longitude intersections were marked by crosses on the face of the map and . . . a grid was added. Even if the references had to be by cumbersome full co-ordinates . . . a modern reference system was there at last.[2]

Work had started on the 'Fifth Edition' in 1931 and by 1938, apart from most of Kent and much of Sussex, it covered the area approximately south of Oxford: at this point all further activity was suspended.

The Davidson Committee and the wartime 1:63 360 maps

The Davidson Committee recommended that the 1:63 360 map should be retained. It was to be replotted on the national projection and also to incorporate the National Grid system in metres. It was this requirement which led to the abandonment of the 'Fifth Edition' before its completion. Production of the 'Sixth Edition', known as the 'New Popular Edition', was put in hand in 1939 but was interrupted later in the same year by the outbreak of World War II. In an emergency situation 'War Revisions' were produced with the same sheet lines, with one or two exceptions, as the Popular Edition. In southern England the maps were derived from the available 'Fifth Edition' sheets and, in northern England, from the 'Fourth Edition' – yet incorporating over the country as a whole such revision materials as were available from various sources. All the wartime 1:63 360 maps (even for military use) were issued on Popular Edition sheet lines. In 1945 a rapid publication programme was reactivated for the 'New Popular' Edition. This series was recast on the National Grid and published in a standard format, measuring 631 mm (24.85 in) from east to west and 710 mm (27.96 in) from north to south; sheets represented an area of 40 × 45 km or approximately 700 sq miles.[3]

The whole of Great Britain was to be covered in a single series comprising 190 sheets but only the 115 sheets for England and Wales were actually published. Scotland was served by sheets derived from the 'Fourth Edition' with the National Grid superimposed; the fact that these maps were reproduced photographically from existing materials, rather than being redrawn, contributed to their somewhat 'heavier' style.

1 *A Description of Ordnance Survey Small Scale Maps* (Southampton, 2nd edn., 1920), 3.

2 G. C. Dickinson, *Maps and Air Photographs* (London, 1969), 84.

3 *A Description of Ordnance Survey Small Scale Maps* . . . 1957, 3; G. Cheetham, (1946), 211–24; G. R. Crone, 'The New Edition of the One-Inch Map', *The Geographical Journal*, **105** (1945), 207–9.

THE SEVENTH SERIES

A completely new edition of the 1:63 360 maps – the Seventh Series[1] – was authorized in 1947. It was to be based on field revision undertaken at 1:10 560 scale and the design of the maps was rethought from first principles. A primary objective was to cover Great Britain with a uniform series of maps which, owing to the recommendations of the Davidson Committee followed by the interruptions of war, had not been available since the 'Fourth Edition'. The basic sheet layout of the 'Sixth Edition' was retained, although with modification to improve the overlap between some sheets. By 1948 the preliminary design and specification had been completed and drawing commenced. The component First Series 1:25 000 sheets covering the area of each 1:63 360 sheet were reduced photographically to 1:40 000, which was the drawing scale for outline, water detail, and contours. Data from field revision were incorporated on these drawings which were assembled on a grid and reduced to 1:63 360, at which scale names, roads, house fillings, and vegetation were completed prior to printing. Proofs of a pilot sheet[2] were circulated in 1949 to a variety of map users – private individuals, government departments, and educational institutions – and in 1951 the specification was finalized. The first sheets in the new series were published in 1952.

The major changes from the 'Sixth Edition' can be summarized under three headings. First, to enhance their readability, the Seventh Series maps were printed in ten colours as compared with seven on the previous edition. A solid grey replaced black for house fillings; a second (darker) grey was introduced for National Grid lines and vegetation symbols; red, brown, and yellow were employed for roads instead of red and orange; the names of water features were printed in blue rather than in black; and red was adopted to indicate National Trust properties and Youth Hostels. Second, to help 'lighten' the look of the maps, several symbols and the style of lettering were redesigned and, in addition, some categories of information were omitted altogether. Post office telephone and other call boxes were retained only in open areas or in built-up areas where space permitted; all post offices, except those in towns, were depicted by symbol; and public houses were not distinguished within built-up areas. Third, however, some additional features – including a more up to date road classification, symbols for bus and coach stations, and distances to destinations on adjacent sheets – were incorporated in an effort to meet changing user requirements.

The design of the Seventh Series continued to develop after its inception. On the first thirty-eight sheets to be published, for example, following the practice on earlier editions, all names had been handwritten but, after 1953, letterpress was adopted with considerable economies in both time and cost of preparation. Letterpress names and names produced by photo-typesetting methods were also used for names which had to be added to or changed on earlier sheets at the time of their revision, so that some maps exhibit a mixture of styles. A more fundamental change took place in 1961 when the number of colours was reduced from ten to six – with corresponding economies in printing. The colours eliminated were light blue for water tints (replaced by a stipple of the dark blue used for solid detail and water names), light grey for house fillings (replaced by a stipple on the black plate), dark grey for grid and vegetation symbols (thereafter printed in solid black and screened black respectively), and the brown filling for secondary roads (replaced by the brown used for contours). The colour combination for the current Seventh

1 See Appendix B.

2 No. 142, Hereford.

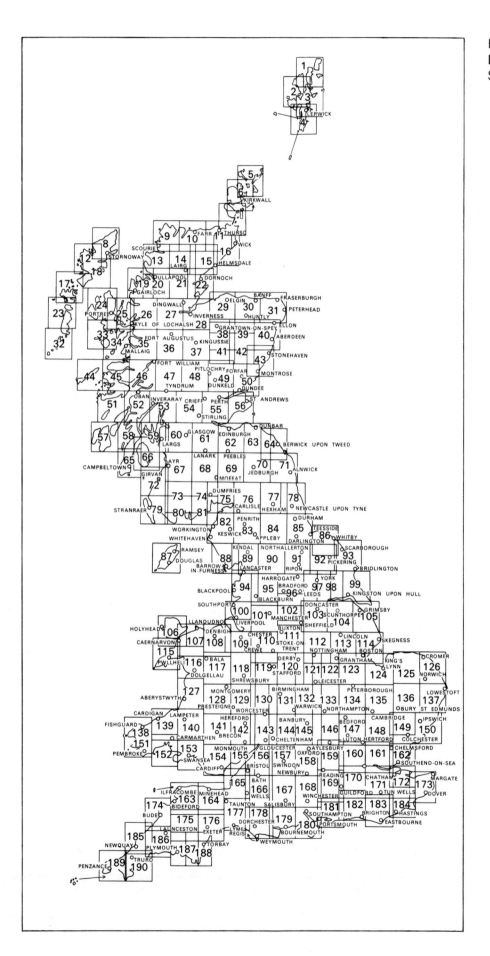

Figure 25
Index to 1:63 360
Seventh Series

Series sheets in publication in 1973 was as follows:

Black   outline, outline names and grid; house fillings and vegetation (screened).

Blue   water and water names; watertint (screened).

Brown   contours, contour values, and secondary roads.

Yellow   road fillings for roads which are not classified by the Department of the Environment (Roads Division), but which have 14 feet of metalling or over; or which are tarred if under 14 feet of metalling; National and Forest Park boundaries (vignetted[1]).

Green   fillings for all woods.

Red   motorways, trunk and main roads and all road numbers, railway stations and halts, bus and coach stations, Youth Hostels, danger areas, the boundaries and abbreviations for National Trust properties[2] and public rights of way.

The first publication of the Seventh Series was completed in 1961 and thereafter a regular system of cyclic revision was adopted for all sheets according to the likelihood of change in particular areas. Before the advent of the 1:50000 series fully revised editions were being produced at the rate of approximately twelve a year. By October 1972, out of the 189[3] sheets in the series, 134 had been fully revised. Many of these had been revised more than once and three (78, 153, and 154) had been revised three times. The remainder, all Scottish sheets, had never warranted a full revision.

Format, referencing and marginalia

The maps are published in fully coloured editions either as flat sheets or as folded versions supplied with laminated covers. The inner cover of the latter was originally devoted to a description of 'The National Grid as a Reference System and Map Index' and a diagram showing the 100 km squares in the National Grid system (Figure 8), but now carries Ordnance Survey publicity material. The outer cover, which is in the Ordnance Survey house style introduced in 1968, carries a diagrammatic map showing the area included in the particular sheet and an index to the sheet lines of the Series as a whole (Figure 25). All 189 sheets – with one exception – represent an area 40 km east to west by 45 km north to south or 1800 sq km (approximately 700 sq miles). These sheets measure 631 mm (24.85 in) × 710 mm (27.96 in) within the neat lines. One sheet, combining the Fishguard and Pembroke sheets (138 and 151), represents an area of 48 × 51 km. Of the total, 147 sheets have some overlap, in order to minimize inconvenience arising from large areas of sea or the splitting of larger towns. Insets are incorporated in some sheets (for example, the Isles of Scilly in sheet 189, Lands End) and the inset is designed with its own border containing grid and graticule values.[4]

National Grid lines are inserted at intervals representing 1 km with the 10 and 100 km intervals being emphasized in a thicker gauge line. Full grid values are given at sheet corners, and the intervening values in kilometres by the last two figures of the kilometre value from 00 to 99 inclusive. Simple instructions on how to give a grid reference correct to 100 m are printed at the bottom of each sheet. The National Grid framework on the Seventh Series maps also serves to index some of the larger scale Ordnance Survey series: in so far as each kilometre square represents the area covered by one National Grid 1:2500 single format map or four 1:1250 maps, and each 10 km square

1 A gradual shading-off of the density of a colour or tone.

2 After 1964 the abbreviation for National Trust (opening restricted) was shown in blue.

3 Sheets 138 and 151 were combined as a single sheet in 1964.

4 Except where the detail in the inset also appears in another sheet which gives the geographical position, in which case the graticule values are omitted from the border round the inset, but grid values are shown.

has the same relationship to one 1:25 000 First Series map or four 1:10 000 (or 1:10 560) maps, the 1:63 360 provides a simple index to these series.

All 1:63 360 maps print information on latitude and longitude in the outer border of the sheet. Full values of latitude and longitude are recorded at the 5 minute intervals nearest to the sheet corners, for example, 'w Long 1°05''. The remaining 5 minute and 10 minute intervals, although marked by short lines intersecting the border at right angles, are given in minutes only; the border is also subdivided by black and white bars to represent 1 minute divisions. Over the map as a whole, where they do not confuse important detail, the intersections of 5 minute intervals of latitude and longitude lines are marked by small black crosses.

A diagram (Figure 7) showing the relation between true north, magnetic north and grid north appears as a footnote to each sheet, together with a tabulation of the actual differences to the nearest minute between grid north and true north at the sheet corners. Sheets 31, 40, 64, 71, 77, 84, 90, 131, 144, 157, 167, and 179, which lie on Longitude 2° West, the central meridian of the National projection, have two footnote diagrams to show the relation between true, magnetic, and grid north at both the east and west edges of the sheet. The difference between magnetic north and grid north at the centre of the sheet – estimated to the nearest ½° – relates to the June of the year in which the sheet was printed; if a sheet is printed after 31 October the difference relates to the June of the following year.

Landscape at 1:63 360

As an original standard map of the Ordnance Survey the 1:63 360 series is so familiar to many map users that there is sometimes a tendency to accept its portrayal of the landscape without establishing its precise terms of reference. In common, however, with all other Ordnance Survey maps the Seventh Series is drawn to a precise specification to ensure a standard treatment of the same features on different sheets. The methods of compilation of the 1:63 360 series are also distinctive. Unlike larger scale maps produced by direct photographic reduction, the 1:63 360 series is to a greater extent eclectic in its sources. Its standard data included not only the 1:25 000 series and the 1:10 560 survey materials for the small scale revision programme, but also sources such as the latest Admiralty charts and Admiralty lists of lights, British Rail timetables, the definitive maps of public rights of way maintained by local authorities (county councils) in England and Wales, the 1:100 000 and 1:250 000 administrative series, the official list of post offices, Department of the Environment (Roads Division) data, census of population reports, and up to date information from such organizations as the National Trust and the Youth Hostels Association. Such information can be amended where appropriate on new printings of a sheet, and does not depend on the state of revision of basic topography.

The conventional signs and main abbreviations (Plate 26) for the Seventh Series are printed in the footnotes to each sheet. During the life of the Series their scope and design has altered, as, for example, in 1960, when public rights of way in England and Wales were added to the range of information depicted, in 1961 when the colour conventions were redesigned, and after 1963 when vegetation types were reclassified. In general, however, the Series has maintained a standard approach to the depiction of landscape features.

The limitations of scale have made it necessary not only to simplify the representation of many surface features and to reduce the number of features depicted either by name or abbreviation, but also to exaggerate deliberately other features such as roads. Some of the major methods by which a difficult balance is struck between detail and clarity at 1:63360 scale are discussed in relation to particular features.

Contours and altitudes

On the Seventh Series 1:63360 maps the vertical contour interval is 50 ft, as opposed to the 25 ft intervals on some of the 1:25000, 1:10000, and 1:10560 series. All contours, even interpolated ones, are shown by a continuous line with every 250 ft contour drawn in a thicker gauge line. The basic source for 1:63360 contours is the 1:25000 series and, although the draughtsman reduces this detail as faithfully as possible, the delineation is as much a result of cartographic judgement as of mechanical reduction. Contour lines are carefully adjusted to fit spot heights, and are broken where contour values are inserted, at railway embankments, cuttings, quarries, large rock formations, and at streams depicted by a double line; they are also sometimes broken where, because of very steep ground, they would be too close to show each line clearly. Contour values are selected by the draughtsman to reconcile the need to provide enough values to enable the height of any contour to be read easily, with that of preventing over-crowding or the obliteration of other detail. In hilly or mountainous districts where the contours are close together, it is sometimes the practice to label only the thickened 250 ft contours, inserting, for example, one value at the bottom and one at the top of a slope; in open lowland country, however, individual contours can be numbered. Values are placed with the top of the number uphill and are located so as to be read easily.

Spot heights are generally calculated in feet above the mean sea level at Newlyn, although the heights on some Scottish sheets – excluding values associated with trigonometrical points – have been based on Liverpool datum.[1] A distinction is made between heights 'surveyed by levelling' and those 'not surveyed by levelling': the former are shown by bold upright numbers, the latter by finer sloping numbers. Where the distinction was not clearly made on the most up to date of the published 1:10560 maps, then the 'surveyed' category was taken to include all heights with decimal points on the 1:10560 maps, together with other heights falling on probable lines of levels between such points – as along roads with bench marks or along clearly defined lines of levels across country. The remaining heights, including those about which there was any doubt, were placed in the 'not surveyed' category. When heights fall on a parish boundary their position is marked by an open circle rather than a dot.

Definite principles govern the selection of spot heights. Firstly, unless they have been cancelled or revised, all heights appearing on the 'Sixth Edition' are also included on the Seventh Series: with discrepancy between these heights and those on the 1:25000 map, the authority of the latter was accepted, and the 1:25000 series was also the source of any additional heights. Secondly, all heights associated with trigonometrical stations are shown as 'surveyed' heights, but published as ground level heights as distinct from heights in the trigonometrical list.[2] Thirdly, where a further selection of heights was necessary it was customary to retain heights associated with

1 H. Collier, 55.

2 That is, making allowance for the height of the flush bracket.

prominent features in the landscape, such as isolated spurs and saddles, valley junctions, and – along roads – either at the tops and bottoms of hills or at road junctions.

1:63 360 is the largest scale at which submarine contours are shown off the coast. The data, published at 5 and 10 fathom limits, are derived from the latest Admiralty charts and a statement to this effect appears in the footnotes of the sheets concerned. Where available, bathymetric contours, with values in feet, are also published for inland lakes: the source is again acknowledged in the sheet footnotes, but in so far as neither the Ordnance Survey nor any other national body has a regular programme of bathymetrical survey, this is often derived from a previous edition of the map.

Antiquities

The scale of 1:63 360 limits the amount of archaeological information which can be shown. The generalization is in relation to factors such as age, intrinsic archaeological importance, and prominence as landscape features (see Chapter 10). In practice this means that all large and visible field monuments – such as hill forts, castles, or long barrows (Table 21) – appear on the 1:63 360 series. This may be true even if their inclusion causes some interference with other map detail. Less imposing antiquities, however, such as small tumuli, fish ponds, or standing stones, are published only if there is no interference with other – i.e. usually modern – map detail. Even smaller sites may find a place only if they are of the Roman period; while 'found' objects, including Bronze Age hoards, coins, implements, and a whole miscellany of odd finds, are usually omitted altogether. Roman roads are shown by a single pecked line. Archaeological periods are distinguished by the type face used in naming the features, with Spartan for Roman antiquities and Lutheran for non-Roman antiquities, the size of lettering varying with importance.

Boundaries and administrative areas

Although the treatment of boundaries is selective, especially compared with the 1:25 000 Second Series, there was a statutory obligation at 1:63 360 scale to show certain boundaries, i.e. those of counties and civil parishes or their equivalents (Table 18).

Table 18   Boundaries shown on the 1:63 360 Seventh Series

England and Wales

National, geographical county, administrative county, county borough, London borough,* civil parish†, national park, and National Trust

Scotland

National, geographical county, county of city, civil parish, forest park, and National Trust for Scotland

Isle of Man

Borough, town, sheading, village district, parish district, and Manx National Trust

* The special symbol only appears on sheets 160, 161, 170, and 171 and is therefore omitted from the panel of conventional signs for the Seventh Series as a whole.

† A civil parish is usually coincident with its borough area and is not separately distinguished. Where two or more exist in boroughs and these are in close areas they are not shown. No civil parishes, as such, exist in Greater London.

Other boundary conventions at the 1:63 360 scale are designed to preserve clarity while retaining the maximum information. Where, for example, a parish boundary is coincident with a footpath, the former is drawn to one side: where, however, a stream is involved, the boundary symbol is always placed in its correct position irrespective of whether the stream is shown by a double or single line. The width of a channel may be exaggerated in an estuarine stretch of a river, to avoid the parish boundary symbol merging with the dots used in the depiction of mud and sand.

The areas for which boundaries are shown are identified by the appropriate names either in the margin or on the body of the map. Conventions vary with the type of boundary. The names of countries and counties are printed in the sheet margin on either side of the boundary line which is continued beyond the map area. When a town straddles a sheet edge, however, the name of the town is shown in the body of the sheet which contains the greater portion: in the adjoining sheet the town name is shown parallel to the sheet edge.

Settlement status and size are also represented by different type faces and, for example, the typography used for parish names differs from that used for villages within parishes, from detached parts of parishes and so on. Where a parish and village bear the same name, the parish name is not shown but the village name is shown in upright type in a size appropriate to its population. Where the parish is named differently, or where it differs in spelling from the village, both names are shown, the village name being in sloping type of an appropriate size. The type face for names of administrative areas varies in size with the population. Sometimes it may be necessary to apportion the population of an administrative area such as an urban district between its component towns for which no separate figures are available, or even adopt the total figure for the whole district, but many towns fit into the simple system in Figure 26 by which data from the latest census enables six numerical bands to be distinguished with a different point size for the lettering in each category.

Buildings

At 1:63 360 scale the amount of detail relating to buildings and similar features which can be shown in built-up areas is limited. This applies particularly to individual buildings. Even churches and chapels which as a general rule are shown by symbols, have had to be omitted occasionally because of lack of space. Given a choice between retaining one of several churches, the order of preference is churches with spires, churches with towers, and churches without spire or tower. Disused churches are not identified but sometimes a 'Church in ruins' may have been included. Individual hotels, inns, and public houses are distinguished where space permits but in towns and large villages where it is assumed that such facilities exist they are generally omitted unless located among a few houses on the outskirts or in a detached suburb.

In generalizing areas of housing from 1:25 000 to 1:63 360 the draughtsman worked to numerical criteria. Where, had they been drawn to scale, a row of detached houses would have become closer together than 0.75 mm, they were coalesced as a single terrace with a black outline and grey stippled filling. The same threshold applied to the tolerated space between terraces and other groups of buildings, which were often amalgamated into single blocks. Some

I

Towns by population over 500 000	LEEDS	Principal parks, forests	*FOREST*
200 000 to 500 000	CARDIFF	Minor parks, forests and woods	*Rufford Park*
100 000 to 200 000	BRIGHTON	Headlands, mud and sandbanks	FORELAND *Basta Ness* Breaksea Point
30 000 to 100 000	CAERPHILLY	Island (large and medium)	ISLAND ISLAND *Island*
10 000 to 30 000	PENARTH		
under 10 000	*PENISTONE*	Railway stations	WENVOE STA
Parish when differing from names of villages within it	*RHIGOS*	Remains of etc	(remains of)
Villages when bearing the same name as parish	Harston	Descriptive names	Colliery
		County names (detached portions)	HUNTS
Other villages	*Coity* *Blackwood*	County names (in border)	HAMPSHIRE
		Country names (in border)	(England)
Hamlets and small districts	Lockwood	Road directions (in border)	Neath 10 miles
Mansions	*Merthyr Castle*	Civil Airports	Lydd Airport
Farms	Court Fm		
Districts in towns	West Bank	Principal lakes, bays, channels, and tidal portions of rivers	*SOLENT* *LAKE*
Hills, valleys, fens, levels, moors, commons, reclaimed marshes, plains and districts in open areas	VALLEY FEN VALE Rhymney Valley	Other rivers, lakes, marsh, bays and all names and descriptions applicable to water	*RIVER* *R Taff* Ebbw Fach R Waterfall

minor roads in towns may also have been eliminated, if, for example, their inclusion would have resulted in an over-reduction of the acceptable space between blocks of buildings. Isolated houses – shown in solid black – had a different specification: even where they occupied 0.75 mm square or less on the map (and at the same time were separated from the nearest building by 0.75 mm or over) they were drawn to scale down to a minimum side on the map of 0.5 mm.[1]

Apart from the public buildings given standard symbols (Plate 26), other public buildings within the built-up area are shown in solid black[2] (as opposed to a grey stipple) and they are always named either fully or with a standard abbreviation. They were defined as including cathedrals (unless too small when they are given the appropriate church symbol), government and municipal offices, hospitals, law courts, museums, art galleries, observatories, royal palaces, schools, colleges and universities, town halls, and civic centres.

In selecting names preference is given to administrative areas and to the names of public buildings, although, with the latter, where space was limited, one abbreviation may have served to describe a related range of features (TH; Town Hall, for example, applying equally for Guildhall, Shire Hall, and Civic Centre). Other features are not named at all at 1 : 63 360 scale. They include rectories and vicarages in England and Wales (unless of particular interest as an antiquity), manses in Scotland, sports, cricket, and football grounds and electricity sub-stations.

1 For some comments on earlier specifications see Henry Rees, 'The Representation of Housing Patterns on the Fifth and Sixth Editions of the Ordnance Survey One-inch Map', *Geography*, **31** (1946), 110–16.

2 The main block only and not necessarily the whole complex is shown in this way.

Figure 26
Styles of type on the 1:63 360
Seventh Series map

Communications

ROADS

Because of the relatively large area it covers, the 1:63 360 sheet was regarded as especially suitable for emphasizing the communications network. Its specification reflects this emphasis, through specially designed symbols for roads and railways (Plate 26) and in the prominence they are allowed in the map detail as a whole. All roads are drawn at *conventional* widths, regardless of their width on the ground. At the same time, despite the need to generalize and exaggerate, every effort is made to preserve correct alignment and to depict features such as major bends and roundabouts as faithfully as possible.

During the life of the Seventh Series maps there have been several changes in the representation of roads. On the earlier printings three road fillings – red, brown, and yellow – were used to distinguish (the then) Ministry of Transport Class 1 and 2 roads, respectively, and other tarred roads.[1] On sheets published after *c*. 1960, however, a more sophisticated road classification was adopted. Following changes in Ministry of Transport practice, it distinguished between motorways, Ministry of Transport trunk roads, Ministry of Transport Class 1 roads, Ministry of Transport Class 2 roads, roads with 14 ft of metalling and over (where not included in the higher categories), tarred roads with under 14 ft of metalling, untarred roads with under 14 ft of metalling and, finally, unclassified roads including private roads, roads to farms, carriage drives, cart tracks, and other minor roads in towns and built-up areas. In Scotland a special category of 'Narrow Class 1 roads with passing places' was distinguished. Further changes in road nomenclature on Ordnance Survey maps resulted from the Local Government Act, 1966, which again revised the officially accepted terms. With implementation after 1 April 1967, Ministry of Transport motorways, trunk, Class 1 and Class 2 roads were referred to as motorways, trunk, principal, and classified roads and the Ordnance Survey has adopted as equivalent terms motorway, trunk, main, and secondary roads. The change was effective on Seventh Series maps published since April 1968.

Road numbers positioned on the map and in the border where roads leave the sheet are used to identify classified roads. Motorways and trunk roads[2] are further distinguished by the letters (M) and (T) placed after the road number, for example A465(T). Road destinations with distances in miles are also printed in the border. On motorways, trunk, and main roads, they are omitted where converging roads are sufficiently close to leave no doubt that they lead to the same town, but otherwise they record the nearest town of urban status or above; on secondary roads, directions are normally given to the nearest town or village of importance but, when a road does not lead to such a place – serving for example as a connecting link between main roads – destinations may be omitted.

Particular care is taken in the delineation of motorways. Junctions and the relationship of subsidiary roads to the motorway are shown with the greatest degree of factual accuracy compatible with the scale. Motorway service areas are named as such, elevated sections are shown by diamond symbols at intervals of 7 mm. Cuttings and embankments of 3 m and over in depth or height (as on all roads) are shown by slope symbols. Motorways under construction in common with other major roads are shown by double pecked lines. Half-mile or more stretches of dual carriageways on trunk, main, and secondary roads, are differentiated by thicker edging lines, and roundabouts,

1 *A Description of Ordnance Survey Small Scale Maps* . . . 1957, 4.

2 When a trunk road passes through a county borough it generally reverts to its 'A' number, in which case it is maintained by the local authority. There are, however, exceptions to this where the road is maintained by the Department of the Environment.

unless so large as to be shown true to scale, are depicted conventionally. Gradients of 1 in 7 or steeper are shown by arrows on all classified roads; 1 in 5 and steeper are double arrowed.

PUBLIC RIGHTS OF WAY

The 1:63 360 Seventh Series map is one of the three Ordnance Survey series – together with the 1:25 000 Second Series and 1:50 000 – on which such public rights of way information (see p. 101) is published. The symbols currently in use – whether for roads used as public paths, bridleways, or footpaths – are printed in red, with the qualification in the sheet footnotes that the depiction is 'subject to the limitations imposed by the scale of the mapping'.[1] The information is derived from the definitive rights of way maps prepared by local authorities as directed by the National Parks and Access to the Countryside Act, 1949, and as approved by the Department of the Environment or the Welsh Office. The first 1:63 360 sheet to show rights of way appeared in 1960 and, by 1972, the majority of the sheets in England and Wales had been published with such details incorporated.[2] This is not to say, however, that a national cartographic record of public rights of way is now in existence. Many of the definitive maps still have to be completed and the Ordnance Survey has adopted the criterion that public rights of way information would be incorporated on the revision of any 1:63 360 sheet when as little as 5 per cent of its area was covered by definitive maps.

'Long-distance paths' are also shown and are annotated in black as, for example, 'Cleveland Way'; where the path is undefined it may, for lengths greater than 1.5 km, be described as 'Cleveland Way undefined'. Paths which have no legal status as rights of way may also be shown by a black pecked line, but, this is replaced by the rights of way symbol when the legal status of a right of way is notified.

RAILWAYS AND CANALS

For standard gauge multiple and single track railways, the same symbols are employed as on the 1:25 000 First Series. A different symbol is, however, used for lines of below standard gauge and a further symbol represents mineral lines, tramways, and sidings[3] (Plate 26). Electric lines and privately owned railways are depicted by normal symbols but the latter are named, for example, 'Bluebell Railway'. Passenger stations are shown to scale where they are large enough and otherwise by symbols; in towns with more than one station the principal station is distinguished by the rectangular symbol. Goods stations are not identified except in the case of the main goods stations in London. Cuttings and embankments of 2 m or over in depth or height are depicted. Destinations (i.e. next major town) of multiple track railways are shown in the border, if there is room, or it is not apparent from road destinations.

In the representation of former railways a distinction is made between dismantled and disused lines. The alignment of dismantled railways is shown by a pecked line and cuttings and embankments are retained: the feature is named 'Tk of old rly'. When, however, a railway line is disused, but the rails have not been removed the appropriate symbol for an active railway remains in use but is qualified by the description 'disused'. There are also rules for classifying stations as either open or closed. A station is shown as open, that is by a symbol with a red filling, when it is open in any way to passenger traffic,

1 Where public rights of way impinge on military areas the description 'danger area' is added in appropriate cases.

2 Ordnance Survey, *Annual Report 1972–73* (1973). Plate 4, is an index map with coverage of 1:63 360 sheets incorporating public rights of way information. On 31 March 1973 the information still had to be added to sheets 74, 87, 99 and 105.

3 The term sidings includes all short feeding lines as to mines, quarries, and factories.

even if some of its former services or lines have been discontinued. It is shown as closed, that is by a symbol without a red filling, when passenger services have ceased. No symbol is employed when a station is closed for all traffic and all staff and facilities have been withdrawn; in this case the station is treated as a normal building if it is still standing.

Tramways are shown by the symbol for mineral lines, but across open country they are included only where the length to be depicted on the map is long enough to associate the name 'Tramway' printed at its normal point size. Tramways in roads are not indicated, but they may be shown in large quarries.

Ship canals are drawn to scale. The banks of the tidal stretches of such canals, together with their inland docks, are depicted in black, although the rest of the canal and any associated names appear in blue. All other canals are drawn to a standard width and the detail (apart from locks shown in black) is printed in blue; towing paths are shown by black pecked lines alongside the canal. Former canals from which the water has drained are shown by means of slope symbols (printed in black) and are named 'Old Canal'. All canal bridges, in common with bridges on roads and railways, are depicted on the 1:63 360 series. Other bridges – for example those across drainage ditches – may not be shown by the bridge symbol unless they have a span of 8 m or over.

Vegetation

At the 1:63 360 scale some small areas of vegetation have to be excluded altogether and fewer categories of vegetation can be differentiated. Within the areas covered by these categories further reductions of vegetation types may be necessary. The problem of deciding which areas to omit at this scale was largely resolved by the application of minimum thresholds. These vary with the vegetation type. With woods a pruning of small areas takes place on the 1:40 000 drawings and they have to cover 3 sq mm or over at this scale to qualify for the final map; where patches of woodland exceed this but have a minimum side of less than 1 mm, then this side is exaggerated to a conventional width of 1 mm. With orchards, bracken, heath, and rough grassland, the threshold was calculated on the ground area of the vegetation: this has to be at least 20 acres but exceptions are made to embrace smaller areas of historical and scientific interest or which form important landmarks. With parkland the area has to be 50 acres or more to qualify for the use of the special parkland symbol, although areas between 20 to 50 acres are treated as ordinary woodland in suitable cases.

The process of simplification also included a sharp reduction in the number of vegetation types, and therefore separate symbols, which were in use. All 'allied' vegetation types were grouped, with a single symbol made to serve for bracken, heath, and rough grassland;[1] another single symbol is used for marsh, reeds, osiers, and saltings; and a third for woods, although here more distinctions are made in practice (as between coniferous and non-coniferous for example) than might be inferred from the symbol in the panel of conventional signs (Plate 26).

Further simplification of content was made within these areas. This is especially so with woodland: tree symbols are omitted from areas on the map too small to accommodate one complete tree symbol within enclosures (but these

[1] After 1963, in line with the larger scales, the vegetation categories were amended on fully revised sheets, and once-familiar categories such as rough pasture, furze, and moor disappeared from the 1:63 360 map.

retained a green tint); minor names of individual woods are shown only very selectively; and firebreaks appear only when they are 20 m wide or over, form a natural division between coniferous and non-coniferous woodland, or alternatively, serve as tracks, occupation roads, or shooting rides. The perimeter of vegetation is indicated in various ways. Woodland enclosed by fences or walls, etc., is delineated by a continuous line or if unenclosed by a pecked line. The limits of bracken, heath, and rough grassland are shown by dotted lines, and the vegetation symbol alone defines the extent of marsh, osiers, and saltings.

Water features

Water features and water names are printed in blue. For rivers and streams a further step in simplification was that 8 m (instead of 5 m as on the 1:25 000 First Series) became the width at which a scale depiction changed to representation in conventional terms only. At 8 m and over rivers and streams were shown by double lines as far as possible true to scale: under that width they are shown in 'atlas' style by single tapering lines. In generalizing a dense network of drains and dykes, it was the practice, as well as retaining the wider channels, to include at 1:63 360 scale such features as are named on larger scale maps. Single drains are omitted where they form the edge of a road.

Revision

A systematic revision for the Seventh Series was commenced in 1958. Previous editions of the 1:63 360 map had suffered from lack of revision partly owing to the fact that the necessary information was largely obtained from the large scale surveys, so that when this basic revision fell behind as it did after 1914, work on the up-dating of all derived maps was correspondingly delayed. To overcome this, small scale maps were maintained by 'small scales' field revision designed to supplement the flow of information from the revision of the large scales (see p. 12); and later to provide a source of information in areas not yet covered by National Grid large scale maps subject to continuous revision.

In so far as the 189 sheets in the Seventh Series covered markedly different types of district, ranging from industrial and urban regions to the Highlands of Scotland, varying cycles of periodic revision were applied to them but with the overall aim that each sheet was fully revised at least once every twenty-five years. Sheets were designated for revision purposes as heavy, medium, or light depending on the amount of urbanization and rate of change that was likely. The pattern for the series as a whole was:

19 heavy sheets	Full revision once every 7–8 years
113 medium sheets	Full revision once every 15 years
57 light sheets	Full revision once every 25 years.

Before the introduction of the 1:50 000 series approximately twelve sheets were revised in any one year of which the majority were in the first two categories.

For this cyclic programme, which was varied to meet special circumstances, field revision was carried out at a scale of 1:10 560. The procedure was to revise all ground detail appropriate to the 1:63 360 specification, either by new survey, or by checking on the ground detail taken from air photographs, or by detail transferred from larger scale maps. The information was then positioned to a degree of accuracy comparable with the 1:10560 series. Names and road classifications were also verified, but a full check of contours was not made although obvious errors were corrected.

Sheets were also reprinted with revision of major features between full revisions. For this purpose a special survey, independent of the cyclic revision, is carried out to record new motorways, changes to major roads and railways, extensive urban development or afforestation and the building of reservoirs – changes which, if unrecorded, would seriously impair the usefulness of the map. Public rights of way information was also inserted, where available. Reprints were made every two to five years, depending on the demand for a sheet. The sheet footnotes were amended to record the alterations that had been made (Appendix B).

SPECIAL EDITIONS OF THE 1:63 360 MAPS
Outline edition

Ever since the introduction of colour to the 1:63 360 maps at the end of the last century, the Ordnance Survey has published 'outline' editions to cater for specialist users who require a base suitable for over-drawing. As far as the Seventh Series is concerned, outline edition maps are printed on heavier paper in black only.[1] They contain all the information appearing in black on the coloured series but with the addition of water and water names. Thus contours, road fillings, woods, public rights of way, and National Trust information are missing. Because of the omission of public rights of way the footnotes are amended. The outline edition is published as flat sheets only and the words OUTLINE EDITION are printed in the north margin of the sheet.

Administrative areas maps

A new 1:63 360 administrative map of Greater London was published in 1966 to replace the old London and Middlesex Administrative Areas Diagram (see p. 143). This map, the current edition of which was published in 1973, shows the administrative and parliamentary constituency boundaries in the area of the Greater London Council. A map on the same base but showing petty sessional divisions and local government areas within the Metropolitan Police District was published in 1967; this map was also revised in 1973. A 1:63 360 administrative areas map of Glasgow and District, showing administrative and parliamentary constituency boundaries was also published in 1966.

Tourist maps

'Tourist' maps were first developed from the sheets of the 'Popular Edition' 1:63 360 in the inter-war period; one of the Snowdon area in 1920 was the first sheet to be published. Currently there are nine Tourist maps based on the reproduction material of the Seventh Series maps.[2] They cover the areas in Figure 27 and are on sheet lines specially drawn to cover the area of tourist interest.[3]

1 Before 1961, when the Seventh Series maps were printed in ten colours, the outline edition consisted of a black printing together with the housefillings shown in grey.

2 It may be noted that the 1:126720 map of Snowdonia National Park and the 1:250 000 map of Wales and the Marches (see p. 135) were also derived from the Seventh Series 1:63 360 detail.

3 Cambridge was withdrawn in 1971 and Greater London in 1973. Sheet 87 in the 1:63 360 series, relating to the Isle of Man, is not officially designated as a Tourist sheet, but the 1970 edition contained several innovations which make it comparable to mainland tourist sheets. They included the addition of 'dark-side shading' to hills to show the mountainous nature of the countryside, as well as an indication of camping sites, parking sites, viewpoints, and the location of tourist information offices. A list of places of special interest such as archaeological and ecclesiastical sites, beauty spots, and museums was also included on the map.

The series is of more than passing interest in showing the development of Ordnance Survey attitudes and techniques since the 1950s. The maps have provided an opportunity to experiment with the representation of those features which are of particular interest to users such as walkers, climbers, skiers, and anglers and in some cases the innovations pioneered in Tourist maps have been adopted into regular map series. In a detailed study of 1:63 360 Tourist maps published since 1959,[1] it was shown how newly published sheets often embodied innovations in relief depiction or, after consultation with tourist agencies, local organizations and other interested bodies, in the conventions for features of tourist interest. The covers and reference panels of the sheets have been designed not only to carry extra tourist information, such as lists of selected places of interest, but also to enhance their marketability, so that folded sheets have a laminated cover with an artist's impression of a well-known local scene.[2] From the mid 1960s onwards new symbols were added for tourist features. On the maps of the Cairngorms (1964), Cambridge (1965), and the New Forest (1966), for example, over twenty items of tourist interest – in addition to those covered by standard symbols – were shown by symbols. They included those for angling and fishing, for boating and canoeing, for pony treking and licensed riding stables, and for chair lifts and rope tows associated with ski slopes. Where there was no symbol for a tourist feature, explanatory notes in red were printed on the maps, as with ski school, mountain rescue post, and rock climbing (Cairngorms sheet) or camping office and keeper's cottage (New Forest sheet). In areas where tourist sheets covered National Parks, Forest Parks, or Nature Reserves special conventions were used to depict the limits of these areas.

The 1:63 360 Tourist series is also notable for its experimental depiction of relief. Contours, hypsometric tints, hill shading, and graded tints have been used on various sheets, separately and in combination, to depict surface terrain. Two main styles of hill shading, for example, both drawn from an oblique light, have been published. First, in a style developed on the Peak District map (and also used on the North York Moors sheet) a blue shadow was printed in half-tone over the layer tinted map – but with the layer tints chosen so as to reduce any 'step' effect. Second, in the Lake District (Plate 27) and Loch Lomond sheets, a more naturalistic delineation was aimed at: there was no layer system, but two printings in purple-grey tones (for the shadow side of the hills) and one printing in yellow (for the illuminated side) were added.[3] There have been other combinations and the Tourist maps, taken as a whole, illustrate a fair cross-section of Ordnance Survey innovation in small scale cartography during the post-Davidson period. In doing so they have lived up to one of Davidson's exhortations that '. . . new features must be introduced experimentally from time to time which may or may not be generally accepted. Only by a constant series of changes can the maps keep pace with modern needs.'[4]

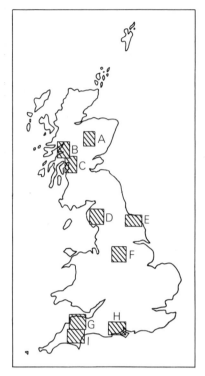

Figure 27
Coverage of Tourist sheets at the 1:63 360 scale 1973

A   Cairngorms
B   Ben Nevis and Glen Coe
C   Loch Lomond and the Trossachs
D   Lake District
E   North York Moors
F   Peak District
G   Exmoor
H   New Forest
I   Dartmoor

1   G. McGrath, 'United Kingdom Ordnance Survey Tourist Maps at One Inch Scale: A Review . . .', *The Cartographer*, **4** (1967), 136–56.

2   The back cover shows an outline diagram of the area covered by the sheet.

3   L. J. Harris, 'Hill-shading for Relief Depiction in Topographical Maps with Some Recent Applications', *The Scottish Geographical Magazine*, **76** (1960), 14–20.

4   *Final Report* (1938), 16; quoted by McGrath, 146.

The 1 : 50 000 series

The advantages of a 1 : 50 000 series were unsuccessfully canvassed on several occasions in the nineteenth century.[1] They were again aired by the Davidson Committee but with the conclusion that metricated maps were appropriate only to a country operating a full metric system: 'a statement such as one inch to a mile conveys a clear meaning to everyone [they argued] whereas a fraction such as 1 : 50 000 does not'.[2] Notwithstanding this decision the Ordnance Survey continued to gain experience in working with metric units and, by the early 1960s, when the metrication question was coming into the public eye, the metre had been used by the Ordnance Survey for a number of years for survey and mapping, for publishing co-ordinate values of the mapping control, for the National Grid, and in effect, therefore, for defining the sheet lines of all series. The problem of converting other aspects of the maps to a metric system could accordingly be viewed optimistically.

Although the Hodgson Committee (1951) was unanimously in favour of a consistent adoption of the metric system,[3] not until 1965 did the Government announce a programme of metrication and fix a general target for its completion at the end of 1975.[4] The Ordnance Survey had meanwhile set up a working party to consider the metrication of the large scale map series and, in 1964, the decision was taken that in future they would be published with metric units of measurements, and that the 1 : 10 560 (six-inch) would be converted to the 'rational' scale of 1 : 10 000 to make it more suitable for use with metric units. The first metric sheets at 1 : 1250 and 1 : 2500 scales were published in October 1969.

The next stage in the programme of metrication was to consider the best replacement for the Seventh Series 1 : 63 360 maps. A number of alternatives were examined including the possibility of maps at 1 : 100 000, 1 : 75 000, and 1 : 62 500 scales but, for a variety of reasons, both technical and on grounds of economy, they all had disadvantages.[5] The adoption of a 1 : 50 000 scale seemed to offer the best solution. Its advantages included the facts that it was widely used by foreign mapmakers; that the scale could be expressed in a simple relationship of centimetres to kilometres; that it had already been recommended by the International Standards Organization, and, not least, that it lent itself to the production of an interim edition by 1976. In reaching a final decision on such an important question it was clearly necessary to consult the potential users of any new series as fully as possible and in 1970 a market research project was commissioned to appraise existing small scale maps to see how they should be modified to meet future requirements. It reported that the vast majority of users considered that a map at 1 : 50 000 scale would be the most suitable successor for the 1 : 63 360 series: it would be welcomed by motorists and walkers and it would also be universally accepted for educational purposes[6] and for military use. Thus for the first time since the 1940s, the Ordnance Survey was given the opportunity to design a completely new map.

To have produced a completely redrawn map series at 1 : 50 000 scale within a short space of time would not have been possible with the manpower resources available. The alternative of publishing a 1 : 50 000 series over a much longer period as cyclic revision on the 1 : 63 360 sheets fell due was not practicable because the changes both in the scale and in the sheet line coverage would have created insoluble problems for map users. The method adopted was a compromise in which full coverage of the country was to be achieved

1 See, for example, *Correspondence Respecting the Scale* . . . 1854 . . ., 284; *Report of the Departmental Committee* . . ., 1893.

2 *Final Report* (1938), 10.

3 *Report of the Committee on Weights and Measures Legislation.* Cmd. 8219. (HMSO, 1951).

4 Department of Trade and Industry, *Metrication*, White Paper, Cmd. 4880 (HMSO, 1972), for background to these events.

5 For example, neither the 1 : 75 000 nor the 1 : 100 000 would allow the standard of the 1 : 63 360 to be maintained and the step between the 1 : 100 000 and the 1 : 25 000 was in any case too large; the 1 : 62 500, although providing an apparently easy solution, did not conform to the International Standards Organization scale.

6 In 1971 the Ordnance Survey had made available for schools a number of special metric editions of 1 : 63 360 sheets. The series consisted of eight sheets – numbers 47, 50, 91, 107, 135, 154, 170, and 180 – enlarged directly to 1 : 50 000, but with contours and spot heights relabelled to the nearest metre. The sheets were selected to cover a wide range of physical features in Great Britain and were printed in the same colours and format as the Seventh Series 1 : 63 360 maps. Examination map extracts were also made available in the same style. See [Ordnance Survey] 'Metric Maps for Schools' leaflet (Southampton, n.d.).

in two blocks each of about 100 sheets. Thus a First Series, as it came to be called, was planned for completion in two stages by 1976, based on a photographic enlargement of existing 1:63 360 material recompiled on new sheet lines; there was to be no major alteration in the amount of detail shown from that on the Seventh Series 1:63 360. Thereafter a Second Series was to be introduced as a completely redesigned and redrawn map taking up to twenty years to cover the whole country. The southern block of the series up to an east–west line across Lancashire and Yorkshire (northing line 460 000), was to be published in 1974 and the block of sheets to the north in 1976. The Seventh Series 1:63 360 maps were to remain in print and to be fully available throughout the country until their 1:50 000 replacements were published.

FIRST SERIES

Format, referencing and marginalia

First Series 1:50 000 maps are published in fully coloured editions either as flat sheets or as folded versions supplied with laminated covers. The outside cover is designed, as was the one-inch series, to carry the Ordnance Survey house style. On the front is a diagrammatic representation of the area covered by each sheet and on the reverse side an index to the series. The cover is, however, immediately distinguishable from the one-inch by its new lavender colour replacing the traditional one-inch red. The inner cover is used to give an explanation of the changeover from the 1:63 360 to the 1:50 000 series.

In designing the new sheet lines for the 1:50 000 series several factors were taken into consideration. These included the limitations imposed by existing printing and ancillary equipment, the convenience of users handling the map, the need to depict major towns and tourist areas on one sheet (or at least on as few sheets as possible), the elimination of unused sea space, and the minimizing of overlaps so as to keep the total number of sheets in the series as small as possible. By balancing such considerations, a sheet representing an area of 40×40 km, giving a size of 800×800 mm within the neat lines was selected. By comparison with the 1:63 360 (189 sheets at 45×40 km) there are 204 sheets in the redesigned 1:50 000 series. Thus despite an increase of about 25 per cent in the scale there are only fifteen additional sheets in the series and the new layout has made possible a saving of about 4 per cent on overlaps and unused sea areas. The overlaps with adjacent sheets are indicated by a diagram in the east margin of each sheet. Insets designed with their own border are still incorporated on a few coastal sheets, and the border is sometimes broken to reduce the number of sheets.

National Grid lines in blue are inserted at intervals representing 1 km, with the 10 and 100 km intervals emphasized in a thicker gauge line. Full grid values are given at the sheet corners, and the intervening values in kilometres by the last two figures of the kilometre values 00 to 99 inclusive. Instructions on how to give a grid reference correct to 100 m are printed in the east margin of the sheet. National Grid lines on the 1:50 000 also serve to index the larger scale Ordnance Survey map series: as each kilometre square on the map covers the same area as one National Grid 1:2500 single format sheet, and each 10 km square has the same relationship to the area of a 1:25 000 First Series sheet, in both cases the 1:50 000 supplies a simple index to these series, and, equally, to the 1:1250 and 1:10 560/1:10 000 series.

Compared with the Seventh Series 1:63 360, the 1:50 000 sheets have a some-what simplified graticule and border (Plate 23). Information on latitude and longitude is, however, printed in the outer border of the sheet: full degrees are printed in heavy type wherever they occur; degrees and minutes are inserted near each corner, for example Lat. 53° 45′ N; and other values are published in minutes only at every 5 minute interval. The 5 minute intervals are marked by short blue lines intersecting the border at right angles; 1 minute divisions are also shown, without values, by (shorter) blue lines in the outer border. Over the map as a whole the intersections of 5 minute intervals of latitude and longitude are, as on the Seventh Series 1:63 360, marked by small crosses.

A new design feature is that marginal information is printed in an extended east margin. The change has the effect of producing a sheet in landscape as distinct from the portrait style of the one-inch, which is more convenient for most users of folded maps, and of reducing the number of creases that pass through the legend when the map is folded allowing information to be tabulated in convenient block headings. The blocks are arranged with all map symbols appearing in the upper part of the legend in the order (from top to bottom) roads and paths, public rights of way, railways, water features, general features, relief, boundaries, abbreviations, and antiquities (Plate 24).[1] A scale is printed beneath the panel for symbols, graduated in kilometres (above) and miles (beneath); and, below that, in turn, a diagram showing the incidence of adjacent sheets, data on true, grid and magnetic north, and notes on compilation and revision. An index map to the 1:50 000 series as a whole (Figure 28) appears at the bottom of the map margin.

Landscape at 1:50 000

1:50 000 First Series sheets are basically an enlargement (to about 1¼ inches to 1 mile)[2] of the material of the Seventh Series 1:63 360 sheets. As a result, apart from the changes in scale, colour, and sheet lines the content specification of the 1:63 360 map applies to this series. The description which follows should therefore be read in conjunction with appropriate sections in Chapter 7: the same criteria for generalizing features from the parent scales are applicable, as are the conventions of exaggerating other features such as roads to ensure a bold delineation. A simple enlargement would tend to give a coarse appearance to the line work. This has been overcome by using a photographic technique which cuts back the width of all lines until the 0.005 in line, the most commonly used for the 1:63 360 series, is not actually thickened by the enlargement process.

Colours

The most striking way in which the 1:50 000 differs from its predecessors is in the range of colour conventions. Six colours are still employed but they have been used differently, not only to keep in step with changing public taste and to meet past criticisms of colour combinations on the Seventh Series, but also to take account of recent research on map users' perception. Particular care was also taken to ensure that the colours finalized for the First Series 1:50 000 could be used without modification for the Second Series.[3] A systematic study of maps published in other countries at similar scales was undertaken to gather ideas on their use of various colour combinations and

1 On the northern block of sheets the format of the legend will be changed to bring it into line with the design for the Second Series.

2 Change of scale from 1:63 360 to 1:50 000 also gives about 60 per cent more *space* on the map; for example, 1 sq km at 1:63 360 = 2.5121 sq cm; 1 sq km at 1:50 000 = 4.000 sq cm.

3 Of the southern block, 103 sheets published in 1974, three – 115 Caernarvon and Bangor, 176 West London, and 177 East London – appeared in the Second Series format from the outset.

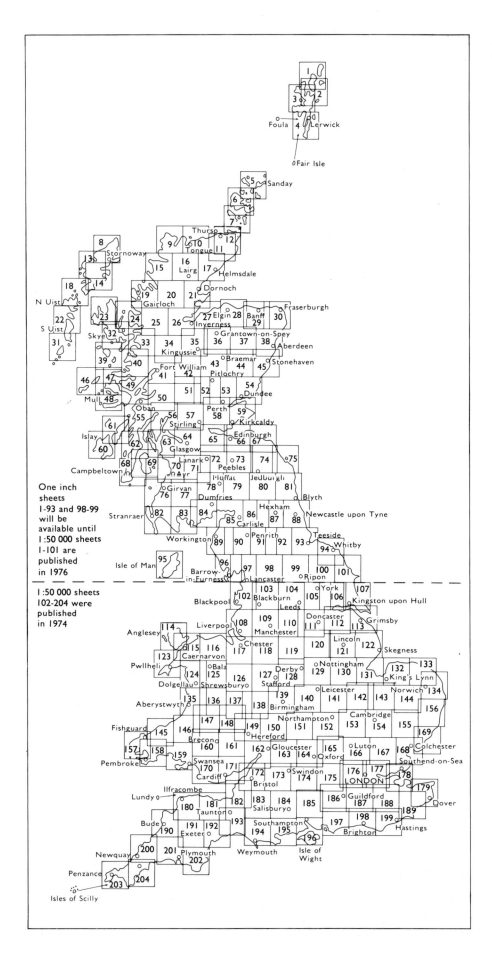

Figure 28
Index to the 1:50 000 series

experimental printings were run with successive prototype maps. These trial sheets were used in market research. The final selection of colours reflected a general move away from black, grey, and brown, and a greater use of low intensity colours in the blue to yellow range which have the advantage of causing minimum interference with other detail. They combine as follows:

Black   Black names, border, county and civil parish or equivalent boundaries, outline

Red   Bus and railway stations, danger areas, National Trust information (always open), trunk and main roads, rights of way, roads numbers, Youth Hostels

Orange   Contours,* secondary roads,* house fillings*

Yellow   National Parks, other metalled roads

Blue   Glasshouses, grid lines and values,* motorways,* trig stations, National Trust information (opening restricted), water, water names, water tints

Green   Orchards,* woods* (varying screens are applied to distinguish these features).

* denotes a change for this feature from the 1:63 360 colour scheme.

Symbols

A similar study was carried out as to the suitability of 1:63 360 symbols for the design of the 1:50 000 map. Symbols were grouped systematically according to their main categories such as communications and water features and the effectiveness of each symbol was then evaluated to decide whether it was still required or whether a new symbol would improve clarity and help to reduce the cost of production and revision. Because the First Series 1:50 000 map was enlarged from the 1:63 360 the changes which could be made, as is indicated in the account which follows of the portrayal of particular features, were limited. In the Second Series, however, which is completely redrawn, more changes are being introduced in both the range and design of conventional signs. Some of these innovations are described in the final part of the chapter.

Contours and altitudes

Spot heights and contours are renumbered on the First Series to the nearest metre[1] and, on both map and legend, they appear simply as numbers (and are not qualified by 'm' to denote metre). They are straight conversions and the actual contour interval of the 1:63 360 series – 50 ft – remains the same, as does the selection of spot heights which have been included. Conversion factors are given in the legend as:

1 metre   = 3.2808 feet
15.24 metres = 50 feet.

Contour intervals created thus have necessitated some changes in design. One problem is that some of the metric contour values especially 61, 91, 168, 686, 869, 899, 991, and 1006 can be misread when inverted and, to avoid confusion, these values are printed only on the south-facing (i.e. sw to se) slopes. They are omitted from other slopes and such omissions are compensated for by adding values above and below those which have been deleted. Another difficulty is that an interval of 15 or 16 m does not allow an easy identification of an unnumbered contour by counting from the nearest

1 Whole-foot values on the 1:63 360 are converted by multiplying them by 0.3048 and then rounding up or down to the nearest metre.

labelled one and, to overcome this, more values are inserted than were required on the 1:63 360 series.

A new feature of the design is that contours and contour values are printed in orange. Black has been retained for spot heights, but the typographical distinction on the 1:63 360 map between those spot heights which had been surveyed by levelling (printed in bold upright figures) and those which had not (shown in finer sloping figures) has been discontinued. Bathymetrical contours on inland lakes were also relabelled in metres, but fathom lines in coastal areas, shown on the 1:63 360, have been omitted.

Boundaries

Planning for the range of administrative boundaries on the 1:50 000 was complicated by changes which were due to take place under the Local Government Reorganization Act (1972). Its implementation on 1 April 1974 called for important revisions to be made to the boundary information on the 1:63 360 material as the statutory obligation to show county and parish boundaries on the 1:50 000 remained.

The position of the national borders, together with their symbol, is the same as on the Seventh Series 1:63 360 map, apart from the block of sheets affected by the decision in the 1972 Act that Wales should receive Monmouthshire as the new county of Gwent. County boundaries on the southern block of the 1:50 000 were, however, more radically revised to show those which became effective on 1 April 1974. To reduce redrawing the symbol is that employed on the 1:63 360 map, the county boundary being taken as the limit of both civil parish and non-parish areas (Plates 24 and 26). Civil parish boundaries are also those of the 1:63 360 map but again variously modified to agree with the Act: in Wales all civil parishes, urban and rural, became 'Communities'; in England the civil parish was retained in rural areas but the Act made all urban civil parishes obsolete; at the same time it left the parish boundary structure incomplete and some anomalies were not resolved in time for publication on the 1974 sheets.[1] The same was true of the boundaries of the new districts created by the Act which were not finalized in time to appear on the southern block of 1:50 000 sheets. Finally, the boundaries of Greater London and of the Isles of Scilly were not affected by the Act and the depiction of their boundaries remains the same as on the 1:63 360 map.

Buildings

The main change in the depiction of buildings on the First Series 1:50 000 – which considerably enhances the legibility of other detail in built-up areas – is that a screened orange colour is used instead of the screened black infilling of the 1:63 360 map. Public buildings are still distinguished in solid black and are named; isolated buildings are also shown in solid black.

Communications

ROADS

The emphasis given to the depiction of the road network on the 1:63 360 is maintained on the 1:50 000 with additional justification derived from the market research undertaken by the Ordnance Survey.[2] This revealed that

1 On the Second Series maps parish boundaries are shown only on the outline edition of the 1:50 000.

2 Betty Drewitt, 'The Changing Profile of the Map User in Great Britain', *The Cartographic Journal*, **10** (1973), 42–8.

motorists were likely to be the largest single group of users for the new series and that continuing attention ought therefore to be paid to their needs.

A conspicuous blue colour was adopted for the motorway symbol; its prominence was justified both on the grounds that motorways form major landmarks in many parts of the country, and also because of their importance in the road system as a whole. Blue was selected to match the blue signs on the motorway, a convention which had been used successfully on some European maps, and also by the Ordnance Survey on its own Route Planning Map (see p. 137) (Plate 34). Separate symbols were introduced to show projected motorways with statutory approval, motorways under construction, elevated stretches of motorway, service areas, and motorway junctions, together with their reference numbers. The two categories of incomplete motorways are depicted by a pecked blue line for a projected motorway (but without the deletion of the under-lying detail), to which the road casing is added when construction begins. When the motorway is opened a continuous infill can be inserted without complete redrawing, which reduces the cost of revision. Motorway numbers, printed in blue, follow the 1:63 360 practice and are placed to one side of the road. A darker shade of red than on the 1:63 360 is used to depict trunk and main roads, but secondary roads, shown in brown on the 1:63 360 map, are printed in orange on the 1:50 000. The distances to road destinations are published in the sheet margin in kilometres and miles.

PUBLIC RIGHTS OF WAY

Public rights of way information is shown within the same legal framework and to the same classification as on the 1:63 360 series. After experiments with the use of a green colour, which had several advantages from a design point of view, red symbols similar to those used for rights of way on the 1:63 360 (albeit in a darker shade) were adopted.

Vegetation

The principal change on the First Series 1:50 000 was a simplification of the manner in which woodland and orchard are shown. Black tree symbols, which had tended to obscure other detail in some areas, were omitted. Instead of these symbols a green tint, varied by the intensity of screen used in printing the two categories, was introduced. The omission of tree symbols has meant that the distinction on the 1:63 360 map between deciduous and coniferous wood is no longer recorded on the 1:50 000.

Revision

Revision methods for the 1:50 000 Series have developed from those once current for the 1:63 360 map which were based on special field surveys at a 1:10 560 scale and supplemented by continuous revision material from the larger scale maps. Each 1:63 360 sheet was fully revised at least once in every twenty-five years and, according to need, in many parts of the country, on shorter periodic cycles. In designing a revision system for the 1:50 000 series additional considerations included the increasing difficulty of keeping abreast of new road developments on some sheets, and also the rising costs of surveying and cartographic work. Such factors contributed to several changes in practice.

The base map used in the field revision of the 1:50 000 sheets is at 1:25 000 scale (enlarged from 1:63 360 outline edition material), rather than at 1:10 560 as formerly employed for 1:63 360 maps. A cyclic system of full revision has been retained, but with some adjustment to suit the organization of work in the field and drawing office. The 1:50 000 cycles are as below:

22 heavy sheets	Full revision once every 8 years
121 medium sheets	Full revision once every 16 years
61 light sheets	Full revision once every 24 years

In addition two categories of 'special' and 'intermediate' revision were introduced to supplement the process of full cyclic revision, of which the former is an entirely new category. It is without set frequency and, depending solely on an assessment of the changes that are likely to occur, it can be undertaken as soon as one year after the publication of the previous edition. Emphasis is placed on changes to motorways and trunk roads, on correcting errors, and on the insertion of detail which does not require field effort. 'Intermediate' revision, on the other hand, is a new name for the 'special' revision previously undertaken for the 1:63 360 sheets. It was carried out as a matter of routine before any sheet was reprinted, enabling major changes to communications and urban development to be included on any new issue of a sheet. In a manner analogous to full revision, intermediate revision had been organized on a cyclic basis, with heavy sheets being up-dated alternatively by full and intermediate revision once every four years, medium sheets once every eight years, and light sheets once every twelve years. The essentials of this approach have been retained for the 1:50 000, but with greater flexibility, and with implementation tied more closely to the new information likely to be available for a particular sheet. A more frequent up-dating of the road network is possible as a result of these policies, but, at the same time, expensive minor revisions are avoided, especially on 'heavy' sheets, where they make relatively little contribution to the overall usefulness of the sheet.

SECOND SERIES

The Second Series 1:50 000 has allowed the Ordnance Survey a chance to make further design changes more in tune with technical developments and trends in user requirements. Innovation in the First Series was restricted by the fact that it was basically an enlargement of 1:63 360 material, but the Second Series is completely rescribed allowing more freedom to experiment. At the same time, the planning of the First and Second Series has (of necessity) been two stages in the same process. As much from a marketing as from a technical point of view it was desirable that the Second Series should have a recognizable relationship with the First Series and design experiments were started concurrently with the production of the First Series sheets. In practice this has meant that the sheet lines and colour combinations which have already been introduced were designed to serve both series.

The main changes introduced for the Second Series fall under two headings; those relating to the design of the map and those affecting its content. So far as design is concerned firstly, a more modern type face, Univers, replaces[1] Gill Sans, first adopted by the Ordnance Survey in the 1920s. Univers, patented in 1957, had already been adopted for the Route Planning Map,

1 With the exception of the sheet name.

with the advantage that it is more robust, better able to withstand modern printing processes, and also that the squarer nature of its rounded letters gives a more integrated appearance to the type face. Secondly, the remaining hand-drawn symbols, expensive to scribe, which still characterized the 1:63 360 map, are being phased out. These comprised symbols for dunes, foreshore, and for park or ornamental ground: dunes will be annotated rather than drawn and the other symbols will be replaced by dot screens on the black plate. Other minor design changes include public buildings where a heavy black outline infilled with a screened orange colour replaces solid black; and the 'v' symbols on electricity transmission lines which instead of alternating from side to side are shown on one side only.

Yet other symbols are either to be further emphasized or simplified. Communications are particularly affected. More prominent symbols for motorway features have already been introduced on the First Series, and on the Second Series dual carriageways are shown by more easily discernible treble lines. There is a common symbol for all railways except sidings; at level crossings there is no tapering of the road casing; and old canals, previously indicated by slope symbols where the ground justified it, are indicated by blue pecked lines.

A number of new symbols are also introduced. They include those for the administrative districts created by the Local Government Reorganization Act 1972, which become part of the standard boundary information at the same time as civil parish boundaries (except on the outline edition) are omitted. A range of symbols is also added to cater for out-of-door and leisure activities. The demand for such features (some of which are already included on Tourist and Outdoor Leisure maps) to be shown on the main series Ordnance Survey maps was revealed by market research. The new symbols include separate conventions for golf courses, heliports, and telephones (black for public telephones and blue for those belonging to the AA and RAC); and also for beauty spots and viewpoints, together with other places of tourist interest such as historic houses, ancient monuments, camp, caravan, picnic and parking sites, and information centres. To provide for the increased use of the 1:50 000 series by foreign visitors (and to promote sales in Europe) a multilingual panel in the legend will give an explanation of the main symbols in French and German.

The 1:50 000 Second Series thus embodies new emphases as well as some new features of design. The content of the map and the presentation of its data are linked closely to the known requirements of the map user. The simplification of some features will make for more economical production and revision. A major objective has been to design a dynamic map, so that, although the series may remain standard for a number of years, its specification can be adapted to the changing patterns of user activity.

OUTLINE EDITION

In common with other Ordnance Survey small scale map series an outline edition of the 1:50 000 map is published, in flat sheet style only. This shows all the detail to be found on the fully coloured edition, apart from contours, road fillings, railway stations, Youth Hostels, National Trust information, danger areas; and rights of way information.[1]

1 On Second Series sheets civil parishes, or equivalent boundaries, are shown on the outline edition only, not on the coloured edition.

K

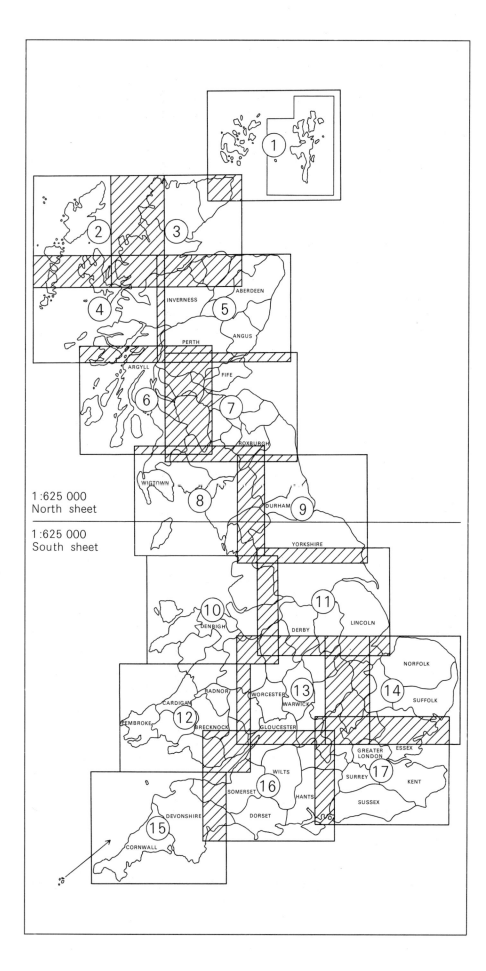

Figure 29
Index to the 1:250 000
Fifth Series and
1:625 000 sheets

The quarter-inch, 1:625 000
and other small scale map
series

9

For the last century, in addition to its topographical maps in the range 1:63 360 to 1:500, the Ordnance Survey has published a number of smaller scale map series. The data for these maps were derived from the basic scales of the Ordnance Survey, or from information collected in their preparation, but to a greater extent than other map series they were designed to focus on the needs of specialist users. Some small scale maps, notably the national half-inch (1:126 720) series, are no longer published,[1] but other series, in particular the 1:625 000 and the 1:250 000 continue as an integral part of the publication programme.

THE QUARTER-INCH TO ONE MILE MAP OF GREAT BRITAIN

Historical background

The first map series to be published by the Ordnance Survey at a scale smaller than 1:63 360 was the true Quarter-inch (1:253 440). Work started on the new series in 1859, but in 1872, engraving was suspended to allow draughtsmen to concentrate on the 1:63 360 series, and the maps were not completed until 1888. Twenty-five sheets on the Cassini projection covered England and Wales and a further seventeen sheets on the Bonne projection related to Scotland. The series was revised in 1898, retaining the same specification for topographical detail, but introducing new sheet lines to give eighteen sheets in England and Wales and nine in Scotland. A further version known as the 'Large Sheet Series' (the number of sheets in England and Wales was to be reduced to ten) was commenced in the same period but was not completed.

The 'Second Edition' was launched in 1912 with the publication of sheet 12 covering Kent. Its production was interrupted by World War I, and the series was not completed until after 1918, when a process of helio-zincography was substituted for copperplate engraving. The country was covered in twenty-one sheets and, on this occasion, on a uniform Cassini projection. In 1928 a 'Third Series' began publication. It was designed primarily as a map for motorists and, with its twenty-one sheets arranged with appropriate overlaps, it incorporated Ministry of Transport road numbers and directions at sheet edges. Town traffic diagrams were added to sheets published in the mounted and folded style.[2]

A 'Fourth Series' was put in hand in 1933. The sheet lines were again re-designed to reduce the number of sheets to nineteen and to allow some variation in sheet size. The series was especially successful as a motoring map and, like its predecessors, went into several printings, often incorporating new elements of design, as after 1945 when the National Grid was added to all sheets.[3] The maps were published in several formats including a coloured edition (flat and folded with covers), an outline edition, a series of county maps, known as Civil Parish Indexes, showing Petty Sessional Divisions, a 'Civil Air Edition', and also several 'District' maps.[4]

1 The 1:126 720 series was authorized in 1902 and the First Edition, covering England and Wales only, was published from 1903 onwards on 103 small sheets (18 × 12 in) based on the current 1:63 360 series, and produced by photo-etching on copper plates. The colour scheme showed detail in black, water in blue, contours and hills in brown, woods in green, and roads in burnt sienna (yellow was added for Second Class roads later). This series was superseded between 1905 and 1911 by larger sheets covering England and Wales in forty sheets (measuring 27 × 18 in) and by thirty-four sheets covering Scotland (measuring 24 × 18 in). These early editions were all printed in three forms, distinguished by method of relief portrayal – hill shaded, layer coloured, and with hill shading and layering combined. District maps of special areas of Great Britain were also published – such as the sheets relating to the Cotswolds, Birmingham and District, and the Island of Skye. Although the versions with hill shading were dropped, publication of the layered map, with various revisions, continued until World War II when most of the reproduction material was destroyed by enemy action and the series had to be discontinued. A completely new series was started in 1957 and was designed to cover the whole of Great Britain in fifty-one sheets. It was not completed and in 1961 (as reported in the *Ordnance Survey Annual Report 1961–62* (1962), 8), it was abandoned as a national series although a few sheets on independent sheet lines and covering tourist areas – currently only Snowdonia National Park, first published in 1956 – were continued.

2 See H. St J. L. Winterbotham, *A Key to Maps* (London, Second Edition, 1939), 81–2, on the historical background to the series.

3 *A Description of Ordnance Survey Small Scale Maps* ... 1947, 11, describes this version.

4 A proper bibliographical study of the various Quarter-inch series from maps, official catalogues and descriptions is needed before such statements can be other than tentative.

FIFTH SERIES

The current 'Quarter-inch' map is known as the Fifth Series, the planning for which was started after World War II, with the first sheet being published in 1957. The opportunity was taken to produce a new specification, so that sheets at this scale would be clear and easy to read (Fourth Series sheets were becoming overcrowded), would reveal the main physical features of the country, and in particular would depict main lines of communications, both road and rail, in a clear and prominent manner. To conform to European standards the scale of the series was changed from 1:253 440 to the rational scale of 1:250 000. The number of sheets was reduced to seventeen and the projection changed to the Transverse Mercator.

The basic data for the compilation of the Fifth Series[1] were derived mainly from the Seventh Series 1:63 360 map. The method of drafting as finally adopted was to generalize separately the details of contours, water, and of outline at 1:63 360 scale, followed by redrawing and then reduction to 1:250 000 scale. The remaining details as of names and hill shading were added at the final scale.

Since the Fifth Series was launched a succession of changes in design have met the needs of revision, economy or particular user requirement and have taken advantage of technical developments in production processes. Modifications were introduced after the appearance in 1957 of sheet 10, covering North Wales and Lancashire and Cheshire, and the first to be published. It was a pilot sheet in several respects and reaction to its design led to a changed specification for the series as a whole. The most noticeable innovations were in the treatment of relief. Contours, omitted from the first printing of sheet 10, were included on the redesigned map, while the scheme of layer colours was altered to improve clarity. In addition, the gauge of all road symbols was increased to aid in the production of a map of maximum utility to motorists. In 1962 sheet 10 was republished in its redesigned form.

A later change, affecting all published sheets, was to reduce the number of colours used in printing. All first editions had been printed in ten to twelve colours, depending on the number of layer tints on the sheets concerned. In 1964 the colours were reduced to eight. In 1973 as a further aid to motorists a blue infill was introduced for motorways.

Format, referencing and marginalia

Fifth Series 1:250 000 maps are published in fully coloured editions either as flat sheets or as folded versions supplied with laminated covers. The inner cover of the folded version currently carries Ordnance Survey publicity material. The outer cover, which is in the Ordnance Survey house style, shows a diagrammatic map of the particular sheet area and (on the back) an index to the sheet lines of the series as a whole (Figure 29). All seventeen sheets are a standard size, representing an area of 190 km east to west by 150 km north to south, and the sheet lines were arranged to make each sheet cover an area considered most convenient to motorists and other users. Sheets measure 760 × 600 mm within the neat lines. Insets are incorporated in a number of sheets – for example the Isles of Scilly on sheet 15 and the Shetland Isles on sheet 1.

National Grid lines are at intervals representing 10 km, with the 100 km

1 D. L. Griffith and J. J. Kelly, 'The Quarter Inch to One Mile Map of Great Britain' in Imhof, E. (ed.), *International Yearbook of Cartography*, 5 (1965), 94–102, discuss the production of the series.

intervals being emphasized in thicker line gauge. Full grid values are given at sheet corners, and the intervening values in tens of kilometres from 0 to 9 inclusive. The 10 km squares on the 1:250 000 serve as a complete index to the 1:25 000 series.

1:250 000 sheets also publish information on latitude and longitude in the outer borders. Full values are recorded at the 30 minute interval nearest to the sheet corners and the remaining 10 minute values are rendered in minutes only. The border is further subdivided by alternate black and white bars at 2 minute intervals. The intersections of 30 minute intervals of latitude and longitude lines are marked by small black crosses over the map as a whole, except where they would confuse important detail.

Conventional signs and other legend are concentrated in the southern margin. A series of diagrams (from left to right) show county boundaries and the incidence of 1:63 360 sheets falling within the sheet; the adjacent sheets and their overlaps and the National Grid reference letters over the area; and the relationship between true, grid, and magnetic north.[1] There are, in addition, a linear scale in imperial measures (top) and kilometres (bottom), a description of how to give a grid reference correct to 1 km, a column of layer tints depicting altitude bands (keyed in both feet and metres) and conventional signs (Plate 32).

Landscape at 1:250 000

The 1:250 000[2] scale requires not only a considerable simplification and generalization of the detail on the parent 1:63 360 map but also a deliberate emphasis of some features such as the major relief patterns and the road network at the expense of others. The process of simplification has been taken further than on the Fourth Series. Some features have been abandoned to improve clarity; these include water pipelines, churches and chapels (with tower or spire), and railway stations which are closed to the public. There has also been generalization of other features: in villages and hamlets, for example, only buildings in the main part of the village but not detached outlying houses appear; similarly, woodland areas have been further simplified and many smaller woods excluded (on the Fourth Series woods were shown as faithfully as possible and even small groups of trees were depicted).

Coupled with such simplification (which had the effect of 'cleaning up' the map), reduction from 1:63 360 to 1:250 000 required the omission of many minor categories of information. With antiquities, for example, the 1:250 000 map employs special symbols only for 'native fortresses', battle sites, and the course of Roman roads; with administrative information, only national boundaries and those of counties are shown; villages off the selected road network are omitted; and many abbreviations and descriptive names disappear as well. Decisions about particular features, as on the larger scale maps, are reached with the help of a standard specification stipulating lengths or areas below which features are omitted. Such thresholds are calculated at either 1:63 360 or 1:250 000 scale and are exemplified in Table 19.

The final content of the 1:250 000 series does not reflect simply a solution to the problem of eliminating detail from the parent scale. While some information disappears, this has allowed an emphasis on aspects related to the main purpose of the series, to provide a map of communications especially useful

1 Sheets on which the 2° meridian (meridian of origin of the National Grid) appear, namely 1, 5, 7, 9, 11, 13, and 16, show two north point diagrams – one for each of the east and west sheet lines.

2 The discussion deals with the series in general. At this relatively small scale the detailed description of each feature given in earlier chapters with map series at larger scales is omitted.

Table 19   Thresholds on the 1:250 000 map

Feature	Threshold below which feature is omitted at 1:250 000 scale
Buildings (Built-up Areas)	5 sq mm
Buildings (Outside Built-up Areas)	0.4 mm sq solid symbol
Coastal cliffs	2.5 mm
Dismantled Railways (where visible on the ground)	12 mm
Foreshore	1 mm between high and low water marks
Lakes, ponds, reservoirs	1 sq mm with a minimum side of 0.5 mm
Marsh	2 sq mm
Rock Area (Foreshore)	3 sq mm
Sandhills	5 sq mm
Woods	5 sq mm with a minimum side of 1 mm

to motorists. It led to the introduction of several categories of information new at this scale. They include telephone call boxes (except in towns and villages) lettered 'T' (for PO), 'A' (for AA), and 'R' (for RAC), steep gradient signs on trunk, main, and secondary roads, narrow gauge railways, tolls, and selected aerodromes and ferry routes for vehicles, including sea ferries.

Roads are shown in as much detail and prominence as possible. Although the method of depiction is basically the same as on the Fourth Series, the width of the road casing was increased to make them stand out. Until 1973, when the motorway blue colour filling replaced red, the widest casing was used for motorways. Trunk and main roads are still shown in red, secondary roads in brown, and unclassified roads left uncoloured. In built-up areas roads are generally restricted to those classified by the Department of the Environment but, in large towns, a selection of roads classified by yellow filling on the 1:63 360 map, giving preference to through routes, are included where other detail permits. Although it is a standard motoring map, it does not set out to show every minor road and, in both rural and urban areas, the user should realize that some detail has been excluded.

It is also a general physical map. Relief features are emphasized by a combination of contours, layer colouring, hill shading, and spot heights, which together give a clear contrast between different height ranges. The contour interval is 200 ft and the treatment smooths out minor bends and isolated areas of particular contours. Layer colours are applied in steps of 200 ft up to a height of 1000 ft above which intervals occur at 1400 ft, 2000 ft, and 3000 ft. The lowest layer is light green, followed by three tones of yellow and then five tones of buff – with brighter and clearer effect than on Fourth Series maps. Hill shading was introduced (on the 1:250 000) for the first time on the Fifth Series maps. The technique assumes that (as on a relief model) a light is shining at an angle of 45° from the north-west corner of the sheet.[1] The method is applied consistently throughout the series and the intensity of shading generally decreases down mountain slopes to the 600 ft level. Between 600 and 400 ft hill shading is faded out completely.

1 L. J. Harris, 'Hill-shading in the New Quarter-inch Ordnance Survey Map', *The Geographical Journal*, **123** (1957), 237–9.

Revision

Quarter-inch maps are republished at more frequent intervals than any of the larger scale series, but revision does not always imply a systematic updating of the whole map. A distinction is made between special revision, to deal quickly especially with major road developments, and full revision when all features on a sheet are brought up to date. While construction of a motorway could in itself be sufficient cause for revising a sheet, as a general rule, revision is carried out periodically according to the likelihood of change. Sheets are placed in three categories: 'heavy', 'medium', and 'light' depending on the expected rate of change. These categories are subject to modification but in 1973 the pattern for the series was:

5 heavy sheets	Revision every 3 years with annual reprint with special revision.
5 medium sheets	Revision every 4 years but with reprint with special revision every 2 years.
7 light sheets	Revision every 6 years with reprint every 3 years with special revision.

The principal material for such revision is provided by the cyclic revision programme for the 1:63 360/1:50 000 series, supplemented by special road surveys where these are necessary.

SPECIAL EDITIONS

Wales and the Marches

A map covering the whole of Wales and the Borderland, in either a flat or folded format, is the only remaining special map published at 1:250 000 scale. It is similar in style to the standard 1:250 000 map, but instead of showing relief by the usual layer tints, a gold tint with a dark-side shading is added to areas above 200 ft; a light green tint is used below 200 ft. Contours are at vertical intervals of 200 ft. The 1971 edition shows the boundaries of the three National Parks within Wales – Brecon Beacons, the Pembrokeshire Coast, and Snowdonia – by colour bands; and there is also a short glossary, introduced in 1962, of Welsh terms and their English equivalents. The cover of the map includes a list of places of interest to tourists.

Outline edition

Fifth Series 1:250 000 sheets are also published as an outline edition, printed in black, from a combination of the black, blue (less water tint), and green plates, the last of which is screened. The details on the outline edition are identical with the coloured edition, apart from the absence of contours, road fillings, water and layer tints, and hill shading. They are published on heavier paper as flat sheets only; OUTLINE EDITION is printed in the north margin of the sheet.

Quarter-inch Atlas and Gazetteer of Great Britain

The seventeen coloured sheets of the 1:250 000 map are also published in atlas form. This has hard covers, but a loose-leaf binding so that revised printings of any sheet can be inserted.[1] The dimensions of the Atlas are

1 Standing orders may be placed with the Ordnance Survey for the supply of updated sheets on publication.

approximately 680 × 450 mm, with sheets folded and trimmed to fit this size. The full map area is of course retained, but trimming removes the legend in the south margin of the ordinary sheet. Conventional signs, together with an index to the sheets in the Atlas, are printed on a special title page, the reverse of which includes (i.e. in 1973) an index map to the 1:250 000 sheets in relation to the National Grid, a similar diagram for the sheet lines of the 1:63 360 map, a description of the National Grid Reference System and of the 1:63 360 and 1:25 000 maps.

The reverse of the title page also describes the Gazetteer to the Atlas. This lists all names – about 33 000 – on the 1:250 000 sheets. Names, listed alphabetically, are identified by the number of the sheet on which they appear and also by their National Grid reference to the nearest kilometre. Large features such as Salisbury Plain are shown to the nearest 10 km; for linear features, such as ancient roads, rivers, or earthworks, adequate references are given for them to be traced across a map. Names are always listed in the form in which they appear on the map. For example, *Ashdown Forest* appears under *A*, while *Forest of Bere* is under *F*. Similarly *Beaulieu River* appears under *B* but *River Thames* is under *R*. When the definite article precedes a name, the name appears first: thus, *The Wash* becomes *Wash, The* and is listed under *W*. An exception is made for Gaelic and Welsh names. These are listed under the initial letter of the Welsh or Gaelic definite article, for example, *An Ceannich* is listed under *A*, and *Y Lethr* is listed under *Y*. When a name appears more than once, it is distinguished by the appropriate county (either full or abbreviated), for example, *Whitchurch (Somerset)*, *Whitchurch (Hants)*.

Apart from standard abbreviations for county names, other abbreviations in the Gazetteer identify the nature of some named features. They comprise:

ant	Antiquity	mt	Mountain, mount or hill
chan	Channel or arm of the sea	pt	Point or headland on coast
dist	District or name of an area	sbk	Sandbank.
is	Island		

The Gazetteer may also be used with the 1:63 360 and 1:25 000 maps published by the Ordnance Survey, although it does not include all the place-names on these series. As it was compiled and is kept revised by automatic data processing methods it may also be supplied on magnetic tape,[1] in which form it is as up to date as the most recently revised 1:250 000 sheet. The Gazetteer is also published as a separate book.

MAPS AT THE TEN-MILE SCALE

After the 1:63 360 and 1:10 560 series, the 10 mile to 1 inch (1:633 600) is one of the oldest scales of the Ordnance Survey. A general map covering part of southern England and Wales was first engraved in the 1820s as an index to the *Old Series* 1:63 360 maps. Successive editions were published recording the progress of the 1:63 360 map but not until 1899 was a general topographical map authorized at this scale. This was completed in twelve sheets in 1904 and was published with one version in outline but with water features in blue and another with hill shading and roads coloured sienna. By eliminating sea areas and joining sheets it was later possible to reduce the sheets to eight and, in a new edition, published in 1926, to three, with overlaps, at a size of 38 × 26 in, although this format had the disadvantage of

1 The Ordnance Survey can supply copies of the Gazetteer magnetic tape in ICL or IBM readable form. By using this tape it is possible to print selected data in various forms; for example, it would be a simple matter to extract the names for a given map sheet and produce an index in alphabetical order for the area.

splitting Scotland. Two sheets were introduced in the 1930s and the current layout (Figure 29), dates from 1956. A rational scale of 1:625 000 (9.86 miles to 1 inch) was adopted in the early 1940s, first by enlarging the true ten-mile map photographically and later by redrawing. The presence of the National Grid enables the 1:625 000 sheets to serve as convenient indexes to larger scale map series.

Owing to its relatively small scale the 1:625 000 map has often served as a base for specialist rather than for general topographical maps. Much of its interest, in the past and as a current publication, lies in its adaptation to specialized data. As early as 1860 a ten-mile 'Rivers and Catchment map' was prepared by the Ordnance Survey for a Royal Commission on Salmon Fisheries;[1] and, in 1927, a special 'Eclipse Map', showing the path of the shadow during the total eclipse of 29 September 1927, was published in collaboration with the Royal Society and Royal Astronomical Society.

Current and recent 1:625 000 maps are described below, with the exception of the archaeological and historical maps at this scale (Chapter 10). All sheets are a standard size, measuring 39 × 30 in, but when both sheets of each map are mounted as a single wall map it measures 42 × 64 in. The North Sheet includes Scotland and England north of Kendal (with insets for the Shetland and Orkney Islands), and the South Sheet covers the rest of England and Wales. The map is plotted on the Transverse Mercator projection and carries National Grid lines at 10 km intervals. Latitude and longitude are shown in the outer border with full values near the sheet corner and intervals of 30 minutes marked in the intervening border.

Route Planning Map

In terms of current importance the Route Planning Map takes pride of place in the 1:625 000 series partly because it is an annual official record of the changing major road network of the country, and also because the changes in its design for successive editions have produced innovations of general value, some of which have been adopted in other standard map series.[2] The origin of a Route Planning Map can be traced to the inter-war years. In 1931 a ten-mile map of Great Britain was published in three sheets, on a base modified to eliminate some names and contours and showing Ministry of Transport Class A and B roads and AA and RAC telephone boxes.[3] A revised edition appeared in 1933. In 1937, in a further edition, the scale of 1:633 600 was retained, but the map was recast in two sheets.

During World War II this map was integrated into the series of 'Planning' maps (see below), published by the Ordnance Survey in collaboration with various government departments. The scale was enlarged to 1:625 000 and the edition published in 1946 became known as 'The Road Map'. Like its pre-1939 parent, of which it was an up-dated version on a similar topographical base, it distinguished by different colours[4] trunk roads and routes, Class 1 and 2 roads with Ministry of Transport numbers, and AA and RAC telephone boxes; a larger scale inset covered the London area. Both base map and road conventions were revised and redesigned in the editions of 1953 and then 1956, which remained as the standard 'Roads' map, with regular revision, until 1963.[5]

An advisory committee on survey and mapping (1963) criticized the existing ten-mile 'Roads' map on grounds of 'general appearance and lack of

1 Quoted by H. St J. L. Winterbotham (1936), 79.

2 For example, the use of blue for motorways, since adopted for the 1:50 000 and 1:250 000 series.

3 [Anon.] 'The New Road Map of Great Britain', *The Geographical Journal*, **81** (1933), 438–9.

4 *A Description of Ordnance Survey Small Scale Maps* . . . 1947, Plate 16 shows the design at that date.

5 *A Description of Ordnance Survey Small Scale Maps* . . . 1957, Plate 13 shows the design of this edition.

clarity'. It was decided not to reprint it and instead a new policy was formulated:

... to provide motorists and transport operators with an up to date map showing motorways, trunk and all Class 1 or A roads at a smaller scale than the Quarter-inch Series and to present users with such additional information as will enable them to plan routes to suit best their individual requirements.

The result was a new map designed from first principles, to be republished annually with full revision. It was given a new name: the Route Planning Map.[1] The two sheets of the first edition, available in flat and folded versions with covers, were published on 1 January 1964. New features were designed to help motorists. Layer colouring was simplified so that roads and road numbers stood out; base detail was toned down from black to grey; motorways were shown in blue; insets at 1:250 000 were included of road networks in larger conurbations, for Glasgow, Edinburgh, Newcastle upon Tyne, London, Manchester, and Birmingham; a triangular mileage chart and the location of British Rail motorail services formed new insets; and, on the body of the map, National Parks, Forest Parks, and areas of outstanding natural beauty were shown in green.

The success of the map was such that it was reprinted three times in 1964.[2] At the same time, it retained some characteristics of its predecessors and design experiments continued, to achieve the best balance between readability and the maximum of motoring information. The second and third editions, published in 1965 and 1966, were modelled on the first, but the fourth edition, published in January 1967, made important changes. The most significant, resulting in a new look, stemmed from the decision to make Ministry of Transport primary routes, popularly known as 'Green Routes', a feature of the map. The roads were signposted in green and, following the convention with motorways, a similar colour was adopted on the map. Green, however, was not clearly distinguishable against the layer colouring for relief, and the less so against the green for National Parks, Forest Parks, and areas of outstanding natural beauty. To overcome a potential colour clash, the layers were reduced to pale yellow and the green for National Parks was omitted entirely. Other new features included the numbering of motorway junctions and an explanation of basic conventional signs in French and German.

Further modifications were made in the four editions published between 1968 and 1971. They included the reinsertion (but in diagrammatic form in the margin) of the location of National Parks, Forest Parks, and areas of outstanding natural beauty (1968) and the printing of information about National Grid references in French and German (1969). Changes in the 1972 edition were more far reaching: road casings were omitted to reduce drawing time during revision and to assist with colour register when printing; road numbers were boxed and placed across the road; inter-town mileages were incorporated on the body of the map; and diagrams of motorway junctions with limited interchange facilities were shown for the first time. The layout of marginal information was also redesigned.

On the 1973 edition the search for an optimum design continued. The layer system for relief was replaced by hill shading and Univers type-face was substituted for the Times Roman, Gill Sans, and Italic of the previous editions. Town insets, hitherto based on the 1:250 000 series, were redrawn in 'town-plan' style and additional limited interchange junctions on

1 On the first edition, the title ' "Ten Mile" Map of Great Britain' with 'The Route Planning Map' as a subtitle, was adopted; in the second edition 'The Route Planning Map' became the title.

2 *The Ordnance Survey Annual Report, 1963–64* (1964), 8.

motorways were inserted. The development of the Route Planning Map since its inception is an instructive case study in the range of considerations faced by the Ordnance Survey in designing maps for the 1970s and beyond. Techniques change but so do user demands. The Route Planning Map has become firmly established as a map used in road vehicles and as such its design requires continuous close attention to the needs of the motoring community.

Planning series

After 1940, an important series of maps, designed for planning purposes, was produced by the Ordnance Survey at the 1:625000 scale.

The series was initiated by the advisory maps committee of the Ministry of Works and Planning (later the Ministry of Town and Country Planning), the members of which included representatives of the British Association and the National Atlas Committee, appointed to advise on the preparation of maps for planning purposes.[1] All maps in the series were published at 1:625000 scale, covering Great Britain in two sheets, and, in some cases, accompanied by explanatory texts, published as separate pamphlets. The aim was to produce a related series of maps depicting at a national level principal physical, social, and economic facts of importance in planning decisions. While the series was sponsored by the Departments concerned with planning, including the Department of Health for Scotland, it also included, for example, maps prepared by the Ministry of Agriculture, the Geological Survey, and independent research organizations such as the Land Utilization Survey. The series was used by schools and colleges, business men, and administrators as well as by planners: until at least the mid 1950s it was regarded as the nucleus of a national atlas. The maps listed in Table 20 were published.

In 1955, after the publication of a new edition of the 'Topographical Map', a completely new policy was adopted for the 'Planning Series'. The majority of the specialized maps became a direct responsibility of their sponsoring departments and only five maps, later reduced to four with the withdrawal of the Topographical Map, were reclassified as of sufficiently general interest to be published by the Ordnance Survey. This is the present policy. The four maps are:

Administrative areas map   This consists of a grey topographical base map with overprints in colour showing administrative units of local government. See p. 142.

Outline map   This is printed in black without relief and road filling. It is designed to be a base map on which to plot other data. An index to the 1:10560/1:10000 sheets is produced as an overprint to the outline edition.

Physical map   This was introduced at 1:625000 to replace the Physical Map at 1:1000000 which was withdrawn from publication in 1965 (see p. 141). Relief is indicated by layer colouring at 200, 400, 600, 800, 1000, 1400, 2000, and 3000 ft above sea level. Sea-bed contours are also shown at 5, 10, 20, 40, and 100 fathoms and are emphasized by varying shades of blue, which colour is also employed for other water features. The selection of names also favours the principal physical features.

Route planning map   (described in pp. 137-9).

1 *A Description of Ordnance Survey Small Scale Maps* . . . 1947, 12.

Table 20   Ordnance Survey 1:625 000 Planning series

Map	Date of last edition	Available in 1973 from*
Administrative Areas	1973	OS
Coal and Iron	1945	DOE
Electricity: Statutory Supply Areas	1946	DOE
Gas Board Areas	1944	Not available
Gas and Coke	1949	DOE
Gravel and Associated Sands (South sheet only)	1965	Not available
Igneous and Metamorphic Rocks	1948	Not available
Iron and Steel	1945	DOE
Land Classification†	1944–5	DOE
Land Utilization	1944	DOE
Limestone (North sheet only)	1955	DOE
Local Accessibility†	1955	DOE
Outline	1969	OS
Physical	1957	OS
Population: Changes by Migration 1921–31	1949	DOE
Changes by Migration 1931–38/39	1949	DOE
Changes by Migration 1938/39–47	1954	DOE
Population Density 1931	1944	Not available
Population Density 1951†	1960–1	DOE
Population: Total Changes 1921–31	1949	DOE
Total Changes 1931–38/39	1948–9	DOE
Total Changes 1938/39–47	1954	DOE
Total Changes 1951–61	1966	DOE
Population of Urban Areas, 1951	1954	DOE
Railways	1946	Not available
Rainfall: Annual Average 1881–1915	1949	DOE
Annual Average 1916–50†	1957	DOE
Road Map (replaced by Route Planning Map 1964)	1956	Not available
Solid Geology (The Ten-Mile Geological Map of Great Britain)	1957	OS
Topography	1955	Not available
Types of Farming	1944	DOE
Vegetation: Grasslands of England and Wales† (South sheet only)	1945	DOE
(Supplementary strip to cover remainder of England)	1946	DOE
Vegetation: Reconnaissance Survey of Scotland†	1953	DOE

* Maps marked as available 'DOE' can be obtained from the Map Library, Department of the Environment.
A fuller description of earlier sheets was included in *A Description of Ordnance Survey Small Scale Maps* (1947), 12–16.

† An explanatory booklet has been published and is available from the Map Library, Department of the Environment.

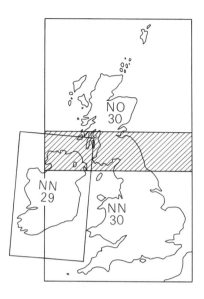

Figure 30
Index to the 1 : 1 000 000
International Map of the World
relating to the British Isles

ORDNANCE SURVEY MAPS 1:1 000 000 SCALE

The publication of maps at the 1 : 1 000 000 scale (in which 1 mm represents 1 km) has grown out of an involvement with the International Map of the World. The original proposal for such a map on a 1 : 1 000 000 scale was put forward by Dr Albrecht Penck in 1891 at the Fifth International Geographical Congress but not until 1909, despite sporadic mapping in some countries, was a preliminary specification drawn up. This was finalized in 1913 and, with minor changes introduced in 1928, it survived as the basis of the specification until 1962 when a new design was adopted.[1] From the start the project ran into problems, unresolved by a series of international conferences, and stemming not only from the complexity of co-operation between independent national map-making organizations but also from technical difficulties such as those created by the choice of a modified polyconic projection or that of devising layer colours to accommodate terrain from the Himalayas to south-east England. In 1939, of an approximate total of 975 sheets required to cover the land surface of the world, 405 had been published, but of these only 232 conformed to the international specification.[2] World War II, coupled with the development of air navigation,[3] was a further stimulus to the development of international mapping at 1 : 1 000 000 and some sheets continue to be published to the standard agreed in 1962.

Without exercising either administrative or technical control, the Ordnance Survey exerted an important influence on the early development of the 1 : 1 000 000 map. A central bureau for the project was located within the Ordnance Survey Office[4] and remained there until 1953, when it was transferred to the Cartographic Office of the United Nations in New York.

The Ordnance Survey was among the first to complete its obligation to the International Map. As far as Great Britain was concerned, however, international sheet lines were inconvenient. The country fell on no less than seven sheets and to produce a practical working map for the UK market these were amalgamated in the 1920s into north and south sheets with an overlap (Figure 30). The sheets could be mounted as a wall map measuring 32 × 57 in.

From 1945 until 1965 the 1 : 1 000 000 sheets relating to Great Britain were published by the Ordnance Survey in two styles:

(a) In the style of the INTERNATIONAL MAP, according to its original specification,[5] but incorporating the National Grid and with contours deleted to improve clarity. The map was described as follows:

. . . *layer colouring brings out the relief with great clearness and streams, rivers and canals are clearly shown in blue. Communications are also very well delineated, the principal roads being shown by means of strong red lines and secondary roads by finer red lines. Railways are shown in black, double and single tracks and narrow gauge and light railways being distinguished.*[6]

It was seen to offer a good general picture of the main features of the country, the usefulness of which was enhanced by its comparability with foreign sheets in the same series.

(b) As a PHYSICAL MAP, but with some differences between the sheets relating, respectively, to England and Wales, and to Scotland. Layer colours were stepped at 50, 100, 200, 400, 800, 1200, and 2000 ft on the map of England and Wales, with the lower levels in graduated shades of green and the higher

1 This is the design for the present Ordnance Survey sheets at 1 : 1 000 000.

2 G. R. Crone, *Maps and Their Makers, An Introduction to the History of Cartography* (London, 2nd edn., 1962), 163–5; also G. R. Crone, 'The Future of the International Million Map of the World', *The Geographical Journal*, **128** (1962), 36–8.

3 R. A. Gardiner, 'A Re-appraisal of the International Map of the World (IMW) on the Millionth Scale', *International Yearbook of Cartography*, **1** (1961), 31–49.

4 M. N. MacLeod, 'The Present State of the International 1/M Map', *Ordnance Survey Professional Papers* (London, New Series, No. 10, 1926), 11–13.

5 UN Cartographic Office, *World Cartography*, **4** (1954), prints the specification in full.

6 *A Description of Ordnance Survey Small Scale Maps* . . . 1947, 17; Plate 17 for a specimen.

ones in a series of red and brown tints. Sea-bed contours were also shown at 5, 10, 20, 30, 40, 50, and 100 fathoms and emphasized in shades of blue; rivers and streams were also coloured blue. Conventions and colour scheme sought to emphasize the principal physical features, for a market which was regarded as primarily educational.

The Physical Map of Scotland was designed to the same specification, but with additional layers for 3000 and 4000 ft and with an overlap into the area of the sheet to the south.

In 1965 the Physical Maps at 1:1 000 000 scale were withdrawn.

Current 1:1 000 000 maps

In 1965 two sheets – NN 30 covering England and Wales and NO 30 covering Scotland – for which the United Kingdom was responsible in the redesigned International Map of the World at 1:1 000 000 were published. Each sheet measures 33 × 40 in but, unlike other Ordnance Survey maps which cover Great Britain only, both sheets extend west to incorporate Northern Ireland. In line with the 'Bonn specification' of the United Nations[1] a new range of colours for hypsometric and bathymetric layer tints was introduced. All printing screens were likewise designed to new specifications and colour values were related to standard Mansell colours. The series tends to emphasize communications, centres of population (classified according to size and importance), physical features and international boundaries (Plate 38).

Archaeological and historical maps published at the 1:1 000 000 scale are described in Chapter 10.

SPECIAL ADMINISTRATIVE MAPS PUBLISHED BY THE ORDNANCE SURVEY

In addition to a statutory obligation to depict administrative boundaries on regular map series, the Ordnance Survey publishes administrative diagrams which emphasize boundaries and names of administrative areas. Some of these maps (as at the 1:63 360 scale of administrative areas in London and Glasgow and of London at the 1:25 000 scale) have already been described, but most special administrative maps fall in the range of small scale maps dealt with below.

1:625 000 administrative areas map

As with other 1:625 000 maps Great Britain is covered in North and South Sheets. A grey base similar to the outline edition 1:625 000, which incorporates national and geographical county[2] boundaries, is overprinted with a further three colours to distinguish boundaries and names of local authorities (excluding civil parishes). The boundaries concerned are:

England and Wales	administrative county, county borough, London borough, municipal borough, urban district, and rural district.
Scotland	county of city, burgh, and district council area.
Isle of Man	borough and town.

1 As agreed at the United Nations Technical Conference on the International Map of the World at 1:1 000 000 held at Bonn in August 1962. The 1965 map of the United Kingdom, though still in publication in 1974, has not been revised.

2 The geographical county, or county at large, includes all its relevant subdivisions such as the administrative county or counties, county boroughs, municipal boroughs, urban and rural districts and civil parishes. It is defined, Yorkshire excepted, as the area under the jurisdiction of the lord lieutenant and is also the limit for judicial areas under the commission of assize.

Insets at enlarged scales show the details within larger conurbations: Greater London, Manchester, Birmingham (South Sheet); and Glasgow, Edinburgh, Newcastle upon Tyne (North Sheet). The South Sheet also shows the Metropolitan Police District. A new edition of the map was published in 1965[1] and required fewer colours than the superseded edition.[2] Both North and South Sheets, with boundaries revised to 1 April, are currently republished annually.

1:100 000 administrative areas maps of England and Wales

From their introduction in the late nineteenth century until 1965, the administrative areas maps of England and Wales had been published at a scale of 1:126 720. Each county was given a separate map, but Devon and Yorkshire consisted of more than one sheet. After 1945 the series was available in two styles. The first was 'fully coloured' printed on a grey base and showing in red areas of administrative counties, county and municipal boroughs, urban and rural districts, civil parishes, and catchment areas; in green, parliamentary areas relating to the parliamentary county, county division, parliamentary boroughs, and the divisions of parliamentary boroughs; and, in black, the National Grid. A second style depicted local government boundaries only in red on a grey base together with the National Grid in black.

The first sheet (Hampshire) of a new 1:100 000 administrative areas series was published in 1965 and publication was completed in 1972. The series is kept up to date by periodical reprinting. All the geographical counties of England and some of Wales are shown separately, but some maps such as those of Devon and Yorkshire consist of two or more sheets. The base was derived from the Seventh Series 1:63 360 map and administrative boundaries, from counties down to civil parishes, are overprinted in red: parliamentary constituencies are printed in blue. The following areas are therefore shown: administrative county, county borough, municipal borough, urban district, rural district, rural borough, civil parish, county constituency, and borough constituency (Plate 33a).

A second series of 1:100 000 maps, depicting petty sessions areas, was developed along with the 1:100 000 administrative areas maps. The first sheet was published in 1967 and they now cover the whole of England and Wales. They employ the same base and format as the administrative areas maps but, instead of boundaries of parliamentary constituencies, they include (in blue) those relating to judicial areas. The boundaries on this series therefore comprise: administrative county, county borough, municipal borough, urban district, rural district, rural borough, civil parish, Metropolitan Police district, county commission of peace, petty sessional division, quarter session borough, commission of peace borough (Plate 33b).

As it relates to geographical counties no index map is necessary for the 1:100 000 series.

In addition to the coloured administrative diagrams, 1:100 000 scale base maps printed in grey are available without overprinting.

1 *The Ordnance Survey Annual Report 1964– 65* (1965), 9.

2 Described and illustrated in *A Description of Ordnance Survey Small Scale Maps . . . 1947.*

1:250 000 administrative areas map of Scotland

In Scotland a special administrative areas map is published at 1:250 000. The whole country is included on nine sheets, the grey base detail of which is derived from the standard 1:250 000 series. The boundaries and names of local government areas are overprinted in red and those of parliamentary divisions in blue. The following boundaries are therefore published: geographical county, county of city, burgh, district council area, civil parish, county constituency, and burgh constituency.

An index map is available for the series.

Archaeology and the archaeological and historical maps

10

The investigation, recording, and surveying of archaeological features has always been a concern of the Ordnance Survey. In so far as massive earthworks of any age are prominent landscape features their survey (it may be said) was inevitable, but the development of a systematic approach to mapping antiquities owed more to the enthusiasm of successive officers with an archaeological bent than to cartographic expediency. In this respect the Survey was fortunate in that one of its founders, General William Roy (1726–90), was a keen archaeologist and author of a survey of the military antiquities of Roman Britain.[1] Roy's interest was aroused by encountering the Antonine Wall in the course of the military survey of the Scottish highlands (1747–55) and his influence helped to imprint archaeology on Ordnance Survey thinking. Even if there was uncertainty about methods, the nineteenth century was characterized by a real development of the department's archaeological activities.

On the first 1:63360 maps published before 1824, antiquities were depicted unconvincingly, often depending on the special interest of the field surveyor. In the 1:10560 survey of Ireland, however, carried out between 1824 and 1845, they were specifically included and received careful treatment under the guidance of the Irish scholar John O'Donovan.[2] Irish maps served as a model for the large scale survey of Great Britain and, by the mid nineteenth century, the importance of antiquities as landscape features was fully recognized. Archaeological details on the County Series 1:2500 and 1:10560 maps indicate that antiquities were systematically surveyed, classified, and given a range of symbols in the second half of the nineteenth century. If the results were variable,[3] this was owing not so much to lack of keenness (as witness the activities of Sir Henry James when Director General and the large archaeological content of the Ordnance Survey Library[4]) as to the lack of a co-ordinating system for the department's archaeological activities.

Only with the appointment of O. G. S. Crawford as Archaeology Officer (1920–45) was this need met and the Ordnance Survey's archaeology put on a professional basis. Crawford's tenure of office was distinguished by important pioneer work in air photography applied to archaeology,[5] and the development of the 'Period Map' as a vehicle for communicating archaeological information. He laid down the general principles of the Survey's approach to archaeology and the foundations of the present Archaeology Division.[6]

The Archaeology Division was founded in 1947 under C. W. Phillips who succeeded Crawford as Archaeology Officer. Thereafter, to facilitate a proper treatment of archaeological topography on the large scale maps, the Ordnance Survey launched a research and survey programme covering Great Britain, important not only for the accuracy of the archaeological details on Ordnance Survey maps but also for archaeological research in general. It has been described as providing the:

. . . last chance to make an accurate field survey of most of the surviving field antiquities in all but the remote and relatively unpopulated parts of Britain. The varying forms of assault on the countryside induced by population pressure and empowered by the use of new machinery have put an immense number of sites in danger, and we have a wider appreciation of the extent of the threat because so many important sites, hitherto unknown, have been revealed by air photography.[7]

1 Major-General William Roy, *The Military Antiquities of the Romans in Britain* (London, 1793).

2 Sir Charles Close, 134–7; and H. St J. L. Winterbotham, . . . 1934, 85–7, give an account of the early development of the depiction of antiquities on Ordnance Survey maps.

3 F. J. Haverfield, (1906), 165–76, summed up some of the criticisms.

4 D. A. Johnston, *Classified Catalogue of Books in the Library of the Ordnance Survey Office, Southampton* (HMSO, London, 1904).

5 Ordnance Survey Professional Papers, *Air Survey and Archaeology* (New Series, **7**, 1928); and *Air Photography for Archaeologists* (New Series, **12**, 1929).

6 Crawford's own account of the period appears in his autobiography *Said and Done: The Autobiography of an Archaeologist* (London, 1955); an early comment from him appears in 'Archaeology and the Ordnance Survey', *The Geographical Journal*, **59** (1922), 245–58.

7 C. W. Phillips, 'The Special Archaeological and Historical Maps Published by the Ordnance Survey', *The Cartographic Journal*, **2** (1965), 27–31.

The Ordnance Survey's archaeology policy

A policy for archaeology was developed against this background and is defined as one which will result in the depiction of appropriate archaeological information on all Ordnance Survey maps between the scales of 1:1250 and 1:1 000 000 as well as the publication of special archaeological and historical maps. To ensure that the published archaeology is properly supported by reliable and immediately available information,[1] the Ordnance Survey compiles a systematic topographical record of features of archaeological and historical interest throughout Great Britain. It also checks and assesses this information and the record is kept up to date from recent research.

Within this general policy, however, the Ordnance Survey does not seek to compile, or to publish on its maps, a definitive record of antiquities. The archaeological record in Great Britain spans some quarter of a million years and typological categories can be multiplied indefinitely so that this would be impossible. The working instructions for archaeology are defined more narrowly and features are excluded on various grounds. The three main categories of antiquity coming within the terms of reference, together with their limiting qualifications and exceptions, are as below:

(a) Artificial features or their sites, and artificial portable objects and their find spots.

(b) Natural features and places associated with (i) well-known historical events and folk-lore traditions, such as battlefields, scenes of political events of major significance, and features associated with important historical characters, saints, etc., (ii) human dwelling-places and human or palaeontological remains such as those found in caves and rock shelters.

In order to be recorded, features included in (a) and (b) must not be of a date later than A.D. 1714[2] and, in addition, selected features *earlier* than A.D. 1714 are also excluded from consideration. These comprise (i) Post-Norman Conquest domestic buildings, such as dwelling houses, manor houses, granges, schools, vicarages, mills, almshouses, tithe barns, inns, and cruck-framed cottages, unless they are outstanding examples of their type or are of considerable historical interest; (ii) minor finds or features which are subsidiary to other antiquities; (iii) Post-Roman roads and tracks; (iv) Post-Norman Conquest churches and chapels, except where they are derelict or the site only is being marked; (v) bridges, unless they are of special visual or architectural interest; (vi) for 'area antiquities', such as forests, parks and field systems, which cover large areas but may lack definite archaeological importance, only abridged records are kept.

(c) In addition to (a) and (b), a number of artificial features or their sites dating from A.D. 1714 to c. 1850, are systematically recorded. The principal items, many of them of interest to industrial archaeologists, include canals and associated features, turnpike roads and their toll houses, derelict railways, docks and harbours (a site obscured by later dock or harbour installations is not recorded), buildings and working sites associated with the introduction of a revolutionary technological process, the dwelling, work place, or birthplace of their inventors, the homes and birthplaces of other famous people (famous in this context implying a national reputation), major country seats or their sites, and deserted villages, townships, or hamlets (but only exceptionally Highland depopulation sites).

Three other qualifications may influence the final list of antiquities eligible

1 The Survey's supporting evidence for the publication of antiquities, accumulated since the mid nineteenth century, was originally recorded in the 'Object Name Books'. These were largely destroyed in the air raid on Southampton in 1940, and of those dealing with the first survey only the volumes for Scotland and parts of the northern English counties survived and are preserved in the Ordnance Survey.

2 On older maps this date was 1688 – the end of the Stuart period. 1714 (the date of accession of George I) was adopted by the Ordnance Survey c. 1950, following the practice implemented in 1913 by the Royal Commission on Ancient Monuments. See *Fifth Report of Select Committee on Estimates. Historic Buildings and Ancient Monuments*, 1956-60 (HMSO, London, 1960).

for recording by the Ordnance Survey, although, as with the other 'rules', they are never dogmatically enforced where there is good evidence which invalidates them.

(*a*) A pre-1715 item scheduled as an antiquity by the Inspectorate of Ancient Monuments is always included.

(*b*) Items already published as antiquities on Ordnance Survey maps are included with the exception of those such as 'Submarine Forests' and 'Rocking Stones', no longer regarded as of archaeological interest. Features claimed in reputable literature to be pre-1714 antiquities are also recorded.

(*c*) Minor items in built-up areas are excluded and as a result, many post-1066 features are not recorded unless they are outstanding examples of a type of monument rare in a district. In villages, however, well-preserved relics of early community life, such as a cross or village stocks, qualify for inclusion.

Records and their compilation

The archaeological records of the Ordnance Survey created by this policy are designed to establish the existence, or previous existence, of antiquities. This includes locating their sites or find spots, assigning modern archaeological terminology to them, allocating them to periods or dates, and establishing their proper names. The records are thus compiled by a programme of research into archaeological literature and documentary sources and by systematic examination of air photographs. This is followed by field investigation, with the emphasis on typological assessment on the spot, and survey and photography where feasible. Close liaison is maintained with other government departments, such as the Inspectorate of Ancient Monuments, and with universities, learned societies, and individuals engaged in archaeological research.

The results of this work are incorporated in a card index. Each 'antiquity' (in this sense a convenient subject for a single record, which may, for example, be a Roman town, a group of barrows, or the find spot of a flint' arrowhead) is allocated a separate card and given a unique number within the 1:10 560 or 1:10 000 sheet on which it falls. A different system is used for 'linear antiquities', such as Roman roads or boundary dykes, the information relating to which is entered on strip-maps. Each card or linear record is also classified archaeologically and a separate skeleton index maintained in the classified order. The records, comprising index cards (Figure 31) and 1:10 560 and 1:10 000 sheets and folders containing details of linear antiquities, are all available for consultation by bona fide research workers. Copies of the cards are also available at (and can be purchased from) the National Monument Record Branch of the Royal Commission on Historical Monuments.[1]

Publication of antiquities on standard maps

The index material is used in two ways: first, by publication on standard Ordnance Survey maps of all scales from 1:1250 to 1:250 000 and, secondly, by producing the special archaeological and historical maps described below.

[1] Fortress House, 23 Savile Row, London, W1X 2AA.

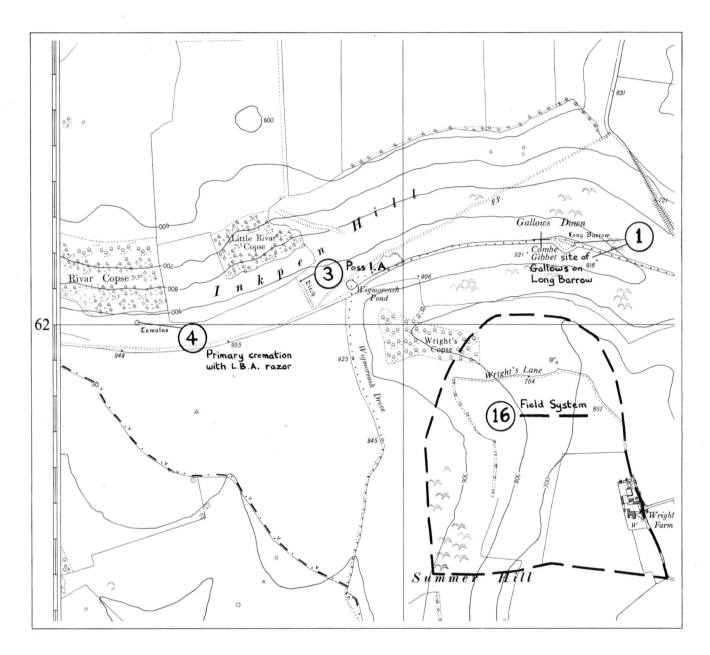

Figure 31
Part of an Archaeology
Division record map, and card

Antiquity No.	County	Parish	BA		1
SU 36 SE 4	BERKS	INKPEN			

Ditched bowl barrow containing cremation, bone implements and LBA razor
[SU 35226200]   Tumulus   [GT]

A ditched bowl barrow opened by Crawford in Sep 1903 and listed by him as Inkpen 4. It had been dug into six or seven years earlier by a Mr Annetts of Inkpen who removed 20 cartloads of flints.
The barrow seems to have been composed of chalk contained by a flint wall c 31 ft in diameter and surrounded by a ditch. A central pit contained a flint lined cist in which was found a cremation burial, three bone implements, a bone needle and a bronze razor (listed as LBA by Piggott). Three bone implements (Acc No OA 285), the needle (Acc No OA 284), and the razor (Acc No 1909/116) are in Newbury Museum.

A central hollow is the only sign that the barrow has been dug. It is otherwise well preserved with a mound 1.4m high and ditch 0.9m deep.
Surveyed at 1:2500.

O.S. 495   P

SU 3522 6200   P

1. OS 6" 1961

2. Trans Newbury Dist FC 10 1954
21-22 (O G S Crawford)
3. PPS 12 1946 137 (C M Piggott)
4. Newbury Museum (Card Index)

GHP F1 30 9 63

5. G H Pitcher F1 30 9 63

NVQ

Naming of antiquities

It has long been an Ordnance Survey practice to use some form of Old English or Gothic lettering for the descriptive or proper names of antiquities.[1] The convention was developed by Crawford, who, in 1923, standardized Old English text for pre-Roman antiquities, Gothic text for post-Roman antiquities, and Egyptian capitals for Roman antiquities. In 1958, however, Gothic (now Lutheran) text was extended to pre-Roman antiquities, on the grounds that it was difficult to distinguish between Old English and Gothic and the cost of two separate type faces could not be justified. The use of sloping Egyptian types (now Gill Sans Roman) for lettering associated with find spots, irrespective of the date of object found, also originated in the nineteenth century. Gill Sans Roman is also currently used for parts of written archaeological entries other than proper or descriptive names. Where both proper and descriptive names are available for publication it is usual to publish the proper name only, printed in its period type, provided that it clearly describes the nature of the antiquity. If there is any ambiguity both names are published with the descriptive name printed in antiquity type.

Marking of antiquities

The antiquity symbol ₒ⅋ₒ was first brought into official use during the survey of Ireland. By marking sites and find spots of antiquities, it conveys the meaning that nothing, or very little, is to be seen on the ground. Visible earthwork antiquities, on the other hand, are depicted by slope hachures. This type of hachuring always indicates a slope downward from the 'head' to the 'tail' of the symbol but it has led to some confusion on small scale maps where the representation of small mounds inevitably resemble asterisks. Antiquity buildings are now shown in the same style as other buildings on the large scale maps, and the former convention of indicating ancient buildings by double line walls has been abandoned.[2]

Selection of antiquities for publication

Other considerations govern the final choice of antiquities. It will already be obvious from Chapters 3 to 9, that a regularly decreasing scale cannot result in the shedding of detail by neat geometrical progression. Factors such as the rarity of an antiquity, its condition, its local fame, its value as a spectacle, and the amount of space for its portrayal, have to be taken into account as well as the scale of the map. Standard Ordnance Survey maps fulfil many practical purposes and sheets cannot be saturated with archaeology at the expense of other detail: as a general rule, in a clash of interest, modern features take precedence over those of the past. At the same time, the demand for archaeology in map form is genuine, and ranges from the needs of amateur enthusiasts to that of serious students, or local authorities relying on large scale maps to help discharge their duty to preserve field monuments.[3] The Ordnance Survey is faced with satisfying professional users and yet providing a record of the past which is of wide interest.

The selection of antiquities for different scales is assisted by the relative historical and archaeological importance of the features themselves. Although there is no rigid gradation of 'importance' such a concept obviously underlies the selection of detail for derived maps, and is reflected in the summary

1 J. B. Harley (ed.), *Reprint of the First Edition of the One-inch Ordnance Survey . . .* sheet 24, Holyhead and Bangor (Newton Abbot, 1970); it seems to have originated in the survey of North Wales, *c.* 1820.

2 In 1951 the practice was discontinued.

3 *Report of the Committee of Enquiry into the Arrangements for the Protection of Field Monuments*, 1966–8 (HMSO, London, 1969), 26.

Table 21   A guide to the publication of antiquities on the standard Ordnance Survey map series

Categories of Antiquities	Examples*	Large scales**†	Small scales			
			1:25 000 †	1:63 360 §	1:50 000 §	1:250 000
1.1 Large imposing extant monuments	Hillforts, castles, henges, monasteries and abbeys, Roman forts, large historic houses	PPP	PPP	PPP	PPP	PPP
1.2 Smaller but imposing extant monuments	Long barrows, chambered cairns, mottes, large tumuli, smaller historic houses, disused churches, strong moats	PPP	PPP	PP	PP	P
1.3 Extensive but unimposing extant monuments	Enclosed settlements, deserted villages, field systems, manorial earthworks	PP	PP	P	P	X
1.4 Small and unimposing extant monuments	Small tumuli, fish ponds and moats, pond bays, disused chapels, standing stones	PP	PP	P	P	X
2.1 Sites of what were large imposing monuments	As for 1.1, but not historic houses	PP	PP	P	X	X
2.2 Sites of what were smaller but imposing monuments‡	As for 1.2, but not historic houses	PP	PP	PR	X	X
2.3 Sites of what were extensive but unimposing monuments‡	As for 1.3, also burial grounds	P	P	PR	X	X
2.4 Sites of what were small and unimposing monuments‡	As for the pre-1066 items under 1.4	P	P	PR	X	X
3.1 Found objects of general interest	Bronze Age hoards, hoards of coin or treasure, extensive debris, superior stone and bronze implements	PP	PP	X	X	X
3.2 Found objects of little general interest	Miscellaneous odd finds	X	X	X	X	X

PPP Publish even if considerable interference with other map detail.

PP Publish even if some interference with other map detail.

P Publish only if no interference with other map detail.

PR Publish but Roman sites only‡.

X Do not publish.

* No publication is ever made unless the siting is secure.

** Large scales: 1:1250; 1:2500; 1:10 560 and 1:10 000.

† Publication on the large scale maps and on the 1:25 000 is normally copied from the largest (basic) scale. Loss of space in reductions is compensated for by a smaller type-face.

‡ Roman sites, particularly villas, are traditionally favoured on the 1:63 360.

§ An antiquity publication entry on 1:63 360 or 1:50 000 will often be a condensed version of the form on larger scales, in the interests of space economy.

in Table 21. This offers little more than an illustration of the application of common sense, and it is a guide, not a rigid specification, for indicating the information depicted at different scales.

SPECIAL ARCHAEOLOGICAL AND HISTORICAL MAPS

A secondary use of the records compiled by the Ordnance Survey has been to provide material for special maps devoted to aspects of archaeology and history. Until 1966 these were known as the 'Period Maps', but thereafter as the 'Archaeological and Historical Maps'. They can be defined as specialized distribution maps, printed on bases of appropriate scale with modern detail either toned down or thinned out. Symbols and conventions for particular facets of prehistoric or historic cultures are used to plot the sites and positions of relevant monuments and finds. Maps in the series are an overall index to the state of knowledge at the date of their publication.

Archaeological and Historical Maps were encouraged by the Davidson Committee in 1938,[1] but their publication has been fitful. There is no statutory obligation to produce them and, consequently, they take second place to the maintenance of archaeology on the regular scales. There is, moreover, a current requirement that new maps in the series are only initiated where they are likely to be commercially self supporting.

Historical development

A sense of cultural obligation extending beyond the simple publication of antiquities on standard maps was strongly manifest in the Ordnance Survey's thinking by the mid nineteenth century. Between 1860 and 1880, for example, numerous facsimile copies of state documents (including the Domesday Book) were made by photo-zincography, and, in 1874, a facsimile was published of the fourteenth century Gough map of Great Britain. Sir Henry James, Director General from 1854 to 1875, in particular attempted to foster archaeology through example[2] and by exhortation to fellow officers.[3] In retrospect many nineteenth century publications were little more than amateur exercises, in line with the undeveloped status of archaeology as a discipline. Credit for the concept of the Period Map as a scientific tool belongs largely to O. G. S. Crawford. He was responsible for compiling fourteen such maps altogether, which are set out in Table 22.

All the maps on this list were published with the exception of the Amesbury sheet of the Celtic earthworks of Salisbury Plain, which reached only proof stage, and the Forth, Clyde, and Tay map, all the material for which was destroyed in 1940 by the air raid on Southampton. None of these maps is now in print.

In addition two other maps were in preparation in 1940:
Neolithic North East Britain,
Monastic Britain.
Material for the former was destroyed in the air raid but that for the latter was saved by the fact that its compiler, Mr Neville Hadcock, worked away from Southampton.

1 *Final Report* (1938), 18.

2 Sir Henry James, *Notes on the Great Pyramid of Egypt, and the Cubits used in its Design* (Southampton, 1869).

3 In Sir Henry James, *Plans and Photographs of Stonehenge, and of Turusachan in the Island of Lewis, with Notes Relating to the Druids, and Sketches of Cromlechs in Ireland* (Southampton, 1867), for example, the work was to be '. . . circulated for the information of the Officers on the Ordnance Survey, in the hope that it may stimulate them to make Plans and Sketches, and to give Descriptive Remarks of such objects of Antiquity as they may meet with during the progress of the Survey of the Kingdom'.

Table 22 'Period' maps compiled under the direction of Crawford, 1923–38

Date	Subject	Scale
1923	A Map of Ancient Winchester, the Celtic Caer Gwent and Roman Venta Belgarum	1:5280
1924	Map of Roman Britain, First Edition	1:1 000 000
1930	Seventeenth century England	1:1 000 000
1930	International Map of the Roman Empire, Sheet NN 30 (covering the Midlands and south Scotland)*	1:1 000 000
1931	Map of Roman Britain, Second Edition	1:1 000 000
1932	Neolithic Wessex	1:253 440
1933	Map of the Trent Basin showing the distribution of long barrows and megaliths (Neolithic map)	1:253 440
1934	International Map of the Roman Empire, Sheet NO 30 (covering north Scotland)*	1:1 000 000
1935	Britain in the Dark Ages, South sheet	1:1 000 000
1936	Map of South Wales showing the distribution of long barrows and megaliths (Neolithic map)	1:253 440
1936	Scotland in Roman Times: Forth, Clyde and Tay area	1:253 440
1937	Celtic Earthworks of Salisbury Plain, Old Sarum sheet	1:25 000
c. 1938	Celtic Earthworks of Salisbury Plain, Amesbury sheet	1:25 000
1938	Britain in the Dark Ages, North sheet	1:1 000 000

* R. A. Gardiner, 'The International Map of the Roman Empire', *The Geographical Journal*, **139** (1973), 107–11, for a description and index.

The pre-1939 'Period Maps' met with varied success. One or two titles were outstandingly popular, but others, although well justified as archaeological exercises, did not reach a wide public. The most successful map was Roman Britain. The first edition was a modest affair, showing little more than the road system, with the towns and principal sites, but it was so enthusiastically received that Crawford was encouraged to prepare a second edition. This was more ambitious, increasing the features shown by symbols and adding a hypothetical reconstruction of the forest areas of the Roman period. It continued to be a successful map until after 1945. The map Seventeenth century England, on the other hand, departed from Crawford's original concept and, drawing on historical as well as archaeological data, portrayed a relatively modern period. Specific features were the road system, derived from Ogilby's *Britannia* (1675), the sites of Civil War battles, as well as the main towns, ports, mining and other centres. It was unfortunately a financial failure. A series of Neolithic maps, planned to cover the whole country at 1:253 440 scale, and laying emphasis on the distribution of long barrows and chambered cairns, were likewise only of limited appeal, as was the Salisbury Plain 'Celtic' map, a reconstruction of the Iron Age Romano-British landscape of a classic archaeological hunting ground but, inevitably perhaps, more of academic than of popular interest.

Owing partly to lack of success with some maps, in Britain in the Dark Ages, the last important map to be produced before 1940, Crawford re-verted to the original approach of the 'Period Maps'. Like Roman Britain, the two sheets of the new map covered the whole country and portrayed its life pattern in the period A.D. 410 to 871. They enjoyed a considerable measure of success.

During World War II there was a gap in archaeological work, and the preparation and publication of 'Period Maps', in common with other tasks, ceased. After 1945 the production of the map of Monastic Britain was completed but, at the same time, a new policy was evolved. New editions were approved for the maps of Roman Britain and Britain in the Dark Ages, with the possibility of their scales being enlarged from 1:1 000 000 to 1:625 000 when new editions were being prepared, but other pre-1939 maps were not to be renewed. Future maps were to fall into three categories:

(a) General maps covering all, or a great portion, of the whole of Great Britain, dealing with specific periods or cultures in all their aspects capable of cartographic expression (i.e. 'Period Maps' as originally conceived such as Roman Britain);

(b) Thematic maps showing the distribution and character of features having a greater or lesser currency through the country for varying periods of time (i.e. distribution maps such as Monastic Britain);

(c) Individual monuments (e.g. Hadrian's Wall).

A programme was prepared in the light of these principles and a complete list of the post-1945 Archaeological and Historical Maps so far produced is shown in Table 23.

The future will be influenced as much by commercial considerations as by the desirability of new projects or the need to revise existing maps. All the current maps will eventually need revising as new archaeological research becomes available and, in turn, this growing mass of detail makes an increase of scale essential if some maps are to continue to show the same features (there is sufficient data, for example, to publish a map of Roman Britain at least at 1:625 000 scale). Resources permitting, there also are gaps which could be plugged in the present list both in geographical terms (completing a map of Iron Age Britain, for example) and in terms of time period.

Table 23 Archaeological and Historical maps published since 1945

Date	Subject	Scale
1950	Monastic Britain (South sheet), First edition	1:625 000
1950	Monastic Britain (North sheet), First edition	1:625 000
1951	Ancient Britain (South sheet)	1:625 000
1951	Ancient Britain (North sheet)	1:625 000
1954	Monastic Britain (South sheet), Second edition	1:625 000
1955	Monastic Britain (North sheet), Second edition	1:625 000
1956	Roman Britain, Third edition	1:1 000 000
1962	Southern Britain in the Iron Age	1:625 000
1964	Hadrian's Wall, First edition	1:31 680
1964	Ancient Britain (South sheet), Second edition	1:625 000
1964	Ancient Britain (North sheet), Second edition	1:625 000
1966	Britain in the Dark Ages, Second edition	1:1 000 000
1969	The Antonine Wall	1:25 000
1972	Hadrian's Wall, Second edition	1:31 680
1974	Britain before the Norman Conquest	1:625 000

ARCHAEOLOGICAL AND HISTORICAL MAPS CURRENTLY AVAILABLE

The notes which follow give brief descriptions of the archaeological and historical maps currently available from the Ordnance Survey.[1]

Southern Britain in the Iron Age

The map of Southern Britain in the Iron Age is published at a scale of 1:625 000 and covers the area south of an east/west line through Richmond (Yorkshire). The sheet measures $41\frac{1}{2} \times 33\frac{1}{4}$ in and is available in either a flat or folded form. Like the maps of Roman Britain and Britain in the Dark Ages, it gives a composite picture of the archaeological evidence for a long period, from the beginning of the fifth century B.C. to the middle of the first century A.D. The base is a physical map, on which are imposed twenty-two different symbols using four colours, black, red, purple, and brown, to distinguish four cultural phases of Iron Age life and, by combination of symbols, the occurrence of foreign imports. Contemporary tribal areas are indicated and also the names of coastal and water features according to Ptolemy. Otherwise the only names are those of rivers printed in blue and the modern names of sites and features to help with identification. The folded map is accompanied by an explanatory text, which includes a chronological table of the period, a study (with eight distribution maps) of the find spots of pre-Roman coins, and a gazetteer listing sites arranged in categories according to the map symbols, and in numerical order of the National Grid with the numbers added of the appropriate 1:63 360 sheet.

Roman Britain

The third edition of the map of Roman Britain, published in 1956 at a scale of 1:1 000 000 is a direct successor to Crawford's map, preserving something of its style and basic approach. It measures $32\frac{1}{2} \times 42\frac{1}{2}$ in and is available either as a flat sheet or as a folded version. The period of Roman occupation is defined as A.D. 43 to 410 and one reflection of an increasing knowledge of its archaeology is that the symbols employed on the map have risen from nineteen in 1931 to thirty-four in 1956. The current map offers a closer definition of site character: Crawford's general class of villas, for example, is broken down into three categories: 'undoubted villas', 'bath houses', and 'buildings of uncertain purpose'. Archaeological features are still printed on a coloured physical base map, but the stipple indicating forest on the second edition has been omitted, partly to help clarify a map which was becoming overcrowded, and partly because modern research did not support the existence of so much contemporary woodland. The 1931 map extended north to Aberdeen to cover all areas seriously affected by Roman penetration but the 1956 edition covers the whole of Great Britain. It shows land and water communications, military sites, settlements, temples, villas and other buildings, with the additional refinement that coloured symbols distinguish between classes of features such as military sites (red), civil sites (black), industrial sites (purple), and agricultural areas (dark green).

The folded map is accompanied by an explanatory text which includes a chronological table for the period 55 B.C. to A.D. 446, five supplementary distribution maps, an index of Roman place-names and their identifications,

[1] Fuller details in some cases will be found in papers by C. W. Phillips, former Archaeology Officer of the Ordnance Survey. These include 'The Ordnance Survey and Archaeology 1791–1960', *The Geographical Journal*, **127** (1961), 1–9; 'The Special Archaeological and Historical Maps Published by the Ordnance Survey', *The Cartographic Journal*, **2** (1965), 27–31; and 'The Period Maps of the Ordnance Survey', Chapter 4 of J. B. Harley and C. W. Phillips, 35–41.

and a topographical index in which sites are arranged in categories according to the symbols used on the map. Within each category these sites are listed in numerical National Grid reference order, together with the number of the 1:63 360 sheet on which they fall.

Britain in the Dark Ages

The map of Britain in the Dark Ages is at a scale of 1 : 1 000 000 and, although the first edition was issued in two sheets, the second edition was published in 1966 as one sheet. It is available in either flat or folded form with the flat sheet measuring $32\frac{1}{2} \times 44\frac{1}{2}$ in. Following the style of the second edition of the map of Roman Britain, the archaeology is printed on a physical base, including a reconstruction of the inferred distribution of ancient forest. The map covers the period A.D. 410 to 871 and employs forty-five symbols to represent a wide variety of features, including cemeteries, crosses, memorial stones, and (in Scotland) Pictish symbol stones. All evidence of Celtic activity is printed in blue; pagan Anglo-Saxon features are printed in black; and those of the Christian age in red. Place-names are in contemporary spellings and the Roman road system is also incorporated.

The folded map is accompanied by an explanatory text, containing a bibliography and a gazetteer listing separately the different types of features shown on the map by parishes, with their National Grid references and 1:63 360 sheet numbers.

Britain before the Norman Conquest

The map of Britain before the Norman Conquest is to be published in 1974 in two sheets, North and South, both at a scale of 1:625 000. Each sheet measures $41\frac{3}{4} \times 33$ in and while the flat sheets are each available separately without the text, the version bound in hard covers, which contains the text, includes *both* North and South sheets in a pocket at the back of the book. The map is a direct sequel to Britain in the Dark Ages and covers the period from A.D. 871 to 1066. Its principal aim is to portray the distribution of evidence for Anglo-Saxon, Scandinavian, and Celtic features in the two centuries before the Norman Conquest. The scope of the map extends to both archaeological and place-name evidence, with this historical detail being printed on a modern base showing relief and drainage. To this the Roman road system has been added and symbols employing blue for Celtic features, red for Scandinavian features, and black for Anglo-Saxon features are combined to show information common to the whole map (i.e. to both North and South sheets), and also that peculiar in turn to England, to Wales and to Scotland and Man. The symbols for towns are graded according to category. An inset map shows the Welsh Cantrefs.

The text describes the compilation of the map and includes a historical summary of the period, a general account of the Scandinavian settlement in Britain, and a fuller history of Norse activity in Scotland, Wales and the Isle of Man. Other sections deal with towns and fortifications in late Anglo-Saxon England, and with the Church in Britain, A.D. 871 to 1066. There is a bibliography and a classified index of places and features on the map: the latter gives National Grid references to six figures, names of counties in which places or features occur, and the numbers of the 1:63 360 sheets on which they are located.

Ancient Britain

The map of Ancient Britain was first published in 1951 in two sheets, North and South, both at a scale of 1:625 000. Each sheet measures $42\frac{1}{2} \times 33\frac{1}{2}$ in and they are available in either flat or folded versions. The original purpose of the map was as a guide to the antiquities of Britain for visitors in the 1951 'Festival of Britain' year. It depicts the principal archaeological sites older than A.D. 1066 (over 1000 in all) which are worth visiting because they have visible remains. The archaeological detail is published on a modern topographical base to facilitate the planning of visits to sites, printed in grey and with relief indicated by layer colours. Special symbols distinguish seven main periods between the Palaeolithic[1] and the Dark Ages, and other symbols indicate museums, linear earthworks (including Roman roads), and sites of uncertain age. A revised edition was published in 1964.

The folded version includes an explanatory text which provides a bibliography, a list of museums, and an index in alphabetical order giving a short description and the 'age' of each antiquity, together with its National Grid reference and the number of the 1:63 360 sheet on which it falls.

Monastic Britain

The map of Monastic Britain, like that of Britain before the Norman Conquest, was published at a scale of 1:625 000 in two sheets, North and South, each measuring $42\frac{1}{2} \times 33\frac{1}{2}$ in and likewise available in either flat or folded versions. Monastic Britain was largely compiled by 1940 but, owing to World War II, the first edition was not published until 1950. Its aim was to show the distribution and character of all known monastic sites in Britain which existed between A.D. 1066 and 1539. A modern base map, derived from the topographical sheets of the regular 1:625 000 series, was printed in grey, but the main design problem was to represent the complexity of the distribution of the religious orders. Symbols representing no less than thirty-seven variables had to be devised. Using black and red printings they were combined to distinguish establishments belonging to monks, nuns, friars, military knights, and alien priories dependent on continental houses; the relative importance of such houses (using three sizes of symbols and lettering); and also to differentiate between religious houses which were dissolved or had moved by A.D. 1500 and those which had survived beyond that date. The movements of some houses and collegiate churches were also represented by special symbols. The intricacy of ecclesiastical boundaries (dioceses, especially in Scotland and south-east England, often included detached and fragmented areas known as 'peculiars') required a system of abbreviations (for example c for Canterbury), also overprinted in red. New editions of the sheets, which incorporated new research, especially in Scotland, were published in 1954–5.

The folded sheets are accompanied by an explanatory text including a bibliography and an index showing the relevant map references. The text of the North sheet applies only to Scotland.

Hadrian's Wall

The map of Hadrian's Wall, depicting a single monument at a relatively large scale, was a new development among the archaeological maps of the Ordnance Survey. A scale of 1:31 680 was selected to show the whole length

1 On the North sheet the sequence of periods begins with the Neolithic.

of the feature, running from the mouth of the Tyne to the Solway Firth nearly due east and west for 90 miles across the north of England. The base consisted of a series of strips of the regular 1:25 000 maps covering the area, slightly reduced in scale, and placed successively on a sheet measuring $42 \times 32\frac{1}{2}$ in, so that the eastern end of the feature began at the top right corner and the western end finished at the bottom left of the map. The scale was sufficiently large, subject to its general limitations, to allow many details to be shown in simplified plan form. Forts and camps and lesser features of the Wall, such as mile-castles and turrets, could be depicted in this manner. It was also possible to indicate the limits of civil settlements and to plot the lines of aqueducts with precision. Symbols were only required for minor features such as bridges, quarries, shrines, watermills, and milestones. Since a knowledge of the relationship of the Wall to ground relief enhances an appreciation of its siting, hill shading was added to reinforce the contours on the base maps. Features still visible on the ground are printed in black; the sites of former features appear in red. There is no separate explanatory text but the cover of the folded version includes a bibliography on the Wall and a schedule listing features under the protection of the Ancient Monuments Act. A second edition was published in 1972.

The Antonine Wall

The map of the Antonine Wall is a companion to that of Hadrian's Wall. Archaeological data are plotted on a base derived from the standard 1:25 000 series, but, in this case, without reduction. The material is again arranged as a series of strips showing the line of the Wall, with the composite map measuring $42 \times 33\frac{1}{2}$ in. Methods of representation are similar to those on the map of Hadrian's Wall: relief is strengthened by hill shading, for example, and remains identifiable on the ground are printed in black, with other sites in red. A brief description of the Wall is given on the map, which is available either flat or folded with an integral cover.

Field Archaeology in Great Britain

No description of the archaeological publications of the Ordnance Survey would be complete without reference to this book which is not only a textbook on principles of field archaeology but also enshrines much of the Survey's approach to archaeological matters. The first edition of *Field Archaeology* (1921), was largely written by Crawford as an Ordnance Survey Professional Paper. The text was substantially revised for the second and third editions of 1932 and 1951, respectively, and again for the fourth edition of 1963 and for the current fifth edition published in 1973. An Introduction describing the purpose and scope of the book is followed by a section on field techniques, including the use of air photographs and the recognition of archaeological sites on the ground, and an illustrated note on time scales. There follow period-by-period descriptions of the main recognizable antiquities of Britain, with emphasis laid on the characteristics by which they are distinguished. The prehistoric, Roman, and medieval periods are covered, with an extension into industrial archaeology. The book is illustrated with twenty-eight line drawings depicting the ground plans of a variety of representative antiquities ranging from stone-age tombs to medieval earthworks. The book concludes with a comprehensive bibliography and an index.

Facsimile editions of early maps

The Ordnance Survey still publishes three reproductions of early maps. Such reproductions were first developed under Sir Henry James in the 1860s and the first map to be published, by photo-zincography in c. 1861, was of the escheated counties of Ulster, 1609–10. It was followed in the next decade by the Bodleian map noted below.

BODLEIAN MAP OF GREAT BRITAIN c. A.D. 1360

The map of Great Britain, variously known as the 'Gough Map', the 'Anonymous Map', and the 'Bodleian Map', was first published by the Ordnance Survey, using photo-zincography, in 1874. The original has been dated to c. 1360 and such was its wealth of detail, particularly of the contemporary road system, that it may have been an administrative map for royal officials.[1] It was to exert a crucial influence, which persisted into the sixteenth century, on the content of subsequent maps of Great Britain. The Ordnance Survey 'facsimile' is in effect a hand copied transcription rather than a direct photographic copy. Outline and other details are printed in black and ancient names are transcribed and printed in red. The reproduction, available as a flat sheet only, measures $42\frac{1}{2} \times 24$ in.

SYMONSON'S MAP OF KENT

'A New Description of Kent', surveyed by Philip Symonson, and engraved by Charles Whitwell, was published in 1596. Although it owed much to the earlier map of Christopher Saxton, it was one of the most detailed English regional maps to appear before 1600. Not only was it the earliest map of Kent to show roads, but degrees of latitude and longitude were incorporated in its border, and a remarkably successful attempt was also made to represent the true appearance of churches and windmills by means of pictograph drawings. The copy reproduced by the Ordnance Survey, first published in 1914 and reissued in 1968, is not printed from the first edition but from a later version reissued by London map-seller Peter Stent (*fl.* 1641–65) and bearing his imprint.[2] The impression in the facsimile can therefore be dated to c. 1650. It measures 38×30 in and is available as a flat sheet only.

ORDNANCE SURVEY ONE-INCH MAP OF THE SOUTHAMPTON AREA

Sheet 11 of the Ordnance Survey *Old Series* 1:63 360 maps, named Winchester, was published on 10 April 1810. The sheet covers an area bounded by Lymington, Chichester, and Winchester, including Southampton and Portsmouth, and it was engraved on a single copper plate in a style characteristic of the early cartography of the Ordnance Survey. After 1810 the copper plate was revised periodically for the addition of railways and other new developments, and sheets were printed from electrotype copies of the original copper plate as late as the 1890s.[3] The Ordnance Survey reproduction is printed from the 'Index to the Tithe Survey' version, for which a duplicate electrotype plate was probably made c. 1850, and a principal characteristic of which is the addition of parish boundaries omitted from earlier printings. A number of railways had also been added to the plate by this date, but otherwise it shows much of the original topography of c. 1810. The sheet measures $32\frac{1}{2} \times 26\frac{1}{2}$ in and is available in flat form only.

1 An authoritative account of the map prefaces another facsimile edition, edited by E. J. S. Parsons, *The Map of Great Britain, c. A.D. 1360 known as the Gough Map* . . . (Oxford, Bodleian Library and Royal Geographical Society, London, 1958).

2 A recent discussion of the map is by R. A. Gardiner, 'Philip Symonson's "New Description of Kent", 1596', *The Geographical Journal*, **135** (1969), 136–7, and ibid. **136** (1970), 312–13.

3 J. B. Harley (ed.), *Reprint of the First Edition of the One-inch Ordnance Survey* . . ., sheet 86, Winchester (Newton Abbot, 1969), gives a fuller description of the printing history of the sheet, setting the Ordnance Survey reproduction in a fuller bibliographical context.

The accuracy of Ordnance Survey maps

11

In so far as earlier chapters have dealt with the specifications and methods of production of the main map series of the Ordnance Survey a discussion of accuracy is implicit throughout the book. Map users have been introduced as much to the limitations as to the potentialities of different map series to help in choosing appropriate applications for practical and academic purposes. But accuracy is such a fundamental issue and of universal concern in one way or another that a general chapter devoted to its meaning in relation to current Ordnance Survey maps is a suitable ending to a book of this nature. Accuracy is a relative rather than an absolute concept as far as cartography is concerned. It cannot be endowed with a rigid definition such as 'in exact conformity to truth' or 'free from error or defect';[1] not only are maps deliberate generalizations of reality, 'representational models of the real world'[2], but all survey and map production processes inevitably introduce error at some stage. What the map user as well as the map maker should be concerned with is a systematic study of factors affecting error, and to seek to establish their causes and variability and the statistical parameters by which error is characterized. It must be recognized that tolerable error is deliberately related to the required accuracy of the end product and is then achieved by the use of appropriate methods and equipment but without providing unnecessary accuracy for the specification. The cost of surveying and map production is also a major constraint and to double the accuracy of a large scale map series would, it has been estimated, far more than double its cost. Both survey and production costs have to seek the best compromise between technical and economic variables.

The concept of accuracy

A whole range of answers can therefore be given to the simple question 'How accurate is the map?' We have already seen how the varying attributes of Ordnance Survey maps are influenced by the surveying and production processes (Chapter 1), by the projection employed for the national surveys as a whole (Chapter 2), as well as by the detailed specifications for individual map series (Chapter 3–10). Levels of accuracy obviously vary with scale, but not uniformly so, and features are often emphasized at the expense of others. Even on the basic scales therefore, not a single, but groups of interrelated yet variable standards of accuracy exist: the more precise question, 'Accuracy of what?', has to be asked about any map. There may be different tolerances (as will be demonstrated) for accuracy of position, for data on altitudes, and for various types of topographical detail, each non-comparable yet all compounded in the concept of map accuracy. Differential accuracies may also occur within the same class of data as with primary, secondary, and tertiary levelling and if we add to these possibilities accidental errors arising from human or mechanical failing, it will be seen that accuracy has many facets. It is only possible in practice to consider specific aspects of the accuracy of maps and Ordnance Survey research into accuracy has been focused on a series of routine tests concerned with specialized attributes of the basic scale maps.

Map users must also pose the question 'Accuracy for what?' A potential difficulty is that the more specialized a map becomes, the less likely is it to meet the accuracy requirements of non-specialist users, with the converse that on a multi-purpose map series, the specialist may find information which

1 *Standards of Accuracy and Limits of Error for Plans and Surveys of Mines* (Joint Report of the Committees of the Chartered Surveyors' Institution and the Institution of Mine Surveyors, London, The Chartered Surveyors' Institution, 1935).

2 C. Board, 'Maps as Models' in R. J. Chorley and P. Haggett (eds.), *Models in Geography* (London, 1967), 671–725.

interests him most is shown to an insufficient level of accuracy or detail. While, for example, the accuracy of contours as shown by the Ordnance Survey, is perfectly acceptable to the ordinary user, to a civil engineer or to a geomorphologist engaged in morphometric analysis of terrain it may fall below a useful standard.

Similarly, although the outline of a patch of woodland may have been surveyed to a standard appropriate for use by a solicitor in a document of conveyance, if for some reason it had been wrongly classified in botanical terms, then the information would be of little value to a student of ecological change in woodland areas. The fact that a national survey organization sometimes has to choose between conflicting interests of majority and minority users makes it even more dangerous to make glib generalizations about the accuracy of its maps.

Ordnance Survey policy on accuracy testing

It is current Ordnance Survey policy to carry out routine accuracy tests on its basic maps. Even if the concept of accuracy ought not properly to embrace 'whole' maps, it is essential to ensure that single features are shown, as far as possible, to the same accuracy level throughout a standard map series. The main role of current accuracy tests is to monitor the published maps and, at the same time, to provide information on the accuracy of completed surveys for dissemination to users and for planning future surveys and map production. With this in mind, over the last decade or so, basic surveys have been tested in their finished form by statistical analysis of sample accuracy tests using methods superior in accuracy to the original survey. Such methods have largely developed since 1956 when the accuracy of 1 : 1250 maps produced by various methods was first investigated. Tests were later extended (1960) to the 1 : 10 560 series but, until 1970, accuracy testing was carried out largely on an *ad hoc* basis.

After 1970 a new programme of regular tests was developed. They are carried out for the following:

(*a*) 1 : 1250 resurvey and continuous revision (planimetric)[1]

(*b*) 1 : 2500 resurvey and continuous revision (planimetric)

(*c*) 1 : 10 000 resurvey and continuous revision (planimetric and contour)

(*d*) 1 : 2500 overhaul and continuous revision (planimetric)

(*e*) contouring for the derived 1 : 10 000

For all these categories sufficient testing is currently undertaken to provide statistically sound evidence of their accuracy. Tests are given to approximately 3 per cent of the maps (or information) in each category. These are generally selected at random but include any with alleged excessive errors reported by a reliable source.

It will be appreciated that the standards which are currently accepted have grown up, like the practice of testing, in an *ad hoc* fashion. They were not set down prior to launching new map series and thereafter adhered to: the mode of development of the Ordnance Survey, constantly incurring a legacy of survey data and published maps, has inhibited an 'ideal' situation in which standards were pre-determined and then all maps made to conform. On the contrary, Ordnance Survey map-makers have always had to work within the constraints of inherited triangulations, levellings, topographical

1 In Ordnance Survey usage accuracy of position.

field sheets, and published maps. The fact, for example, that much of the post-1945 large scales programme has taken the form of an overhaul of a pre-1939 survey has, despite experiments to achieve the best method of adaptation,[1] imposed absolute limits to the accuracy which can be achieved. The role of earlier survey operations in determining present-day accuracies should always be borne in mind.

Methods of accuracy testing of the detail survey

Accuracy of position, as determined by triangulation, has always concerned the Ordnance Survey in so far as it provides the framework on which maps at all scales rest. Even with sophisticated instruments and skilled observers it is a starting assumption that the horizontal (or planimetric) control must (and does) suffer from errors of position, scale, and orientation. Inaccuracies in the control framework can be assessed and monitored in the field by new measurements made between trigonometrical points.

In the case of the primary triangulation, it has proved more convenient to state the estimated errors in terms of scale and azimuth, rather than of position by means of co-ordinates. To this end – to provide evidence for scale assessment – electromagnetic distance measurements of over 190 sides of the primary triangulation have been made since the early 1960s. The results suggest that on average the primary triangulation is 15 parts per million (ppm) too large and, to obtain a better accuracy, triangulation lengths computed from published co-ordinates should be reduced by this amount. It appears from the evidence of astronomical observations that the azimuths of the primary triangulation may be in error by up to 5 seconds.

The great bulk of accuracy testing relating to points of detail, is, however, done by comparing the accuracy on the basic maps with an independent survey, to establish the displacement of map details compared with their surveyed positions. Such accuracy tests were first carried out on the field documents (butt-joint plates for the 1:1250 scale resurvey and transparent plastic sheets for the 1:2500 overhaul) and were later repeated using the same check points on published paper maps. The problem of distortion in the paper map was largely avoided during these tests by reading map co-ordinates from the nearest grid intersection, and the investigation revealed that the fair drawing and reproduction processes had introduced only negligible errors on the 1:1250 and 1:2500 series. Accuracy tests could therefore be carried out on published paper copies, albeit with a disadvantage that the co-ordinates so measured evaluate only the final accumulation of error of all stages in the survey and production processes.

The main strategy in accuracy testing is to compare the co-ordinates of randomly selected points of detail on the map being tested with the National Grid co-ordinates of the same points computed from instrumental field survey or supplied by aerial triangulation. There is no hard and fast rule about the number of check points. In 1:1250 areas an attempt is made to check all types of detail, both control detail and field completion detail. A sample of up to 150 points of each type of detail may be selected for a test and an individual area under investigation could have 500 or more test points. For 1:2500 overhauled maps the co-ordination of check points is done by aerial triangulation methods using suitable strips of photography, generally at 1:7500 scale, and with triangulation control at the end of the strips. Aerial

1 Ordnance Survey, *The Overhaul . . .*, *passim.*

M

triangulation generally requires control on every eighth stereogram along the strip, and this sometimes needs extra ground control by instrumental methods. As the co-ordinates produced by these accuracy tests – irrespective of the exact method – are derived from a check by an order of survey higher than the original survey, they are taken to be without error for the purposes of the test. The differences between the check co-ordinates and the map co-ordinates are accordingly considered as errors rather than residuals. From these values three separate measures of accuracy can be derived:

ROOT MEAN SQUARE ERROR

As the errors (since there is no mean) cannot be considered in terms of standard deviation, the root mean square error is calculated by

$$r = \sqrt{\frac{\Sigma x^2}{n}}$$

where x_1, x_2, . . .x_n are the errors at n check points.

This can be used to evaluate the overall accuracy of the survey, with the root mean square error being calculated in either metres on the ground or millimetres on the map. Errors in contouring may be expressed in the same way.

SYSTEMATIC ERROR

It may also be necessary to examine the consistency of the survey on one or a group of sheets. If the errors are random then

$$\Sigma x = 0$$

and the consistency of the survey is its root mean square error.

If, however,

$$\Sigma x \neq 0$$

it means that an overall shift has been introduced (with systematic errors in eastings and northings being related, for example, to the inaccurate graphic fixation of a triangulation station) and this average error (systematic error) is given by

$$s = \bar{x} = \frac{\Sigma x}{n}.$$

STANDARD ERROR

The consistency of the survey is then found by taking this systematic error from the individual errors at each check point and this gives

$$\sigma = \sqrt{\frac{\Sigma(x-\bar{x})^2}{n}}.$$

This value, in Ordnance Survey usage, is called the *Standard Error* and it can also be expressed

$$\sigma = \sqrt{(r^2 - s^2)}.$$

From this it can be seen that Standard Error can never exceed the root mean square error; in fact it is always less, except when $s = 0$. By use of Standard Error the random or accidental component in the inaccuracy can be isolated and the Standard Error provides an estimate of the range on either side of the best results by fallible observations within which the true results may be expected to lie. The results of a typical routine accuracy test, embodying the three measures of accuracy, are set out in Table 24.

Table 24 Results of routine accuracy test undertaken on the 1:1250 map relating to Lowestoft, Suffolk

Edition	Number of points	Number of plans	Root mean square error			Systematic error			Standard error			Max Vector
			E	N	Vector*	E	N	Vector*	E	N	Vector*	RMSE
A	34	3	±0.32	±0.24	0.40	+0.09	+0.07	0.11	±0.31	±0.23	0.39	1.02
B	71	3	±0.33	±0.27	0.43	+0.15	+0.06	0.16	±0.29	±0.26	0.39	1.24
C	91	3	±0.33	±0.29	0.44	+0.13	+0.04	0.14	±0.30	±0.29	0.42	1.24
D	129	3	±0.30	±0.28	0.41	+0.13	+0.04	0.14	±0.27	±0.28	0.39	1.24
E	126	2	±0.28	±0.25	0.38	+0.13	+0.06	0.14	±0.25	±0.24	0.35	1.24
F	72	1	±0.34	±0.28	0.44	+0.17	+0.03	0.17	±0.29	±0.28	0.40	1.24

All distances are in metres.

* The vector is the distance between the 'true' position (revealed by the check survey) and its position on the map.

E Eastings
N Northings
RMSE root mean square error

The tests reported in this table were designed to determine the accuracy of successive revisions in an area where five or six editions of a map had been produced. The number of points co-ordinated in the test was 176, equivalent to 235 points per km square. The result was that the systematic and standard errors, and therefore the differences between editions, were within the normal[1] limits to be tolerated at this scale. There was no evidence to suggest that accuracy had deteriorated with successive editions and all values were in general equal to the accuracy of the initial survey.

Accuracy testing of a sample of new sheets thus provides a statistical yard-stick by which the accuracy of map detail, both in different parts of the country and through time, can be assessed and maintained as new surveys are published. As well as the routine testing of new surveys – the data from which can either be tabulated or the vectors shown in map form (Figure 32) to pinpoint the location of accidental error at a glance – tests can be initiated in special circumstances. These include reported difficulties in carrying out Land Registry surveys; those owing to discrepancies between Ordnance Survey maps and work undertaken by commercial air survey firms; and as part of the Ordnance Survey's own research programme into new techniques and materials for map-making.

Probabilities of error in planimetric position

The example of an accuracy test given in Table 24 related to the testing of maps in a small area, but, taken together, the programme of accuracy tests has enabled a number of general statements to be made about the planimetric accuracy of Ordnance Survey maps at the basic scales. The most important is that the basic surveys can be given numerical criteria relating to their expected accuracies and above which they are reinvestigated as unacceptable (Table 25).

In this table criteria of acceptability are quoted in terms of root mean square error. Although some map users require to know the relative accuracy between points of detail, indicated by the standard error, the development of electromagnetic measuring equipment has meant that it is now much more common for professional surveyors to measure between triangulation stations across sheet edges and triangulation block boundaries. To evaluate the accuracy of such measurements it is necessary to have a knowledge of the

[1] The Normal Distribution of error is assumed to be:

Multiple of standard error σ		% of points falling within this multiple of σ
0.6745 σ	(pe)	50.0
1.0 σ		68.3
1.5 σ		86.6
2.0 σ		95.5
2.5 σ		98.8
3.0 σ		99.7

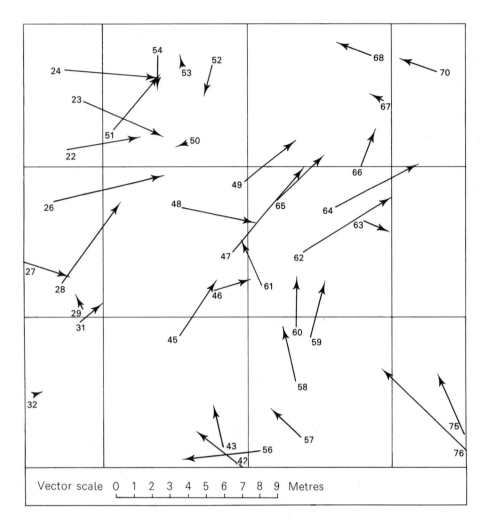

Figure 32
Vectors plotted from an
accuracy test on a 1:2500
overhaul map

The vectors are a diagrammatic
representation at 1:25 000 of map
detail errors on 1:2500 maps in part
of an area subjected to a test of
accuracy. The test was initiated to
determine if the accuracy of the map
detail, after gridding, was of an
acceptable standard to commence
revision. The vector numbers are in a
sequence order related to an area
larger than the diagram.

Table 25   Criteria of acceptability for maps at the basic scales

Type of Survey	Root mean square error
1:1250 resurvey and continuous revision	0.4 metres
1:2500 resurvey and continuous revision	0.8 metres
1:2500 overhaul and continuous revision	2.5 metres
1:10 000 resurvey and continuous revision	3.5 metres

systematic error (imposed by such factors as the malpositioning of the grid)
and thus it is the root mean square error which is the relevant criterion.

The maximum expected error in any test accepted by the field accuracy
testing group of the Ordnance Survey is defined as three times the standard
error plus the systematic error. It has already been noted that in a normal
test up to 150 points of each type of detail might be selected and this could
produce some 500 check points or more; the probability of the error at a
single point falling outside $2\frac{1}{2} \times$ the standard error is approximately 1 in 80,
and outside $3 \times$ standard error is 1 in 375: therefore $3 \times$ standard error is
accepted as being reasonable for the maximum expected random error.
When, in any test, the criterion of acceptability is exceeded, further investigations are conducted to determine at what stage of the survey the error was
incurred. The mixing or modifying of surveying processes, such as the use of
air machine survey to assist 1:2500 overhaul methods, the change of meridian

boundary within a 1:2500 overhaul map, or the use of different types of instrumental survey within a 1:1250 map, are factors which can lead to the tracing of unacceptable errors in map sheets. A resurvey may be authorized with the check survey providing additional points of control. Table 25 also stresses that differences in accuracy of Ordnance Survey basic maps are a direct reflection of survey methods. The greater errors in the 1:2500 over-hauled series are related to the fact that they were originally surveyed between 75 and 115 years ago and over this period have accumulated errors during the processes of revision, drawing, and reproduction largely because suitable non-distorting materials for drawing were not available until after 1945. When the overhaul method was adopted as a result of the recommendation of the Davidson Committee, the consequent lower standard of accuracy had to be weighed against the urgent need for up to date maps and the far longer time it would have taken to complete a resurvey.

The position of detail on the basic maps of the Ordnance Survey is thus accurate within *defined* limits and therefore for specific purposes. For most users the standards of the overhauled 1:2500 maps are adequate and they are suitable, for example, for management of land, for planning, and for keeping records. If, on the other hand, a greater precision of position is required the maps may be inadequate. When, for example, the National Coal Board needs to establish a relationship between underground workings and surface features, perhaps when a rescue operation has to be planned, a higher accuracy is necessary.

Accuracy testing of levelling and contours

For the same reason as accuracies of position can vary, so too does the accuracy with which the information on height is rendered on the basic maps of the Ordnance Survey. The variables include the order of levelling and particular technique from which the values are derived and, similarly with contours, the method of their survey and plotting. The published values of height also depend on the datum which was in use (see p. 55), but it should be remembered that the practical information required by surveyors, as when choosing a line of levels, is frequently the relative difference of height between adjacent bench marks, a figure which is independent of datum. The estimates below provide an assessment, as established by surveying techniques of varying reliability, of the maximum error in these height differences.

Spirit levelling

As far as bench marks are concerned the following maximum errors (Table 26) between bench marks on the same levelling line up to 2 miles (3.25 km) apart are currently accepted:

Table 26 Estimated maximum errors in the difference of height between landmarks (on levelling lines up to 2 miles (3.25 km) in length)

For distances under 1 mile take √miles = 1.00
For distances under 1.6 km take √km = 1.26
The maximum error between adjacent bench marks 0.25 mile (0.5 km) apart is ±0.03 ft (±9 mm).

Type of levelling	Error in feet		Error in metric	
Geodetic	±0.01 ft	√miles	±2 mm	√km
Secondary	±0.02 ft	√miles	±5 mm	√km
Tertiary	±0.05 ft	√miles	±12 mm	√km

Where spot heights have been obtained by spirit levelling a lower degree of accuracy is likely to be achieved. As spot heights occur on a levelling line they represent the positions of the staff and, although the heights are initially as accurate as any bench mark, their plan positions are not surveyed so accurately. The combination of these errors of position and of the error introduced by rounding to the nearest foot, gives a maximum error for the height values recorded on the 1:1250 and 1:2500 maps of ±0.3 m.[1]

Trigonometrical heights and the heights of mountains

Theodolite observations were employed to provide the heights of some triangulation stations, the final values for which to the nearest foot are published by the Ordnance Survey in its National Grid Triangulation Lists. The available accuracy checks on the method as by comparison with spirit levelling suggest that the listed values are correct to ±2 ft, with the majority accurate within ±1½ ft. The fact remains, however, that the heights of triangulation stations are still derived both from spirit levelling and from trigonometrical observations which sometimes cannot be accurately evaluated and no *general* figure can be quoted by the Ordnance Survey for the accuracy of heights of triangulation stations published on its maps.

Some aspects of the same problem are illustrated by the controversy which periodically surrounds the heights of mountains appearing on Ordnance Survey maps. During the mid 1960s the Ordnance Survey published revised heights, *inter alia*, for a number of well-known peaks in Scotland and the Lake District and this produced a lively reaction from mountaineering and countryside organizations. In the ensuing correspondence the Ordnance Survey explained that changes were attributable to one or more of several causes; to a change in the datum to which heights are related, to improvements in the techniques of height measurement, and to a change of point to which the height is referred. The change from Liverpool to Newlyn datum, for example, required adjustment of published heights, but a particular cause of misunderstanding stemmed from confusion as to the exact position to which the height refers. Height is usually determined to and from a triangulation pillar at or near the summit of the mountain, and it is normal practice to publish the height of ground level at the foot of the pillar. Where the pillar is located at the summit the published height is therefore the height of the highest point of natural ground on that particular mountain. On other peaks, however, the triangulation point has not been placed on the summit, but near it, owing, for example, to the fact that the summit may be occupied by a man-made structure such as a cairn, a mound, or a monument, which makes it impossible to occupy for triangulation purposes. On such mountains where the triangulation pillar does not coincide with the summit, and if lack of space at the 1:63 360 scale (and on Tourist maps) makes the publication of two heights difficult, the Ordnance Survey sometimes print only ground level height at the base of the triangulation station. This was the case with the Lake District peaks as shown in Table 27.

On revised editions of 1:10 000 and 1:25 000 maps it will be possible to show both pillar and summit heights although (owing to other factors) summit heights, as the table indicates, may have undergone revision from those published on previous editions of maps.

1 Where spot heights were surveyed by telescopic alidade observations, the maximum error is calculated to be ±1.0 m, although in many cases the result may be better.

Table 27   Heights of some Lake District peaks

Mountain	National Grid reference	Height at ground level of triangulation pillar (in ft)	Revised height of summit (in ft)	Height of summit formerly published by os
Scafell Pikes	NY 2107	3206	3210	3210
Helvellyn	NY 3415	3113	3116	3118
Coniston Old Man	SD 2797	2631	2635	2635
Loughrigg Fell	NY 3405	1099	1100	1101

The traditional heights of the more famous mountains have an almost mystical significance, and it is Ordnance Survey policy to avoid changing their height unless the validity of the change can be fully established. Every case is considered on its merit. The summit of Scafell Pikes, for example, is covered by a large cairn with a war memorial plaque set into it; ground height at the base of the cairn was determined as 3209 ft and, as it was reasonable to assume that additional height existed beneath the cairn, the decision to leave the old summit height of 3210 ft undisturbed was justified. In the case of Helvellyn, however, the summit was determinable by new and accurate observations, and there was no valid reason for continuing to accept the old value of 3118 ft. Since the 1960s these heights have been converted to metres and published to the nearest metre.

Heights and contours derived from air machine survey

Air machine survey, as noted in Chapter 1, produces spot heights and contours from air photography. Current Ordnance Survey policy lays down that contour standard errors shall not exceed one quarter of the contour interval. Since 1962 this has been monitored by a programme of systematic accuracy testing, involving checking points on the ground, which have been shown on the map as contours cutting across detail preferably at right angles. By scaling distances along the map detail and using a microptic alidade and staff to measure the same horizontal distances on the ground, the map points are established on the ground and marked by a peg. This is subsequently heighted by traversing with a microptic alidade and staff from the nearest bench marks. Table 28 shows the results of such a routine test on the air-machine contours published on the Provisional 1 : 10 560 sheets relating to the Tiverton area.

The test indicates that the contours in the Tiverton block of sheets were well within the permissible tolerance for countryside of medium relief. The differences did not exceed one quarter of the vertical interval (1.90 m for 25 ft vertical interval; 1.25 m for 5 m vertical interval) and as such were acceptable.

Systematic testing is not extended to spot heights derived by aerial plotting machines but, from such evidence as is available, their maximum error as recorded on the 1 : 10 000 series is ± 3.3 m; smaller errors are to be expected for the majority of spot heights.

Table 28   Accuracy tests on air machine contours in the Tiverton area

National Grid sheet number	Number of machine contour checks	Systematic error (in ft)	Maximum error (in ft)	Root mean square error (in ft)
ST 00 SW	77	+0.6	+6.5 −4.2	2.9 (0.88 m)
SS 90 NW	88	0	+11.3 −7.7	3.6 (1.10 m)
SY 09 SW	69	−1.4	+5.2 −6.2	2.5 (0.76 m)
Whole area	234	−0.2	+11.4 − 7.7	3.1 (0.94 m)

Conclusion

The chapters in this book have tried to show that in one way or another the processes of the Ordnance Survey are designed, in the light of particular specifications, to obtain standard accuracies in its maps. From the primary triangulation down to the measurement of the shortest line, the surveyors work within established tolerances. To ensure that the detail survey has been carried out correctly its accuracy is monitored in the field by means of a 'final examination', in which the examining surveyor checks a sample of instrumentally surveyed detail and of that derived from other processes such as those providing names, house numbers, boundary mereings, and antiquities. Detail is carefully matched across the abutting edge of all contiguous maps. Even with systematic checks made at each stage errors inevitably creep into the published maps and where discovered, either by users or through continuous revision, there are standard procedures so that they can be investigated and accorded a priority depending on their seriousness in the work of revision.

But not all features can be treated in this way. Very often it is the qualitative as much as the quantitative defects in a map which will cause concern to users. Much of the correspondence which the Ordnance Survey receives from the public relates to non-quantitative matters and more heat is likely to be generated (for example) over the spelling of a Celtic name than over the height of a contour. Features such as names, antiquities, or vegetation types indeed embody a different concept of 'accuracy' and the user needs to be familiar equally with the Ordnance Survey policy on their depiction as with survey tolerances in the narrow sense. A fair amount of misunderstanding about the true nature and limitations of maps is still abroad. There is a tendency to confuse, for example, lack of revision at the basic scales with inaccuracy; or to expect to find detail (or a level of positional accuracy) on a derived map, the level of generalization and specification of which explicitly excludes these expectations. The correct decodification of the information on any map series requires a thorough knowledge of its basic data and specification at both survey and production stages and Ordnance Survey maps are no exception. The present study is offered as an introduction to a wider understanding of their characteristics from both the map maker's and map user's point of view.

Abbreviations for Ordnance Survey maps

This appendix is in five parts:

(a) Normal abbreviations in use

(b) Abbreviations concerning boundary information

(c) Obsolescent abbreviations

(d) County names abbreviations

(e) County names 1972 Act abbreviations

The plural may be indicated by the addition of the letter 's' in lowercase when appropriate and where the detail is so close that the abbreviation cannot be repeated for each object because of space or appearance.

Special rules apply to boundary mereings and only the more common ones are listed.

Normal abbreviations in use

Feature	Abbreviation	1:1250 and 1:2500	1:10560	1:10000	1:25000 1st	1:25000 2nd	1:50000 and 1:63360	1:250000	Route Planning Map
Air Light Beacon	ALB	○							
Allotment Gardens	Allot Gdns	○	○	○	○	○			
Ambulance Station	Amb Sta	○	○	○					
April	Apr	○				○	○	○	
August	Aug	○				○	○	○	
Automobile Association	AA	○	○	○			○	○	○
Avenue	Ave or Av	○	○	○					
Bank (building)	Bk	○	○						
Baptist	Bapt	○	○						
Barracks	Bks	○	○	○	○	○	○		
Battery	Bty	○	○						
Beer House	BH	○	○		○				
Bench Mark	BM	○	○	○					
Bollard	Bol	○							
Boundary	Bdy	○	○	○		○			
Boundary Mark	B Mk	○	○	○					
Boundary Mound	B Md	○	○	○					
Boundary Post or Plate	BP	○	○	○	○	○			
Boundary Stone	BS	○	○	○	○	○			
Bridge	Br	○	○	○	○	○	○		
Building	Bldg	○					○		
Burial Ground	Burial Gd	○	○	○			○		
Calvinist	Calv	○	○						
Capstan	Cn	○							
Castle	Cas	○	○	○	○	○	○	○	
Cathedral	Cath	○	○	○	○	○	○		
Cemetery	Cemy	○	○	○	○	○	○		
Centre (Social, etc.)	Cen	○	○	○	○	○			
Chapel	Chap	○	○	○			○		
Chimney	Chy	○	○	○	○	○	○		
Christian Science Church	Chr Sc Ch	○	○						
Church	Ch	○	○	○			○		
Church of Christ Scientist	Chr Sc Ch	○							
Church of England	C of E	○	○						
Church of Scotland	C of S	○	○						
Church in Wales	C in W	○	○						
Cinema	Cin	○	○						
Cistern	Cis	○	○	○					
Civil Parish	CP	○	○	○	○	○	○		
Close	Cl	○	○	○					
Club House	CH	○	○	○	○	○	○		
Coastguard Station	CG Sta	○	○	○	○	○	○		
Co-educational	Co-ed	○							
College	Coll	○	○	○	○	○	○		
Colliery	Colly	○	○	○	○	○			

Feature	Abbreviation	1:1250 and 1:2500	1:10560	1:10000	1:25000 1st	1:25000 2nd	1:50000 and 1:63360	1:250000	Route Planning Map
Congregational	Congl	O	O						
Convalescent Home	Conv Home	O	O	O	O	O			
Convent	Cvt	O	O	O	O	O	O		
Corporation	Corpn	O	O						
Corporation Yard	Corpn Yd	O	O	O					
Cottage	Cott	O	O	O	O	O	O		
Council (not in conjunction with County)	Cnl	O	O						
Course	Cse	O	O		O	O	O		
Court	Ct	O	O	O			O		
Crane	C	O							
Crematorium	Crem	O	O	O	O	O	O		
Crescent	Cres or Cr	O	O	O					
December	Dec	O				O	O	O	
Department	Dept	O	O	O	O	O			
Detached	Det	O	O	O	O	O	O	O	O
Disused	Dis	O	O	O	O	O	O	O	
Dock	Dk	O	O	O	O	O			
Drinking Fountain	D Fn	O							
Drive	Dr	O	O	O					
East	E	O	O	O	O	O	O	O	
Electric or Electricity	El	O	O	O		O			
Electricity Generating Station	El Gen Sta	O	O	O		O			
Electricity Pillar / Electricity Pole	El P	O							
Electricity Sub Station	El Sub Sta	O	O	O					
Electricity Transformer	El Tfmr	O	O	O					
Electricity Transformer Station	El Tfmr Sta	O	O	O		O			
Electricity Transmission Line	ETL	O							
Electricity Works	El Wks	O	O	O		O	O		
Employment	Emp	O	O	O		O			
Employment Exchange	Emp Ex	O	O	O		O			
Engineering Works	Eng Wks	O	O	O	O	O	O		
Exchange	Ex	O	O	O		O			
Farm	Fm	O	O	O	O	O	O		
February	Feb	O				O	O	O	
Ferries – Vehicular, Foot	Ferry V or F	O	O	O	O	O	O		
Filter Bed	FB	O							
Fire Alarm	FA	O							
Fire Alarm Pillar	FAP	O							
Fire Engine Station	FE Sta	O	O	O					
Fire Station	F Sta	O	O	O	O	O			
Flagstaff	FS	O							
Foot Bridge	FB	O	O	O	O	O			
Fountain	Fn	O	O	O					
Free Church	F Ch	O	O						
Fundamental Bench Mark	FBM	O							

Feature	Abbreviation	1:1250 and 1:2500	1:10560	1:10000	1:25000 1st	1:25000 2nd	1:50000 and 1:63360	1:250000	Route Planning Map
Gardens	Gdns	○	○	○	○	○			
Gas Valve Compound	GVC	○		○					
General Post Office	GPO	○	○	○	○	○			
Generating Station	Gen Sta	○	○	○	○	○			
Government	Govt	○	○	○		○	○		
Grave Yard	G Yd	○	○	○					
Greater London Council	GLC	○							
Ground	Gd	○	○	○	○	○			
Grove	Gr	○	○	○					
Guide Post (signpost)	GP	○	○	○	○				
Head	Hd	○	○	○	○	○		○	○
Head Post Office	HPO	○	○	○	○	○			
Headquarters	HQ	○	○	○	○	○			
Hectares	ha	○							
High Water Mark	HWM						○		
High Water Mark (Springs)	HWM(S)						○		
Hospital	Hospl	○	○	○	○	○	○		
House	Ho	○	○	○	○	○	○		
Hydrant	H	○							
Hydraulic	H	○	○	○	○	○			
Independent	Indpt	○	○						
Infant	Inft	○	○						
Infirmary	Infmy	○	○	○	○	○	○		
Inshore Rescue Boat Station	IRB Sta	○	○	○		○	○		
Institute	Inst	○	○	○	○	○			
Institution	Instn	○	○	○	○	○	○		
Island, Isle	I	○				○	○	○	○
Isolation Hospital	Isoln Hospl	○	○	○	○	○	○		
January	Jan	○				○	○	○	
July	Jul	○				○	○	○	
Junction	Junc	○	○	○	○		○		
June	Jun	○				○	○	○	
Kilometre Post	Km P	○							
Kilometres	km	○					○		
Lake	L	○	○	○			○	○	○
Lane	La	○	○	○					
Letter Box	LB	○							
Level Crossing	LC	○							
Library	Liby	○	○	○		○			
Lifeboat House	LB Ho	○	○	○		○			
Lifeboat Station	LB Sta	○	○	○	○	○	○		
Lighthouse	L Ho	○	○	○	○				
Lighting Tower	L Twr	○							
Lime Kiln	LK	○	○	○					

Feature	Abbreviation	1:1250 and 1:2500	1:10560	1:10000	1:25000 1st	1:25000 2nd	1:50000 and 1:63360	1:250000	Route Planning Map
Loading Gauge	LG	○							
Loch	L	○	○	○	○	○	○	○	○
Lock	L	○	○				○		
Locomotive Shed	Loco Shed	○	○	○					
Lodge	Lo	○	○	○	○	○	○		
London Borough	LB	○	○	○	○	○			
London Transport	LT	○	○	○					
Lower	Lr	○					○		
Low Water Mark	LWM						○		
Low Water Mark (Springs)	LWM(S)						○		
Magnetic Variation	Mag Var				○				
Mail Pick-up	MPU	○							
Manhole	MH	○			○				
Manor	Mr	○	○	○	○	○			
March (month)	Mar	○				○	○	○	
Market	Mkt	○	○	○	○	○			
Market House	Mkt Ho	○	○	○					
May	May	○					○	○	
Mean High Water	MHW	○	○	○		○			
Mean High Water Springs	MHWS	○	○	○		○			
Mean Low Water	MLW	○	○	○		○			
Mean Low Water Springs	MLWS	○	○	○		○			
Mean High and Mean Low Water	MH & MLW	○	○	○		○			
Mean High and Mean Low Water Springs	MH & MLWS	○	○	○		○			
Memorial	Meml	○	○	○	○	○	○		
Mental Hospital	Mtl Hospl	○					○		
Meteorological Station	Met Sta	○	○	○	○	○			
Methodist	Meth	○	○						
Metres	m	○		○	○	○			
Metropolitan	Met	○							
Mile Post	MP	○	○	○	○	○	○		
Miles	M	○							
Mile Stone	MS	○	○	○	○	○	○		
Mission	Misn	○	○						
Mission Church	Misn Ch	○	○						
Monument	Mon	○	○	○	○	○	○		
Mooring Post	MP	○							
Mortuary	Mort	○	○	○	○	○	○		
Mountain	Mt	○	○	○				○	
Municipal	Munl	○	○	○		○			
Museum	Mus	○	○	○	○	○	○		
National Coal Board	NCB	○	○	○		○			
National Trust	NT	○	○	○	○	○	○		
National Trust for Scotland	NTS	○	○	○	○	○	○		
Nonconformist	Noncon	○							
Normal Tidal Limit	NTL	○	○	○		○			
North	N	○					○	○	○

Feature	Abbreviation	1:1250 and 1:2500	1:10560	1:10000	1:25000 1st	1:25000 2nd	1:50000 and 1:63360	1:250000	Route Planning Map
November	Nov	○				○	○	○	
Number	No	○	○	○		○			
Observatory	Obsy	○	○	○	○	○			
October	Oct	○				○	○	○	
Omnibus	Bus	○	○	○					
Palace	Pal	○	○	○	○	○	○		
Pavilion	Pav	○	○	○	○				
Permanent Traverse Station	ts	○							
Pillar	P	○							
Place	Pl	○	○	○					
Plantation	Plantn	○	○	○	○	○	○		
Point	Pt	○	○	○			○		
Pole	P	○							
Police Call Box	PCB	○			○				
Police Station	Pol Sta	○	○	○		○			
Police Telephone Pillar or Post	PTP	○							
Post	P	○							
Post Office large scales	PO	○	○	○					
small scales	P				○	○	○		
Presbyterian	Presb	○							
Presbytery	Presby	○			○	○			
Public Convenience	PC	○	○	○		○	○		
Public House	PH	○	○	○	○	○	○		
Public Library	Liby	○	○	○	○	○			
Pump	Pp	○							
Pump House	Pp Ho	○	○	○					
Pumping Station	Ppg Sta	○	○	○					
Pylon	P	○							
Railway	Rly	○	○	○	○	○	○		
Railway Station	Rly Sta	○					○		
Recreation	Recn	○	○	○	○	○			
Recreation Ground	Recn Gd	○	○	○	○	○	○		
Rectory	Rec	○	○	○	○	○			
Remains of	Rems of	○	○	○	○	○	○		
Reservoir	Resr	○	○	○	○	○	○	○	○
Revision Point	rp	○							
Rifle Range	Range						○		
River	R	○	○	○	○	○	○	○	○
Road	Rd	○	○	○					
Road House	RH	○	○	○					
Roman Catholic	RC	○	○		○				
Royal Automobile Club	RAC	○	○	○			○	○	○
Saint	St	○	○	○	○	○	○		
Saints	SS	○							
Salvation Army	SA	○							
Sanatorium	Sanatm	○	○	○	○	○	○		

Feature	Abbreviation	1:1250 and 1:2500	1:10560	1:10000	1:25000 1st	1:25000 2nd	1:50000 and 1:63360	1:250000	Route Planning Map
School	Sch	○	○	○	○	○	○		
September	Sep	○				○	○	○	
Signal Box	SB	○	○						
Signal Bridge	S Br	○	○	○					
Signal Gantry	S Gantry	○	○	○					
Signal Light	SL	○							
Signal Post	SP	○							
Signal Station	S Sta	○	○	○					
Sluice	Sl	○	○	○					
Smithy	Smy	○							
Sound	Sd	○	○	○				○	○
South	S	○					○	○	○
Spring	Spr	○	○	○	○	○			
Square	Sq	○	○	○					
Standard	Std	○							
Station	Sta	○	○	○	○	○	○		
Stone	S	○							
Street	St	○	○	○					
Sunday School	Sun Sch	○	○						
Sundial	SD	○							
Tank	Tk	○	○	○					
Technical College	Tech Coll	○	○	○	○	○	○		
Telephone Call Box:									
Public large scales	TCB	○	○	○					
small scales	T				○	○	○	○	○
AA large scales	AA	○							
small scales	A				○	○	○	○	○
RAC large scales	RAC	○							
small scales	R				○	○	○	○	○
Telephone Call Post or Pillar	TCP	○	○	○					
Telephone Exchange	Tel Ex	○	○	○			○		
Telephone Pole	Tel P	○	○						
Television Station	TV Sta	○	○	○		○	○*		
Terminus	Ter	○	○	○	○	○			
Terrace	Terr	○	○	○					
Territorial Army	TA	○	○	○	○	○			
Territorial and Army Volunteer Reserve	TA	○	○	○	○	○			
Territorial and Army Volunteer Reserve Centre	TA Centre	○	○	○	○	○			
Toll Gate or Bridge	Toll	○	○	○			○	○	○
Tower	Twr	○	○	○			○	○	
Town Hall	TH	○	○	○	○	○	○		
Track	Tk	○	○	○					
Travelling Crane	Trav C	○	○	○					
Traverse Station	ts	○							
Trough	Tr	○							

Feature	Abbreviation	1:1250 and 1:2500	1:10560	1:10000	1:25000 1st	1:25000 2nd	1:50000 and 1:63360	1:250000	Route Planning Map
Undenominational	Undenom	○							
Under Construction	Under Constn		○	○	○	○	○		
United Reformed Church	U Ref Ch	○	○						
University	Univ	○	○	○	○	○	○		
Upper	Upr	○	○	○			○		
Valve	V	○							
Valve House	V Ho	○							
Ventilator	Vr	○							
Vicarage	Vic	○	○	○	○	○			
Voluntary Assisted	VA	○							
Voluntary Controlled	VC	○							
War Memorial	War Meml	○	○	○	○	○			
Water Board	Wr Bd	○							
Water Point	Wr Pt	○	○						
Water Tap	Wr T	○							
Water Tower	Wr Twr	○	○	○			○		
Water Works	Wr Wks	○	○	○					
Waterfall	Fall	○	○	○		○			
Weighbridge	WB	○							
Weighing Machine	WB	○							
Well	W	○	○	○	○	○			
Wesleyan Methodist	Wes Meth	○							
West	W	○	○	○	○	○	○	○	○
Wind Electricity Generator	Wd El Gen	○	○						
Wind Pump	Wd Pp	○	○	○	○	○			
Wireless Station (Transmitting or Receiving)	WT Sta	○	○	○		○	○		
Works	Wks	○	○	○	○	○	○		
Yard	Yd	○	○	○					
Young Men's Christian Association	YMCA	○	○	○					
Young Women's Christian Association	YWCA	○	○	○					
Youth Hostel	Y	○			○	○			

Abbreviations concerning boundary information

Feature	Abbreviation	1:1250 and 1:2500	1:10 560	1:10 000	1:25 000 1st	1:25 000 2nd
ADMINISTRATIVE NAMES, DESCRIPTIONS, ETC						
Administrative County (England and Wales only)						
Margin	Admin Co	○	○	○		○
Description	Ad Co	○				
Borough Constituency						
Body	BC	○				○
Margin and description	Boro Const	○	○			○
Boundary	Bdy	○				
Boundary Mark	B Mk	○				
Boundary Mound	B Md	○				
Boundary Post or Plate	BP	○	○	○	○	○
Boundary Stone	BS	○	○	○	○	○
Burgh Constituency						
Body	BC	○				
Margin and description	Burgh Const	○				
Civil Parish	CP	○		○		○
County Borough						
Body and description	CB	○	○			○
County Constituency						
Body	CC	○				
Margin and description	Co Const	○		○		○
County Council (Scotland only)						
Margin	County	○				
Description	Co Cnl	○				
County of City						
Description	Co of City	○				
Detached	Det	○				
District						
Description	Dist	○				
London Borough	LB	○				
Municipal Borough	MB	○		○		○
Rural Borough	RB	○				
Rural District	RD	○		○		○
Urban District	UD	○	○	○		○

MEREINGS

Special rules apply to boundary mereings and only the more common ones are listed.

Baulk, Bank, Base, Basin Bridge, Broad	B	○	
Cam, Canal, Causeway, Centre of, Channel, Cliff, Conduit, Cop, Course of, Covered, Culvert, Cut	C	○	
Dam, Ditch, Dock, Double, Down, Drain	D	○	
Defaced	Def	○	
Double Ditch or Drain	DD	○	
Double Fence	DF	○	
Edge of, Eyot	E	○	

Feature	Abbreviation	1:1250 and 1:2500
Mereings continued		
Face of, Fence, Fleet, Foot, Freeboard	F	○
Feet	Ft	○
Harbour, Hedge	H	○
Inches	ins	○
Kerb	K	○
Lade, Lake, Lead, Loch, Lockspit, Lynchet	L	○
Marsh, Mere, Moat	M	○
Mean High Water Springs (Scotland only)	MHWS	○
Mean High Water	MHW	○
Mean Low Water	MLW	○
Mean Low Water Springs (Scotland only)	MLWS	○
Metres	m	○
Old	O	○
Passage, Path, Plate, Pond, Post	P	○
Race, Railway, Ride, River, Road, Root of	R	○
Scar, Sewer, Side of, Slope, Sluice, Stone, Stream	S	○
Top of	T	○
Track	Tk	○
Undefined	Und	○
Wall, Weir	W	○

The following are examples of combined abbreviations

Base of Bank	BB	○
Centre of Bank, Basin, Baulk, Broad	CB	○
Centre of Canal	CC	○
Centre of Covered Stream	CCS	○
Centre of channel at Low Water	CCLW	○
Centre of Drain	CD	○
Centre of old course of stream	COCS	○
Centre of Railway, River, Road	CR	○
Centre of Road	CR	○
Centre of Stream	CS	○
Edge of Kerb	EK	○
Face of Fence	FF	○
Face of Wall	FW	○
Root of Hedge	RH	○
Side of River	SR	○
Top of Bank	TB	○
Track of Hedge	Tk H	○
Track of Stream	Tk S	○

Obsolescent abbreviations

Feature	Abbreviation	1:1250 and 1:2500	1:10560 and 1:10000	1:25000
Cart Track	CT	○	○	
Footpath	FP	○	○	○
High water Mark of Ordinary Tides	HWMOT	○	○	○
High water Mark of Ordinary Spring Tides	HWMOST	○	○	○
High water Mark of Medium Tides	HWMMT	○	○	○
Highest Point to which Medium tides flow	HP to which MTs flow	○		
Highest Point to which Ordinary tides flow	HP to which OTs flow	○		
Highest Point to which Ordinary Spring tides flow	HP to which OSTs flow	○		
Lavatory	Lav	○		
London County Council	LCC	○		
Low water Mark of Ordinary Tides	LWMOT	○	○	○
Low water Mark of Ordinary Spring Tides	LWMOST	○	○	○
Low water Mark of Medium Tides	LWMMT	○	○	○
Ministry of Technology	Min Tech	○		
Parish	Ph	○	○	

County Names Abbreviations

ENGLAND

Bedfordshire	Beds
Berkshire	Berks
Buckinghamshire	Bucks
Cambridgeshire and Isle of Ely	Cambs and Isle of Ely
Cheshire	Ches
Cornwall	Corn
Cumberland	Cumb
Derbyshire	Derby
Devonshire	Devon
Dorset	Dorset
Durham	Durham
Essex	Essex
Gloucestershire	Glos
Greater London	Greater London
Hampshire	Hants
Herefordshire	Here
Hertfordshire	Herts
Huntingdon and Peterborough	Hunts and Peterborough
Kent	Kent
Lancashire	Lancs
Leicestershire	Leic
Lincolnshire	Linc
Monmouthshire	Monm
Norfolk	Norf
Northamptonshire	Northants
Northumberland	Northum
Nottinghamshire	Notts
Oxfordshire	Oxon
Rutland	Rut
Shropshire	Salop
Somerset	Somer
Staffordshire	Staf
Suffolk	Suff
Surrey	Surrey
Sussex	Sussex
Warwickshire	Warw
Westmorland	Westm
Wiltshire	Wilts
Worcestershire	Worc
Yorkshire	Yorks
Isle of Man	I of M

WALES

Anglesey	Angle
Brecknockshire	Breck
Caernarvonshire	Caern
Cardiganshire	Card
Carmarthenshire	Carm
Denbighshire	Denb
Flintshire	Flint
Glamorgan	Glam
Merionethshire	Meri
Montgomeryshire	Mont
Pembrokeshire	Pemb
Radnorshire	Rad

SCOTLAND

Aberdeenshire	Aber
Angus	Angus
Argyllshire	Argyll
Ayrshire	Ayr
Banffshire	Banff
Berwickshire	Berwick
Buteshire	Bute
Caithness	Caithness
Clackmannanshire	Clackmannan
Dumfriesshire	Dumfrie
Dunbartonshire	Dunbar
East Lothian	E Lothian
Fife	Fife
Inverness-shire	Inver
Kincardineshire	Kincar
Kinross-shire	Kinross
Kirkcudbrightshire	Kirkcud
Lanarkshire	Lanark
Midlothian	Midloth
Morayshire	Moray
Nairnshire	Nairn
Orkney	Orkney
Peeblesshire	Peebles
Perthshire	Perth
Renfrewshire	Renfrew
Ross and Cromarty	Ross and Crom
Roxburghshire	Roxb
Selkirkshire	Selk
Stirlingshire	Stirl
Sutherland	Suther
West Lothian	W Lothian
Wigtownshire	Wigtown
Zetland	Zetland

County names 1972 Act abbreviations

ENGLAND

Avon	Avon
Bedfordshire	Beds
Berkshire	Berks
Buckinghamshire	Bucks
Cambridgeshire	Cambs
Cheshire	Ches
Cleveland	Cleve
Cornwall	Corn
Cumbria	Cumbr
Derbyshire	Derby
Devon	Devon
Dorset	Dorset
Durham	Durham
East Sussex	E Susx
Essex	Essex
Gloucestershire	Glos
Greater London	Gtr London
Greater Manchester	Gtr Mches
Hampshire	Hants
Hereford and Worcester	Here and Worc
Hertfordshire	Herts
Humberside	Humbs
Isle of Wight	I of W
Kent	Kent
Lancashire	Lancs
Leicestershire	Leic
Lincolnshire	Lincs
Merseyside	Mers
Norfolk	Norf
North Yorkshire	N Yorks
Northamptonshire	Northants
Northumberland	Northum
Nottinghamshire	Notts
Oxfordshire	Oxon
Salop	Salop
Somerset	Somer
South Yorkshire	S Yorks
Staffordshire	Staffs
Suffolk	Suff
Surrey	Surrey
Tyne and Wear	Tyne and Wear
Warwickshire	Warw
West Midlands	W Mids
West Sussex	W Susx
West Yorkshire	W Yorks
Wiltshire	Wilts

WALES

Clwyd	Clwyd
Dyfed	Dyfed
Gwent	Gwent
Gwynedd	Gwyn
Mid Glamorgan	Mid Glam
Powys	Powys
South Glamorgan	S Glam
West Glamorgan	W Glam

OTHER AREAS

Isle of Man	I of M
Isles of Scilly	Is of Sc

In 1947 the Ordnance Survey began to introduce a new system of edition letters and footnotes to enable map series, first and subsequent editions of individual sheets, and reprints embodying significant change, to be readily identified. For map users concerned with recent changes in the landscape for whom the information may be of vital importance and for map stockists, the purpose of this appendix is to explain the basis for these practices and the form in which they are applied at present.

Definitions

The meaning of the word *edition* has changed within Ordnance Survey usage. Until the period after World War II it usually referred to maps at one scale and made to a common design and specification as, for example, the 1:63360 Sixth or New Popular Edition. Current practice substitutes the term *series* for *edition* (in its original usage) and, to identify the specification to which a map of given scale is produced, a series number is employed as with the 1:63360 Seventh Series. The terminology applies to maps at all scales, except that National Grid 1:1250 and 1:2500 maps, which are subject to continuous revision, are simply known as '1:1250 (and 1:2500) National Grid Series'.[1]

The word *edition* is now used to define a version of a published map, which has been re-edited to incorporate systematic revision (i.e. full revision of all detail over the whole or a substantial part of that map or, alternatively, full revision of the elements in a map which constitute its main purpose);[2] *edition* is also applied to a new version of a map which, with or without revision, has undergone metric conversion. Systematic revision may be cyclic as with small scale maps or continuous as for maps at basic scales.

A *reprint*, on the other hand, is taken to mean a fresh printing of an existing map, for the purpose of replenishing stocks, not incorporating systematic revision or metric conversion, but which may (or may not) include changes or corrections of varying importance to miscellaneous topographical detail especially on the 1:10000 and smaller scale series. The different forms of reprint are explained below.

Current notation practice

NEW EDITIONS

The edition of a map is indicated by a capital letter printed in the left-hand side of the bottom margin of small scale maps and, on the 1:10560 and larger scale maps, also in the right-hand side of the top margin. The year of publication to which the edition letter refers is shown in the publication footnote printed in the bottom margin of the sheet. Thus a map first published in 1970 would show in the lower margin.

Edition Letter	Publication footnote
A	*Made and published by the Director General, Ordnance Survey, Southampton, © Crown Copyright 1970.*

Subsequent editions of this map, fully revised in whole or part or converted to the metric system with or without revision, are indicated by advancing the edition letter by one letter at each new edition to B, C, etc.[3] and by amending the year in the publication footnote to conform.

1 The name of the map series is printed on the top margin of all flat sheets, but is trimmed off all folded maps except the 1:250000 before they are put into covers. Apart from the 1:25000 Second Series, which is so described on the covers to distinguish it from the 1:25000 First Series, folded maps currently bear no indication of the series on the covers.

2 For example, on the Route Planning map, road and ferry network may be revised in producing a new edition, but not necessarily base detail; a similar situation can exist with maps overprinted with administrative areas detail.

3 The alphabetical sequence of letters used in edition notation omits 'I' and 'O'.

REPRINTS

Facsimile reprints (i.e. without any changes being made), or reprints incorporating the correction of only minor errors, are not acknowledged in either footnotes or notation system. If more important changes (short of the revision required for a new edition) are made, however, and depending on their nature, the following alterations are made to edition letters and footnotes

(a) Where significant topographical information such as a section of a new major road has been added which might justify superseding existing stock or when rights of way information has been added to the sheet for the first time, an additional footnote is added, for example:

Reprinted with major road revision

A bar with an asterisk is added below the edition letter thus $\underline{A}_*$

(b) Where miscellaneous topographical changes have been made which do not justify superseding stock, an additional footnote is added as follows:

Reprinted with minor changes

A bar is added below the edition letter thus $\underline{A}$

(c) Where changes are limited to the correction of errors in names or detail shown at the time of the previous printing, no additional footnotes are added but a bar is shown below the edition letter as in (b) above.

New editions and reprints with significant changes (that is those which show the notation ___* beneath the edition letter) have been notified in the Ordnance Survey monthly Publication Report since January 1963. Facsimile reprints, and reprints upon which alterations are limited to the correction of small errors and to minor changes, are not included in the Report.

The Ordnance Survey replaces its agents' stocks of 1 : 10 560 and larger scale maps as soon as possible after a new edition or reprint with significant changes has been published. Stocks of maps at small scales held by agents or other retailers are not replaced and earlier versions may continue to be on sale after a new publication has been noted in the Ordnance Survey Publication Report.

Changes since 1947

An edition lettering system has been in use on large scale plans and medium scale maps (as they were then called)[1] since 1 January 1947, and on small scale maps since 1 April 1953. After 1947, and up to October 1952, all changes, whether major or minor made on reprint of large scale plans were acknowledged by advancing the edition letter. Since October 1952 for large scale plans, and since January 1956 for medium and small scale maps, changes or corrections carried out at reprint, but not amounting to systematic revision, have been acknowledged by adding the bar beneath the edition letter. The acknowledgement of the incorporation of important topographical information such as a new major road by means of the bar and asterisk beneath the edition letter has been in use since May 1960 and, for public rights of way information, since February 1963.

1 In 1966 the term 'large scale map' was substituted for 'large scale plan', and, at the same time, the categorization of the 1 : 10 560 and 1 : 25 000 maps as 'medium scales', introduced after 1945, was abandoned. See *The Ordnance Survey Annual Report* (1967), iii; the 1 : 10 560 was thereafter designated as a 'large scale map' and the 1 : 25 000 as a 'small scale map'.

A select bibliography

No attempt is made in this bibliography to give a comprehensive list of books and articles about the Ordnance Survey but, as well as the principal references in the text, it includes a short selection of other studies supplementing the main themes in the book.

ANDREWS, J. H. 1974. *History in the Ordnance Map. An introduction for Irish readers.* Dublin, Ordnance Survey Office, pp. 63.

ARTHUR, D. W. G. 1955. A stereocomparator technique for aerial triangulation. (*Ordnance Survey Professional Paper, New Series*, no. 20). London, HMSO. pp. 59.

AYLWARD, J. 1971. The retail distribution of Ordnance Survey maps and plans in the latter half of the nineteenth century—a map seller's view. *The Cartographic Journal.* Edinburgh. Vol. **8**, no. 1, pp. 55–8.

BALCHIN, W. G. V. and COLEMAN, A. M. 1966. The consultative machinery of the Ordnance Survey. *The Cartographer.* Toronto. Vol. **3**, no. 1, pp. 48–51.

BECKINSALE, R. P. 1946. Correspondence on the new Popular Edition grid. *Geography.* London. Vol. **31**, pt. 2, pp. 79–80.

BREWARD, R. W. 1972. A mathematical approach to the storage of digitised contours. *The Cartographic Journal.* Edinburgh. Vol. **9**, no. 2, pp. 82–6.

CAREY, MAJOR-GENERAL L. F. DE VIC. 1960. The Ordnance Survey. *The Geographical Magazine.* London. Vol. **32**, no. 11, pp. 564–76.

CARR, A. P. 1962. Cartographic record and historical accuracy. *Geography.* London. Vol. **47**, pt. 2, pp. 135–44.

CHEETHAM, MAJOR-GENERAL G. 1945. The post-war programme of the Ordnance Survey of Great Britain. *Empire Survey Review.* London. Vol. **8**, no. 57, pp. 93–102.

CHEETHAM, MAJOR-GENERAL G. 1946. New medium and small scale maps of the Ordnance Survey. *The Geographical Journal.* London. Vol. **107**, nos. 5–6, pp. 211–24.

CLARKE, A. R. 1858. *Ordnance Trigonometrical Survey of Great Britain and Ireland. Account of the observations and calculations of the principal triangulation* . . . London, Board of Ordnance. 2 vols., pp. xvii, 782; pl. XXVIII.

CLARKE, R. V. 1969. The use of watermarks in dating Old Series One-Inch Ordnance Survey maps. *The Cartographic Journal.* Edinburgh. Vol. **6**, no. 2, pp. 114–29.

CLAYTON, K. M. 1953. A note on the twenty-five foot 'contours' shown on the Ordnance Survey 1:25000 map. *Geography.* London. Vol. **38**, pt. 2, pp. 77–83.

CLAYTON, K. M. 1971. Geographical reference systems. *The Geographical Journal.* London. Vol. **137**, pt. 1, pp. 1–13.

CLOSE, COL. SIR CHARLES. 1926. *The Early Years of the Ordnance Survey.* Reprinted, with an introduction by J. B. HARLEY, 1969. Newton Abbot, David & Charles. pp. xxxv, 164.

CLOSE, COL. SIR CHARLES. 1932. The public use of large scale Ordnance Survey maps. *Conference of Empire Survey Officers 1931. Report of Proceedings.* London, HMSO. pp. 23–4.

COLLIER, H. 1972. A short history of Ordnance Survey contouring with particular reference to Scotland. *The Cartographic Journal.* Edinburgh. Vol. **9**, no. 1, pp. 55–8.

Correspondence respecting the scale for the Ordnance Survey, and upon contouring and hill delineation. 1854. British Parliamentary Paper. XLI, 187.

CRASTNER, J. E. E. 1925. Photo-mechanical processes of map production. *The Geographical Journal.* London. Vol. **65**, no. 4, pp. 301–14.

CRASTNER, J. E. E. 1934. Cylindrical map projections. *Empire Survey Review.* London. Vol. **2**, no. 14, pp. 493–6.

CRAWFORD, O. G. S. 1922.
Archaeology and the Ordnance
Survey. *The Geographical Journal.*
London. Vol. **59**, no. 4, pp. 245–58.

CRAWFORD, O. G. S. 1928. Air survey
and archaeology. Second edition.
(*Ordnance Survey Professional Papers,
New Series, no. 7*). London, HMSO.
pp. 42, pl. XIII.

CRAWFORD, O. G. S. 1929. Air photography for archaeologists. (*Ordnance
Survey Professional Papers, New Series,
no. 12*). London, HMSO. pp. 44, pl. XIX.

CRAWFORD, O. G. S. 1955. *Said and
Done. The autobiography of an
archaeologist.* London, Weidenfeld &
Nicolson. pp. 316.

CRONE, G. R. 1945. The new edition
of the One-Inch map. *The
Geographical Journal.* London. Vol. **105**,
no. 6, pp. 207–9.

CRONE, G. R. 1962. The future of the
International Million Map of the World.
The Geographical Journal. London.
Vol. **128**, pt. 1, pp. 36–8.

CRONE, G. R. 1968. *Maps and their
Makers. An introduction to the history of
cartography.* Fourth (revised) edition.
London, Hutchinson University
Library. pp. 184.

CROOK, H. T. 1892. *The Maps of the
Ordnance Survey: as they are and as they
ought to be.* London, Simpkin, Marshall,
Kent & Co. Manchester, J. E. Cornish.
pp. 42.

DAVIES, E. (Ed.) 1958. *A Gazetteer of
Welsh Place-names.* Cardiff, University
of Wales Press.

DENNETT, J. R. B., HOBBS, L. H. E.
and WHITE, B. F. 1967. Cartographic
production control. *The Cartographic
Journal.* Edinburgh. Vol. **4**, no. 2,
pp. 93–103.

DEPARTMENT OF TRADE AND INDUSTRY.
1972. *Metrication.* White Paper. Cmd.
4880. London, HMSO.

DICKINSON, G. C. 1969. *Maps and Air
Photographs.* London, Edward Arnold.
pp. xi, 286.

DREWITT, B. 1973. The changing
profile of the map user in Great
Britain. *The Cartographic Journal.*
Edinburgh. Vol. **10**, no. 1, pp. 42–8.

EDGE, Major-General R. C. A. 1968.
Annual Livery Lecture. [On the
Ordnance Survey,] 16 November
1967. London, The Worshipful
Company of Stationers and Newspaper
Makers. pp. 14.

*Eighth Report from the Estimates
Committee . . . Session 1962–63.*
Ordnance Survey. London, HMSO.
pp. xxvi, 177.

FAGAN, P. F. 1972. Photogrammetry
in the National Survey. *The
Photogrammetric Record.* London. Vol. **7**,
no. 40, pp. 405–23.

FARQUHARSON, Col. Sir John. 1900.
Twelve years' work of the Ordnance
Survey, 1887 to 1899. *The Geographical
Journal.* London. Vol. **15**, no. 6,
pp. 565–98.

*Fifth Report of Select Committee on
Estimates. Historic Buildings and Ancient
Monuments.* 1956–60. London, HMSO.
pp. vii.

*Final Report of the Departmental
Committee on the Ordnance Survey.* 1938.
London, HMSO. pp. v, 39, 3 maps.

FORBES, J. and ROBERTSON, I. M. L.
1967. Population enumeration on a
grid square basis: the Census of
Scotland–a test case. *The Cartographic
Journal.* Edinburgh. Vol. **4**, no. 1,
pp. 29–37.

GAITS, G. M. 1969. Thematic mapping
by computer. *The Cartographic Journal.*
Edinburgh. Vol. **6**, no. 1, pp. 50–68.

GARDINER, R. A. 1950. The use of air
photographs by the Ordnance Survey.
Empire Survey Review. London. Vol. **10**,
no. 76, pp. 242–55.

GARDINER, R. A. 1961. A re-appraisal
of the International Map of the World
(IMW) on the millionth scale.
Internationales Jahrbuch für Kartographie.
Gütersloh. Vol. **1**, pp. 31–49.

GARDINER, R. A. 1969. Philip
Symonson's 'New Description of
Kent', 1596. *The Geographical Journal.*
London. Vol. **135**, pt. 1, pp. 136–7.

GARDINER-HILL, R. C. 1972. The
development of digital maps.
(*Ordnance Survey Professional Papers,
New Series, no. 23.*) Southampton,
Ordnance Survey. pp. 14.

GARDINER-HILL, R. C. 1973. Automated cartography in the Ordnance Survey. *Conference of Commonwealth Survey Officers, 1971. Report of Proceedings*. Part I. London, HMSO. pp. 235–41.

GENERAL REGISTER OFFICE. 1970. *1971 Census Information Paper 1*. (Mimeographed.)

GENERAL REGISTER OFFICE. *1971 Census Information Paper 5*. (Mimeographed.)

Glossary of Technical Terms in Cartography. 1966. London, The Royal Society. pp. 84.

GRIFFITH, D. L. and KELLY, J. J. 1965. The Quarter Inch to One Mile map of Great Britain. *International Yearbook of Cartography*. London. Vol. 5, pp. 94–103.

H M LAND REGISTRY. 1971. *Registration of Title to Land*. London, HMSO. pp. 18.

HACKMAN, F. 1972. Scaling the heights. *The Geographical Magazine*. London. Vol. 44, no. 11, pp. 778–80.

HACKMAN, G. A., WILLATTS, E. C. and WORTH, J. 1972. Instant maps for planners. *The Geographical Magazine*. London. Vol. 44, no. 11, pp. 775–7.

HALLIDAY, A. J. D. 1960. The re-survey of the six-inch maps of Scotland. *The Photogrammetric Record*. London. Vol. 3, no. 16, pp. 320–37.

HALLIDAY, LIEUT.-COL. E. 1968. Possible causes of systematic error in the geodetic levelling of England and Wales with particular reference to the heating of levelling staves by direct sunlight. *Conference of Commonwealth Survey Officers, 1967. Report of Proceedings*. Part I. London, HMSO. pp. 144–53.

HARLEY, J. B. and PHILLIPS, C. W. 1964. *The Historian's Guide to Ordnance Survey Maps*. London, The Standing Conference for Local History. pp. 51.

HARLEY, J. B. 1968. Error and revision in early Ordnance Survey maps. *The Cartographic Journal*. Edinburgh. Vol. 5, no. 2, pp. 115–24.

HARLEY, J. B. (Ed.) 1969–71. *Reprint of the First Edition of the One-Inch Ordnance Survey of England and Wales*. Newton Abbot, David & Charles.

HARLEY, J. B. 1971. The Ordnance Survey and the origins of official geological mapping in Devon and Cornwall. In *Exeter Essays in Geography*, edited by K. J. Gregory and W. L. D. Ravenhill. Exeter, University of Exeter. pp. 105–23.

HARLEY, J. B. 1971. Place-names on the early Ordnance Survey maps of England and Wales. *The Cartographic Journal*. Edinburgh. Vol. 8, no. 2, pp. 91–104.

HARRIS, L. J. 1957. Hill-shading in the new Quarter-Inch Ordnance Survey map. *The Geographical Journal*. London. Vol. 123, pt. 2, pp. 237–9.

HARRIS, L. J. 1959. Hill-shading for relief depiction in topographical maps. *The Chartered Surveyor*. London. Vol. 91, no. 9, pp. 515–20.

HARRIS, L. J. 1960. Hill-shading for relief depiction in topographical maps with some recent applications. *The Scottish Geographical Magazine*. Edinburgh. Vol. 76, no. 1, pp. 14–20.

HARRIS, L. J., BIDDLE, C. A., THOMPSON, E. H. and IRVING, E. G. 1964. British maps and charts: a survey of development. *The Geographical Journal*. London. Vol. 130, pt. 2, pp. 226–40.

HAVERFIELD, F. J. 1906. The Ordnance Survey maps from the point of view of the antiquities shown on them. *The Geographical Journal*. London. Vol. 27, no. 2, pp. 165–76.

HOTINE, M. 1937. The re-triangulation of Great Britain. *Empire Survey Review*. London. Vol. 4, no. 25, pp. 130–6.

Interim Report of the Departmental Committee on the Ordnance Survey, 1936. London, HMSO. pp. 16.

IRWIN, M. St G. 1971. Developments in automated cartography at the Ordnance Survey. *The Cartographic Journal*. Edinburgh. Vol. 8, no. 2, pp. 133–8.

JACK, E. M. 1926. The work of the Ordnance Survey. *The Scottish Geographical Magazine.* Edinburgh. Vol. **42**, no. 4, pp. 220–7.

JAMES, Col. Sir Henry. 1867. *Plans and Photographs of Stonehenge, and of Turusachan in the Island of Lewis; with notes relating to the Druids, and sketches of cromlechs in Ireland.* Southampton, Ordnance Survey.

JAMES, COL. Sir HENRY. 1869. *Notes on the Great Pyramid of Egypt and the cubits used in its design.* Southampton, Thomas Gutch & Co. pp. 13.

JOHNSTON, COL. D. A. 1899. *Ordnance Survey Maps of the United Kingdom. A description of their scales, characteristics, etc.* London, HMSO.

JOHNSTON, COL. D. A. 1904. *Classified Catalogue of Books in the Library of the Ordnance Survey Office, Southampton.* London, HMSO. pp. vii, 314.

JOHNSTON, LIEUT.-COL. W. J. 1920. The new One-Inch and Quarter-Inch maps of the Ordnance Survey. *The Geographical Journal.* London. Vol. **55**, no. 3, pp. 192–200.

KELLAWAY, G. P. 1970. *Map Projections.* London, Methuen & Co. pp. 127.

McCAW, G. T. 1938. The Transverse Mercator projection: a critical examination. *Empire Survey Review.* London. Vol. **4**, no. 27, pp. 275–81.

McGRATH, G. 1967. United Kingdom Ordnance Survey Tourist maps at one-inch scale: a review. Some Canadian implications. *The Cartographer.* Toronto. Vol. **4**, no. 2, pp. 136–56.

MacLEOD, M. N. 1926. The present state of the International 1/Million Map. (*Ordnance Survey Professional Papers, New Series no. 10.*) London, HMSO. pp. 11–13.

MacLEOD, M. N. *et al.* 1936. Ordnance Survey maps. *The Geographical Journal.* London. Vol. **87**, no. 4, pp. 308–27.

MacLEOD, M. N. *et al.* 1939. Discussion on the Final Report of the Departmental Committee on the Ordnance Survey. *The Geographical Journal.* London. Vol. **93**, no. 4, pp. 314–32.

MALING, D. H. 1973. *Coordinate Systems and Map Projections.* London, George Philip & Son. pp. xi, 255.

MATHIESON, J. 1932. The new One-Inch to a mile Ordnance Survey map. (Popular Edition.) *The Scottish Geographical Magazine,* Edinburgh. Vol. **48**, no. 2, pp. 98–103.

MONKHOUSE, F. J. 1950. The new Ordnance Survey map series scale 1:25000. *The Town Planning Review.* Liverpool. Vol. **21**, no. 2, pp. 70–81.

MUMFORD, I. and CLARK, P. K. 1968. Engraved Ordnance Survey one-inch maps – the methodology of dating. *The Cartographic Journal.* Edinburgh. Vol. **5**, no. 2, pp. 111–14.

MUMFORD, I. 1968. Engraved Ordnance Survey One-Inch maps: the problem of dating. *The Cartographic Journal.* Edinburgh. Vol. **5**, no. 1, pp. 44–6.

MUMFORD, I. 1972. Lithography, photography and photozincography in English map production before 1870. *The Cartographic Journal.* Edinburgh. Vol. **9**, no. 1, pp. 30–6.

NEALE, G. A. 1968. The large scale surveys of Great Britain. *American Congress on Surveying and Mapping. Papers from the 28th Annual Meeting.* Washington, DC. pp. 571–80.

1931. The One-Inch to the Mile Ordnance Survey map of England. *The Geographical Journal.* London. Vol. **78**, no. 4, pp. 353–6.

1933. The new road map of Great Britain. *The Geographical Journal.* London. Vol. **81**, no. 5, pp. 438–9.

OGILVIE, A. G. 1939. The future work of the Ordnance Survey: a review. *The Scottish Geographical Magazine.* Edinburgh. Vol. **55**, no. 2, pp. 107–11.

ORDNANCE SURVEY. 1857. *Report on the Ordnance Survey of the United Kingdom for 1855–56.* London, HMSO. pp. 27, pl. 28.

ORDNANCE SURVEY. 1875. *Account of the Methods and Processes Adopted for the Production of the Maps of the Ordnance Survey of the United Kingdom . . . London,* HMSO. pp. 214.

ORDNANCE SURVEY. 1902. *Contouring with the Water Level.* Department instructions. pp. 8.

ORDNANCE SURVEY. 1919. *The Ordnance Survey and the War, 1914–1919.* Southampton, Ordnance Survey Office.

ORDNANCE SURVEY. 1919. *Report of the Progress of the Ordnance Survey to the 31 March 1919.* London, HMSO. pp. 22.

ORDNANCE SURVEY. 1920. *A Description of the Ordnance Survey Small Scale Maps.* Second edition. Southampton, Ordnance Survey. pp. 32.

ORDNANCE SURVEY. 1922. *The Second Geodetic Levelling of England and Wales. 1912–1921.* London, HMSO. pp. 62; pl. XLVI.

ORDNANCE SURVEY. 1936. *Instructions for the Revision and Drawing of the One-Inch (Fifth Edition) Map.* Southampton, Ordnance Survey. pp. 31.

ORDNANCE SURVEY. 1947. *A Description of Ordnance Survey Medium Scale Maps.* Chessington, Ordnance Survey. pp. v, 21.

ORDNANCE SURVEY. 1950. *Constants, Formulae and Methods used by the Ordnance Survey for Computing in the Transverse Mercator Projection . . .* London, HMSO. pp. 31.

ORDNANCE SURVEY. 1950. *Projection Tables for the Transverse Mercator Projection of Great Britain.* Reprinted, 1967. London, HMSO. pp. 80.

ORDNANCE SURVEY. 1951. Field archaeology. Some notes for beginners . . . (*Ordnance Survey Professional Papers, New Series, no. 13.*) London, HMSO. pp. vii, 176.

ORDNANCE SURVEY. 1954. *A Description of the Ordnance Survey Large Scale Plans.* Chessington, Ordnance Survey. pp. v, 21; pl. x.

ORDNANCE SURVEY. 1955. *A Description of Ordnance Survey Medium Scale Maps.* Chessington, Ordnance Survey. pp. iv, 20; pl. XIV.

ORDNANCE SURVEY. 1957. *A Description of Ordnance Survey Small Scale Maps.* Chessington, Ordnance Survey. pp. iv, 12; pl. 17.

ORDNANCE SURVEY. 1960. *The Ordnance Survey Annual Report. 1959–60.* London, HMSO. pp. 18; pl. XII.

ORDNANCE SURVEY. 1961. *The Ordnance Survey Annual Report. 1960–1.* London, HMSO. pp. 18; pl. XII.

ORDNANCE SURVEY. 1963. *The Ordnance Survey Annual Report. 1962–63.* London, HMSO. pp. 11; pl. IX.

ORDNANCE SURVEY. 1965. *The Ordnance Survey Annual Report. 1964–65.* London, HMSO. pp. 19; pl. IX.

ORDNANCE SURVEY. 1967. *The History of the Re-triangulation of Great Britain. 1935–1962.* London, HMSO. 2 vols. pp. xix, 395; pl. 20.

ORDNANCE SURVEY. 1967. *The Ordnance Survey Annual Report. 1966–67.* London, HMSO. pp. v, 6; pl. VIII.

ORDNANCE SURVEY. 1969. *Annual Report. 1968–69.* London, HMSO. pp. 10; pl. v.

ORDNANCE SURVEY. 1969. *Place Names on Maps of Scotland and Wales.* Southampton, Ordnance Survey. pp. 23.

ORDNANCE SURVEY. 1970. Reduction service. (*Ordnance Survey Leaflet no. 6.*) Southampton.

ORDNANCE SURVEY. 1970. Enlargement and reduction service for 1:10560 and 1:10000 scale maps. (*Ordnance Survey Leaflet no. 12.*) Southampton.

ORDNANCE SURVEY. 1970. Supply of transparencies. (*Ordnance Survey Leaflet no. 14.*) Southampton.

ORDNANCE SURVEY. 1970. Supply of enlargements of large scale maps. (*Ordnance Survey Leaflet no. 15.*) Southampton.

ORDNANCE SURVEY. 1970. 35 mm microfilm service. (*Ordnance Survey Leaflet no. 33.*) Southampton.

ORDNANCE SURVEY. 1971. *Annual Report. 1970–71.* London, HMSO. pp. 10; pl. 5.

ORDNANCE SURVEY. 1972. The overhaul of the 1:2500 county series maps. (*Ordnance Survey Professional Papers, New Series, no. 25.*) Southampton, Ordnance Survey. pp. 30.

OUGHTON, M. 1963. Ordnance Survey Map Users' Conference. *Geography*. London. Vol. **48**, pt. 4, pp. 422–3.

PALMER, H. S. 1873. *The Ordnance Survey of the Kingdom; its object, mode of execution, history and present condition* . . . London, Edward Stanford. pp. 77.

PARSONS, E. J. S. 1958. *The Map of Great Britain circa 1360, known as the Gough Map*. Oxford, printed by Oxford University Press for the Bodleian Library, and Royal Geographical Society. pp. 38.

PHILLIPS, C. W. 1961. The Ordnance Survey and Archaeology 1791–1960. *The Geographical Journal*. London. Vol. **127**, pt. 1, pp. 1–9.

PHILLIPS, C. W. 1965. The special archaeological and historical maps published by the Ordnance Survey. *The Cartographic Journal*. Edinburgh. Vol. **2**, no. 1, pp. 27–31.

PROCTOR, D. W. 1962. Adjustment of aerial triangulation by electronic digital computers. *The Photogrammetric Record*. London. Vol. **4**, no. 19, pp. 24–33.

REDFEARN, J. C. B. 1948. Transverse Mercator formulae. *Empire Survey Review*. London. Vol. **9**, no. 69, pp. 318–22.

REES, H. 1946. The representation of housing patterns on the Fifth and Sixth Editions of the Ordnance Survey One-Inch map. *Geography*. London. Vol. **31**, pt. 3, pp. 110–16.

REIGNIER, F. 1957. *Les Systèmes de projection et leurs applications à la geographie, à la cartographie, à la navigation, à la topometrie, etc*. Paris, Institut Géographique Nationale. 2 vol.

Report from the Select Committee on Ordnance Survey (Scotland) . . . British Parliamentary Paper. 1851. X, 359.

Report from the Select Committee on Ordnance Survey of Scotland . . . British Parliamentary Paper. 1851. XIV, 361.

Report from the Select Committee on the Cadastral Survey . . . British Parliamentary Paper. 1861. XIV, 93.

Report from the Select Committee on the Cadastral Survey . . . British Parliamentary Paper. 1862. VI, 1.

Report of the Committee of Enquiry into the Arrangements for the Protection of Field Monuments. 1966–8. British Parliamentary Paper. Cmd 3904, 1963–9. XXXII, 739.

Report from the Registration and Conveyancing Commission. British Parliamentary Paper. 1850. XXXII, 1.

Report of the Committee on Weights and Measures Legislation. British Parliamentary Paper. Cmd. 8219. 1951. 1950–1. XX, pp. iv, 146.

Report of the Departmental Committee Appointed by the Board of Agriculture to Enquire into the Present Condition of the Ordnance Survey. British Parliamentary Paper. 1893. 1893–4. LXXII, 305.

Report of the Ordnance Survey Commission. British Parliamentary Paper. 1857–8. XIX, 585.

Report to the Lord Chancellor on H.M. Land Registry for the Year 1972–1973. 1973. London, HMSO. pp. 22.

ROBERTSON, I. M. 1970. The national grid and social geography. *Geography*. London. Vol. **55**, pt. 4, pp. 426–33.

ROBINSON, A. H. 1952. *The Look of Maps*. Madison, The University of Wisconsin Press. pp. 105.

ROBINSON, A. H. and SALE, R. D. 1969. *Elements of Cartography*. Third edition. New York, London, etc., John Wiley & Sons. pp. 415.

ROSING, K. E. and WOOD, P. A. 1971. *Character of a Conurbation. A computer atlas of Birmingham and the Black Country*. London, University of London Press. pp. 126.

ROY, MAJOR-GENERAL W. 1793. *The Military Antiquities of the Romans in Britain*. London, Society of Antiquaries. pp. xvi, 206; pl. LI.

Select Committee on Land Titles and Transfers. British Parliamentary Paper. 1857. Sess. 2. XXI, pp. vii, 457.

SEXTON, F. M. 1968. The adoption of the metric system in the Ordnance Survey. *The Geographical Journal*. London. Vol. **134**, pt. 3, pp. 328–42.

SEYMOUR, W. A. and IRWIN, B. St G. 1965. Continuous revision of Ordnance Survey plans. *The Geographical Journal.* London. Vol. **131**, pt. 1, pp. 76–85.

SHEWELL, H. A. L. 1951. Accuracy of contours. *Journal of the Royal Institution of Chartered Surveyors.* London. Vol. **84**, no. 4, pp. 195–215.

SKELTON, R. A. 1962. The origins of the Ordnance Survey of Great Britain. *The Geographical Journal.* London. Vol. **128**, pt. 4, pp. 415–30.

SKELTON, R. A. 1967. The military survey of Scotland, 1747–1755. *The Scottish Geographical Magazine.* Edinburgh. Vol. **83**, no. 1, pp. 5–16.

STEERS, J. A. 1965. *An Introduction to the Study of Map Projections.* Fourteenth edition. London, University of London Press. pp. 292.

SWEENEY, C. J. and SIMPSON, J. A. 1967. The Ordnance Survey and land registration. *The Geographical Journal.* London. Vol. **133**, pt. 1, pp. 10–23.

WALMESLEY-WHITE, A. 1970. Printing on demand and other Ordnance Survey developments. *International Yearbook of Cartography.* London. Vol. **10**, pp. 64–73.

WHEELER, R. P. 1948. The 1/1250 re-survey of Great Britain. *Empire Survey Review.* London. Vol. **9**, no. 68, pp. 234–47.

WILLIAMS, E. P. J. 1972. Digitised Ordnance Survey maps. *The Geographical Magazine.* London. Vol. **44**, no. 11, pp. 780–1.

WILLIAMS, E. P. J. 1973. The publication of urban topographic surveys in Great Britain. *The Cartographic Journal.* Edinburgh. Vol. **10**, no. 1. pp. 49–53.

WILLIS, J. C. T. 1932. *An Outline of the History and Revision of 25-inch Ordnance Survey Plans.* London, HMSO. pp. 18.

WILLIS, J. C. T. 1956. The Ordnance Survey and the public. *The Geographical Journal.* London. Vol. **122**, pt. 2, pp. 145–55.

WILSON, COL. SIR CHARLES W. 1891. Methods and processes of the Ordnance Survey. *The Scottish Geographical Magazine.* Edinburgh. Vol. **7**, no. 5, pp. 248–59.

WINTERBOTHAM, BRIG. H. St. J. L. 1932. The small scale maps of the Ordnance Survey. *The Geographical Journal.* London. Vol. **79**, no. 1, pp. 17–31.

WINTERBOTHAM, BRIG. H. St. J. L. 1932. Sheet-lines. *The Geographical Journal.* London. Vol. **80**, no. 6, pp. 512–18.

WINTERBOTHAM, BRIG. H. St. J. L. 1933. The use of the new grid on Ordnance Survey maps. *The Geographical Journal.* London. Vol. **82**, no. 1, pp. 42–54.

WINTERBOTHAM, BRIG. H. St. J. L. 1934. The national plans. (*Ordnance Survey Professional Papers, New Series, no. 16.*) London, HMSO. pp. 106; pl. 21.

WINTERBOTHAM, BRIG. H. St. J. L. 1934. The replotted counties . . . (*Supplement to Ordnance Survey Professional Papers, New Series, no. 16.*) Southampton, Ordnance Survey Office. pp. 25.

WINTERBOTHAM, BRIG. H. St. J. L. 1936. *A Key to Maps.* London and Glasgow, Blackie & Son. pp. ix, 208.

WINTERBOTHAM, BRIG. H. St. J. L. 1938. 50 years and 150 meridians. *Empire Survey Review.* London. Vol. **4**, no. 28, pp. 322–6.

WINTERBOTHAM, BRIG. H. St. J. L. 1938. The town plans. *Empire Survey Review.* London. Vol. 4, no. 29, pp. 425–30.

WINTERBOTHAM, BRIG. H. St. J. L. 1942. The Ordnance Survey. *Empire Survey Review.* London. Vol. **6**, no. 46, pp. 450–8.

WITHYCOMBE, J. G. 1925. Recent productions of the Ordnance Survey. *The Geographical Journal.* London. Vol. **66**, no. 6, pp. 533–9.

WITHYCOMBE, J. G. 1929. Lettering on maps. *The Geographical Journal.* London. Vol. **73**, no. 5, pp. 429–46.

WOODROW, H. C. 1967. The use of colour photography for large scale mapping. *The Photogrammetric Record.* London. Vol. **5**, no. 30, pp. 433–60.

Index

Demand 938385 5/75 K 160

Plates

SHETLAND Is.

Foula

ORKNEY Is.

Cape Wrath Dunnet Head

HEBRIDES

LEWIS

CAITHNESS

Cleisham

SUTHERLAND

Ben Clibrig

Moray F.

ROSS AND
CROMARTY

Findlay Seat

NAIRN

MORAY

BANFF

Sgur-na-
Lapich

Cairn
Glasher

The Buck

ABERDEEN Aberdeen

INVERNESS
Ben Auler

KINCARDINE

ANGUS

Craigowl

PERTH
Ben Cleuch

KINROSS

Firth of Tay

CLACKMANNAN

FIFE

DUMBARTON

Broadfield

STIRLING

WESTLOTHIAN
Firth of Forth

MIDLOTHIAN

The Buck

Cruach-na-Sleaghi

RENFREW

Lanark
Ch. Sp.

LANARK

EAST
LOTHIAN

BERWICK

Derrington Great Law

Berwick

PEEBLES

SELKIRK

Dunrich

Sandhope Heights

ARRAN

AYR
Brown
Carrick

ROXBURGH

Roxburgh is on the Lanark
Church Spire Meridian.

Firth of
Clyde

Hart Fell
DUMFRIES

KIRKCUDBRIGHT

NORTHUMBERLAND

Newcastle
Sunderland

WIGTOWN

Solway F.

CUMBERLAND
High Pike

DURHAM

Brandon R. Tees

Forest

Middlesbro'

ISLE OF MAN

WESTMORLAND

South Berule

NORTH RIDING

Barrow

YORK

York Minster

Flamborough

Bleasdale

EAST RIDING

LANCASHIRE

WEST RIDING

Hull

ANGLESEY

Liverpool

Manchester

Sheffield

Grimsby

R. Humber

Holyhead

Cryn-y-Bram

FLINT

Chester
CHESHIRE

DERBY

LINCOLN

CAERNARVON

DENBIGH

Nantwich
Ch. Sp.

Derby

NOTTINGHAM

Bardsey Is.

MERIONET

Shrewsbury

STAFFORD

Grantham

The
Wash

Cromer

HUNTINGDON

NORFOLK

Aberystwyth

MONTGOMERY

SALOP

LEICESTER

RUTLAND

Danbury Ch. Sp.

CAMBRIDGE

CARDIGAN

RADNOR

WORCESTER

WARWICK

NORTHAMPTON

SUFFOLK

BRECKNOCK

HEREFORD

BEDFORD

Danbury Ch. Sp.

PEMBROKE

CARMARTHEN

MONMOUTH

GLOUCESTER

OXFORD

BUCKINGHAM

HERTS

ESSEX

Highgate

GLAMORGAN

Llangeinor

MIDDLESEX
St. Paul's

R. Thames

Swansea

BERKS

LONDON

KENT

BRISTOL CHANNEL

Cardiff

Bristol

WILTS

SURREY
Leith Hill

Hollingbourne

Dover

Lundy Is.

SOMERSET

HANTS

SUSSEX
Ditchling

Beachy Hd.

Southampton

DEVON

DORSET

Black Down

ISLE OF WIGHT
Dunnose

Rippon Tor

Exeter

CORNWALL

Hensbarrow

Plymouth

ENGLISH CHANNEL

Scilly Isles

Lands End

Lizard

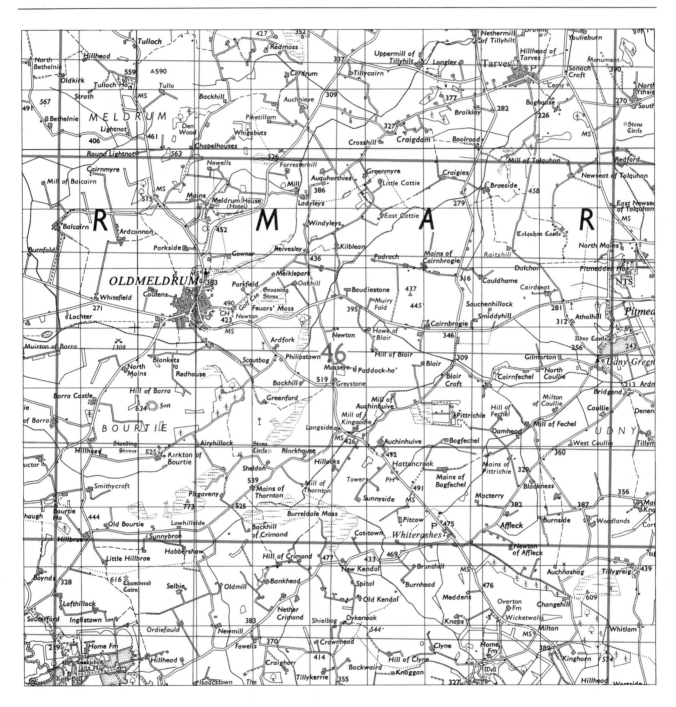

1:2500 SHEETS ON
COUNTY SERIES
SHEET LINES

1	2	3	4
5	6	7	8
9	10	11	12
13	14	15	16

46

SIX-INCH SHEET NUMBER
Sheets of each county are numbered
generally by Roman numerals

EXAMPLE
1:2500 plan
Aberdeen 46/14

Always prefix the plan number with the County name (see example)

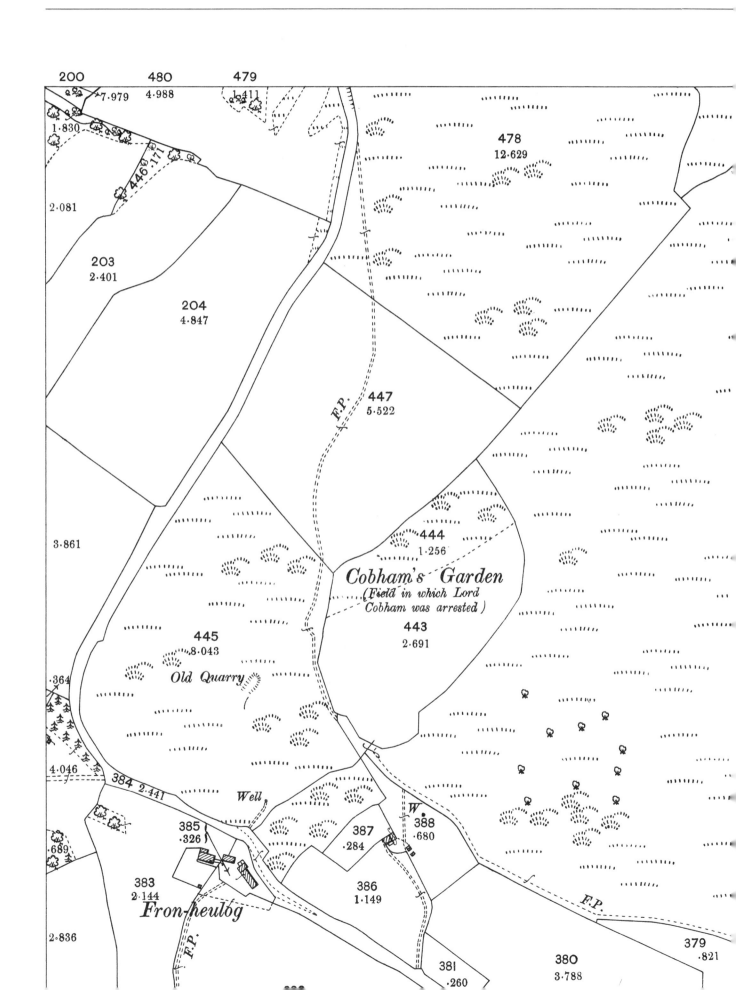

200   480   479

7·979   4·988   ·411

1·830

446·171

2·081

203
2·401

204
4·847

478
12·629

447
5·522

F.P.

3·861

444
1·256

Cobham's Garden
(Field in which Lord
Cobham was arrested)

443
2·691

445
8·043

Old Quarry

·364

4·046   384   2·441

Well

W·
388
·680

·689

385
·326

387
·284

383
2·144

Fron-heulog

386
1·149

F.P.

2·836

F.P.

381
·260

380
3·788

379
·821

Boundaries

Counties

Div^ns of Parly. Boroughs — Div. of Parly. Boro. Bdy.

County & Civil Ph.

Municipal Boroughs — Munl. Boro. Bdy.

Ridings

Municipal Wards — Ward Bdy.

County Boroughs (England) — Co. Boro. Bdy.

Urban Districts — U.D. Bdy.

County Burghs (Scotland) — Co. Burgh Bdy.

Police Burghs (Scotland) — Burgh. Bdy.

Parliamentary County Divisions — Parly. Div. Bdy.

Rural Districts — R.D. Bdy.

Poor Law Unions — Union Bdy.

Civil Parishes

Parliamentary Boroughs — Parly. Boro. Bdy.

Method of shewing the Boundaries in connection with the Detail.

The initials are placed where a change occurs in the nature of the Boundaries, as referred to a road, wall, stream, drain, or fence, and the symbol .... is used for marking the extent of the Boundary to which the initials refer.

1...Centre of Stream — C.S. C.S. 2...Centre of Track of Stream — C. Tk. S. Tk. S.

3...Centre of Road — C.R.

Side of Stream or Drain {

4... S.S.

5... S.D. S.D. — Drain or Stream Straight, Boundary changes Sides

6... S.S. S.S. — Boundary Straight, Stream or Drain changes Sides

7...Track of Hedge — Tk. H. Tk. H.   8...Root of Hedge, Face of Cop, Face of Fence — R.H. R.H.

9...Face of Wall — F.W.

4 feet from Root of Hedge or Fence &c. {

10... 4 ft. R.H.

11... 4 ft. R.H. 4 ft. R.H. — Fence Straight, Boundary changes Sides

12... 4 ft. R.H. 4 ft. R.H. — Boundary Straight, Fence changes Sides

13... 4 ft. R.H. — Stream on the Boundary side of Fence

14... 4 ft. R.H. 4 ft. R.H. — Boundary Straight, Fence changes Sides

15...Centre of Fence, Top of Cop, Centre of Wall &c. — C.F. T.C. C.W.

16...Defaced or Undefined, Track of Stream, Drain, or Fence — Def. Tk. S. Und.

From 4 to 9 the dots should be in contact with the line which represents the Side of Stream or Drain, Root of Hedge, Face of Cop, Face of Fence, Face of Wall.

From 10 to 14 the dots should not be in contact with the line which represents the Hedge or Fence, &c.

No. 15 The dots should be on the continuous line representing Centre of Fence, Top of Cop, Centre of Wall, &c.

Writing

These Examples must vary in size and extent according to the importance of the Districts they refer to.

Counties..⎫
                                                         ⎬ **C**
Ridings...⎭

Districts (Close) in Towns & Suburbs.... 𝔻

Districts (Open) in Towns & Suburbs.... 𝔻

County Boroughs (England)................⎫
                                                         ⎬ **€**
County Burghs (Scotland)..................⎭

Parish Churches & Villages

Other Villages

PARKS & DEMESNES

Gentlemen's Seats

Parliamentary County Divns.................**P**

Manufactories, Mines, Farms, Locks

Local Authority Establishments

Poor Law Unions............................**P**

Bridges (On Main Roads), Bridges (Other)

Isolated Houses

Parliamentary Boroughs....................**P**

BAYS & HARBOURS

NAVIGABLE RIVERS & CANALS

Divisions of Parly. Boroughs................𝔻

Small Rivers & Brooks

Municipal Boroughs.........................𝕄

BOGS, MOORS & FORESTS

Woods & Copses

Municipal Wards............................**W**

RANGES OF HILLS
*(The Names of very extensive Ranges of Hills are not shown
on Large Scale plans)*
Parts of Ranges

Urban Districts............................⎫
                                                         ⎬ **U**
Police Burghs (Scotland)..................⎭

Single Hill Features

Antiquities:‑
Pre & Post Roman *(to A D 1714)*
ROMAN (A.D. 43 to A.D. 420)

Rural Districts............................ℝ.𝔻.

Civil Parishes............................*P*

RAILWAYS. *RAILWAYS (Mineral).* Stations.

Towns (other than the above)..............*T*

Areas

Every parcel is numbered thus **27**

Its area is given underneath in Acres, thus .... **4·370**

Braces, indicating that the spaces so connected are included in the same reference number and area .... *The track in this case is excluded.*

___ „ _____ „ ___ *included.*

Altitudes (in feet)

The Altitudes are above the assumed mean level of the Sea at Liverpool. or Newlyn (as stated).

The Contour altitudes are written thus 200

Surface Levels along roads and to Trig! Stations, obtained by Spirit levelling, are written thus 326⁺, the cross shewing the spot at which the altitude is taken.

Altitudes with the letters B.M. marked ⚊ against them, refer to marks made on Buildings, Walls, Milestones &c., (Bench Marks).

Abbreviations

Electricity Pylon . E.P *or* ▯ E.P
Telephone Call Box . T.C.B
Police ___ „ ___ . P.C.B

Mile Stone .... ⎫ M.S
Pump .... ⎪ P
Signal Post ..... ⎬ . S.P
Guide Post ..... ⎪ G.P
or Board .... ⎪
Letter Box ...... ⎭ L.B

Trig! Station .... △

Altitude at Trig! Station ..... 507 △

Bench Mark .... B.M.325·9 ⚊

Surface Level .... 342 +

Boundary Stone .... B S ⎫
___ „ ___ *Post* .... B P ⎬ ₒ

Foot Bridge .... F.B.
Foot Path .... F.P.
Bridle Road .... B.R.

High or Low Water Mark of Medium Tides .... H.or L.W.M.M.T.
(England)

_____ „ _____ *Ordinary Spring* __ „ ____ H.or L.W.M.O.S.T.
(Scotland)

Sluice .... Sl.
Trough .... ▭ Tr.
Spring .... ⎫ Sp.
Well .... ⎬ₒ W
Mooring Ring .... ⎫ M.R
Mooring Post ..... ⎭ · M.P

Arrow denotes ..... ⟵ ⫷⫷⫷
  flow of water

Antiquities .... ⚓
  (Site of)

Signs

Wood

Marsh

Reeds

Osiers

Rough Pasture

Furze

Fir

Mixed Wood

Brushwood

Orchard

Bush

Ford

Stepping Stones

Ferry

Sloping Masonry

Flat Rock

Lock

Waterfall

Quarry

Sand Pit

Refuse Heap

Shingle

Gravel Pit

Clay Pit

Fences, Walls, Buildings &c.

Railway crossing River or Canal

Railway crossing Road

Embankment

Level Crossing

Road crossing Railway

Open Country

Cutting

27
4·220

28
·190

30
·270

29
3·670

F.P.

Road over single stream

B.R.

**Road over
River or Canal**

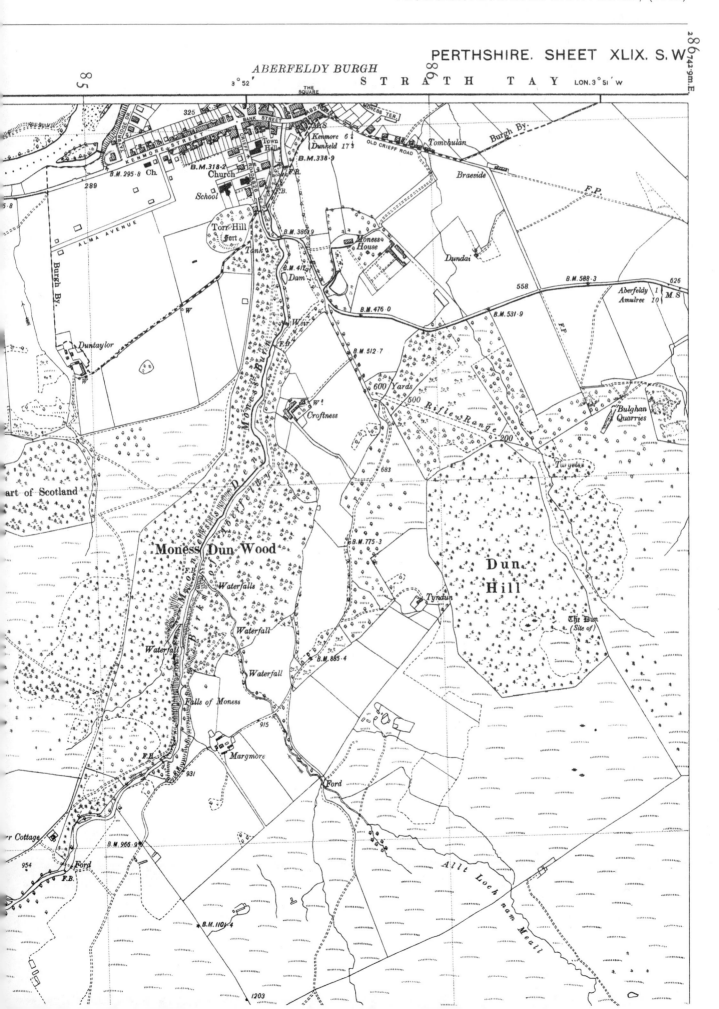

Boundaries

Counties (Geographical)	— — — —
County & Civil Ph.	— · — · — ·
Administrative County & Civil Parish. *(Part of Geographical County)*	+ · + · + · +
County Boroughs (England)	Co. Boro. Bdy. — — — —
County Burghs (Scotland)	Co. Burgh Bdy. — — — —
Parliamentary County Divisions	Parly. Div. Bdy. — — — —
Poor Law Unions (Obsolete since 1930).	Union Bdy. × · · · · · ×
Parliamentary Boroughs	Parly. Boro. Bdy. — — — —
Div^ns of Parly. Boroughs	Div. of Parly. Boro. Bdy. — — — —
Municipal Boroughs	Munl. Boro. Bdy. — — — —
Urban Districts	U.D. Bdy. — — — —
Police Burghs (Scotland)	Burgh Bdy. — — — — —
Rural Districts	R.D. Bdy. ∨ · · · · · ∨
Civil Parishes	· · · · · ·
Catchment Areas	C.A. Bdy. — — — —

Note: Where any Boundary other than County or Administrative County is coincident with Civil Parish Boundary,
the Symbol for the latter is shown, other Areas being denoted by description along the Boundary.

Altitudes (in feet)

The Altitudes are above the mean level of the Sea
at Liverpool or Newlyn (as stated).
The Contour altitudes are written thus ... 200

Altitudes along roads and to Trig! Stations obtained by
Spirit Levelling, are written thus 300·, the dot showing
the spot at which the altitude is taken.

Altitudes with the letters B.M. marked ⚞ against them,
refer to marks made on Buildings, Walls, Milestones, &c.

The Latitudes are given on the margin to every 30 seconds, & the Longitudes to every minute.

Writing

These Examples must vary in size and extent according to the importance of the Districts they refer to.

County Boroughs (England)..........⎫
                                    ⎬ **C**
County Burghs (Scotland)..........⎭

Parliamentary Boroughs .... **P**

Divisions of Parly. Boroughs.......... D

Municipal Boroughs.......... **M**

Urban Districts..........⎫
                         ⎬ U
Police Burghs (Scotland)..........⎭

Civil Parishes.......... **P**

Towns (Other than the above).......... *T*

Districts (Close) in Towns & Suburbs...... ⅅ

Districts (Open) in Towns & Suburbs ...... ⅅ

Antiquities ⎰ ROMAN (*A.D. 43 to A.D. 420.*)
            ⎱ 𝕻re & 𝕻ost 𝕽oman (*to A.D. 1714.*)

Parish Churches & Villages

Other Villages

PARKS & DEMESNES

Gentlemen's Seats

Manufactories, Mines, Farms, Locks

Local Authority Establishments

Bridges (**On Main Roads**), Bridges (*Other*)

Isolated Houses

BAYS & HARBOURS

NAVIGABLE RIVERS & CANALS

Small Rivers & Brooks

* BOGS, MOORS & FORESTS

Woods & Copses

RAILWAYS, *RAILWAYS* (Mineral) Stations

RANGES OF HILLS
Separate parts of Ranges
Single Features

When several Moors, Bogs, Mosses, &c. are included under one general name, or where they are the component parts of a larger though nameless district of Moor, the name of each subordinate or component part is shewn in Roman Print or in Stump Character according to its extent.

Contours

In Red or Blue ⎰ *Instrumental* ⌇‾‾200‾‾⌇
               ⎱ *Sketched* ....225........

In Black ⎰ *Instrumental* ‾‾‾200‾‾‾
         ⎱ *Sketched* ....225........

Before 1895 all contours were shewn by dotted lines.

Signs

Woods

Fir

Deciduous

Mixed Wood

Brushwood

Orchard

Rough Pasture

Furze

Marsh   Reeds   Osiers

Parks

Gravel Pit   Sand Pit

Quarry   Shingle

Other Pits

Railway over Road   Road over Railway   Road over Stream

Level Crossing   Railway over River   Sunken Road

Road over
River or Canal   Road over Stream   Raised Road

Arrow denotes flow of water.......... >

Antiquities, Site of ....

Trigonometrical Station ....

Bench Mark (B.M.)................................

Pump, Guide Post, Signal Post.................

Well, Spring, Boundary Post ....

Surface Level .... ·285

Double Lines of Railway

Single _do_ & Tramways

M.S. (Mile Stone)

Fenced

Main Roads

Minor _do_

Unfenced

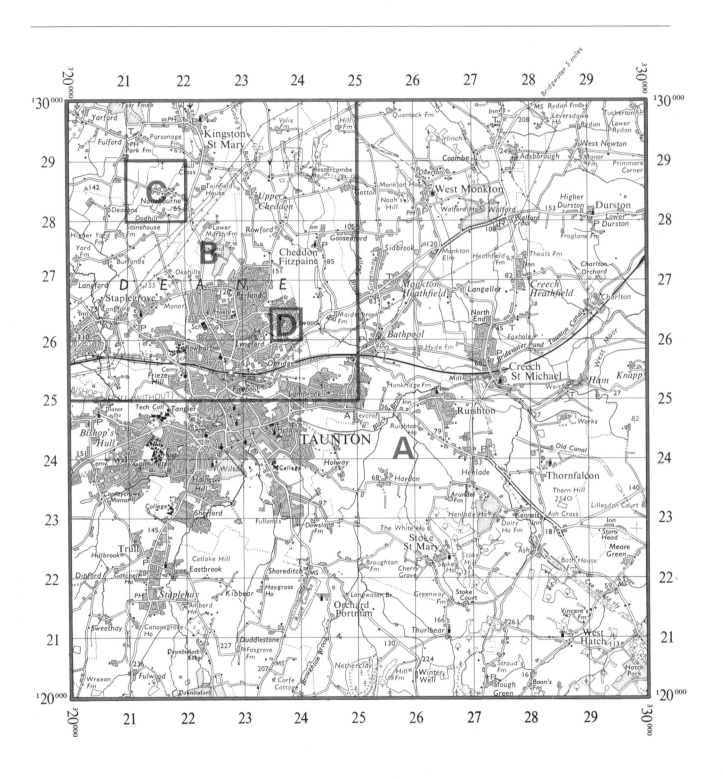

A Represents 1:25 000 sheet ST 22, at 1:63 360 scale

B Represents 1:10 560 sheet ST 22 NW, at 1:63 360 scale

C Represents 1:2500 sheet ST 2128, at 1:63 360 scale

D Represents 1:1250 sheet ST 2326 SE, at 1:63 360 scale

Links 50   0   5   10

259500

Metres

LANARKSHIRE   *COUNTY OF THE CITY OF GLAS*

596   597

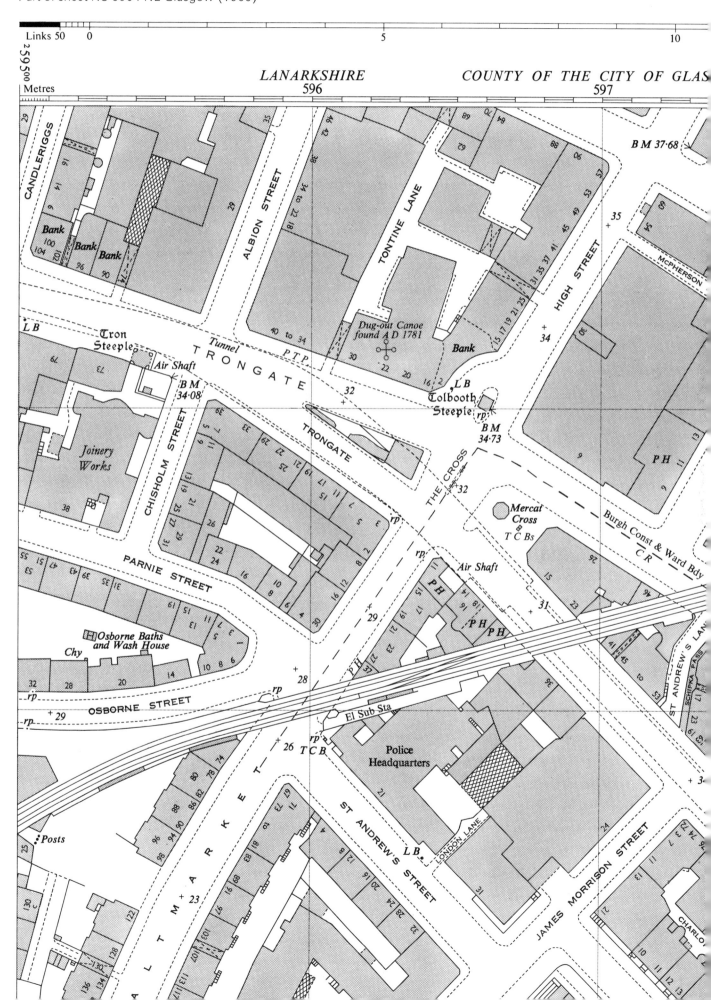

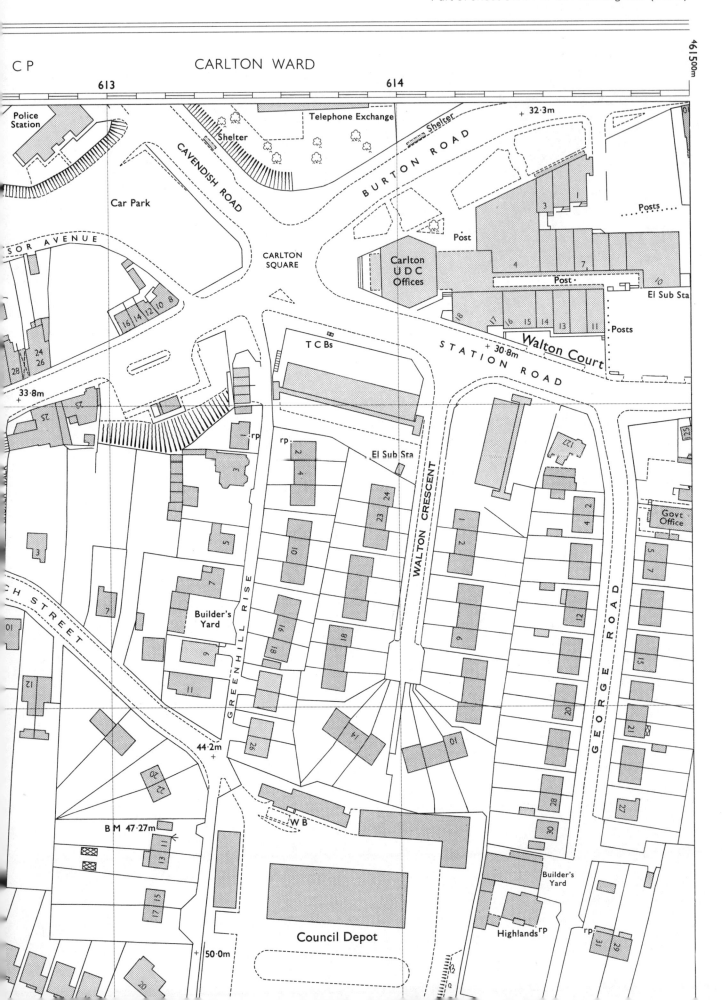

Symbols and signs

.... Bracken		.... Marsh, Saltings	
.... Coniferous Tree *(Surveyed)*		.... Orchard Tree	
.... Coniferous Trees *(Not Surveyed)*		.... Reeds	
.... Coppice, Osier		.... Rough Grassland	
.... Non-coniferous Tree *(Surveyed)*		.... Scrub	
.... Non-coniferous Trees *(Not Surveyed)*		.... Heath	
.... Antiquity *(site of)*		·ts .... Permanent Traverse Station	
.... Direction of water flow		·rp .... Revision Point *(Instrumentally fixed)*	
↑ B M .... Bench Mark *(Normal)*		↑ rp .... Revision Point and Bench Mark *(Coincident)*	
↑ F B M .... Bench Mark *(Fundamental)*		+ .... Surface Level	
⊗ .... Cave Entrance		△ .... Triangulation Station	
✚ .... Electricity Pylon		ʃ .... Area Brace *(1:2500 scale only)*	
━ E T L ━ .... Electricity Transmission Line		Perimeter of built-up area with single acreage *(1:2500 scale only)*	

Slopes

Top

Top

or

Sloping Masonry

Top

Glazed Roof Building

Archway

Roofed Building

Culvert

Boulders

Rock

Cliff

Active Quarry Chalk Pit or Clay Pit

Inactive Quarry Chalk Pit or Clay Pit

or

Walls, other than those of roofed buildings, which are less than 1 metre thick at 1:1250 scale or 1·4 metres thick at 1:2500 scale, are shown by a single line representing the centre of the wall.

Walls which are in excess of these widths are shown by two lines, each representing one face. For roofed buildings, the lines on the plan normally represent the outer face of the walls at ground level.

Thick Wall *Thin Walls* *Represented by*

Building

Boundaries

England & Wales

County Boundary (Geographical)

County & Civil Parish Boundary coterminous

Administrative County or County Borough Boundary

L B Bdy
London Borough Boundary

M B Bdy   U D Bdy   R D Bdy   County District Boundaries based on civil parish

R B Bdy
Rural Borough (Borough included in a Rural District)

Where the boundary of an Admin Co, Co Boro or
Co of City is coincident with that of a geographical county,
the symbol for the latter is shown.

England, Wales & Scotland

Civil Parish Boundary

Boro (or Burgh) Const   Co Const   Parly & Ward Boundaries based on civil parish

Boro (or Burgh) Const & Ward Bdy
Parly & Ward Boundaries not based on civil parish
Co Const Bdy

Scotland

(Not with parish)	(Coincident with parish)	
		County Boundary (Geographical)
Co Cnl Bdy	Co Cnl Bdy	County Council Boundary
Co of City Bdy	Co of City Bdy	County of the City Boundary
Burgh Bdy	Burgh Bdy	Burgh Boundary
Dist Bdy	Dist Bdy	District Council Boundary

Examples of Boundary Mereings

F F
R H
Symbol marking point where boundary mereing changes

Und
Undefined boundary

Def
Original boundary feature destroyed or defaced

C B	Centre of Bank	E K	Edge of Kerb
C C	Centre of Canal, etc.	F F	Face of Fence
C D	Centre of Ditch, etc.	F W	Face of Wall
C R	Centre of Road, etc.	S R	Side of River, etc.
C S	Centre of Stream, etc.	T B	Top of Bank
C O C S	Centre of Old Course of Stream	Tk H	Track of Hedge
C C S	Centre of Covered Stream	Tk S	Track of Stream
4ft R H	4 feet from Root of Hedge		

Abbreviations

B H	Beer House	P	Pillar, Pole or Post
B P, B S	Boundary Post, Boundary Stone	P C	Public Convenience
Cn, C	Capstan, Crane	P C B	Police Call Box
Chy	Chimney	P T P	Police Telephone Pillar
D Fn	Drinking Fountain	P O	Post Office
El P	Electricity Pillar or Post	P H	Public House
E T L	Electricity Transmission Line	Pp	Pump
F A P	Fire Alarm Pillar	S B, S Br	Signal Box, Signal Bridge
F S	Flagstaff	S P, S L	Signal Post, Signal Light
F B	Foot Bridge	Spr	Spring
G P	Guide Post	S, S D	Stone, Sundial
H	Hydrant or Hydraulic	Tk	Tank or Track
L B	Letter Box	T C B	Telephone Call Box
L C	Level Crossing	T C P	Telephone Call Post
L Twr	Lighting Tower	Tr	Trough
L G	Loading Gauge	Wr Pt, Wr T	Water Point, Water Tap
Meml	Memorial	W B	Weighbridge
M P U	Mail Pick-up	W	Well
M H	Manhole	Wd Pp	Wind Pump
M P	Mile Post or Mooring Post	M H or L W	Mean High or Low Water
M S	Mile Stone		(England and Wales)
N T	National Trust	M H or L W S	Mean High or Low Water
N T L	Normal Tidal Limit		Springs (Scotland)

Part of sheet SU 9877-9977 Datchet, Bucks (1968)

Links 100   0   10   20

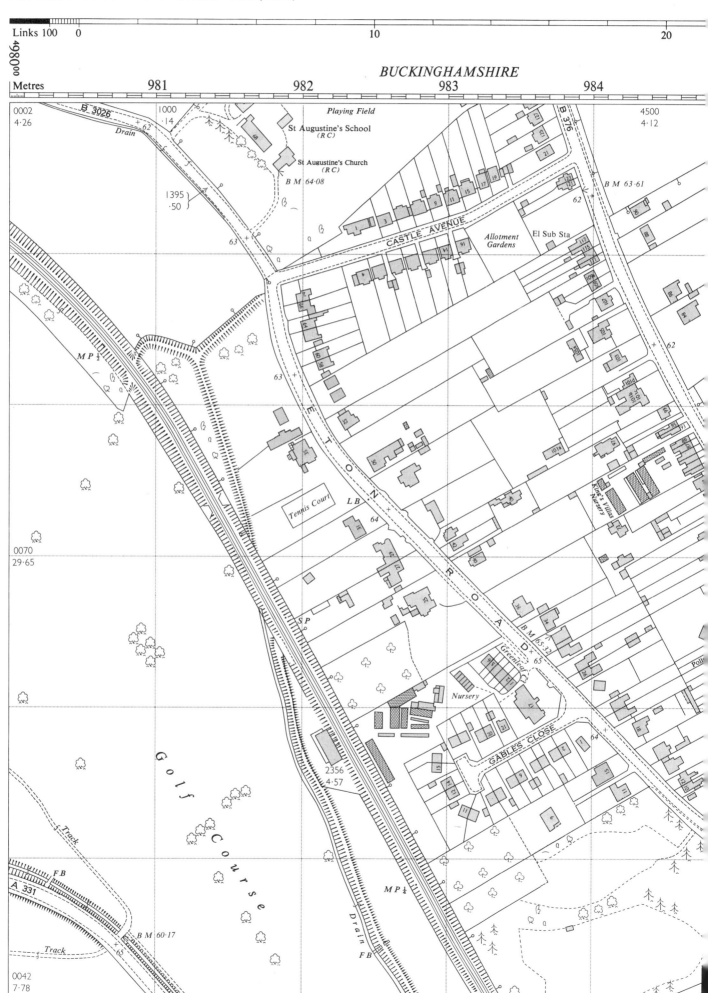

BUCKINGHAMSHIRE

Metres   981   982   983   984

Scale 1:2500
National Grid Metric Series

Part of sheet TQ 0437-0537 Cranleigh, Surrey (1971)

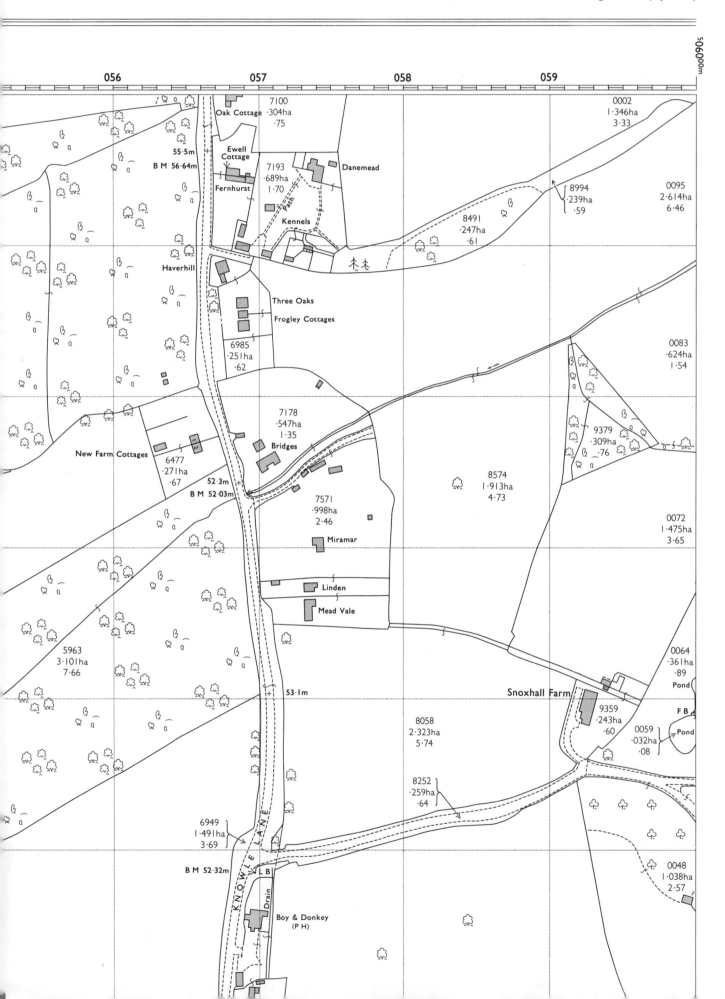

Part of sheet SU 9600-9700 Felpham, Sussex (1961)

Links 100   0   10   20

CHICHESTER R D   YAPTON PH

961   962   963   964

Metres

14

Scale 1:10 560
National Grid Provisional Series

Part of sheet SP 90 NW Wigginton, Herts. (1960)

0   500   0

80

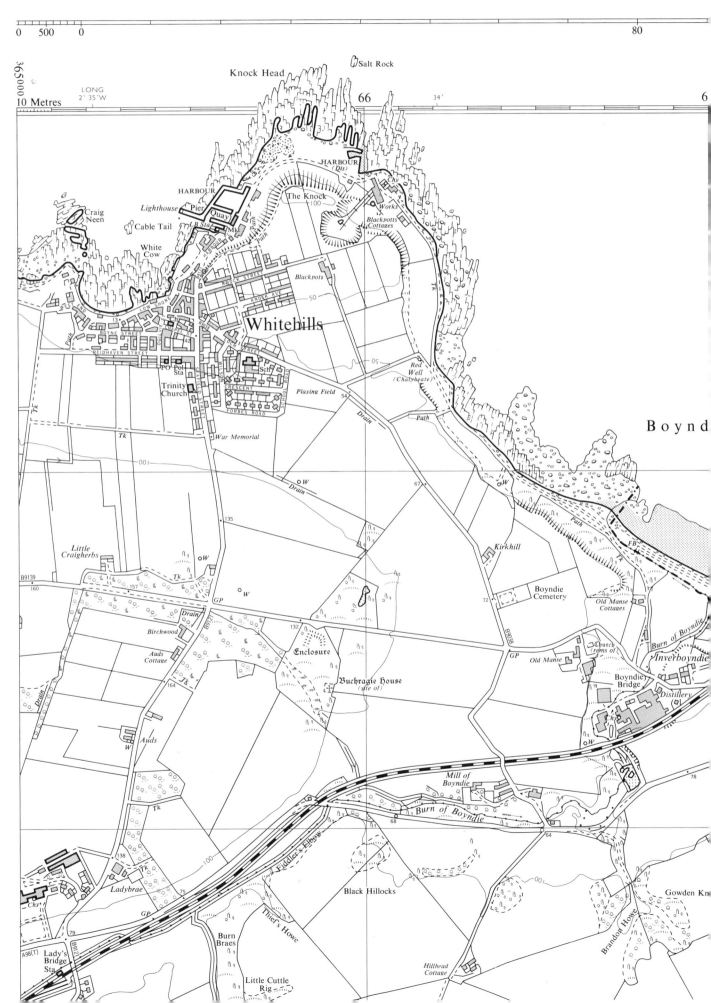

365000

LONG
2° 35'W

10 Metres

Salt Rock

Knock Head

66

34'

6

HARBOUR
(Dis)

HARBOUR

Chy

Craig
Neen

Lighthouse Pier Quay

Cable Tail

LB Sta MW

White
Cow

The Knock
100

Works

Blackpotts
Cottages

Blackpots

KNOCK STREET

KNOCK AVE.

50

Tk

WEST END

LOW SHORE

Whitehills

Chy

BOYNE STREET

Path

Path

Path

REIDHAVEN STREET

13

42

Boynd

PO Post
Sta

Sch

CHAPEL ST.

CRESCENT

FORBES ROAD

SCHOOL ROAD

Trinity
Church

Playing Field

05

54

Red
Well
(Chalybeate)

Path

Drain

Tk

War Memorial

Tk

001

Drain

W

67

W

135

Little
Craigherbs

W

Tk

W

B9139

160

157

GP

Drain

B9121

132

Birchwood

Auds
Cottage

Tk

164

Enclosure

Buchragie House
(site of)

Kirkhill

Boyndie
Cemetery

72

Old Manse
Cottages

B9038

Burn of Boyndie

Church
(rems of)

Inverboyndie

GP

Old Manse

Boyndie
Bridge

Distillery

Auds

W

W

Mill of
Boyndie

78

Tk

Burn of Boyndie

68

64

Fiddler's Elbow

138

Tk

100

001

Chy

Ladybrae

75

Black Hillocks

Gowden Kn

GP

Thief's Howe

Brandon Howe

79

Burn
Braes

A98(T)

Lady's
Bridge
Sta

B9121

Little Cuttle
Rig

Hillhead
Cottage

Symbols and signs

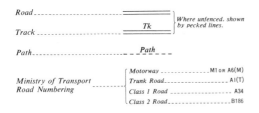

Road .... Where unfenced. shown by pecked lines.

Track .... *Tk*

Path .... *Path*

Ministry of Transport Road Numbering
- Motorway .... M1 OR A6(M)
- Trunk Road .... A1(T)
- Class 1 Road A34
- Class 2 Road B186

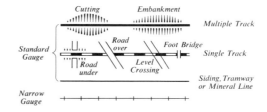

Standard Gauge

Narrow Gauge

Cutting   Embankment   Multiple Track

Road over   Foot Bridge   Single Track

Road under   Level Crossing

Siding, Tramway or Mineral Line

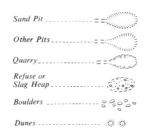

Roofed Building .... ▦

Glasshouse .... ⊠

Ruin .... ⊠

Antiquity (site of) .... ※

Triangulation Station .... △

Sloping Masonry .... ▦

Gravel Pit .... ▦

Sand Pit ....

Other Pits ....

Quarry ....

Refuse or Slag Heap ....

Boulders ....

Dunes ....

Trees, Coniferous ....

 " Non Coniferous ....

Scrub ....

Bracken ....

Heath ....

Rough Grassland ....

Electricity Transmission Line ...... Pylon Pole

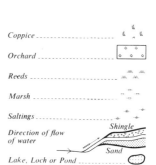

Coppice ....

Orchard ....

Reeds ....

Marsh ....

Saltings ....

Direction of flow of water   Shingle   Sand

Lake, Loch or Pond ....

Boundaries

Geographical County ....

Administrative County, County Borough or County of City ....

Municipal Borough, Urban or Rural Districts, Burgh or District Council ....

The first appropriate symbol in this list is shown when coincidence of boundaries occurs.

Civil Parish .... · · · · · · · · Shown alternately when coincidence of boundaries occurs.

Borough, Burgh or County Constituencies .. Shown only when not coincident with other boundaries.

Heights

Values are given in feet above Mean Sea Level at Newlyn.

Contours are at a varying vertical interval.

Surface heights determined by { ground survey .... •165 air survey .... ·356

Bench Marks and their values are shown on Large Scale plans, and Bench Mark lists containing fuller and possibly later levelling information are obtainable from the Director General, Ordnance Survey.

Rock features

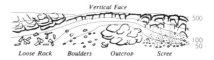

Vertical Face   500   100 50

Loose Rock   Boulders   Outcrop   Scree

Abbreviations

Boundary Post or Stone .... *BP, BS*

Church .... *Ch*

Fire Engine Station .... *F E Sta*

Foot Bridge .... *F B*

Fountain .... *Fn*

Guide Post .... *G P*

Mile Post .... *M P*

Mile Stone .... *M S*

Police Station .... *Pol Sta*

Post Office .... *PO*

Public House .... *PH*

Signal Box .... *SB*

Spring .... *Spr*

Telephone Call Box .... *TCB*

Well .... *W*

Symbols and signs

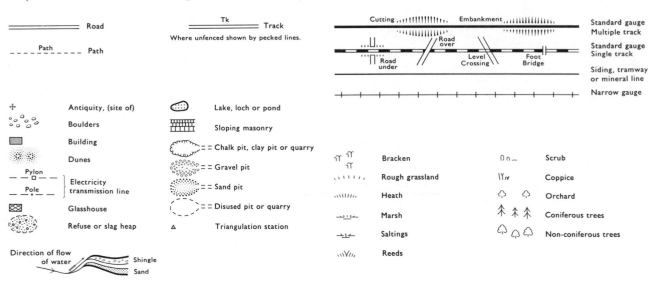

―――― Road

――Tk―― Track
Where unfenced shown by pecked lines.

─ ─ ─ ─ Path ─ ─ ─ ─ Path

Cutting ‖‖‖‖‖ Embankment ‖‖‖‖‖ Standard gauge Multiple track

Road over Standard gauge Single track

Road under Level Crossing Foot Bridge Siding, tramway or mineral line

─┼─┼─┼─┼─┼─ Narrow gauge

‡	Antiquity, (site of)
°°°	Boulders
▣	Building
░	Dunes
Pylon ─□─ Pole ─·─	Electricity transmission line
⊠	Glasshouse
⊚	Refuse or slag heap

Direction of flow of water Shingle Sand

⬭	Lake, loch or pond
▦	Sloping masonry
⬭ = =	Chalk pit, clay pit or quarry
⬭ = =	Gravel pit
⬭ = =	Sand pit
⬭ = =	Disused pit or quarry
△	Triangulation station

⟂⟂	Bracken
⟍⟍⟍	Rough grassland
⟍⟍⟍	Heath
┴┴	Marsh
┴┴	Saltings
⟍V⟍	Reeds

0 0 ‒	Scrub
⟍Y⟍	Coppice
⌂ ⌂	Orchard
♠ ♠ ♠	Coniferous trees
♣ ♣ ♣	Non-coniferous trees

Boundaries

The first appropriate symbol in this list is shown when coincidence of boundaries occurs.

━ ━ ━ ━ Geographical County

━ ━ ━ ━ Administrative County, County Borough or County of City

▬ ▬ ▬ ▬ Municipal Borough, Urban or Rural District, Burgh or District Council

· · · · · · · · Civil Parish
Shown alternately when coincidence of boundaries occurs.

▬ ▬ ▬ ▬ Borough, Burgh or County Constituency
Shown only when not coincident with other boundaries.

Heights

Values are given in metres above mean sea level at Newlyn

Surface heights determined by { ground survey · 165m
air survey · 108m

CONTOUR NOTE
Contours have been surveyed at 25 feet vertical interval but values are given to the nearest metre.

Rock features

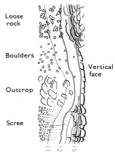

Loose rock

Boulders

Outcrop

Scree

Vertical face

Abbreviations

BP,BS	Boundary Post or Stone	GP	Guide Post	PH	Public House
Ch	Church	MP	Mile Post	SB	Signal Box
CH	Club House	MS	Mile Stone	Spr	Spring
F E Sta	Fire Engine Station	Pol Sta	Police Station	TCB	Telephone Call Box
FB	Foot Bridge	PO	Post Office	TCP	Telephone Call Post
Fn	Fountain	PC	Public Convenience	W	Well

DEVONSHIRE

OFFWELL CP
HONITON CO CONST

DALWOOD CP

WIDWORTHY CP

SHUTE CP

COLYTON CP

Symbols, signs and abbreviations

Roads

Motorway, Trunk and Main Road (Dual Carriageway)	M4 or A6(M)	A123 or A123(T)
Trunk & Main Road	A123 or A123(T)	
Secondary Road	Fenced B2314	Unfenced
Road Under Construction		
Other Roads	Good, metalled	Poor, or unmetalled
Footpaths	FP Fenced	FP Unfenced

Railways, Multiple Track — Station — Road over — Cutting — Tunnel — FB (Footbridge)
Sidings

,, Single Track — Viaduct — Level Crossing — Embankment — Road under

,, Narrow Gauge

London & Glasgow Transport Underground Stations ○   Interchange Stations ⊗

Aerial Ropeway — Aerial Ropeway

Pipe Line (Oil, Water) — Pipe Line

Electricity Transmission Lines (Pylons shown at bends and spaced conventionally) —⊗— — — — —⊗—

Post Offices (In Villages & Rural Areas only) P   Town Hall TH   Public House PH

Church or Chapel with Tower ▮   Church or Chapel with Spire ▮   Church or Chapel without either +

Triangulation Station △   on Church with Tower △   without Tower △

Intersected Point on Chy ○   on Church with Spire ○   without Spire +   on Building ▭

Guide Post GP.   Mile Post MP.   Mile Stone MS.   Boundary Stone BS ○   Boundary Post BP○

Youth Hostel Y   Telephone Call Box (Public) T   (AA) A   (RAC) R   Antiquity (site of) ⚔

Public Buildings	Glasshouses
Quarry & Gravel Pit	Orchard
National Trust Area — Sheen Common NT	Furze
,, ,, ,, Scotland NTS	Rough Pasture Heath & Moor
Osier Bed	Marsh
Reeds	Well W ○
Park, Fenced	Spring Spr ○
Wood, Coniferous, Fenced	Wind Pump Wd Pp .
Wood, Non-Coniferous Unfenced	Contours are at 25 feet vertical interval.
Brushwood, Fenced & Unfenced	Spot Height 123 ·

Ferries — Foot — Vehicle — Sand Hills — Mud — Flat Rock — Slopes — Lake — Bridge — Aqueduct — Towing Path — Lock — Weir — Ford — Dam — FB (Footbridge) — HWMMT — Highest point to which Medium Tides flow — Sand — △ Beacon — Sand — Lightship — Sand & Shingle — Cliff — Lighthouse

(High & Low Water Mark of Ordinary Spring Tides, in Scotland)

Boundaries

County or County Borough	— — — — — — — — —
,, ,, County of City (in Scotland)	
,, ,, ,, ,, ,, with Parish	—·—··—·—··—·—··
Parish	· · · · · · · · · · · · · · · · ·

Roads

M I or A 6 (M)	Motorway
A 31 (T)	Trunk road
A 35	Main road
B 3074	Secondary road
A 35	Dual carriageway
	14 ft of metalling or over (not included above)
	Under 14 ft of metalling, tarred (not included above)
	Under 14 ft of metalling, untarred
	Minor road in towns, drive or track (unmetalled)

Unfenced roads and tracks are shown by pecked lines

.... Path

Public rights of way

} Public paths { Footpath / Bridleway

Road used as a public path

Public rights of way indicated by these symbols have been derived from Definitive Maps as amended by later enactments or instruments held by Ordnance Survey and are shown subject to the limitations imposed by the scale of mapping.
The representation on this map of any other road, track or path is no evidence of the right of way.

Railways

	Multiple track
	Single track
	Narrow gauge
	Siding
	Cutting
	Embankment
	Tunnel
	Road over
	Road under
	Level crossing
	Station

Vegetation

	Coniferous trees
	Non coniferous trees
	Coppice
	Orchard
	Scrub
	Bracken
	Heath
	Rough grassland
	Reeds
	Marsh
	Saltings

Rock features

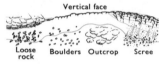

Vertical face

Loose rock · Boulders · Outcrop · Scree

Heights

Values are given in feet above mean sea level at Newlyn.

165 ·	Determined by ground survey
913 ·	Determined by air survey
250 / 200 / 150 / 125	Contours are at 25 feet vertical interval.

Boundaries

— — — — —	Geographical County
— — — — —	Administrative County, County Borough, or County of City
— — — — —	Municipal Borough, Urban or Rural District, Burgh or District Council
··············	Civil Parish
— — — — —	Borough, Burgh or County Constituency

The first appropriate symbol in this list is shown when coincidence of boundaries occurs

Shown alternately with one of the symbols above, when coincidence of boundaries occurs

Shown only when not coincident with other boundaries

Symbols

↑	Church or chapel	with tower	
↑		with spire	
+		without tower or spire	
▭		Building	
▨		Glasshouse	
⬭		Bus or coach station	
○		Chimney	
⊥		Beacon	
⛯		Lighthouse	
⚓		Lightship	
△		Triangulation station	
⛯ ⛯ ⊹		Triangulation point on church, chapel, lighthouse & beacon	
⛯ ⊥			
▭ ○		Triangulation point on building & chimney	

NT	National Trust always open
NT	National Trust opening restricted
VILLA	Roman antiquity (AD 43 to AD 420)
Castle	Other antiquities
✝	Site of antiquity
⚔ 1066	Site of battle (with date)
	Gravel pit
	Sand pit
	Disused pit or quarry
	Chalk pit, clay pit or quarry
	Refuse or slag heap
	Sloping masonry

Electricity transmission line

pylon — pole

Abbreviations

BP	Boundary Post	Sch	School
BS	Boundary Stone	Spr	Spring
CH	Club House	T	Telephone, public
F	Ferry { Foot	A	Telephone, AA
V	Ferry { Vehicle	R	Telephone, RAC
FB	Foot Bridge	TH	Town Hall
Ho	House	Twr	Tower
MP	Mile Post	W	Well
MS	Mile Stone	Wd Pp	Wind Pump
Mon	Monument	Y	Youth hostel
P	Post office		
Pol Sta	Rural areas only { Police Station		
PC	Public Convenience		
PH	Public House		

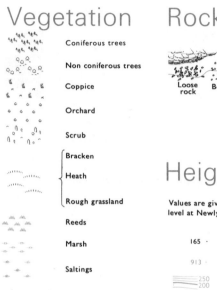

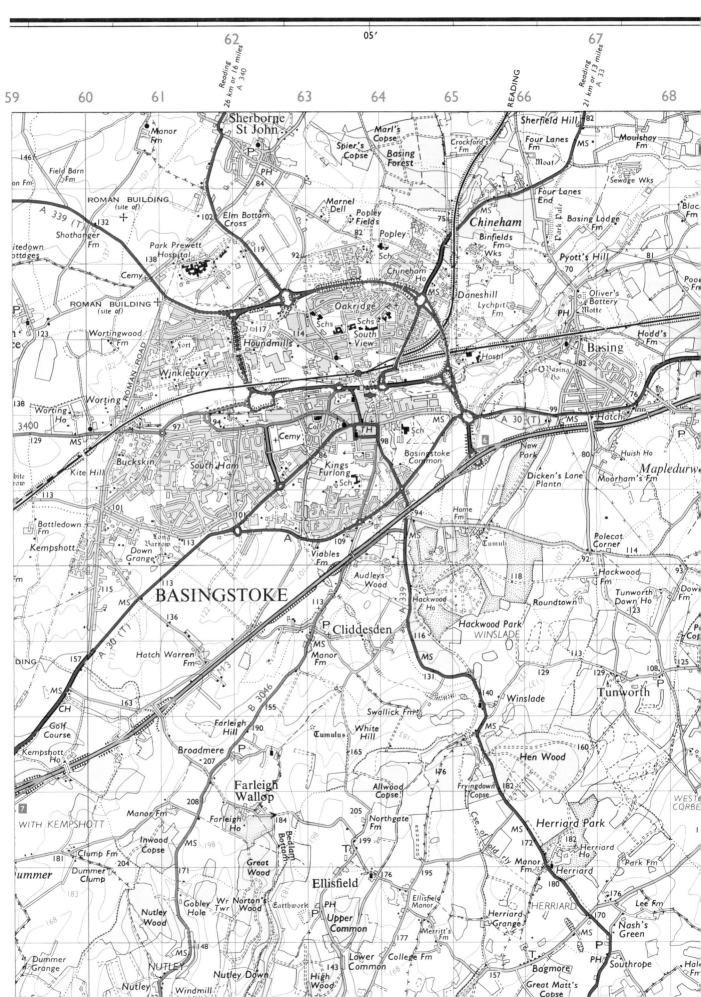

Roads and paths

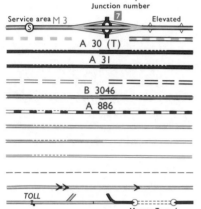

Service area M 3   Junction number   Elevated

A 30 (T)

A 31

B 3046

A 886

TOLL   Mersey Tunnel

Unfenced roads are shown by short pecks

Motorway
Motorway projected; under construction
Trunk road ⎫
Main road ⎬ Single and dual carriageway
Under construction
Secondary road ⎭
Narrow trunk or main road with passing places
4·3 metres of metalling or over (not included above)
Under 4·3 metres of metalling tarred and untarred
Minor road in towns, drive or track (unmetalled)
Path
Gradients: 1 in 5 and steeper   1 in 7 to 1 in 5
Toll gate   Other gates   Entrances to road tunnels

Public rights of way

⎫ Public paths ⎧ Footpath
⎭   ⎩ Bridleway
Road used as a public path or byway open to all traffic

Public rights of way indicated by these symbols have been derived from Definitive Maps as amended by later enactments or instruments held by Ordnance Survey and are shown subject to the limitations imposed by the scale of mapping The representation on this map of any other road, track or path is no evidence of the existence of a right of way

Railways

Multiple ⎫ Standard
Single ⎬ gauge track
Narrow gauge
Mineral line, siding or tramway
Bridge
Foot bridge

a   b
Station (a) principal
        (b) closed to passengers

Viaduct
Level crossing
Tunnel
Cutting
Embankment

Water features

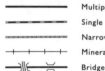
Marsh
Lake or loch
Canal and tow path
Aqueduct

Ferry F
Ferry V
Ferry foot
Ferry vehicle
Foot bridge
Light vessel, lighthouse and beacon

Slopes
Cliff
Flat rock
Sand and mud
Sand and shingle
Low water mark
High water mark
Highest point to which tides flow

General features

Electricity transmission line
(with pylons spaced conventionally)
Pipe line
(arrow indicates direction of flow)

Quarry
Open pit
Wood
Orchard
Park or ornamental grounds
Bracken, heath and rough grassland
Dunes

Broadcasting station (mast or tower)
Bus or coach station
Church ⎧ with tower
  or   ⎨ with spire
Chapel ⎩ without tower or spire
Glasshouse
Graticule intersection at 5' intervals
Triangulation pillar
Windmill (in use)
Windmill (disused)
Wind pump
Youth hostel

Relief

—76—   Contour values are given to the nearest metre. The vertical interval is, however, 50 feet.

.144   Heights are to the nearest metre above mean sea level. Heights shown close to a triangulation pillar refer to the station height at ground level and not necessarily to the summit. Details of the summit height may be obtained from the Ordnance Survey
1 metre = 3·2808 feet
15·24 metres = 50 feet

Boundaries

—+—+—+   National
–o–o–o–o–   London Borough
National Park
—·—·—·—   County or Metropolitan County
············   Civil Parish or equivalent

The county areas and names shown on this map are effective on 1st April 1974
Urban Civil Parishes cease to exist on 1st April 1974

National Trust
NT   always open

NT   opening restricted

Abbreviations

P   Post office
PH   Public house
CH   Club house
.MP   Mile post
.MS   Mile stone
TH   Town hall, Guildhall or equivalent
PC   Public convenience (in rural areas)
.T ⎫   ⎧ PO
.A ⎬ Telephone call box ⎨ AA
.R ⎭   ⎩ RAC

Antiquities

VILLA   Roman
Tumulus   Non-Roman
+   Site of antiquity
×   Battlefield (with date)
1066

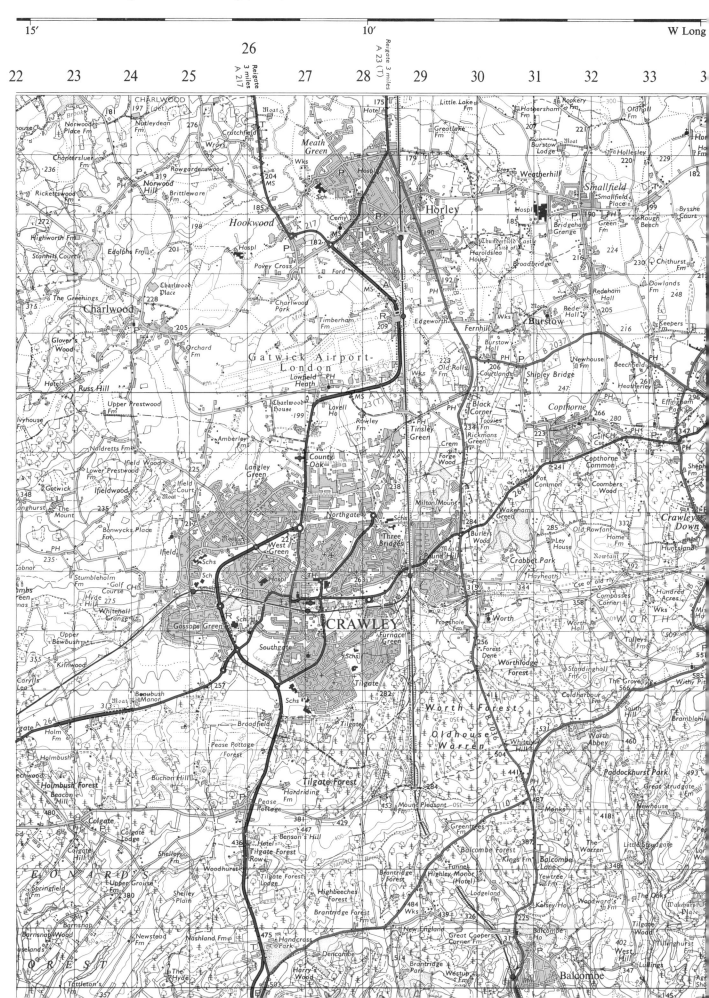

Roads and paths

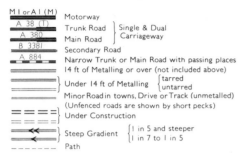

M I or A I (M) — Motorway
A 38 (T) — Trunk Road ⎫ Single & Dual
A 380 — Main Road ⎬ Carriageway
B 338I — Secondary Road
A 884 — Narrow Trunk or Main Road with passing places
— 14 ft of Metalling or over (not included above)
⎫ Under 14 ft of Metalling { tarred / untarred
— Minor Road in towns, Drive or Track (unmetalled)
(Unfenced roads are shown by short pecks)
— Under Construction
◄◄ Steep Gradient { 1 in 5 and steeper / 1 in 7 to 1 in 5
— Path

Boundaries

+—+—+—+ National
— — — County
—..—..—.. County Borough or County with Civil Parish
.... Civil Parish
—●—●— London Borough

England and Wales | Scotland
NT | NTS ⎫ National Trust { always open
NT | NTS ⎬ { opening restricted

National Park Boundary

Public rights of way

.... ⎫ Public Paths { Footpath
— — — — — ⎬ { Bridleway
┬┬┬┬┬┬┬ Road used as public path

Abbreviations

P — Post Office
PH — Public House
CH — Club House
.MP — Mile Post
.MS — Mile Stone
TH — Town Hall, Guildhall or equivalent
PC — Public Convenience (in rural areas)

.T ⎫ ⎫ PO
.A ⎬ Telephone Call Box ⎬ AA
.R ⎭ ⎭ RAC

Railways

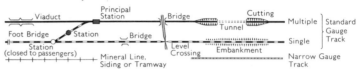

Viaduct — Principal Station — Bridge — Cutting — Multiple ⎫ Standard Gauge Track
Foot Bridge — Station — Bridge — Tunnel — Single ⎬ Gauge Track
Station (closed to passengers) — Mineral Line, Siding or Tramway — Level Crossing — Embankment — Narrow Gauge Track

Miscellaneous

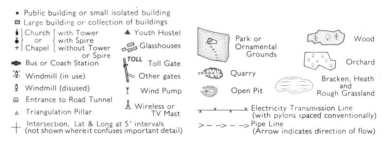

■ Public building or small isolated building
▢ Large building or collection of buildings
▮ Church { with Tower
▮ or { with Spire
+ Chapel { without Tower or Spire
● Bus or Coach Station
☿ Windmill (in use)
♀ Windmill (disused)
∩ Entrance to Road Tunnel
△ Triangulation Pillar
+ Intersection, Lat & Long at 5′ intervals (not shown where it confuses important detail)

▲ Youth Hostel
Glasshouses
TOLL Toll Gate
Other gates
Ψ Wind Pump
Wireless or TV Mast

Park or Ornamental Grounds
Quarry
Open Pit

Wood
Orchard
Bracken, Heath and Rough Grassland

Electricity Transmission Line (with pylons spaced conventionally)
>—>—— Pipe Line (Arrow indicates direction of flow)

Water features

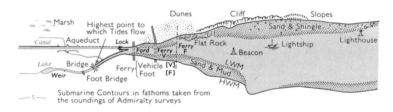

Marsh — Highest point to which Tides flow — Dunes — Cliff — Slopes
Canal — Aqueduct — Lock — Sand & Shingle
Lake — Bridge — Ford — Ferry — Flat Rock — Lightship — Lighthouse
Weir — Foot Bridge — Ferry Foot — Vehicle [V] / Ferry [F] — Sand & Mud — Beacon
LWM — HWM

Submarine Contours in fathoms taken from the soundings of Admiralty surveys

Antiquities

VILLA — Roman Antiquity (AD 43 to AD 420)
Castle — Other Antiquities
+ — Site of Antiquity
⚔ 1066 — Site of Battle (with date)

Relief

Heights in feet above Mean Sea Level

·275 — surveyed by levelling
·1091 — not surveyed by levelling

—250— Contours at 50 ft intervals

Part of Lake District sheet (1971)

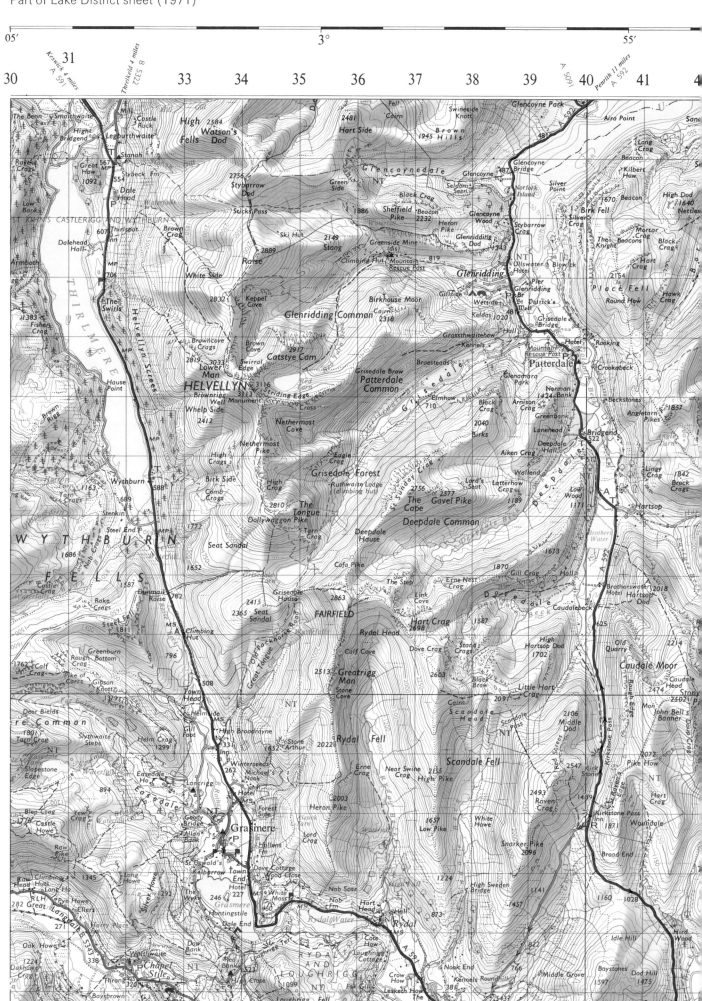

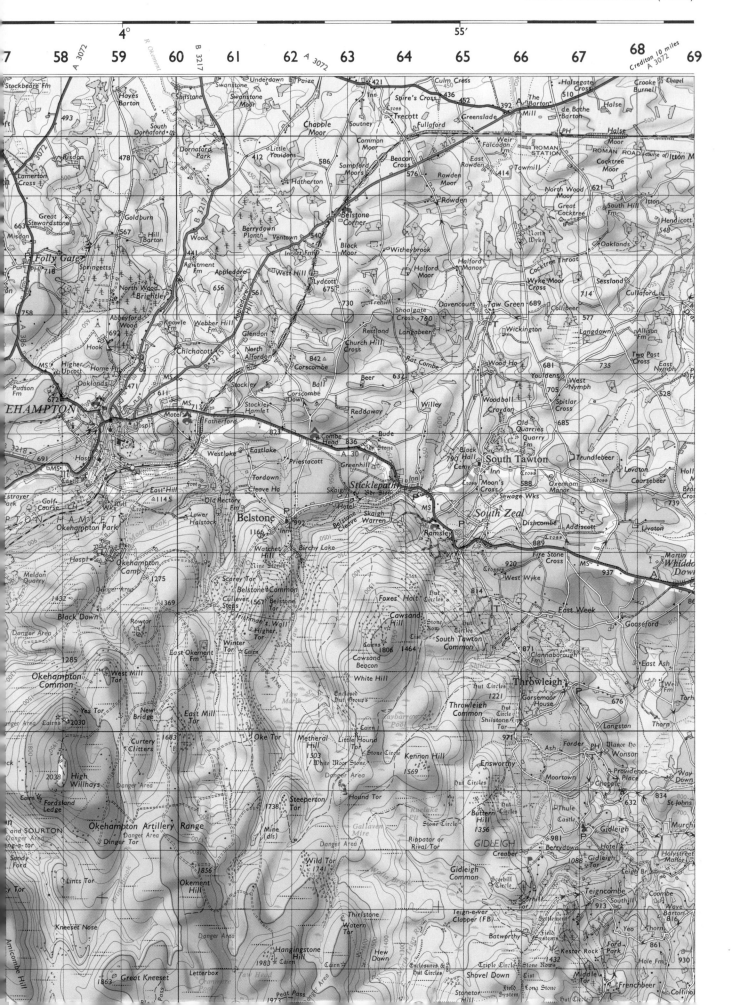

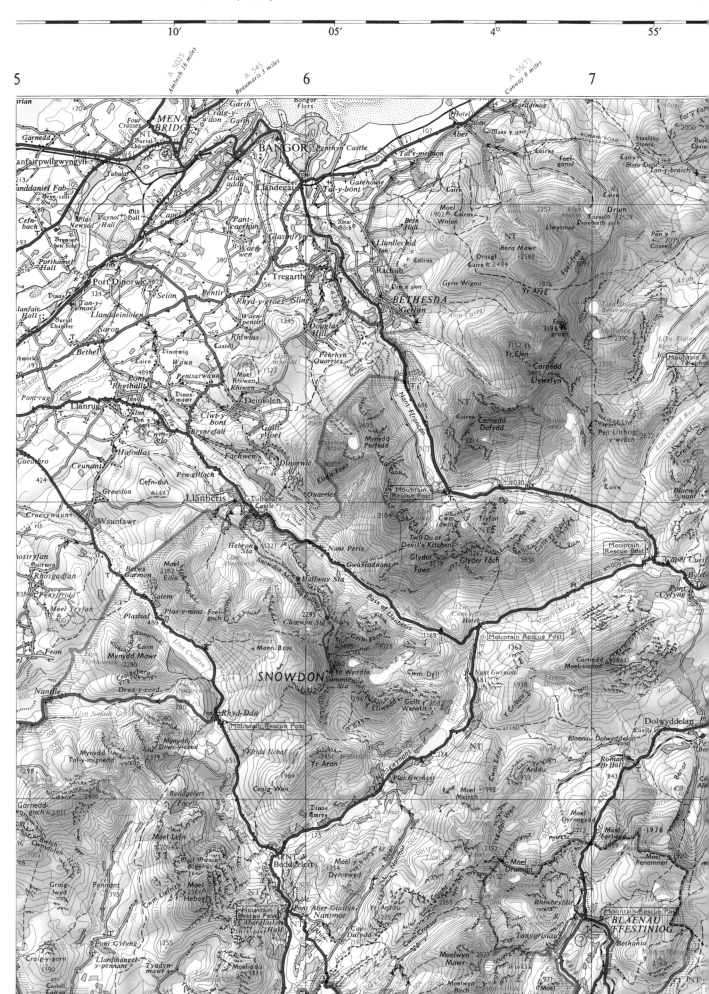

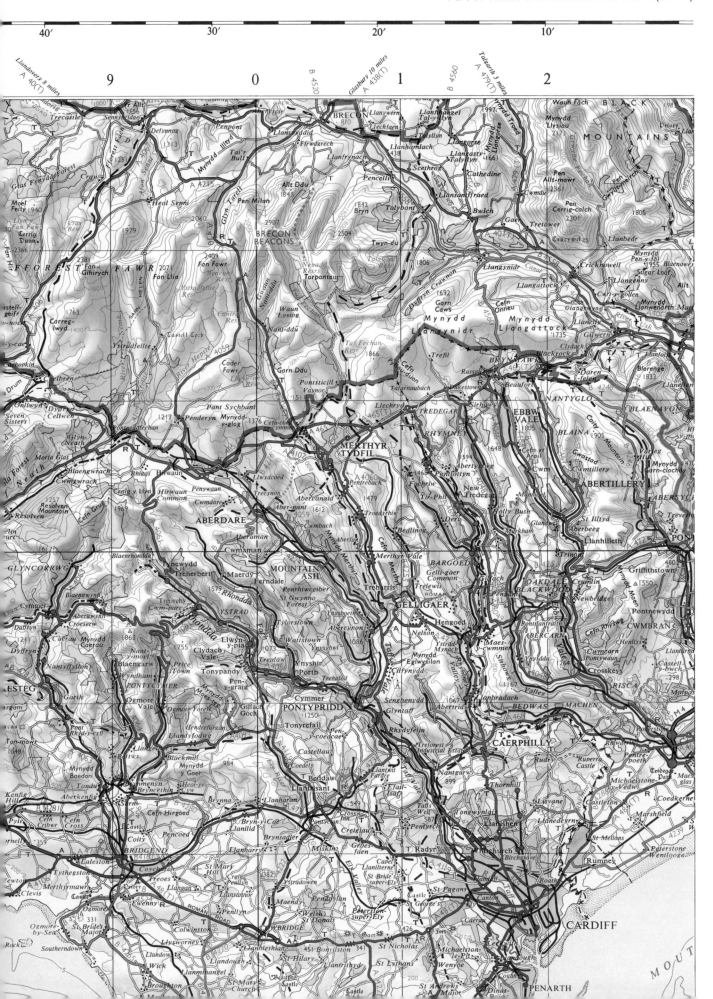

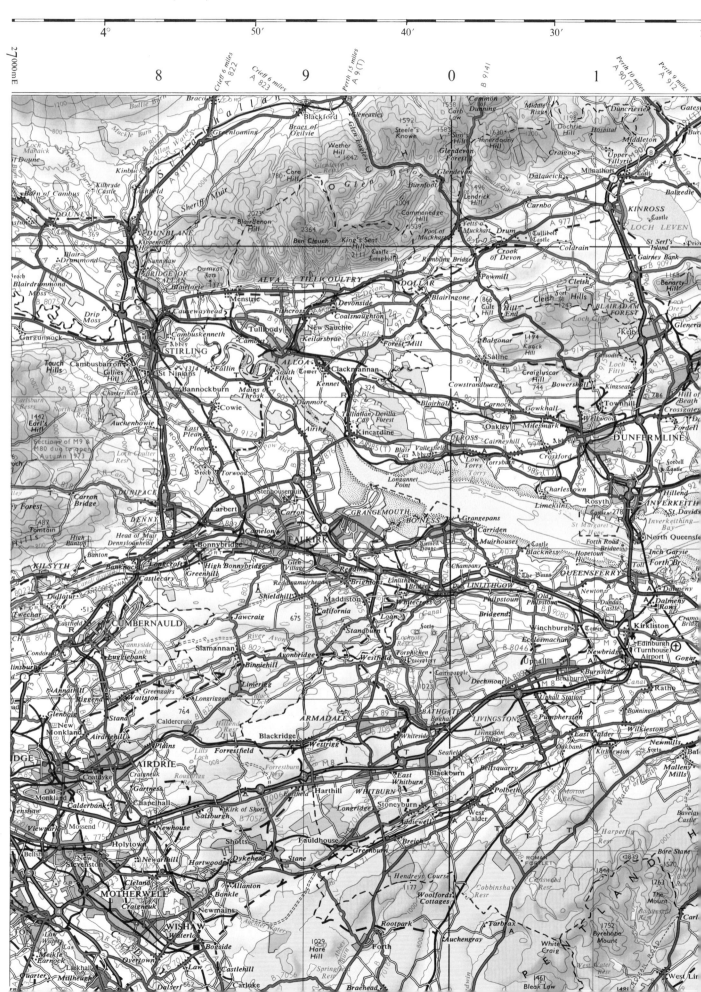

Roads

 Motorway   Service area   Junction with number

Motorway junctions with limited interchange

Motorway under construction

A 1(T)   Trunk road

A 811   Main road

B 6357   Secondary road

== == == ==   Under construction

Single and dual carriageway

A 855   B 885   Narrow road with passing places

Other tarred road   Other minor road

Gradient 1 in 7 and steeper

Toll   Toll   Entrance to road tunnel

Roundabout or multiple level junction

The representation on this map of a road is no evidence of the existence of a right of way

Railways

Standard gauge track

Disused

Dismantled

Narrow gauge track

Road crossing under or over

Level crossing

Tunnel

Open   Station

Miscellaneous

Civil aerodrome

with Customs facilities

without Customs facilities

+   Intersection, latitude & longitude at 30′ intervals
(not shown where it confuses important detail)

Light-vessel

Lighthouse

Windmill

Radio or TV Station

.T
.A   Telephone call box
.R

PO
AA
RAC

Buildings

Wood

Water features

Canal

Marsh

Submarine contours in fathoms taken from the soundings of Admiralty surveys

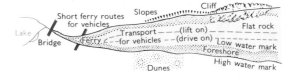

Relief

Feet	Metres
3000	914
2000	610
1400	427
1000	305
800	244
600	183
400	122
200	61
0	0

· 275
Heights in feet above mean sea level

Contours at 200 ft intervals

To convert feet to metres multiply by 0·3048

Boundaries

+ – + – + – + – National

– – – – – – – – Geographical County

Antiquities

CANOVIVM ·   Roman antiquity

Castle ·   Other antiquities

☼   Native fortress

✕
1066   Site of battle (with date)

- - - - - - -   Roman road (course of)

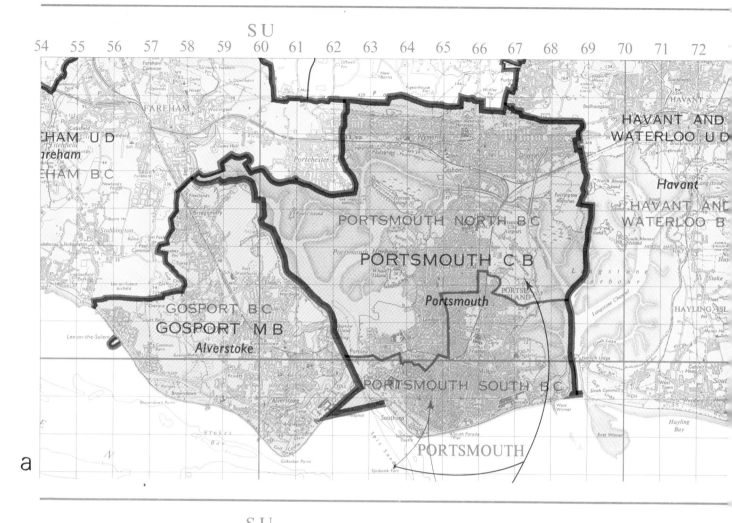

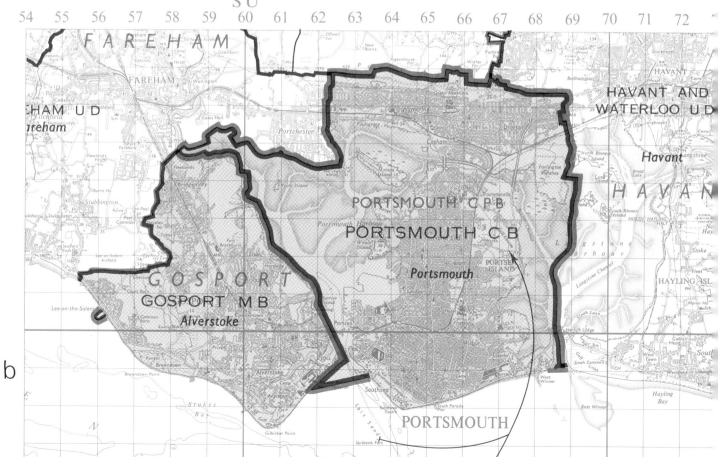

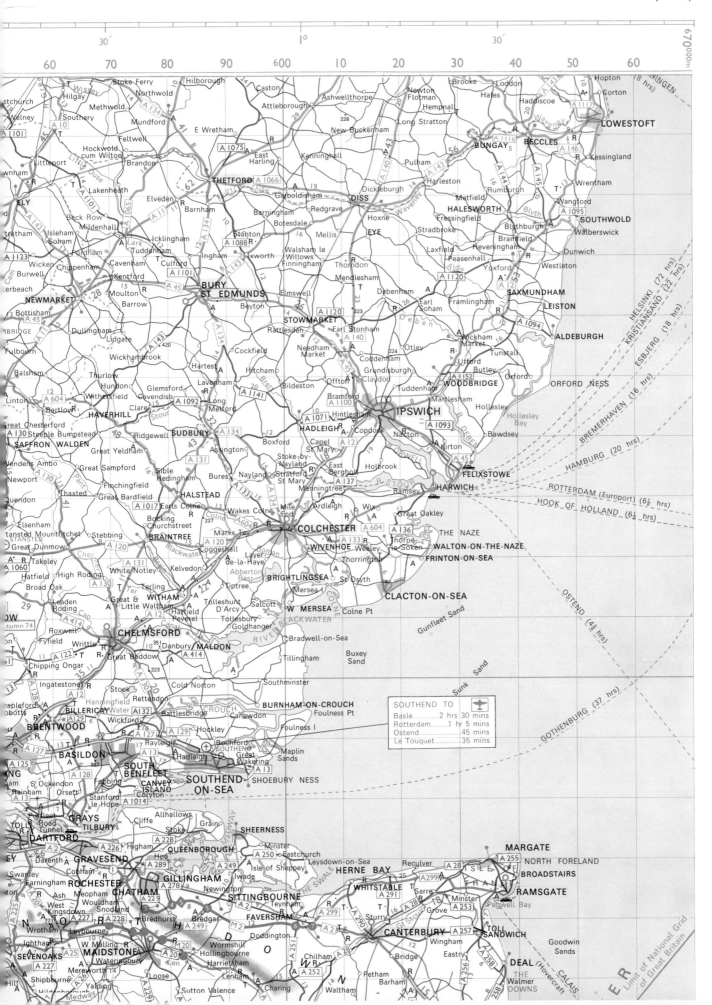

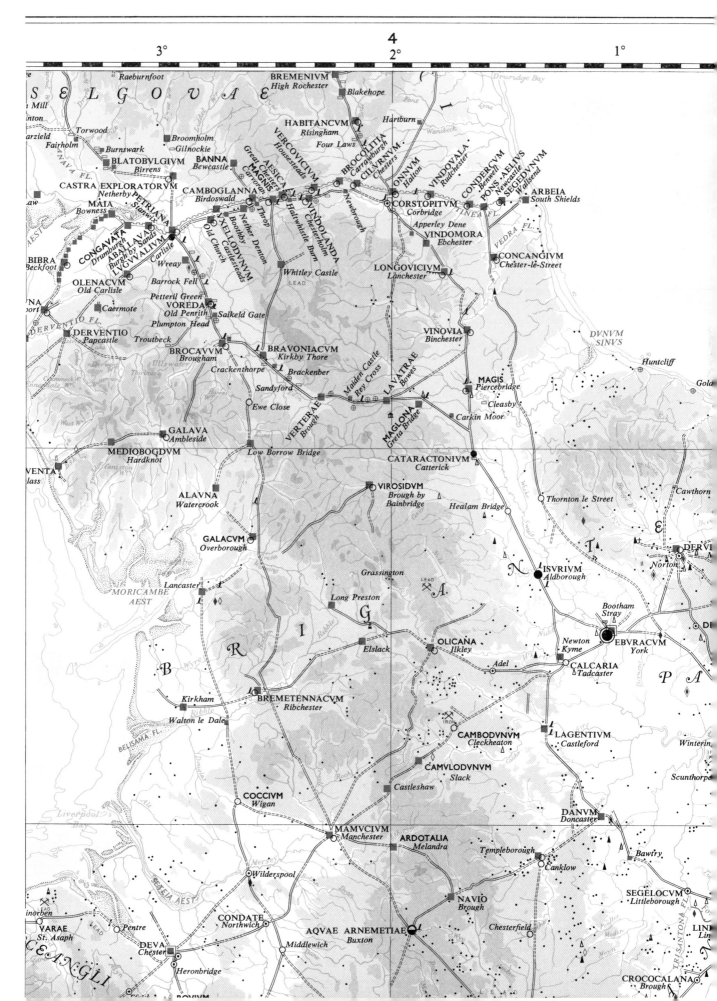

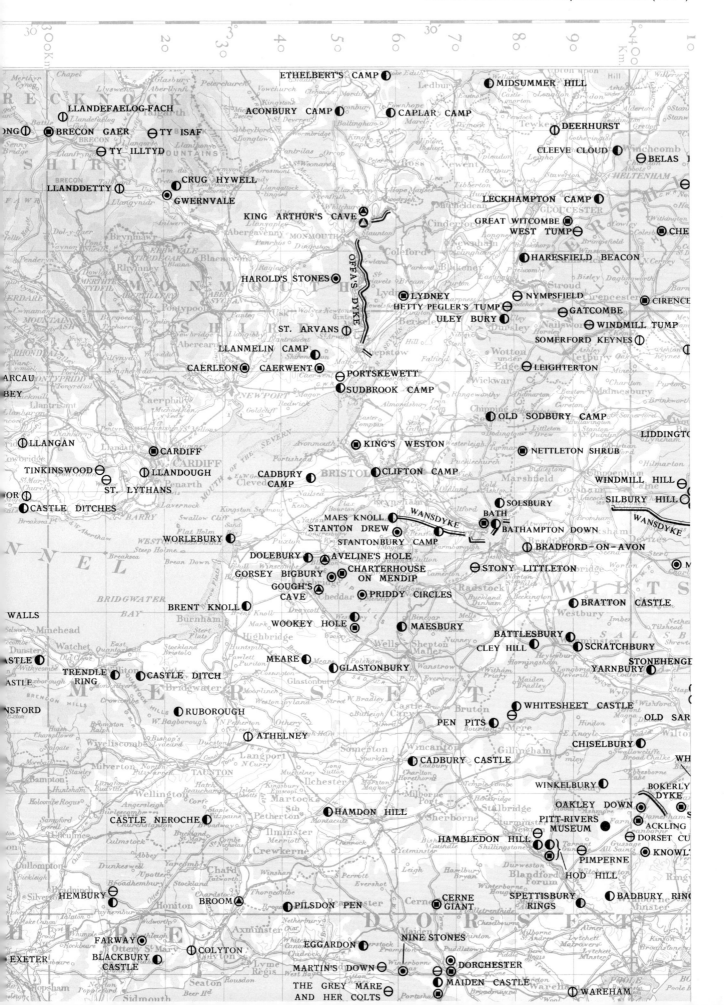

Part of Hadrian's Wall map (1972)

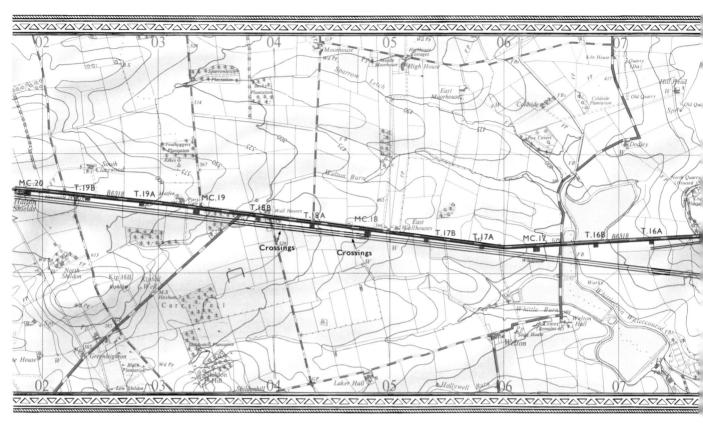

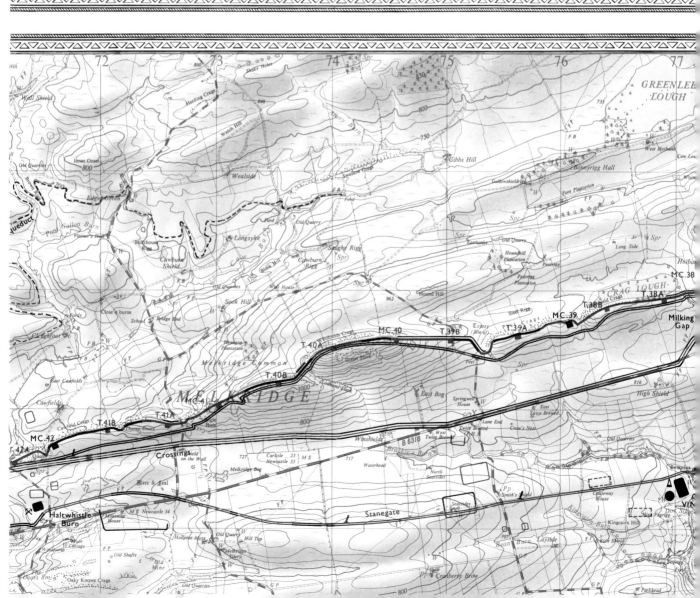

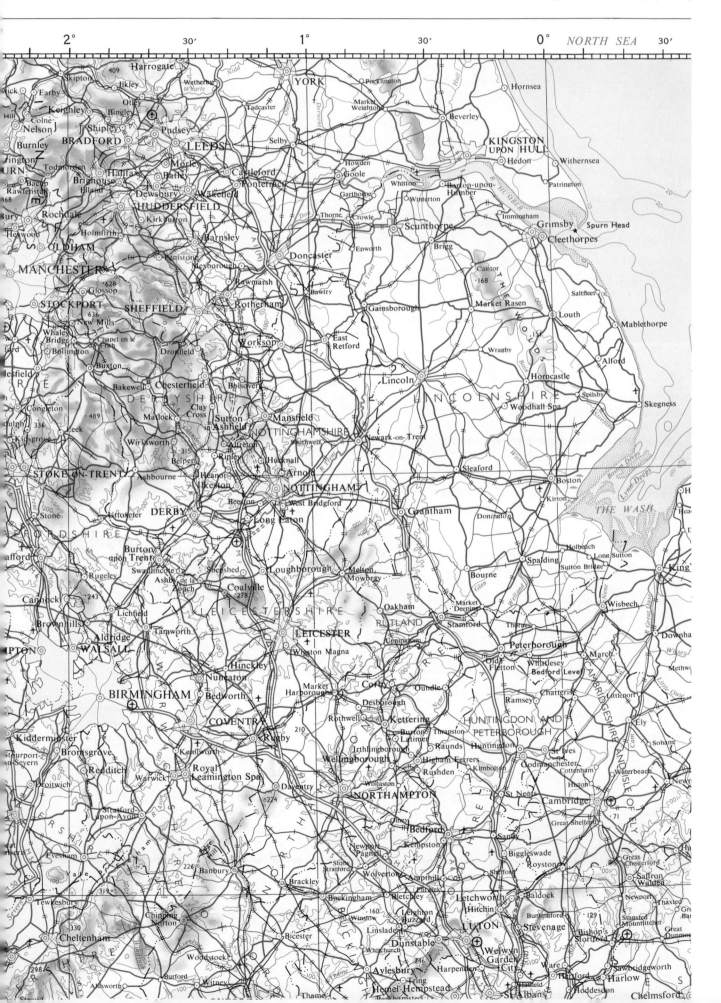

Part of sheet SO 5052-5152 Leominster (1973)

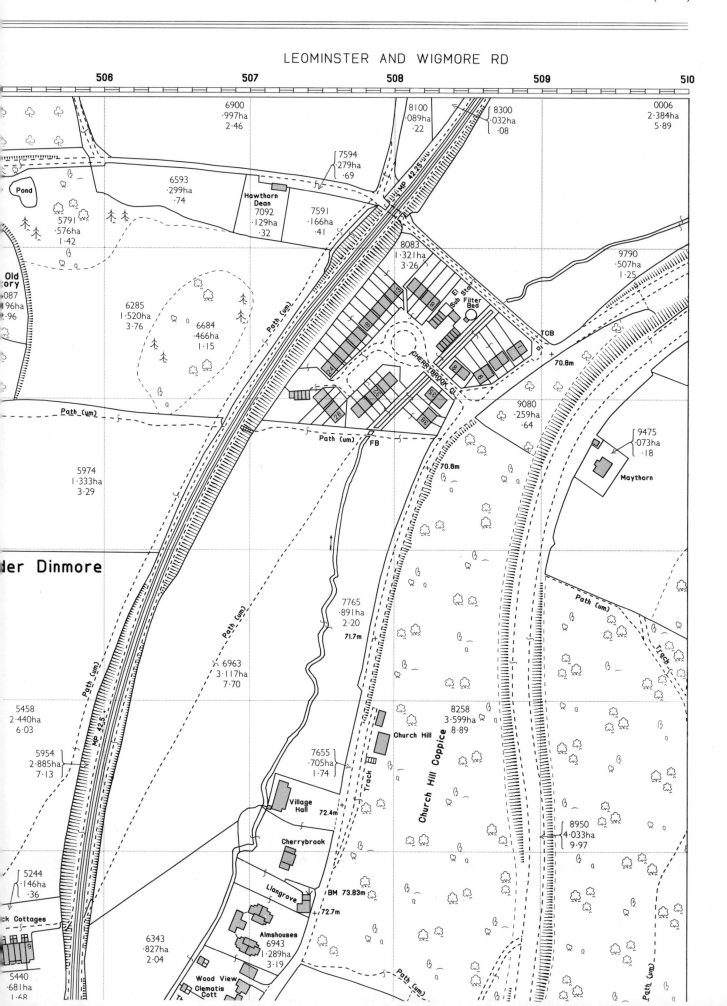